Implementing Sustainable Development Goals in the Service Sector

Vipin Nadda
University of Sunderland, UK

Pankaj Kumar Tyagi
Chandigarh University, India

Rubina Moniz Vieira
St. Mary's University, London, UK

Priyanka Tyagi
Chandigarh University, India

IGI Global
PUBLISHER of TIMELY KNOWLEDGE

A volume in the Advances in Hospitality, Tourism, and the Services Industry (AHTSI) Book Series

Published in the United States of America by
IGI Global
Business Science Reference (an imprint of IGI Global)
701 E. Chocolate Avenue
Hershey PA, USA 17033
Tel: 717-533-8845
Fax: 717-533-8661
E-mail: cust@igi-global.com
Web site: http://www.igi-global.com

Library of Congress Cataloging-in-Publication Data

ames: Nadda, Vipin, 1970- editor. | Tyagi, Pankaj Kumar, 1979- editor. | Moniz Vieira, Rubina, editor. | Tyagi, Priyanka, editor.
Title: Implementing sustainable development goals in the service sector / [edited] by Vipin Nadda, Pankaj Kumar Tyagi, Rubina Vieira, Priyanka Tyagi.
Description: Hershey, PA : Business Science Reference, [2024] | Includes bibliographical references and index. | Summary: "This book will examine the various digital technologies such as the Internet of Things (IoT), Artificial Intelligence (AI), and Blockchain and their applications in the service sector to promote economic growth, create new job opportunities, and improve access to essential services such as education, healthcare, and financial services"-- Provided by publisher.
Identifiers: LCCN 2023047360 (print) | LCCN 2023047361 (ebook) | ISBN 9798369320655 (hardcover) | ISBN 9798369320662 (ebook)
Subjects: LCSH: Social service--Technological innovations. | Sustainable development--Technological innovations.
Classification: LCC HV40 .I45 2023 (print) | LCC HV40 (ebook) | DDC 361.3/20285--dc23/eng/20231201
LC record available at https://lccn.loc.gov/2023047360
LC ebook record available at https://lccn.loc.gov/2023047361

This book is published in the IGI Global book series Advances in Logistics, Operations, and Management Science (ALOMS) (ISSN: 2327-350X; eISSN: 2327-3518)

British Cataloguing in Publication Data
A Cataloguing in Publication record for this book is available from the British Library.

For electronic access to this publication, please contact: eresources@igi-global.com.

Advances in Hospitality, Tourism, and the Services Industry (AHTSI) Book Series

Maximiliano Korstanje
University of Palermo, Argentina

ISSN:2475-6547
EISSN:2475-6555

Mission

Globally, the hospitality, travel, tourism, and services industries generate a significant percentage of revenue and represent a large portion of the business world. Even in tough economic times, these industries thrive as individuals continue to spend on leisure and recreation activities as well as services.

The Advances in Hospitality, Tourism, and the Services Industry (AHTSI) book series offers diverse publications relating to the management, promotion, and profitability of the leisure, recreation, and services industries. Highlighting current research pertaining to various topics within the realm of hospitality, travel, tourism, and services management, the titles found within the AHTSI book series are pertinent to the research and professional needs of managers, business practitioners, researchers, and upper-level students studying in the field.

Coverage

- Leisure & Business Travel
- Tourism and the Environment
- Customer Service Issues
- Casino Management
- Sustainable Tourism
- Travel Agency Management
- Service Management
- Health and Wellness Tourism
- International Tourism
- Service Design

IGI Global is currently accepting manuscripts for publication within this series. To submit a proposal for a volume in this series, please contact our Acquisition Editors at Acquisitions@igi-global.com or visit: http://www.igi-global.com/publish/.

The Advances in Hospitality, Tourism, and the Services Industry (AHTSI) Book Series (ISSN 2475-6547) is published by IGI Global, 701 E. Chocolate Avenue, Hershey, PA 17033-1240, USA, www.igi-global.com. This series is composed of titles available for purchase individually; each title is edited to be contextually exclusive from any other title within the series. For pricing and ordering information please visit http://www.igi-global.com/book-series/advances-hospitality-tourism-services-industry/121014. Postmaster: Send all address changes to above address.

Titles in this Series

For a list of additional titles in this series, please visit: http://www.igi-global.com/book-series/advances-hospitality-tourism-services-industry/121014

Management and Practices of Pilgrimage Tourism and Hospitality
S.K. Gupta (Centre for Mountain Tourism and Hospitality Management, HNB Garhwal University, India) Lilibeth C. Aragon (College of International Tourism and Hospitality Management, Lyceum of the Philippines University, Philippines) Pankaj Kumar (Department of Tourism and Hospitality Management, Mizoram University, India) Madhurima S. (Department of Environmental Science, Mizoram University, India) and Rajesh Ramasamy (Department of Tourism and Hospitality Management, Mizoram Universit, India)
Business Science Reference • © 2023 • 264pp • H/C (ISBN: 9798369314142) • US $250.00

Critical Social Challenges in the Tourism Industry Labor, Commodification, and Drugs
Barış Çıvak (Anadolu University, Turkey) and Engin Bayraktaroğlu (Anadolu University, Turkey)
Business Science Reference • © 2023 • 298pp • H/C (ISBN: 9781668492550) • US $250.00

Prospects and Challenges of Global Pilgrimage Tourism and Hospitality
S.K. Gupta (Centre for Mountain Tourism and Hospitality Management, HNB Garhwal University, India) Lilibeth C. Aragon (College of International Tourism and Hospitality Management, Lyceum of the Philippines University, Philippines) Pankaj Kumar (Department of Tourism and Hospitality Management, Mizoram University, India) Madhurima S. (Department of Environmental Science, Mizoram University, India) and Rajesh Ramasamy (Department of Tourism and Hospitality Management, Mizoram University, India)
Business Science Reference • © 2023 • 291pp • H/C (ISBN: 9781668448175) • US $250.00

Handbook of Research on Innovation, Differentiation, and New Technologies in Tourism, Hotels, and Food Service
Gonçalo Poeta Fernandes (CITUR, Polytechnic Institute of Guarda, Portugal & CICS, Universidade NOVA de Lisboa, Portugal) and António Silva Melo (CiTUR, Polytechnic Institute of Porto, Portugal & CIDTFF, University of Aveiro, Portugal)
Business Science Reference • © 2023 • 389pp • H/C (ISBN: 9781668469859) • US $295.00

Exploring Niche Tourism Business Models, Marketing, and Consumer Experience
Maria Antónia Rodrigues (CEOS.PP, ISCAP, Polytechnic of Porto, Portugal) and Maria Amélia Carvalho (ISCAP, Polytechnic of Porto, Portugal)
Business Science Reference • © 2023 • 397pp • H/C (ISBN: 9781668472422) • US $250.00

IGI Global
PUBLISHER of TIMELY KNOWLEDGE

701 East Chocolate Avenue, Hershey, PA 17033, USA
Tel: 717-533-8845 x100 • Fax: 717-533-8661
E-Mail: cust@igi-global.com • www.igi-global.com

Table of Contents

Detailed Table of Contents

Research had previously identified individual and contextual antecedents, which promote innovative behaviors through implementation in organizational contexts. The purpose of this chapter is to introduce drivers of individual innovative behavior (IIB) by modelling the mediating effect of knowledge sharing behavior through implementation in non-organizational contexts, such as for technology students. The study provided recommendations on how to leverage the individual and contextual antecedents of course design characteristics and self-regulated learning to prompt IIB.

The objective of sustainable logistics management is to ensure enduring economic, environmental, and social stability, leading to long-term sustainable expansion. The global push towards sustainable development is driving the adoption of sustainable logistics practices in the management of tourism-related logistics, with a particular focus on meeting environmental performance targets. Consequently, there is an increasing amount of theoretical and practical discussion surrounding tourism logistics operations. The objective of this chapter is to examine the impact of sustainable tourism supply chain management on the environmental performance of service companies. Through a prospective analysis, the authors investigate the relationship between sustainable logistics practices in tourism and their influence on environmental performance. The findings demonstrate that coordinated, collaborative, and pooled logistics resources can enhance the efficiency of the responsible supply chain within the tourism industry.

This chapter examines the prospects and challenges of homestay accommodation in rural Uttarakhand, India, based on secondary data sources. Homestays are a sort of community-based tourism that provides visitors with an authentic experience of the local culture and way of life by allowing them to stay in the homes of local families. This chapter examines the potential of homestay accommodation to contribute to rural development and tourism promotion in Uttarakhand. The research is based on current literature and studies, as well as government and tourism sector data. The findings indicate that homestay accommodation has significant potential to generate income and provide alternative livelihood options for rural communities in Uttarakhand; but requires greater support and investment from the government and other stakeholders in order to address the challenges facing the homestay sector. The chapter finishes with suggestions for enhancing the viability of homestay accommodations in rural Uttarakhand, including capacity building, infrastructural improvement, and marketing assistance.

In the context of sustainable tourism, the part that tour guides play in influencing visitors' experiences and views has drawn a lot of attention. This study explores the crucial function of tour operators as advocates for ethical behavior in the field of sustainable tourism. The research examines how tour guides operate as change agents, encouraging sustainable practices among tourists, in light of growing concerns regarding the environmental, sociocultural, and economic implications of tourism. This chapter investigates the many duties of tour guides in sharing knowledge about sustainable tourism practices. It does so by drawing on a thorough review of academic literature and case studies. It emphasizes the significance of tour guides' capacity to persuade various tourist groups to adhere to responsible tourism's core values. Tour guides can encourage tourists to adopt more responsible behaviour by raising understanding about the local ecosystems, cultures, and social norms through engaging storytelling.

The present study attempts to make a meaningful contribution to both the academic dialogue and the practical comprehension of how the Sustainable Development Goals can be utilised as a catalyst for profound change within the distinct socio-cultural and environmental context of Uttarakhand. Three heritage sites have been discussed in this context: Natural (Nanda Devi National Park), Built (Kedarnath), and Riverscape (Har ki pauri).The study discovers significant insights that will resonate with policymakers, practitioners, and communities all around the world by conducting an exhaustive study of the complexities of sustainable development in this particular region.

Rural tourism, increasingly recognized as a driver of economic growth in rural areas, acts as a catalyst for local development and sustainability. The purpose of this study is to explore the dynamic interplay between rural tourism supply chains and the sustainable development goals (SDGs), and also gain a deeper understanding of Rural tourism's components important from the prospect of India, its supply chain, and stakeholders in the supply process and potential of rural tourism in its contribution to SDG. By fostering economic growth, preserving cultural heritage, and promoting responsible supply chains, rural tourism can be a catalyst for sustainable development, bringing us closer to achieving the global

The current study aims to determine how social sustainability and tourism are related, and how social sustainability can benefit all parties involved in the tourism industry. The qualitative study employed a theory-based methodology to ascertain the solutions to the question: How can we establish and preserve an economically sustainable tourism system that contributes favourably to social sustainability? How can we use social resources in the tourism industry without increasing them but instead by fostering their development? How do we ensure that the tourism-related mechanisms that promote social sustainability continue to work? The study came to the conclusion that social sustainability through tourism focuses on the core elements of social sustainability, namely improving infrastructure and working conditions, ensuring that men and women have equal access to job opportunities and security, and establishing more secure supply chains.

Education opens numerous revenues to register economic expansion all around the world with specific reference to developing nations. Advancement of India in education indicators has been severely lacking during the previous decades. Decreased financing along with inefficiency in budget expenditure, plus weak management system, have crippled the education sector ensuing poor educational outcomes. Outcome based education (OBE) is widely recognized as a prominent benchmark within contemporary educational system and has recently gained much attention in India as it proposes an influential and interesting option of transforming and organizing hospitality education. OBE is used in hospitality education because it clearly focuses and organizes everything in an educational system around what is necessary for all students to be able to do at the end of their learning. The purpose of this chapter is to look into the extent of quality and mobility of outcome-based education in hospitality education.

Food plays a vital role in the growth and development of human beings and helps fight many diseases, shaping consumers' intentions and actual behaviour. Consumers prefer a healthy lifestyle in the current COVID-19 situation, where immunity is one of the most critical factors in fighting the deadly coronavirus. The constructs of the health belief model (HBM) and the theory of planned behaviour (TPB) plays an essential role in shaping consumers' preferences for food. To identify the determinants of consumers' choice for traditional Indian cooking practices, a mixed-method approach was followed in the study. Qualitative research prepared the base for quantitative research. First, an open-ended personal interview of 12 respondents was conducted to develop a questionnaire used for the quantitative survey. Exploratory factor analysis results helped identify the seven factors, i.e., behaviour, cues in action, social influence, perceived benefits, self-efficacy, perceived susceptibility, and readiness, as determinants of consumers' preference for traditional Indian cooking practices.

This book chapter will explore the role of social media towards promoting wellness tourism to achieve good health and the well-being of the tourists. The first section of the chapter will describe what is social media by providing a few definitions provided by various authors and giving an insight to the evolution of social media. Further, it will present the types of social media and the benefits of using social media. The next section will explain the fundamentals of social media marketing along with definitions, dimension scales, benefits, and the usage of social media according to the recent statistics. It will be followed by one of the popular social media marketing theories, technology acceptance model, analyzing its sub-constructs and its relationships to social media marketing. The subsequent section will explore the sustainability development goal three, which is ensuring good health and well-being for all at all ages listing the targets that they wish to achieve by 2030.

Probabilistic FFS assessments are carried out by integrating damage detection data gathered from inspections and permanently installed monitoring systems. After a negative measurement, it determines the likelihood of a postulated severe defect being present. It is crucial to point out that this distribution of the size of a postulated fault differs from the distribution of the size of a defect. A negative measurement merely eliminates the possibility that defects of the specified size do not exist. As a result, rather than estimating the dimensions of a defect, the distribution gives an estimate of the possible sizes of defects in the component of interest. The work is suggested to make early detection and future prediction damages in the structures. The database considers the initial images of the structure. The present images are mapped to the initial images to estimate the damage that can be caused in the future. It increases the detection by 13.69%.

The rapid advancement of digital technologies has revolutionized various sectors, including healthcare, fostering novel approaches to promote health and well-being. This book chapter provides a comprehensive overview of the integration and application of digital technologies in health and well-being, exploring their transformative potential and the challenges they pose. These innovations have not only enhanced healthcare delivery but also empowered individuals to actively participate in managing their well-being. Mobile health apps, for instance, allow users to monitor their fitness levels, track nutrition, and manage stress, fostering a culture of self-care and health awareness. However, there are issues that need to be resolved among the advantages of digital technologies. The chapter clarifies the significance of data

Preface

In an era where technological advancements are reshaping the landscape of our societies and economies, the service sector stands as a linchpin for sustainable development. Our book, *Implementing Sustainable Development Goals in the Service Sector*, is a comprehensive exploration of the transformative potential of digital technologies in propelling progress towards the United Nations Sustainable Development Goals (SDGs) within the service domain.

The coalescence of digital innovation and sustainability is timely and significant. As the service sector emerges as a critical pillar of global economies, leveraging digital technologies offers a golden opportunity to elevate service delivery while enhancing sustainability measures. Technologies such as the Internet of Things (IoT), Artificial Intelligence (AI), Blockchain, and more, hold immense promise in amplifying economic growth, nurturing novel job prospects, and amplifying access to fundamental services like healthcare, education, and financial services.

Developments in communication, transportation and information technology have nurtured the increase of global travelers, who are looking for unique and tailored experiences that are also innovative and culturally immersive. Service sector providers wish to address these tastes and requirements that require differentiation and innovation-oriented products.

However, with every opportunity comes its own set of challenges. Our book takes a candid approach in addressing these hurdles, from concerns about data privacy and security to the digital divide and the essential need for upskilling and reskilling the workforce. It emphasizes the necessity of a collaborative effort involving policymakers, stakeholders, and service providers to navigate these challenges and ensure that digital technologies serve as catalysts towards achieving the SDGs.

CHAPTER OVERVIEW

Chapter 1 delves into the sustainable adaptability of the library ecosystem within the Fourth Industrial Revolution (4thIR) era, emphasizing its pivotal role in achieving SDG4. Rooted in the Three Pillars of Sustainability Model and Ranganathan Laws of Library and Information Science, the chapter situates Library Ecosystem 4.0 within sustainability research. It highlights the necessity for library professionals to strategically position themselves within the evolving knowledge economy to effectively contribute to SDG4.

Chapter 2 shifts its focus to the UN 2030 Sustainable Development Agenda, particularly emphasizing SDG4's quest for improved education accessibility, heavily reliant on digital technology. The chapter explores the positive impacts of technological advancements on the academic system, emphasizing the role of digital technology in enhancing educational institutions. It presents a comprehensive exploration of the benefits and challenges posed by technological integration in education.

In Chapter 3, the focus shifts to the drivers of Individual Innovative Behavior (IIB), particularly in non-organizational contexts such as technology education. Building on prior research, the chapter models the mediating effect of knowledge sharing behavior on innovative behavior. Recommendations are offered to leverage course design characteristics and self-regulated learning in promoting IIB.

Chapter 4 shifts to the domain of sustainable logistics management in tourism. The chapter examines the impact of sustainable tourism supply chain management on the environmental performance of service companies. By prospectively analyzing sustainable logistics practices in tourism, it showcases how responsible supply chain logistics within the tourism industry can significantly enhance efficiency and sustainability.

Chapter 5 explores the potential and challenges of homestay accommodation in rural Uttarakhand, India. Using secondary data sources, the chapter evaluates the viability of homestay accommodation in promoting rural development and tourism in Uttarakhand. It emphasizes the need for government support and investment to address the challenges faced by the homestay sector and maximize its potential for rural communities.

Chapter 6 sheds light on the pivotal role of tour operators in advocating ethical behavior and sustainable practices in tourism. The research delves into how tour guides serve as change agents, promoting sustainable tourism practices among tourists. Drawing on academic literature and case studies, the chapter emphasizes the persuasive role of tour guides in fostering responsible tourism behaviors.

Chapter 7 delves into the unique socio-cultural and environmental context of Uttarakhand, exploring how Sustainable Development Goals can drive profound change within the region. The study extensively analyzes heritage sites—natural, built, and riverscape—and offers insights resonating with policymakers, practitioners, and communities globally to promote sustainable development.

Chapter 8 focuses on rural tourism supply chains and their dynamic interplay with the Sustainable Development Goals (SDGs), specifically within the context of India. The chapter underscores the potential of rural tourism in contributing to SDGs by fostering economic growth, preserving cultural heritage, and promoting responsible supply chains. A holistic approach to rural tourism development is advocated for maximizing positive SDG impact.

Chapter 9 explores the promising contributions of blockchain technology in overcoming obstacles and achieving the objectives of sustainable tourism. By presenting Indian and international case studies, the chapter unravels the potential of blockchain technology in transforming various aspects of tourism operations and positively impacting sustainability.

Chapter 10 delves into religious tourism, particularly in the colorful and culturally rich province of Rajasthan, India. The chapter provides insights into the historical and present significance of religious places in Rajasthan, highlighting their spiritual and cultural value.

Chapter 11 investigates the vital connection between social sustainability and tourism, aiming to establish an economically sustainable tourism system that positively contributes to social sustainability. The chapter emphasizes the importance of infrastructure improvement, equal job opportunities, and secure supply chains in promoting social sustainability through tourism.

Chapter 12 examines the application and mobility of outcome-based education (OBE) within the hospitality education sector in India. The chapter delves into the potential of OBE in transforming and organizing hospitality education, focusing on enhancing educational quality and mobility.

Chapter 13 investigates consumers' preferences for traditional Indian cooking practices, exploring the determinants shaping these choices. Using a mixed-method approach, the chapter identifies factors influencing consumers' food preferences and sheds light on their role in promoting healthy eating habits.

Chapter 14 delves into the role of social media in promoting wellness tourism for the tourists' overall health and well-being. The chapter explores various aspects of social media, social media marketing, and its application in promoting sustainable tourism practices aligned with SDG3.

Chapter 15 explores probabilistic assessments for damage detection and future prediction in structures, focusing on early detection and predictive maintenance. The chapter emphasizes the utilization of database mapping to estimate damages and enhance detection capabilities.

In Chapter 16, the focus shifts to the integration and application of digital technologies in promoting health and well-being, particularly in the healthcare sector. The chapter offers a comprehensive overview of the transformative potential of digital technologies in empowering individuals to actively engage in managing their health while addressing data privacy and security concerns.

This book endeavors to enlighten and inspire a diverse spectrum of readers. From academicians and researchers to business leaders, managers, and entrepreneurs within service-oriented industries, we aspire to arm you with knowledge and insights to navigate the digital age effectively. Through our collection of case studies, best practices, policy recommendations, and guidelines, we aim to instigate action, foster collaboration, and create a roadmap towards a sustainable future driven by digital innovation.

The book is designed to cater to the knowledge needs of learners at higher education institutions, serving as an invaluable resource for undergraduate and postgraduate students globally. Moreover, it extends its reach to professionals and consultants, inviting them to join the conversation on harnessing the power of digital innovation to effect meaningful transformations in the service sector.

As we delve into the realms of Digital Innovation, Creative Models, Green Energy, Health & Well Being, Smart Infrastructure, Education & Lifelong Learning, Eco-Economics, Meaningful Tourism, Responsible Practices, and Sustainable Adaptability, we invite you on a journey that holds the promise of a brighter and more sustainable future.

With warm regards,

Vipin Nadda
University of Sunderland, United Kingdom

Pankaj Kumar Tyagi
Chandigarh University, India

Rubina Moniz Vieira
St. Mary's University, United Kingdom

Priyanka Tyagi
Chandigarh University, India

Chapter 1
Sustainable Adaptability of the Library Ecosystem in the 4.0 Era:
A Routeway for Achieving Sustainable Development Goal 4 (SDG4)

Oluwabunmi Dorcas Bakare-Fatungase
https://orcid.org/0000-0002-4665-3969
Lead City University, Nigeria

ABSTRACT

The adaptable nature of the library ecosystem into the Fourth Industrial Revolution (4thIR) technological era has been fundamental to its sustainability even in the actualization of sustainable development goals (SDGs) most especially the SDG4 knowing fully well that this is instrumental to the achievements of other SDGs. It is on this premise that this chapter explored the sustainable adaptability of the library ecosystem in the 4.0 era as the routeway for achieving SDG4. The study was underpinned by the three pillars of sustainability model and the Ranganathan laws of library and information science by situating library ecosystem 4.0 within the sustainability research. The study recommended that library professionals should embrace the changing realities of the knowledge economy and strategically situate themselves in achieving SDG4.

INTRODUCTION

Advancement in technology has transcended into the 4.0 era that is characterized by revolutionizing service-oriented institutions globally of which the Library Ecosystem is not an exception. This advancement hinged on the principles of Industry 4.0 also known as the Fourth Industrial Revolution (4^{th}IR) is going a long way in promoting the adaptability of the library ecosystem to fit the dictates of contemporary times to showcase its significance in solving all identified societal problems being the hub of human

DOI: 10.4018/979-8-3693-2065-5.ch001

knowledge. Hence, its sustainability ought to be ensured without compromising the needs of the future generation, which is in tandem with the principles of the Sustainable Development Goals (SDGs) most especially the SDG4 which is meant to ensure inclusive and equitable quality education and promote lifelong learning opportunities for all without any iota of discrimination. This is an absolute opportunity to showcase the institution of the library's adaptability in addition to being the bedrock of the education ecosystem knowing fully well that the 4thIR is indispensable within this domain.

The adaptability of the library ecosystem to different technological eras has always been a contentious issue within the discourse of Library and Information Science (LIS) as Librarians have always fallen into the categories of either innovators, early adopters, early majority, late majority, or laggards based on Rogers Model of Diffusion (Lund et al. 2020). These categories vary whether the librarian is domiciled in the Global South or the Global North as the latter finds technological evolution herculean due to the myriads of challenges the Library ecosystem is facing in these climes. Thus, inhibiting the infusion of 4.0 tech such as Artificial intelligence (AI), Big data analytics, Social Media Technologies (SMTs), Blockchain technology (BTCT), Gamification, Augmented Reality, Data visualization, etc. into the actualization of SDG4 which will be a veritable opportunity of exhibiting the sustainability and adaptability of the library ecosystem across all strata of human existence. For the Global South on the other hand, Librarians in this space accept technological innovations with the heart of making informed decisions (Adekunle, Omoba & Tella, 2007) in the actualization of SDG4 knowing fully well the survival of the library ecosystem is sacrosanct to embracing tech trends of each era.

Bakare (2023, p. 2) averred that even though emerging technologies (EMTs) that make up the 4.0 era are indispensable to the discourse of the sustainability of the library ecosystem, "howbeit, libraries within the Nigerian ecosystem are good in mouthing its adoption in addition to the usage of these technologies but its applicability to the sustainability of the library services is most times a mirage". On the other hand, Igbinovia and Osuchukwu (2018) asserted the indispensable role of Librarians in boosting the attainment of SDGs through proper channels of information dissemination and knowledge sharing which can be uninterrupted in contemporary times due to tech 4.0. More this reason, Bakare and Okuonghae (2022) affirmed an intricate nexus between the activities of the library ecosystem and the actualization of SDGs as librarians are deemed change agents of inestimable value.

Therefore, it is necessary to explicate the sustainable adaptability of the library ecosystem in the 4.0 era as the routeway for achieving sustainable development goal 4 (SDG4). This will factor in sub-themes on the Library as a Critical Component of the Knowledge Economy; Fourth Industrial Revolution (4th IR) as Enablers for Sustainable Development Goals (SDGs); Library Ecosystem and Sustainable Development Goal 4 (SDG 4); Library Ecosystem 4.0 and Customer Experience; Sustainable Adaptability of the Library Ecosystem in the 4.0 Era as the Routeway for Achieving SDG4; and Challenges Associated with Library Ecosystem 4.0 in Achieving Sustainable Development Goal 4 (SDG 4). The discussion from the above is expected to broaden people's horizons on the subject of discourse

LIBRARY AS A CRITICAL COMPONENT OF THE KNOWLEDGE ECONOMY

There is no disputing the fact that the library plays a fundamental role within the knowledge ecosystem which is the foundation on which the knowledge economy is built. This social institution is saddled with the responsibility of ensuring that everyone irrespective of age, creed, or location has unhindered access to varied information resources that meet their information needs. These information resources are provided across different quarters through the Public Library, Academic Library, Special Library, and the National Library which are the different types of libraries deemed as the heritage institution of the human race.

The Public library is the local gateway to knowledge and provides a seamless opportunity for lifelong learning to all members of the community in which the library is domiciled regardless of sexual orientation, nationality, language, status, level, or educational qualification. This library has been known to be a place of learning abode for great leaders like John Kennedy who asserted that For the United States of America (USA) to be wise as well as strong and to achieve destiny, then there is the need for innovative ideas prompting more wise men reading more good books in public libraries. Nnamdi Azikwe as the President of Eastern Nigeria in the 1950s and the first President of Nigeria in the 1960s ensured the establishment of the legal basis for public library development in Nigeria which John Harris who is regarded as the "Father of Nigerian Libraries," opined as utmost significant in the course of library development in the Nigerian state (Aguolu & Aguolu, 2007). Subsequently, Prince Bisi Yusuf, the Executive Chairman of Ayobo-Ipaja Local Council Development Area of Lagos state in 2009 asserted that the public library helps in building Youths' character in society thus becoming a veritable channel for social change.

Academic libraries are situated within an educational environment and deemed the heart of such institutions tailored towards ensuring an academic smooth sail for teaching and learning. These libraries are known as School libraries which are situated in Primary and Secondary school environments aimed to instill the reading culture right from a young age to foster lifelong learning; College libraries are domiciled within Colleges of Education or Polytechnics aimed at ensuring that students are exposed to educational and instructional materials of programs offered in the college thus promoting intelligent, informative and enlightened students; while University libraries is pivotal to the educational and research activities in all disciplines in addition to reflecting the character of the parent institution. As a researcher, academic libraries have been a veritable pedestal for scholarly attainment right from the cradle and building of professional character that has stood the test of time. This is in line with the assertion of Prince Bisi Yusuf who also in 2009 averred the library was a source of inspiration for him to achieve greater height as a student and imbued in him the thirst to place education on his priority list whenever he finds himself in the position of authority. However, Moropa (2010) asserted the varying declining state of academic libraries in Africa while there has been a decline in budgetary allocation of academic libraries in Nigeria (Irenoa, Emilian & Eru, 2019) thus militating its effectiveness and efficiency to the knowledge economy.

The American Library Association (ALA) glossary affirmed special libraries as libraries set up by private organizations, business firms, or government agencies for the sole reason of meeting the specific information needs of their members or clientele weaved around the interest of the parent organization. Librarians working in special libraries are expected to possess core competencies such as information and data retrieval and analysis; information and knowledge asset; information and knowledge systems and technologies; organization of data; information and knowledge services; and enabling competencies such as creativity, innovation, flexibility, adaptability, critical thinking skills, etc. outlined in the checklist of Special Library Association (SLA) that speaks to the main reason of setting up the specialised library. Howbeit, the same issue of lack of appropriate funding is also a bane for special libraries as Otsonu et al. (2016) reinstated poor budgetary allocation as a roadblock for staff development in maximally upskilling themselves in the discharge of their professional duties within the knowledge economy.

The National Library is the mother of every library in any nation and it is called the "Apex Library" as it is instrumental to the strategic deployment of other types of libraries. It is the responsibility of this National social institution to be the pacesetter in ensuring the development of the National Library Ecosystem aimed at the conservation of the nation's heritage through legal deposit, improving the literacy level of the populace by preserving the literary wealth of the nation. Najafqolinejad and Hassanzadeh (2016) affirmed it as the scientific and cultural memory of nations in addition to being heirs of written heritage. It is on this basis that an American astronomer Carl (1996, p.1) asserted "The library connects us with the insight and knowledge, painfully extracted from Nature, of the greatest minds that ever were, with the best teachers, drawn from the entire planet and all our history, to instruct us without tiring, and to inspire us to make our contribution to the collective knowledge of the human species".

The contribution of the Library institution anchored on Librarians within the knowledge economy can be viewed from the lenses of developing institutional framework, innovation systems, education, and training in addition to thriving information infrastructure, thus showcasing the importance of the library within this ecosystem.

Institutional Framework: This implies the foundation on which an organization is built which informs the tenets, clientele, and vision, which goes a long way in informing the organizational structure that is supposed to have a meaningful impact on the immediate environment and society at large. Librarians either in Public, special, or academic libraries who are the custodians of information resources are expected to work hand-in-hand with the management of each organization to develop this framework gathered and provide ample information that is needed.

Innovation systems: There is no doubt that for every organization to thrive in the knowledge economy, innovativeness is required at its peak to ensure competitive advantage. Librarians domiciled in any organizational library should be vast enough in emerging trends that speak to the dictates of such an organization so that an innovative system that will place such an organization on a high pedestal to be able to compete favorably in the knowledge economy is developed. In this respect, Librarians should build up their tech prowess, be in charge of their narratives, and stop being backbenchers so that the Information Communications Technology (ICT) unit of the organization will not relegate them to the background as is the case in most organizations.

Education and Training: With the wealth of information at the disposal of librarians, education and training of organization staff to perform their duties maximally should not be an issue. Librarians are supposed to bring their professional competencies to bear to instill the requisite 21st-century skills in the organization. Organizing capacity development programs like webinars, workshops, hands-on training sessions and also organizing conferences is an opportunity to showcase the significance of librarians as well as the institution in the knowledge economy. This is brought to bear by the Nigerian Library Association (NLA) Oyo State Chapter through different committees such as the Capacity Development Committee and the Young Librarian Professional (YLP) Committee organizes Webinars and hands-on training sessions bi-monthly and once every semester for practicing Librarians and emerging Librarians (Undergraduate and Postgraduate students) respectively.

Information Infrastructure: Librarians in the organization should strategically and intellectually situate themselves in the good book of organizational management so that they can be seen as indispensable in decision-making within the organization. This indication is a green light to the significant role that librarians play in the information infrastructure as a liaison information officer between the organization and the society at large. The invaluable contribution of librarians in the creation, production, dissemination, organization, storage, retrieval, and preservation of information and knowledge for the sustainability of the organization and for future relevance within the knowledge economy should always be at the front burner of the library. The Department of Information Management housing the Lead City University (LCU) Library School does this on a regular basis through her Soft Skill Series Programs in collaboration with the University library to showcase the library as the bedrock of knowledge creation, diffusion, usage, remodification, and storage. This is fostering the synergy between LCU Library School and the University library as the fulcrum of information infrastructure within the University environment.

It is high time librarians in all different types of the library start living with the changing reality of the knowledge economy which should steer them to have a good understanding of how to assess the value of information and knowledge, both within an organization and the wider community.

FOURTH INDUSTRIAL REVOLUTION (4TH IR) AS ENABLERS FOR SDGs

The invaluable contributions of the Fourth Industrial Revolution (4thIR) to all aspects of human endeavour most especially in the achievement of the Sustainable Development Goals (SDGs) cannot be overemphasized. This era in technological advancement ushers in the "New Order" where innovativeness and creativity are boundless and can either follow the bottom-to-top approach, top-to-bottom approach, or middle-to-top approach, that is against the "Old Order" of strictly the top-to-bottom approach. Therefore, it portrays the fact that no human being is useless in the scheme of things if provided with the appropriate technology in a conducive environment. This resonates with the tenets of the SDGs that are tailored towards not leaving anyone behind in ensuring peace and prosperity to overcome all known human global challenges for a sustainable future.

These technologies are laced with emerging technological algorithms that are changing the way and manner we carry out daily activities as humans and at the same time making it easier to perform these tasks. Xu, David, and Kim (2018, p.90) asserted that Klaus Schwab, founder and executive chairman of the World Economic Forum who coined the term 4thIR describes a "world where individuals move between digital domains and offline reality with the use of connected technology to enable and manage their lives". Therefore, there is a synergy in the outlook of the 4thIR and SDGs which are both tailored to ensure the management of human lives effectively without any glitches, though the former is an enabler of the latter.

These 4thIR techs such as Social Media Technologies (SMTs) have provided a fundamental basis for awareness creation and information dissemination by the United Nations (UN), its subsidiaries, and all countries in the actualization of the SDGs. Contents are being created in the form of texts, images, videos, animation, graphics, or sound on the 17 SDGs across different social media platforms to showcase ways that will promote its actualization. The essence of SMTs in improving human lives cannot be quantified in equivocal terms as this technology has transformed all aspects of human endeavour. These platforms have made the world a global village and communication boundless and play a significant role in the actualization of the SDGs both from personal and organizational viewpoints. Economic growth is enhanced via these platforms as big industries are showcasing products and services and Small Scale Enterprises (SMEs) are irrupting with innovations that are providing sustainable jobs irrespective of location. Agricultural initiatives are being provided to show human intolerance to Zero hunger while telemedicine is improving and saving patients' lives with no age limit. Educational institutions are also harnessing these platforms for educational training, webinars, or conferences so that everyone has unhindered access to quality education for improved lives.

Artificial Intelligence (AI) which is a simulation of human intelligence in machines that are programmed to think and act like humans is also an enabler to achieving SGDs. Humans will be doing a disservice to themselves if these AI technologies are not embraced and welcomed with open hands. This is a technology that can bridge the gap between the Global South and Global North countries by fostering global partnerships for sustainable development. This will fill the chasm between the have and have-nots countries through the exchange of ideas, initiatives, and strategies for a sustainable future for the human race. Though within the academic sector, there have been ethical concerns about the usage of ChatGPT and other Generative AI tools its invaluable contribution to both teaching and learning cannot be denied.

The Global South countries are developing strategies to maximally harness AI while the Global North countries are scared these technologies will displace their professional duties thus making education of no significance. Chatbot which is a generative AI tool is making human communication seamless based on natural, conversational exchanges with users, during which it provides information, responds to questions, and offers assistance with a variety of tasks. This technology can therefore be used to provide the needed information for the populace on issues relating to any of the SDGs. Robotics is also making waves as this is also being used in different sectors inclusive of the library environment thus making the educational journey in the usage of information resources seamless.

The Internet of Things (IoT) which is the inter-connectedness of digital devices via the Internet is redefining all facets of human existence. Core to IoT is internet-centrism and user-centrism all weaved together for the sharing and dissemination of data without any inhibition of place, means, and location due to the pervasive nature of the internet. Therefore, since the world has turned into a global village due to the immersion of the internet, IoT is a bedrock for the fulfillment of SGDs in all aspects of human endeavour. Bakare (2023) affirmed a synergy between sustainable library service delivery and IoT as both are hinged on technology that fosters interaction without constraint. This human interaction can be fostered maximally by employing gamification which is a playful as well as intellectual avenue of promoting the SDGs just like Computer playfulness, an anchoring factor in the Technology Acceptance Model (TAM) 3 is showcasing the cognitive spontaneity of humans in microcomputer interactions. These goals can be gamified in such a way that all the tenets of the goals are well infused into the development of the game and should be enjoyable and at the same time goal-oriented towards the achievement of the SDGs.

LIBRARY ECOSYSTEM AND SDG4 IN THE 4.0 ERA

The library is the storehouse of human knowledge and has been playing a fundamental role in human existence right from pre-recorded history. This information ecosystem is weaved around different services such as reference services, marketing services, outreach services, selective dissemination of information services (SDI), user education services, and document delivery services. These services are veritable avenues for promoting Sustainable Development Goals (SDGs), most especially SDG4 which is fundamental to the realization of other SDGs.

The Sustainable Development Goal 4 (SDG4) is aimed at providing quality education for all irrespective of age, gender, or location. It promotes equal access to affordable vocational training, eliminates gender and wealth disparities, and achieves universal access to quality higher education. All these can only be adequately achieved if the library as a social institution whose fundamental role is to create a wealth of knowledge, disseminates and transfer the knowledge for use through various information resources duly plays its significant role through its service-oriented channels.

The image maker of the library is the reference section saddled with the responsibility of providing reference services to clientele. These services can be provided by the different types of libraries most especially the Public library which can be an avenue for vocational training for community members; School libraries providing information resources right for preschool to secondary school pupils; University or College libraries providing capacity development programmes for both lecturers and students of higher institution of learning. It is pertinent to know that these developmental programs stem from community analysis or diagnosis that have been embarked on by librarians through which the information needs of clientele have been gathered over time. Also, users' queries are equally taken into consideration so that holistic information is provided to the academic community when needed.

References services in the present era of the 4thIR have transcended from the physical domain to the virtual space through the usage of emerging technologies such as SMTs, AI, Gamification, Big Data Analytics, etc. These services form the basis of either synchronous or asynchronous reference service delivery. Synchronous reference service delivery is digital reference services provided instantaneously without any delay and this is mostly through video conference, social networks, real-time chat, Chatbot, Robotics, etc. While the asynchronous reference service delivery is not instantaneous there is a bit of delay in the response time, for example, email, web form, Frequently Asked Questions (FAQ). Bakare (2023) asserted that Digital Reference Services (DRS) were quite handy for the provision of sustainable library services on SMT platforms amid the pandemic irrespective of the age cohort. Therefore, emphasizing the fact that sustainable education was provided for all amid the pandemic without any restriction, though the era created a chasm between the rural and urban cities most especially in developing countries like Nigeria where access to internet connectivity and energy production is still a challenge.

The role of library marketing services in the actualization of SDG4 is non-negotiable. Marketing of library services entails the display or showcasing of different library products and services that meet the information needs of clientele in addition to exposing them to trends in their fields of study. In the traditional sense, library marketing can be done within the library via the display shelf while outside the library via library exhibitions. These exhibitions can be moved from one physical location to the other through four wheels known as 'Library on the Move' to display educational resources showcasing the essence of SDG4. But with the advent of digitization, library marketing moved to cyberspace in which librarian does not need to leave the confined of the four walls of the library space before library information products and services are marketed at the click of a button to the global space. The various SMT platforms have been handy in this respect and AI tools such as Chatbots are equally not left out. This type of service in the 4.0 era is called the Digital Marketing Services (DMS) which Bakare (2023, p. 15) affirmed: "can be used to advertise born-digital library products and services which will allow users to know about new library digital compendiums or collections that have gone through the mills of digitization".

For every educational discipline, certain literacy skills are required for students to perform maximally well in their chosen field and the long run be well-equipped in all respects to compete favorably with their peers globally. This will inform the user education services and the information literacy services as both are two sides of the same coin in that it is meant to imbue in the learner and instructor the literacy skills to access, evaluate, organise, and use information from a variety of sources to meet their varied information need. Libraries globally are harnessing the technological innovation brought to bear in the provision of user education and information literacy services to clientele. Libraries in Nigeria were equally not left out in this respect, especially amid the Covid-19 era where there was a transition from fulfilling the tenets of the SDG4 from the traditional face-to-face form of teaching engagement to purely the virtual domain.

Educational institutions most especially Private Universities took up the challenge and had an uninterrupted academic session virtually while Public institutions were found wanting due to the lackadaisical attitude of the government in providing an enabling environment for educators to efficiently perform their duties. Bakare and Ademakinwa (2022) revealed that Lead City University and some other private institutions had both undergraduate and postgraduate classes and examinations virtually seamlessly. Some librarians within this clime also harnessed SMTs to improve the literacy skills of students and society at that time about prevalent societal issues such as bullying and mobile bullying behaviours.

The #LCMBV which is a mnemonic for the hashtag "Librarian Curb Mobile Bully-Victim" was actively involved in promoting the significant roles of librarians within the mobile bullying discourse amid the Covid-19 era. The #LCMBV contents which were in the form of discussions, text, images, graphics, and audio-books across SMT platforms were able to instill the requisite skills in curbing bullying, mobile bullying, gender-based violence, domestic violence, rape, body shaming, gender inequality, ethical issues related to technological usage etc. According to Bakare (2023), Digital Literacy Services (DLS) were an avenue to curb misinformation and disinformation amid the pandemic and the SMT platforms were readily available to correct these false narratives.

Information needs are user-specific to solve an identified query, more reason document service delivery (DSD) is user-centric. Since 21st-century library clientele within the educational space are mostly Gen Z who are comfortable with technology, DSD has to metamorphose into Electronic Document Delivery (EDD) which is an avenue to digitally send a specific information product to a user with the click of a button. This can be done via SMT platforms, ChatGPT, Chatbots, and other generative AI tools which can be built into the library's digital structure to meet the information needs of users on a personalized level.

LIBRARY ECOSYSTEM 4.0 AND CUSTOMER EXPERIENCE

The emergence of the 4thIR technological trend has redefined the library ecosystem in unprecedented ways. This is shown in the types of services provided and the methods of service delivery of its information products. Also, librarians who are core to the delivery of library services as well as other paraprofessionals within the library ecosystem are left with no other option than to embrace the innovativeness of Library 4.0 to provide uninhibited library service to improve customer experience.

Library customers are called Library Patrons who form the cohort of library users. These library users have expectations from the library as an information resource centre which should not be cut short. This is known as the customer experience which over time has created an ennui to library users based on myriads of challenges facing the traditional library system within the Nigerian space. The traditional form of service delivery comes with the bane of not being able to provide 24/7 library services to clientele. But the advent of tech 4.0 ushered in a remodification and remodeling of the library ecosystem and libraries in Nigeria are embracing these innovations in varying degrees. The University of Lagos (UNILAG) Library in Nigeria and the University of Pretoria in South Africa took the giant stride in improving customer experience by adopting and using robotics within the library ecosystem which is therefore bringing a facelift to customer experience. These robots which are named Libby and RoboScholar are increasing library patronage and user experience as it is novel and first of its kind within the Nigerian and South African library space.

Library personnel should ensure they upskill their technological prowess and embrace tech 4.0 within the library space to be able to improve customers' experiences. These customers are the main reason that the library exists and their experience is sacrosanct for the continuity of this knowledge institution. The fact that the library has moved from being collection-specific to being user-centric should be the driving force for ensuring a smooth process of service delivery hinged on tech 4.0

ADVANTAGES AND CHALLENGES ASSOCIATED WITH LIBRARY ECOSYSTEM 4.0 IN ACHIEVING SUSTAINABLE DEVELOPMENT GOAL 4 (SDG 4)

The library ecosystem is core to the achievement of Sustainable Development Goal 4 (SDG 4) as it is deemed the heart of every educational institution. The following are the advantages of Library Ecosystem 4.0 in achieving SDG4:

1. Provision of digital information resources and services that are tailored towards an inclusive and equitable quality education that promotes lifelong learning opportunities for all
2. Provision of digital awareness and sensitization services in ensuring girls and boys complete free, equitable, and quality primary and secondary education leading to pertinent and successful learning outcomes. This implies librarians romancing every actor in the knowledge economy so that our impact is not just read on the pages of literature but felt in the nitty-gritty of knowledge production which is the driving force of the contemporary knowledge economy
3. Providing digitised information products and services that will ensure equal access for all women and men to affordable and quality technical, vocational, and tertiary education, including university
4. Provision of digitised developmental programmes for youth and adults who have relevant skills, including technical and vocational skills, for employment, decent jobs, and entrepreneurship
5. Adopting advocacy using tech 4.0 to draw the attention of the government and all agencies concerned to the upgrading of education facilities that are child, disability, and gender sensitive and provide safe, peaceful, inclusive, and effective learning environments for all
6. Curating into an information products scholarships available to developing countries, in particular least developed countries, as well as partnership opportunities with developed countries most especially the girl child

Challenges of the Library in Achieving SDG4

1. The Nigerian government has not yet come to terms with the major role of the library within the knowledge economy not to talk of having any impact in the processes of achieving SDG4.
2. There is no enabling environment for library professionals to function maximally well in the usage of tech 4.0 as epileptic power supply and internet connectivity is still a problem in most libraries
3. Lack of developmental programs and hands-on training on the usage of tech 4.0 for optimum service delivery to promote the SDG4
4. The complacent attitude of Library professionals towards the usage of tech 4.0 within the library environment

5. Inadequate knowledge of the relevance of library professionals in the accomplishment of SDG4 within the Nigerian space
6. The misconception that 4^{th}IR technological trends most especially AI and other generative tools will displace librarians from their professional duties
7. The misinformation that AI does not need librarians to function in the provision of library services

Library professionals who are supposed to play a fundamental role in curbing misinformation, disinformation, and mal-information should not fall prey to the misconception of the 4^{th}IR revolution technological trends. It should not be forgotten that there is always a human face for any technological development, more reason library professionals cannot be displaced within the information ecosystem. Therefore, it is the responsibility of these professionals to ensure that they have a positive attitude toward this technological change, unlearn, re-learn, and see tech 4.0 as an enabler in making them perform their duties efficiently and effectively.

SUSTAINABLE ADAPTABILITY OF THE LIBRARY ECOSYSTEM IN THE 4.0 ERA AS THE ROUTEWAY FOR ACHIEVING SDG4

The technological creativity of the 4^{th}IR in redefining the library ecosystem is a routeway for achieving SDG4 without any hazel. Library sustainability has been made possible due to improved technology thus meeting the information needs of the present generation without compromising that of the future generation. This implies having a holistic framework that takes into cognizance the information output of the present era which will still be accessible for usage for the future generation though with a touch of remodification, packaging, or repackaging. This framework with the acronym CAAAUF implies:

1. **Collection** Development Policies that Capture the underlining principles of SDG 4: The library management should ensure that a collection development policy that captures the underlining principles of SDG4 is developed and followed to the letter.
2. **Acquisition** of information materials that speak to the tenets of SDG4: These information resources can be both physical and digital which should be processed and then made available to users
3. **Availability** of digital information resources that will broaden clientele horizons about SDG4: Processed information resources should be readily available 24/7 without any inhibition due to the pervasive nature of tech 4.0. The library can develop a Chatbot or even a robot to cater to this to have an uninterrupted service delivery that promotes the SDG4
4. **Accessibility** to digital information resources that cover the SDG4 targets: There should be no restriction on age, religion, academic status, or background in the usage of information resources to ensure the actualization of SDG4.
5. **Use** of electronic information resources that holistically speaks to the actualization of SDG4: Library professionals should provide an enabling physical and digital environment to use these information resources. This will entail creating awareness about these resources, training, and re-training users on how best they can make use of digital information resources, and interacting with the Chatbots, ChatGPT, or robots. Fears should be allayed so that maximum usage can be assured for an efficient learning outcome.

6. **Feedback** from the usage of SDG4 information resources: The library should provide an avenue for clientele feedback on the usage of these information resources. This will go a long way in changing the ennui library patrons have towards the library as they will see that their opinion matters in the types of services offered to them as these are not just dumbed on them without taking their opinions into perspective.

The leadership of the library should carry along the management of the parent institution by letting them know the significant role the library ecosystem plays in the actualization of the SDG4 and their relevance should not only be recognised when the institution wants their courses to be accredited.

THEORETICAL FRAMEWORK

The Three Pillar Model of Sustainability propounded by Gro Harlem Brundtland in 1987 is aimed to showcase the principles underlying sustainable development. The three pillars are economic sustainability, environmental sustainability, and social sustainability which are core to the discourse of the Library and Information Science (LIS) discipline. Therefore, there is a synergy in outlook between the LIS domain and the SDG4 as the former is a driving force for the latter and the latter is a pedestal to showcase the significant roles of the library ecosystem in the overall education of the human race for lifelong learning.

Economic sustainability which is concerned with the purchasing decision by the library management by taking into consideration the collection development and acquisition policy is operationalised as "Acquisition of information resources and tech 4.0 tools by library management in achieving SDG4". Environmental sustainability is weaved around the coordination, practices, and services within the library ecosystem and is operationalised as the provision of service model weaved around tech 4.0 in achieving SDG4. Social sustainability entails the leadership and organizational values of the library ecosystem. This is operationalised as the ability of the library management to embrace a leadership style that is forward-driven to motivate subordinates in working towards the vision, mission, and goals of using tech 4.0 in achieving SDG4.

On the other hand, the Ranganathan Law of Library & Information Science propounded in 1931 has been the bedrock for library service delivery. The five laws are books are for use; every person his/her book; every book its reader; saves the time of the library user, and the library is a growing organism. These are operationalised as every information resource and tech 4.0 in the library ecosystem are for use in achieving SDG4; every information user his/her information resource and tech 4.0 in the library ecosystem for achieving SDG4; every information resource and tech 4.0 its reader in the library ecosystem in achieving SDG4; save the time of the library user by using tech 4.0 in the library ecosystem in achieving SDG4; Library ecosystem 4.0 is a growing organism in achieving SDG4. Therefore, the fusion of the Three Pillar Model of Sustainability and the Ranganathan Law of Library & Information Science is hinged on the tenets of service provision that is sustainable without any constraint, and this is core to the discipline of Library and Information Science. Hence, these theories are contributing to situating Library Ecosystem 4.0 within sustainability research as the routeway for achieving Sustainable Development Goal 4 (SDG4).

CONCLUSION

The adaptable nature of the library ecosystem in each technological era has been fundamental to its sustainability even in the actualization of SDG4. A good understanding of navigating the information ecosystem by library professionals are veritable opportunity for creating knowledge, modifying knowledge, transferring knowledge, and using knowledge to meet users' information needs. This service delivery process is made easy with the advent of 4thIR which is characterized by the utilization of emerging technologies that can be harnessed for the provision of unhindered library services aimed at achieving the actualization of SDG4. The study is impactful to the practice of service delivery within the library ecosystem; to educational policy tailored towards the achievement of SDG4; to the society as knowledge production is now boundless and hierarchy in information structure is blurred and theoretically based on the fusion of the Three Pillars of Sustainability and the Ranganathan Law of Library science to showcase Library Ecosystem 4.0 as the routeway for achieving Sustainable Development Goal 4 (SDG4). Therefore, library professionals need to harness these technologies as a routeway for achieving Sustainable Development Goal 4 (SDG4).

RECOMMENDATIONS

The study recommends that:

1. The significant roles of Library professionals should be recognised as the gatekeepers of human knowledge and they should be involved in the policy-making relating to the SDG4 within the Nigerian space and globally
2. Library professionals should avail themselves with the requisite technological skillset as an arsenal so they can significantly perform their professional duties within the knowledge economy knowing fully well it is a fluid and flexible domain that changes within split seconds
3. Library professionals should embrace the changing reality of the knowledge economy and strategically situate themselves in achieving the SDG4
4. The Leadership of libraries should embrace a transformational leadership style that will motivate library professionals to embrace 4thIR technologies for the achievement of the SDG4
5. Library professionals should be forward-driven in their disposition to tech 4.0 and not live in the delusion of misinformation weaved around these technologies

REFERENCES

Adekunle, P. A., Omoba, R. O., & Tella, A. (2007). Attitudes of librarians in selected Nigerian universities toward the use of ICT. *Library Philosophy and Practice*, *9*(2), 1–8.

Aguolu, C. C., & Aguolu, L. E. (2007). *A force in library development in Nigeria.* World Libraries. https://worldlibraries.dom.edu/index.php/worldlib/article/view/199/154

Bakare, O., & Okuonghae, N. (2022). Information Managers as Change Agents in Achieving Sustainable Development in the 21st Century. *Journal of Environmental Science and Economics*, *1*(2), 58–66. doi:10.56556/jescae.v1i2.97

Bakare, O. D. (2023). Emerging Technologies as a Panacea for Sustainable Provision of Library Services in Nigeria. In *Global Perspectives on Sustainable Library Practices* (pp. 1–21). IGI Global.

Bakare, O. D., & Ademakinwa, M. A. (2021). The Impact of COVID-19 on Mentorship of Graduate Students in Nigerian Universities. *Journal of the Nigerian Pastoral Counselling Association*, *1*(1), 15–19.

Quote Park. (1996, December 23). *Carl Sagan Quotes*. Quote Park. https://quotepark.com/quotes/687730-carl-sagan-books-permit-us-to-voyage-through-time-to-tap-the/

Igbinovia, M. O., & Osuchukwu, N. P. (2018). Predictors of knowledge sharing behaviour on Sustainable Development Goals among library personnel in Nigeria. *IFLA Journal*, *44*(2), 119–131. doi:10.1177/0340035218763445

Irenoa, K. O., Emilian, B., & Eru, J. (2019). Funding Academic Libraries in Nigeria for Effective Services: Alternatives to Resource Development and Library Management. *Communicate: Journal of Library and Information Science*, *21*(1), 104–111.

John F. Kenedy Quotes. (2023). Goodreads. https://www.goodreads.com/quotes/48906-if-this-nation-is-to-be-wise-as-well-as

Library inspired my love for education, says LG Chairman (2009, August 13). Vanguard. https://www.vanguardngr.com/2009/08/library-inspired-my-love-for-education-says-lg-chairman/

Lund, B. D., Omame, I., Tijani, S., & Agbaji, D. (2020). Perceptions toward artificial intelligence among academic library employees and alignment with the diffusion of innovations' adopter categories. *College & Research Libraries*, *81*(5), 865. doi:10.5860/crl.81.5.865

Moropa, R. (2010). Academic libraries in transition: Some leadership issues–a viewpoint. *Library Management*, *31*(6), 381–390. doi:10.1108/01435121011066144

Najafqolinejad, A., & Hassanzadeh, M. (2016). National libraries and regional cooperations: A framework for ECO national libraries. *The Electronic Library*, *34*(2), 196–212. doi:10.1108/EL-07-2014-0118

Otsonu, A. S., Asom, F., Zuwaira, A., & Olije, O. A. (2016). Challenges and strategies to enhance staff development for effective library services in special libraries in Benue State, Nigeria. *International Journal of Education, Learning and Development*, *4*(4), 12–20.

Purvis, B., Mao, Y., & Robinson, D. (2019). Three pillars of sustainability: In search of conceptual origins. *Sustainability Science*, *14*(3), 681–695. doi:10.100711625-018-0627-5

Xu, M., David, J. M., & Kim, S. H. (2018). The fourth industrial revolution: Opportunities and challenges. *International journal of financial research, 9*(2), 90-95.

Chapter 2
Use of Digital Technology in Improving Quality Education:
A Global Perspectives and Trends

Ridhima Sharma
Vivekananda Institute of Professional Studies, India

Amrik Singh
https://orcid.org/0000-0003-3598-8787
Lovely Professional University, India

ABSTRACT

The UN 2030 sustainable development agenda focuses heavily on improving access to high-quality education. This goal can no longer be pursued without heavily relying on digital technology. In addition to reducing emissions through increasing energy efficiency and environmentally friendly alternatives to burning fossil fuels, these methods may be used to completely remove harmful greenhouse emissions from the air. The purpose of technological advances is to improve production and efficiency while reducing waste and harmful effects on the environment. These technological advances have had a significant positive impact on the academic system. Because of the COVID-19 pandemic, the use of computers and other electronic aids in the classroom has increased dramatically. These digital technologies have had a profound impact on educational institutions as a whole. The present study aims to explore the significance of technological advances in education, discussing their principal benefits and the challenges they provide.

INTRODUCTION

Education is critical to the psychological health required for long-term growth. The spread of digital communication technologies is a critical aspect in the present push for educational reform. Smartphones, smartboards, massive open courses on the internet, laptops, tablets, simulations, dynamic representations, and simulated environments are just a few examples of innovative technology-assisted educational

DOI: 10.4018/979-8-3693-2065-5.ch002

resources that have transformed education in educational institutions and schools. The IOT has been demonstrated to be one of the most effective and affordable methods to teach children. It's also an effective method for including everyone in an excellent educational environment (Alghazi et al., 2020; Güler et al., 2022). Companies in the industry of learning technology are always coming up with innovative ways to increase kids' chances of receiving a decent education regardless of whether they do not live in an area with strong schools. When it comes to schooling, social media has come a long way. Many educators and learners now regard social media to be an essential component of the process of e-learning. It's an important forum for addressing current concerns. Social media platforms, in addition to promoting real-time information transmission, provide fertile ground for the creation of professional and private networks (Tasya, 2023; Vega-Muñoz et al., 2022).

Traditional classroom instruction lacks the immediate atmosphere for learning, faster evaluations, and higher engagement when compared with online learning. In contrast, technology and digital educational tools satisfy this demand. Some characteristics of this technology cannot be replicated by more traditional approaches to teaching. Given the broad usage of cellphones and other wireless technology, it seems to reason that such tools would help schools. Modern technology' adaptability and lack of interference have made education more appealing to today's kids. Traditional instructors are sometimes hesitant to incorporate new gadgets and technologies into the classroom since they are concerned that they would distract pupils rather than benefit them (Pakhomova, 2023 ;Barua&Urme, 2023). Students are going to profit from having online access to a class schedule that shows when examinations, presentations, and other significant occasions occur during the semester. Cellphones and clicker gadgets are two instances of pupil reaction technologies that can assist teachers in quickly determining how well their students comprehend a concept or notion and rather or not they require more explanation (Kwaah et al., 2022).

Farming in developed countries will soon experience a revolution due to the effect of computer technology, which will drastically cut the consumption of both water and pesticides. COVID-19- the phrases a global epidemic, lockdown, and confinement have just recently become commonplace. The devastation caused by the coronavirus epidemic is well recognised around the world. At the very least, the school system is surviving the crisis owing to the employment of digital technologies. Students can learn online from the convenience of their personal homes (Daniel &Ndumbaro, 2022). When technology is used in the classroom, students were more likely to stay focused on the content at hand and are less likely to be distracted. Students may discover that using projectors, laptop computers, and other cutting-edge technology devices in the classroom makes learning more interesting and fun. Technology-enhanced activities in the classroom that allow for pupils to speak and encourage student cooperation may make education more engaging and enjoyable for students. There are various methods to engage than talking (Ghobakhloo et al., 2021; Michaels, 2022)

Digital learning is an excellent way to save funds, better use resources, encourage sustainability, and increase student and teacher reach and influence. This is true for a variety of reasons, including the impact on the environment by using fewer pages for handouts and books, in addition to the time savings and ease of research. (Camilleri & Camilleri, 2022; Menon, 2022). There are few aspects of modern society and daily life that weren't influenced by technology. The global digital revolution is beginning to have an impact on the educational system. Technology is rapidly transforming the way pupils learn, and it is commonly expected that this development will make education more inexpensive and readily accessible (Hoffman et al., 2023; Limongelli et al., 2022). This article gives a basic summary of how to use digital technologies in the classroom. We will discuss why it is necessary to utilise technological resources in school, how digital tools can be used in the school environment, and some instances of electronic tools being employed in educational settings in the following three parts. The debate is then followed by a part on the problems of employing such technologies in the classroom today, as well as a segment on the probable future of technological advances in education.

Research Objectives

The following are the key research aims of this paper:

RO1: Research the necessity for technological advances in education;
RO2: Provide an overview of the value of digital classrooms in education and define the function of digital technology applications in education.
RO3: Identifying the major issues of digital technology in education.

TECHNOLOGY ACCEPTANCE MODEL: A FRAMEWORK USED

Researchers have relied on the Technology Acceptance Model (TAM) since it is the most well-studied theoretical model for explaining why people accept new systems and other forms of information technology. The Theory of Reasoned Action (TAM) (Fishbein and Ajzen, 1980) is a straightforward model of IT adoption that postulates that users' perceptions o'f the system's (a) usefulness and (b) ease of use have a significant effect on their (c) view of its use (ATT) and (d) behavioural intentions to use (BI).

To be more precise, "the degree to which a person believes that using a particular system would enhance his or her job performance" is one definition of "performance utility," while "the degree to which a person believes that using a particular system would be free of effort" is another. A person's affective valence (ATT) is how they feel about engaging in a certain behaviour. BI refers to the propensity for behaviour to persist in technological use. So, BI is what makes or breaks a product's marketability.

TAM has grown into a globally accepted model for explaining how societies adopt new technologies. This model has been useful in assisting countries all around the world to get ready for the unforeseeable consequences of the COVID-19 pandemic. The sudden spread of COVID-19 has pushed the development of TAM even farther into other fields of study, notably in higher education.

Figure 1. TAM Model

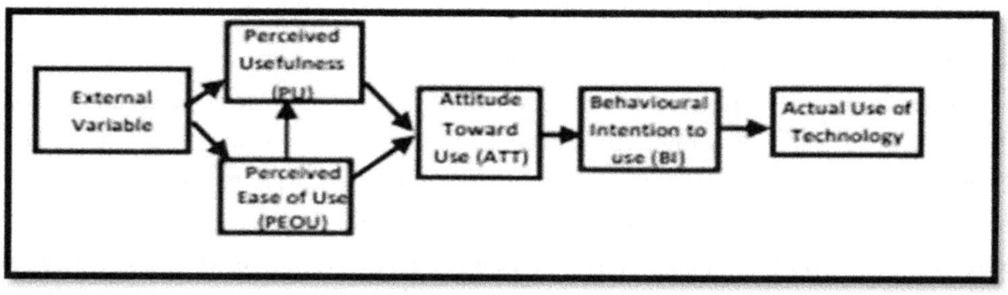

NEED_DIGITAL TECHNOLOGY IN EDUCATION

The use of digital technology in education is already being forced by the trend towards internationalization of classrooms. It was possible to run lessons, distribute materials, administer tests, and manage the day-to-day operations of educational institutions using online platforms. The employment of these mediums, however, was proactive. The COVID-19 Pandemic caused educational institutions to switch to an online-only curriculum. The developed nations were ready for this emergency. However, many emerging nations put in extra effort to fulfil this criterion. The advent of digital technology has been heralded as the educational system's savior (Lee et al., 2022; Jastrow et al., 2022; Singh, 2022; Singh & Bathla, 2023).The current worldwide crisis has made it more important than ever to have a truly globalised educational experience. Skills like issue solving, thinking structure building, and process comprehension, all of which will be essential in the workplace, may be honed with the use of digital tools. They are also getting ready for a future that is more fluid and uncertain, and in which technological advances will play an important part. The skills and knowledge that students gain will be crucial to their future success in the workforce. Digital technologies and other educational resources may help make the classroom experience more engaging for both teachers and students. Further, they provide schools more leeway in adapting their curricula to the specific needs of their students (Bompard et al., 2023; Siakalli et al., 2022; Zviagintsev et al., 2023; Singh, 2022; Singh & Bathla, 2023).

Using technology in the classroom has the potential to pique students' interest in learning. Because modern children are so accustomed to using electronic devices, introducing them into the classroom is a great way to pique their interest and boost their engagement. By incorporating technology into the classroom, teachers are able to keep their students' attention and keep them interested in the material at hand. Students may find learning more engaging and enjoyable if they use projectors, laptops, and other state-of-the-art technological equipment in the classroom. Incorporating technology, student presentations, and collaborative group work into classroom activities may make learning more interactive and interesting for students. There are more ways to participate than talking (Secundo et al., 2021; Deacon at al., 2023; Singh, 2022; Singh & Bathla, 2023).

Students can take more initiative and feel more like they are in the driver's seat when they use desktops and other gadgets in tandem with digital tools (Goodyear et al., 2021; Herro et al., 2013). The teacher assumes the role of facilitator and may verify successful learning. Students have access to a plethora of digital materials and may either upload their own work or get what they need to succeed. Web 2.0 tools (such as wikis, podcasts, and blogs) make it easier for students to create their own content, work together, evaluate one another's efforts, and ultimately engage in co-learning. Learning-enhancing strategies, such as gamification and flipped classrooms, are more accessible than ever thanks to digital technology. With the development of learning landscapes, educators now have the ability to offer students with individualised learning paths that draw from a variety of methods. Using technology in the classroom increases motivation and retention (Zheng et al., 2022; Ferdig et al., 2022; Singh, 2022; Singh & Bathla, 2023).

DIGITAL CLASSROOM

The term "digital classroom" refers to classrooms where pupils are taught utilising digital tools and resources. Today's educational scene has changed for the better as a result of the use of digital technologies. One definition of digital learning is "the use of digital media and technology to accomplish all course requirements in a timely manner" (Watty et al., 2016; Mate, 2022). Teaching in the digital classroom is based solely on the use of digital tools. The majority of today's classrooms have some form of technology or internet-connected device used by the students. Most of the content is presented online through an interesting and dynamic interface, so students don't need to take notes. Despite its complexity, education may be reduced to a form of exchange (Singh, 2022; Singh & Bathla, 2023. As a result of the proliferation of online resources, there are now more ways than ever before to disseminate and get access to instructional materials. Learning is aided by these forms of media and online spaces (Niedlic et al., 2021; Gain, 2023; Singh, 2022; Singh & Bathla, 2023). Figure 1 depicts a digital classroom's many useful features.

Figure 2. Highlights of online classroom

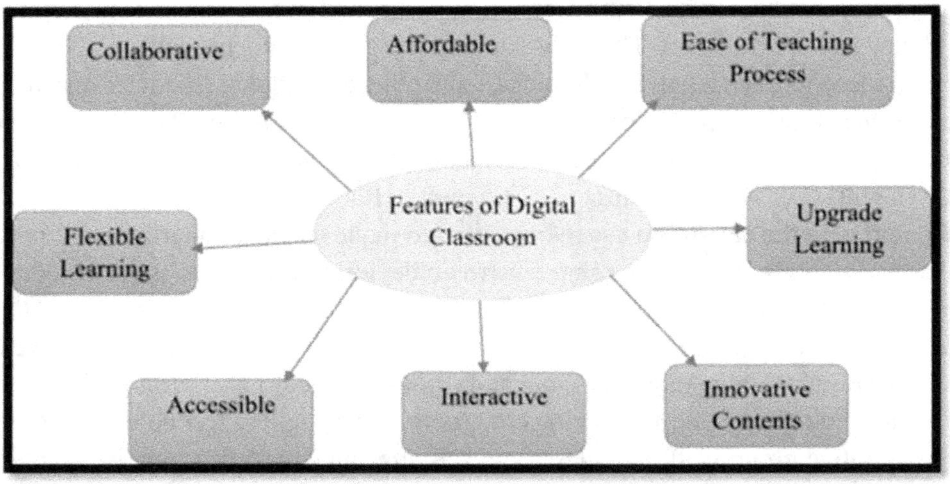

In virtual classrooms, students have access to a variety of educational resources online. A digital classroom requires both feedback loops and technology. For students to get immediate responses from their instructors, feedback loops are crucial. Many variables, including student, lesson, group, etc., can be used by teachers in feedback loops. PowerPoint presentations, videos, e-learning strategies, online instruction, and other digital methods are being utilised more and more in the classroom (Haidabrus, 2022; Crawford &Cifuentes, 2022; Singh, 2022; Singh & Bathla, 2023). Therefore, there is a trend towards increasing student involvement in class. Using the internet and virtual classrooms, students may now educate themselves on a wide range of topics independently. The most effective teaching in the classroom is often represented visually using colour graphs, charts, and models. However, these techniques of teaching are now considered archaic. Reading aloud, having the teacher explain the material on the board, and taking comments in a textbook are all things of the past (Rahman & Amir, 2019; Singh, 2022; Singh & Bathla, 2023).

USING ICT IN EDUCATION

There are many ways in which digital technologies may be used to enhance education. For example, they can facilitate the creation of teaching materials and provide novel approaches to learning and collaboration. The widespread availability of the Internet and the proliferation of smart gadgets that can communicate with it have ushered in a new age. As a result, it will be up to educators and instructional designers to maximise the efficacy and accessibility of education through the use of cutting-edge digital technology (Clemente et al., 2022; Howley, 2022; Singh, 2022; Singh & Bathla, 2023). Outside of traditional classroom settings, computers keeps on to play an integral part in educating children. Learning in a digital environment encourages pupils to think laterally and creatively, leading to more learning. It's encouraging that every country has been able to implement remote learning tools like TV, radio, the internet, and mobile devices. Access to information, the ability to retain that information, the capacity to store additional information, and the quality of information presentation have all been greatly enhanced by these developments; as a result, classrooms have been more engaging, knowledge has been more widely disseminated, and students have shown more interest in acquiring knowledge (Feroz et al., 2022; Singh, 2022; Singh & Bathla, 2023).

Teachers in the modern day need to be able to use numerous devices, such as tablets and smartphones, or they will be left behind. Teachers should make use of any and all digital tools to keep lessons fresh and relevant. There's more to technology than just watching cartoons and playing video games. How well kids, parents, and educators integrate technology into the classroom will decide the benefits. Students are more engaged and have a better time learning when technological advances is used successfully in the classroom (Singh, 2022; Singh & Bathla, 2023). One key factor in the widespread adoption of digital education has been making e-learning platforms accessible on mobile devices like smartphones and tablets. Edutainment products that use animation, gaming, or artificial intelligence to teach students are also featured. Learning of all ages and in all fields has been aided by technological advances. Big data as well as the use of analytics in education are two areas that have received little attention until recently (Bond, 2021; Pregowska, 2021; Singh, 2022; Singh & Bathla, 2023). As the use of e-learning platforms, online tests, and virtual classrooms grows in schools, administrators see the benefit of having access to robust data on student and teacher performance.

CHALLENGES_ICTIN EDUCATION

The introduction and regular use of educational technologies are not without their challenges. Concerns about technology equity, the dangers of too much screen time, and the effectiveness of teachers' use of technology are also brought up. Since the COVID-19 outbreak, the material's importance has grown. Teachers need to create and contribute to instructional content online, with a focus on getting students to consider an subject from several perspectives. In addition, some students do quite well in virtual classrooms, while others have a far more difficult time. A pupil who has experienced hardship in direct interaction with others, for instance, may find themselves in an even more trying scenario now. It's possible that these folks needed assistance that are no more available to them. However, there may be challenges for educators when using online education, especially in contexts where it is not the norm (Schizas et al., 2022; Awan et al., 2022; Singh, 2022; Singh & Bathla, 2023).

Many people have heard of some of the causes of the learning crisis. The low standard of education is a major contributor. Unfortunately, many educators are not well-versed in their subjects and have little training. Technology-based solutions exist, which could be useful for both teacher education and classroom instruction. In-service education can be delivered either solely via technological means or as a hybrid of online and classroom instruction. There is also evidence that teachers need more financial incentives. They have the ability to teach, but not the drive. While it's true that learning has always occurred in settings other than a traditional classroom, the rapid development and expansive nature of digital and distant contexts necessitate substantial change, preparation, support, and involvement. Possibilities for responsive learning and teaching include rethinking participation, reaching, teaching methodologies, correctly addressing an array of unique requirements, motivating students, managing competing time requests, and coping with confined surroundings. (Ghobrini et al., 2022; Troshina et al., 2022; Singh, 2022; Singh & Bathla, 2023).

Evidence also suggests that "instruction at the appropriate level" can be considerably impacted by low-tech interventions. Research is needed to determine either technologically advanced or simple solutions are superior since high-tech solutions are more expensive and financing is limited for developing countries. Teachers are increasingly using video to instruct students, however the quality of instruction may not always be comparable to what students would receive if the teacher were physically there. More MOOCs are being made available and signed up for, but many of them aren't designed for elementary school students and hence don't help with the learning problem. It requires gear and bandwidth at home, which many low-income families lack, making it unavailable to their children. Children may be motivated to study more by using gamification and other techniques. Finally, keep in mind that you might be able to get good results in education without resorting to technology (Yu, 2022; Ozdamli&Karagozlu, 2022; Singh, 2022; Singh & Bathla, 2023).

The transition to online learning has been challenging for some pupils. Some pupils from low-income backgrounds have it particularly tough because their families don't have smartphones. The internet is a vital tool for learning, yet millions of kids lack access to it at home. Young students often have trouble with impaired vision and backaches despite their early adoption of this sophisticated equipment. Some educators have little background working with new media and are also struggling. However, they are making every effort to ensure that their kids get a good education by enrolling them in online programmes. Practical knowledge is not accessible in online programmes(Lu, et al., 2022; Almaiah et al., 2022; Singh, 2022), thus students who study more practical topics than theoretical subjects in college encounter comparable issues.

It is feasible to arrange tasks and evaluations so that it is highly unlikely that students would use technology to cheat. Open-book examinations, on the contrary hand, can place more of a focus on critical thinking and mastery than just memorization. Automation may speed up time-consuming tasks like keeping track of students' attendance and grades. Engagement tools, thanks to their objectivity, can help speed up the grading of writing assignments, chats, and participation, and they can also answer frequently asked questions from students. Students cannot take part in distance education without the necessary ICT tools, access to the internet/mobile networks, instructional materials, and teacher preparation. Students from low-income families, rural regions without enough resources, and urban ghettos are at a greater disadvantage. Students who have special needs or come from homes where English is not spoken may benefit greatly from customised instruction.

DISCUSSION

Students now have the opportunity to travel the world without ever leaving their classrooms thanks to digital technologies. Inviting a subject-matter expert to speak to the class is a great way to liven up the curriculum. Thanks to advances in video conferencing technology, we may easily have a guest lecturer from across the country or around the world join our class for an in-person discussion. Having a video conference with students at another school is simple to set up. Students of various personalities and confidence levels are involved in online surveys and other digital technologies. In order to get student feedback on instructional content and tasks, regular online check-ins are possible thanks to engagement technologies. Understanding where kids are having difficulty may also be gleaned through student perspectives. By encouraging student participation and providing immediate feedback, response systems for the classroom foster good digital citizenship. Closing schools has far-reaching effects on the mental health of a lot of kids and families because of the crucial role they play in our communities. This is a task that can be taken up easily by digital technology. Students may go at their own pace, rewind and replay videos, and dig deeper into topics of interest via online learning.

Education technology may also facilitate the use of quizzes as an active learning technique. With the use of social media platforms, whiteboards that are interactive, and other tools, students may jump right into completing an assignment collaboratively in class and communicate, collaborate, and rebound ideas off of one another. Students are free to work together regardless of their location or socioeconomic status. Technology has also made it easier for students to take part in impromptu discussions and get prompt responses to any queries or concerns they may have about a topic. Students will almost always finish their assignments at different times due to factors like learning rate and individual differences. In such a situation, providing students with access to instructive videos, course-based activities, or interactive educational resources is an easy way to keep their attention. This means that students who work more quickly may continue their studies without having to wait for their slower classmates to finish, and that those who work more slowly are less likely to feel pressured to rush complete their assignments. Schools of the future will use this Education 4.0 curriculum in an effort to raise educational standards and more effectively prepare future generations for leadership roles. In addition, AI will improve the efficiency and lower the emissions of driverless automobiles. Artificial intelligence is being used by material scientists to develop biodegradable plastic alternatives and methods for cleaning up marine environments. Despite their apparent simplicity, recycling and upcycling are powerful tools that may significantly advance the sustainability movement. Whether it's individuals reusing bottles to cut down on plastic waste or corporations repurposing unwanted materials, recycling proves to be a game-changer in environmental friendliness.

FUTURE OF TECHNOLOGIES IN EDUCATION: GLOBAL PERSPECTIVE

A growing number of startups, midsize businesses, and multinational corporations are developing innovative digital solutions for schools. As a result, cutting-edge tools for education will be more widely available and accessible across the country. We anticipate that all language barriers will be eliminated, and that more educational resources will be made available in local languages on the Internet. With the help of e-learning and m-learning programmes, educators and students have access to a wealth of data. While technological advancements will have a significant impact on education in the future, the success of innovative teaching methods will depend on a new crop of teachers who value interpersonal interaction in the classroom. These may pave the way to a rewarding and interesting profession in teaching. Students learn how to take full use of the present and future opportunities presented by advances in educational technology. The rising speed and capacity of the internet will carry the latest educational trends in the next years, making it simpler to implement cutting-edge technology in the classroom. However, nothing can replace face-to-face instruction in a classroom setting. As a result, we have entered the period of hybrid education and instruction, in which online and offline technologies are merged to improve outcomes as predicted by Education 4.0.

In the current context, education has moved online. Education is shifting its emphasis to the acquisition and use of technological skills. E-learning systems facilitate virtual interaction between educators and their students. Innovative technology for communication and information has shifted the focus of higher education from a traditional to a smart educational approach. Smart learning leverages scientific and social progress to facilitate individualised study with the help of cutting-edge tools, most notably mobile and online resources.

Smart learning is gaining traction in the academic world (Ywiołek and Schiavone, 2021). In this COVID-19 lockdown, the e-learning strategy has been universally adopted and has proven its superiority across all levels of education. Radha et al.'s (2020) research suggests that online education will continue to grow in popularity in the near future. Because of the global epidemic, we need teachers who are both tech-savvy and expert level. So, teachers need to get better at using technology, e-learning tools, educational applications, and other online platforms to teach their students. As Internet and telecommunications infrastructures have improved, so too has e-learning. After the advent of the web, e-learning began to grow significantly, and it is still expanding to meet the new demands it faces. The training and education process may be enhanced by the use of e-learning in various ways.As a result, educational institutions will be better equipped to "ensure inclusive and equitable quality education and promote lifelong learning opportunities for all," as UNESCO's fourth Sustainable Development Goal (SDG) states.

CONCLUSION

Accessibility software and devices are examples of digital technology used in the classroom to support students with disabilities. Using modern technology in the educational setting is the most efficient method to lessen a teacher's workload of mundane, time-consuming tasks. By automated or partially automating routine tasks like recording attendance and performance monitoring, learning technology applications may significantly reduce labour and effort demands. Students learn to utilise technology in a responsible and strategic manner, which can aid in their growth as decision makers and self-disciplined individuals. Students may better prepare for a lifetime of learning with the aid of technology in the classroom. By allowing them to learn in a digital environment, these tools provide students more control over their education. Students are able to learn at their own speed with the help of digital content development tools that personalise education. The electronic equipment and software in the digital classroom are used to teach pupils. Technology and the Internet can turn every classroom into an interactive learning environment. With the aid of modern tools, students may monitor their own development and accelerate their learning. Soon, these innovations will be widely used in classrooms to improve students' access to digital resources and their overall academic achievement. Complex analysis and handling of data have been greatly aided by modern technology, allowing for more informed long-term decisions in fields like warming temperatures, water and air security, preservation of biodiversity, disaster resilience, etc. Technologies that take into account natural resources while simultaneously fostering economic and social development are meant here. These are made with the long-term goal of drastically reducing ecological and environmental risks. These innovations lessen environmental impacts including deterioration and pollution.

REFERENCES

Alghazi, S. S., Wong, S. Y., Kamsin, A., Yadegaridehkordi, E., & Shuib, L. (2020). Towards sustainable mobile learning: A brief review of the factors influencing acceptance of the use of mobile phones as learning tools. *Sustainability (Basel), 12*(24), 10527. doi:10.3390u122410527

Almaiah, M. A., Ayouni, S., Hajjej, F., Lutfi, A., Almomani, O., & Awad, A. B. (2022). Smart mobile learning success model for higher educational institutions in the context of the COVID-19 pandemic. *Electronics (Basel), 11*(8), 1278. doi:10.3390/electronics11081278

Awan, K. A., Din, I. U., Almogren, A., & Rodrigues, J. J. (2022). AutoTrust: A privacy-enhanced trust-based intrusion detection approach for internet of smart things. *Future Generation Computer Systems, 137*, 288–301. doi:10.1016/j.future.2022.07.026

Barua, B., &Urme, U. N. (2023). Assessing the online teaching readiness of faculty member. *Journal of Research in Innovative Teaching & Learning.*

Bompard, E., Estebsari, A., Mazza, A., Pons, E., & Solida, L. (2023). Innovative Higher Education Approaches for Power System Courses. *Education Sciences, 13*(1), 92. doi:10.3390/educsci13010092

Bond, M. (2021). Schools and emergency remote education during the COVID-19 pandemic: A living rapid systematic review. *Asian Journal of Distance Education, 15*(2), 191–247.

Camilleri, M. A., & Camilleri, A. C. (2022). The acceptance of learning management systems and video conferencing technologies: Lessons learned from COVID-19. *Technology. Knowledge and Learning, 27*(4), 1311–1333. doi:10.100710758-021-09561-y

Clemente-Suárez, V. J., Beltrán-Velasco, A. I., Ramos-Campo, D. J., Mielgo-Ayuso, J., Nikolaidis, P. A., Belando, N., & Tornero-Aguilera, J. F. (2022). Physical activity and COVID-19. The basis for an efficient intervention in times of COVID-19 pandemic. *Physiology & Behavior, 244*, 113667. doi:10.1016/j.physbeh.2021.113667 PMID:34861297

Crawford, J., & Cifuentes-Faura, J. (2022). Sustainability in higher education during the COVID-19 pandemic: A systematic review. *Sustainability (Basel), 14*(3), 1879. doi:10.3390u14031879

Daniel, J., &Ndumbaro, F. (2022). An assessment of human resource capabilities in supporting digital records preservation: a case of RAMD and RITA, Tanzania. *Records Management Journal.*

Deacon, B., Laufer, M., & Schäfer, L. O. (2023). Infusing educational technologies in the heart of the university—A systematic literature review from an organisational perspective. *British Journal of Educational Technology, 54*(2), 441–466. doi:10.1111/bjet.13277

Ferdig, R. E., Kosko, K. W., & Gandolfi, E. (2022). Using the COVID-19 pandemic to create a vision for XR-based teacher education field experiences. *Journal of Technology and Teacher Education, 30*(2), 239–252.

Feroz, H. M. B., Zulfiqar, S., Noor, S., & Huo, C. (2022). Examining multiple engagements and their impact on students' knowledge acquisition: The moderating role of information overload. *Journal of Applied Research in Higher Education, 14*(1), 366–393. doi:10.1108/JARHE-11-2020-0422

Gain, V. (2023). Informality as a resource: A systems-theoretical take on the open method of coordination in education. *European Educational Research Journal*, 14749041231168952. doi:10.1177/14749041231168952

Ghobakhloo, M., Fathi, M., Iranmanesh, M., Maroufkhani, P., & Morales, M. E. (2021). Industry 4.0 ten years on: A bibliometric and systematic review of concepts, sustainability value drivers, and success determinants. *Journal of Cleaner Production, 302*, 127052. doi:10.1016/j.jclepro.2021.127052

Ghobrini, R. E. A., Benzert, F. Z., & Balas, M. (2022). Educationalizinginstagram for virtual instruction in COVID-19: A pragmatic framework. [IJWLTT]. *International Journal of Web-Based Learning and Teaching Technologies, 17*(6), 1–16. doi:10.4018/IJWLTT.287621

Goodyear, V. A., & Armour, K. M. (2021). Young People's health-related learning through social media: What do teachers need to know? *Teaching and Teacher Education, 102*, 103340. doi:10.1016/j.tate.2021.103340 PMID:34083866

Güler, M., Bütüner, S. Ö., Danişman, Ş., & Gürsoy, K. (2022). A meta-analysis of the impact of mobile learning on mathematics achievement. *Education and Information Technologies, 27*(2), 1–21. doi:10.100710639-021-10640-x

Haidabrus, B. (2022). Information technology and management in higher education and science. *Futurity Education, 2*(4), 26–35.

Herro, D., Kiger, D., & Owens, C. (2013). Mobile technology: Case-based suggestions for classroom integration and teacher educators. *Journal of Digital Learning in Teacher Education, 30*(1), 30–40. doi:10.1080/21532974.2013.10784723

Hoffman, R. R., Mueller, S. T., Klein, G., & Litman, J. (2023). Measures for explainable AI: Explanation goodness, user satisfaction, mental models, curiosity, trust, and human-AI performance. *Frontiers of Computer Science, 5*, 1096257. doi:10.3389/fcomp.2023.1096257

Howley, D. (2022). Experiences of teaching and learning in K-12 physical education during COVID-19: An international comparative case study. *Physical Education and Sport Pedagogy, 27*(6), 608–625. doi:10.1080/17408989.2021.1922658

Jastrow, F., Greve, S., Thumel, M., Diekhoff, H., & Süßenbach, J. (2022). Digital technology in physical education: A systematic review of research from 2009 to 2020. *German Journal of Exercise and Sport Research, 52*(4), 504–528. doi:10.100712662-022-00848-5

Kwaah, C. Y., Adu-Yeboah, C., Amuah, E., Essilfie, G., & Somuah, B. A. (2022). Exploring preservice teachers' digital skills, stress, and coping strategies during online lessons amid covid-19 pandemic in Ghana. *Cogent Education, 9*(1), 2107292. doi:10.1080/2331186X.2022.2107292

Lee, H., Woo, D., & Yu, S. (2022). Virtual reality metaverse system supplementing remote education methods: Based on aircraft maintenance simulation. *Applied Sciences (Basel, Switzerland), 12*(5), 2667. doi:10.3390/app12052667

Limongelli, C., Marani, A., Sciarrone, F., & Temperini, M. (2022). Measuring the similarity of concept maps according to pedagogical criteria. *IEEE Access : Practical Innovations, Open Solutions, 10*, 27655–27669. doi:10.1109/ACCESS.2022.3156662

Lu, J., Schmidt, M., Lee, M., & Huang, R. (2022). Usability research in educational technology: A state-of-the-art systematic review. *Educational Technology Research and Development, 70*(6), 1951–1992. doi:10.100711423-022-10152-6

Mate, M. J. (2022). *Improving the Teaching Staff Capacity to Integrate EdTech in the Teaching and Learning Processes at Eduardo Mondlane University* [Master's thesis, Faculty of Humanities].

Menon, D. (2022). Uses and gratifications of educational apps: A study during COVID-19 pandemic. *Computers and Education Open, 3*, 100076. doi:10.1016/j.caeo.2022.100076

Michaels, S. (2022). *Eligibility, Preparation and Administration of the PASA (Pennsylvania Alternate System of Assessment): Special Education Teacher Perceptions of the Alternate Assessment.* Immaculata University.

Niedlich, S., Kallfaß, A., Pohle, S., & Bormann, I. (2021). A comprehensive view of trust in education: Conclusions from a systematic literature review. *Review of Education, 9*(1), 124–158. doi:10.1002/rev3.3239

Ozdamli, F., & Karagozlu, D. (2022). Online Education During the Pandemic: A Systematic Literature Review. *International Journal of Emerging Technologies in Learning, 17*(16), 167–193. doi:10.3991/ijet.v17i16.32287

Pakhomova, T., Hryhorieva, V., Omelchenko, A., Kalenyk, M., & Semak, L. (2023). The formation of digital competence by means of information and communication technologies among students of higher education. *RevistaEduweb, 17*(2), 78–88.

Pregowska, A., Masztalerz, K., Garlińska, M., & Osial, M. (2021). A worldwide journey through distance education—From the post office to virtual, augmented and mixed realities, and education during the COVID-19 pandemic. *Education Sciences, 11*(3), 118. doi:10.3390/educsci11030118

Radha, R., Mahalakshmi, K., Kumar, V. S., &Saravanakumar, A. R. (2020). E-Learning during lockdown of Covid-19 pandemic: A global perspective. *International journal of control and automation, 13*(4), 1088-1099.

Rahman, F., & Amir, P. (2019). Trends in Reading Literary Fiction in Print and Cyber Media by Undergraduate Students of Hasanuddin University. *International Journal of Education and Practice, 7*(2), 66–77. doi:10.18488/journal.61.2019.72.66.77

Schizas, N., Karras, A., Karras, C., & Sioutas, S. (2022). TinyML for Ultra-Low Power AI and Large Scale IoT Deployments: A Systematic Review. *Future Internet*, *14*(12), 363. doi:10.3390/fi14120363

Secundo, G., Gioconda, M. E. L. E., Del Vecchio, P., Gianluca, E. L. I. A., Margherita, A., & Valentina, N. D. O. U. (2021). Threat or opportunity? A case study of digital-enabled redesign of entrepreneurship education in the COVID-19 emergency. *Technological Forecasting and Social Change*, *166*, 120565. doi:10.1016/j.techfore.2020.120565 PMID:33518821

Siakalli, M., Mousoulidou, M., Christodoulou, A., Savvidou, A., & Kouppa, K. (2022). Secondary Education and COVID-19. *Encyclopedia*, *2*(1), 409–427. doi:10.3390/encyclopedia2010025

Singh, A. (2022). Conceptual framework on Smart Learning Environment for the present and new century-An Indian perspective. *Revista de educación y derecho= Education and law review*, (25), 2.

Singh, A., & Bathla, G. (2023). Fostering Creativity and Innovation: Tourism and Hospitality Perspective. In Embracing Business Sustainability Through Innovation and Creativity in the Service Sector (pp. 70-83). IGI Global.

Tasya, D. H. (2023). The Role Of Technology In English Curriculum Design. *PUSTAKA: Jurnal Bahasa danPendidikan, 3*(4), 42-57.

Troshina, E. P., Dobrova, V. V., & Kozyreva, M. P. (2022). Digital educational platforms: Advantages and disadvantages. In *Digital Technologies in the New Socio-Economic Reality* (pp. 183–188). Springer International Publishing. doi:10.1007/978-3-030-83175-2_25

Vega-Muñoz, A., Estrada-Muñoz, C., Andreucci-Annunziata, P., Contreras-Barraza, N., & Bilbao-Cotal, H. (2022). Validation of a measurement scale on technostress for university students in Chile. *International Journal of Environmental Research and Public Health*, *19*(21), 14493. doi:10.3390/ijerph192114493 PMID:36361366

Watty, K., McKay, J., & Ngo, L. (2016). Innovators or inhibitors? Accounting faculty resistance to new educational technologies in higher education. *Journal ofAccounting Education*, *36*, 1–15. doi:10.1016/j.jaccedu.2016.03.003

Yu, Z. (2022). A meta-analysis and bibliographic review of the effect of nine factors on online learning outcomes across the world. *Education and Information Technologies*, *27*(2), 2457–2482. doi:10.100710639-021-10720-y PMID:34456608

Zheng, L., Long, M., Zhong, L., & Gyasi, J. F. (2022). The effectiveness of technology-facilitated personalized learning on learning achievements and learning perceptions: A meta-analysis. *Education and Information Technologies*, *27*(8), 11807–11830. doi:10.100710639-022-11092-7

Zviagintsev, R., Kersha, Y., Bysik, N., & Kosaretsky, S. (2023). Response to COVID-19 in Remote Russian Schools: Readiness to Online Education and Coping Strategies. In Global Perspectives on Education Research, (pp. 34-65). Routledge.

Żywiołek, J., & Schiavone, F. (2021, September). Perception of the quality of smart city solutions as a sense of residents' safety. *Energies*, *14*(17), 5511. doi:10.3390/en14175511

Chapter 3
Modelling the Mediating Effects of Knowledge Sharing Behavior in the Education Sector:
Drivers of Individual Innovative Behavior

James K. Ngugi
University of South Africa, South Africa

Leila Goosen
https://orcid.org/0000-0003-4948-2699
University of South Africa, South Africa

ABSTRACT

Research had previously identified individual and contextual antecedents, which promote innovative behaviors through implementation in organizational contexts. The purpose of this chapter is to introduce drivers of individual innovative behavior (IIB) by modelling the mediating effect of knowledge sharing behavior through implementation in non-organizational contexts, such as for technology students. The study provided recommendations on how to leverage the individual and contextual antecedents of course design characteristics and self-regulated learning to prompt IIB.

INTRODUCTION

This section will describe the general perspective of the chapter and end by specifically stating the **objectives**.

DOI: 10.4018/979-8-3693-2065-5.ch003

Sustainable Development Goal Advancement Through Digital Innovation in the Service Sector

As part of this book, the chapter intends to explore the role of digital technologies in implementing the United Nations Sustainable Development Goals (SDGs) in the service and education sectors. With the service and education sectors being critical components of the global economy and significant contributors to achieving sustainable development, adopting digital technologies presents an opportunity to enhance service delivery and improve not only **innovation**, entrepreneurship, and **sustainability** for information and communication technology (ICT) students towards the post-COVID-19 era (Ngugi & Goosen, 2021b), but **sustainability** across these sectors. As part of this book, the chapter will examine the various digital technologies such as the Internet of Things (IoT) and Artificial Intelligence (AI), as well as the applications of these in the service and education sectors to promote economic growth, create new job opportunities, and improve access to essential services. It will also discuss how digital technologies can enhance customer experiences, resulting in increased satisfaction and loyalty. However, as part of the book, this chapter will also highlight the **challenges** associated with adopting digital technologies in the service and education sectors, including data privacy and security concerns, the digital divide, and the need for upskilling and reskilling of the workforce. It will provide insights into how policymakers, stakeholders, and service providers can work together to address these **challenges** and ensure that the implementation of digital technologies in the service and education sectors contributes to the achievement of the SDGs. As part of this book, the chapter will offer an overview of the role of digital technologies in implementing the SDGs in the service and education sectors and provides practical **recommendations** for stakeholders on how to leverage these technologies for sustainable development.

Target Audience

Like that of the book that it proposes to form part of, the **target audience** of this chapter includes learners at higher education institutions, especially at undergraduate and postgraduate levels (500+ universities in India and 1000+ universities globally). As part of the book, this chapter will also cater to a **target audience** of academicians, researchers, business leaders, managers, decision-makers, entrepreneurs and startups, as well as professionals and consultants from service-oriented industries, such as tourism, hospitality, etc., who are interested in understanding and harnessing the power of digital **innovation** to drive successful transformation in the service and education sectors.

Recommended Topics

In terms of the **recommended topics** suggested for the book **Sustainable Development Goal Advancement Through Digital Innovation in the Service Sector**, this chapter will especially address those with regard to:

- Digital Technologies for Education and Lifelong Learning

but also:

- Leveraging Digital Technologies for Sustainable Operations

- Digital Technologies for Enhancing Service Quality and Customer Experience
- Digital Technologies for Sustainable Cities and Communities
- Digital Technologies for Enabling Innovation and Collaboration in the Service and Automotive Sectors
- Digital solutions for promoting renewable energy and energy efficiency

Objectives

As part of the book "**Sustainable Development Goal Advancement Through Digital Innovation in the Service Sector**", this chapter aims to explore the potential of digital **innovation** in promoting and achieving the sustainable development goals, specifically within the service and education sectors. As part of the book, this chapter will examine how digital technologies and innovative **solutions** can be harnessed to address various social, economic, and environmental **challenges** faced by the service, education, tourism, and automotive sectors, and more. It seeks to highlight the transformative power of digital innovation in advancing sustainable development **objectives**. Along the key **objectives** of the book, those of this chapter include:

1. **Understanding the role of digital innovation in achieving the SDGs:** As part of the book, this chapter aims to provide insights into how digital technologies can contribute to the accomplishment of specific SDGs, such as industry innovation and infrastructure, sustainable cities and communities, and especially quality education.
2. As part of the book, this chapter may showcase **real-world examples** of where digital innovation had been successfully utilized in the service and education sectors to advance sustainable development goals. It will highlight innovative approaches and lessons learned from different contexts and regions.
3. **Identifying challenges and opportunities:** As part of the book, this chapter will discuss the **challenges** and **barriers** that organizations and policymakers face in adopting and implementing digital innovations for sustainable development. It will also explore the **opportunities** and potential synergies between digital innovation and sustainable development within the service and education sectors.
4. **Policy recommendations and guidelines:** As part of the book, this chapter will provide **recommendations** and guidelines for policymakers, organizations, and practitioners on how to harness digital innovation to accelerate progress towards the SDGs effectively. It could propose strategies for creating an enabling environment, fostering **collaboration**, and promoting the adoption of digital technologies in the service and education sectors.

Overall, in line with the **objective** of the book, that of this chapter is to raise awareness, promote Computer Science (CS) and Information Technology (IT) students' self-regulated learning and **knowledge sharing behavior** as drivers of individual innovative behavior (Ngugi & Goosen, 2021c), and inspire action towards leveraging digital innovation as a catalyst for sustainable development in the service and education sectors.

BACKGROUND

This section of the chapter will provide broad definitions and discussions of the topic on **Modelling** Course-Design Characteristics (CDCs), Self-Regulated Learning (SRL) and **the Mediating Effects of Knowledge Sharing Behavior in the Education Sector** with regard to **Drivers of Individual Innovative Behavior** (IIB) and incorporate the views of others (in the form of a literature review) into the discussion to support, refute, or demonstrate the authors' position on the topic (Ngugi & Goosen, 2018).

Leveraging Digital Technologies for Sustainable Operations

Against the **background** of *Embracing Business Sustainability Through Innovation and Creativity in the Service Sector*, the book edited by Tyagi, Nadda, Bharti and Kemer (2023) pointed out that "the ever-increasing pressure and rivalry in the global business environment" means that "businesses must develop sustainable practices that set them apart from the competition". In the latter book, the chapter by Kemer and Tyagi (2023, p. 125) indicated that rapid technological developments, such as the application of artificial intelligence and robotics, "have affected business areas and caused differences in products and services. The tourism and hospitality" marketing industry had "also been affected by these".

Digital Technologies for Sustainable Cities and Communities

In the context of *inclusive* ***community*** *development through tourism and hospitality practices*, Nadda, Gonzo, Batta and Sharma (2023) pointed out that **sustainable** "tourism should not be limited to environmental preservation; the sociocultural and economic sides should also be considered. There is a need for an integrated approach". According to Daneva and Nadda (2023, p. 20), the United Nations World Tourism Organization (UNWTO) indicated that "annual ecotourism revenues worldwide are estimated to grow from approximately $800 billion to one trillion in 2025." An example of **community** development through ecotourism in a stakeholder analysis of Botevgrad, Bulgaria, was provided in the latter chapter.

The thesis by Moniz Vieira (2022, p. 2) critically examined the multiple tourism and lifestyle mobilities, as well as "travel experiences of the Madeiran **community** that decided to migrate to the Channel Island of Jersey, most during the 1990's".

Digital Technologies for Enabling Innovation and Collaboration in the Service and Automotive Sectors

"The purpose of the study reported on in" the chapter by Bolton, Goosen and Kritzinger (2023, p. 184) in that same book "was to explore and attempt to answer the primary research question: To what extent can embracing business sustainability through" *innovation* and productivity *in the automotive sector* impact creativity, *collaboration*, and the generation of savings?

Understanding the Role of Digital Innovation in Achieving the Sustainable Development Goals

In order to develop an **understanding of the role** of employee-tourist interactions and the value that these have in terms of "an effect on tourist experiences, text" and Big Data analytics were used in the research reported on in the paper presented by Tyagi, et al. (2023, p. 1289) at the 10th international conference on computing for **sustainable** global **development** (INDIACom).

Knowledge Sharing Behavior

Knowledge sharing behavior was found to be a significant mediator of the three (3) antecedents of technology-mediated learning **innovation**: cognizance of technology, ability to explore and intention, as well as to mediate information technology student **innovation** (Ngugi & Goosen, 2021a).

Knowledge Management

In a book on *Knowledge Management and Research Innovation* at *Global Higher Education Institutions* (HEIs), the chapter by Nadda (2023, p. 61) explored "a *framework* to manage the **sharing** of **knowledge**" at "higher education institutions and the role of information and communication" technologies "in promoting and enhancing the" purpose of said chapter "across several key processes and services like the research processes, teaching and learning processes, virtual learning" environments, "student recruitment, engagement, retention and achievement related services, administrative services and processes, and strategic planning and management as an efficient and effective tool at global level."

A *framework* for university partnerships promoting continued support of e-schools was suggested by Vorster and Goosen (2017) in the proceedings of the 46th annual conference of SACLA.

Self-Regulation

Self-regulation is viewed as an important construct that promotes an understanding of the human self (Forgas, Baumeister, & Tice, 2009). Self-regulation, according to Williams (2008, p. 9), "is the ability of the learner to control interest, attitude, and effort toward a task or a goal".

The decision to investigate self-regulatory mechanisms among technology students was supported by the maxim "that people with good self-control do better than others" (Forgas, et al., 2009, p. 5). When applied to technology students, the research posits that students with high levels of self-regulation, outperform others and tend to have innovative tendencies. This lays a basis for exploring students' self-regulatory skills. Consequently, one of the study objectives explored how SRL acts as an antecedent of both knowledge sharing behavior and innovative behavior. The construct of SRL is discussed further in the following paragraphs.

Self-Regulated Learning

According to Hagger, Wood, Stiff, and Chatzisarantis (2009), instructors can support students to engage in self-regulation to monitor their own work, generate their own feedback, and use that feedback to improve their learning and understanding.

Self-Regulated Learning and Innovative Behavior

Lizarraga, Villanueva and Baquedano (2011) established a link between *self-regulation* of *learning* supported by web 2.0 tools and competence on creativity and **innovation**, which implied a link between SRL and *innovative behavior.*

In the proceedings of the 48th Annual Conference of the Southern African Computer Lecturers' Association (SACLA), Goosen and Ngugi (2019a) indicated that **innovation** for computing students matter, while the journal article by Ngugi and Goosen (2021c) how Computer Science and Information Technology students' *self-regulated learning* and **knowledge sharing behavior** acted as drivers of individual *innovative behavior.*

Self-Regulated Learning and Digital Entrepreneurship

In their journal article on *educational technologies* and **society**, Ming-Chou and Ming-Hsiao (2012) were investigating learner affective performance in web-based **learning** by using **entrepreneurship** as a metaphor.

Papers in the proceedings of the South Africa International Conference on *Educational Technologies* (SAICET) described how such technologies were being used for an ICT for Development (ICT4D) Massive Open Online Course (MOOC) *in the 21st century* (Goosen, 2015a) or a community engagement project (Goosen, 2015b), as well as in distance education, to go beyond the horizon with qualitative perspectives (Goosen & Mukasa-Lwanga, 2017) respectively. When rethinking teaching and learning *in the 21st century*, **course design characteristics** towards innovative behavior (Goosen & Ngugi, 2018) consist of *course task characteristics and course knowledge characteristics.*

Overview of the Job Characteristics Model

The *Job Characteristics Model* (JCM) by Hackman and Oldham (1980) presented five (5) intrinsic factors or dimensions for any given job or task. These five (5) dimensions describe the extent of task identity, job feedback, autonomy, skill variety and task significance.

Course Design Characteristics

Within the university sector and setting, a major function of university education is to "assist in the preservation, transmission and increase of knowledge and in the stimulation of the intellectual life and cultural development" (Republic of Kenya, 2012, p. 46). Hence, an investigation of course design characteristics should inform how it acts as a significant driver of students' intellectual and innovative life.

Two papers in the proceedings of Institute of Science and Technology Education (ISTE) conferences on Mathematics, Science and Technology Education described the effects of **course design characteristics**, *self-regulated learning* and **knowledge sharing behavior** in facilitating the development of innovative behavior among technology students at universities (Ngugi & Goosen, 2017); (Goosen & Ngugi, 2019b).

MAIN FOCUS OF THE CHAPTER

Issues, Problems

This section of the chapter will present the authors' perspective on the **issues**, **problems**, **challenges**, etc., as these relate to the main theme of **Sustainable Development Goal Advancement Through Digital Innovation in the Service Sector** and arguments supporting the authors' position on **modelling the mediating effects of knowledge sharing behavior in the education sector** regarding **drivers of individual innovative behavior**. It will also compare and contrast with what has been, or is currently being, done as it relates to the specific topic of the chapter.

Such innovative students would be involved in nurturing and creating novel and improved products and services, as well as providing a seamless supply of innovative human expertise to the society. Consequently, this raises critical **issues** for university education providers and scholars, as the study demonstrated that successful innovative behavior among technology students is partly determined by the contextual antecedent of course design characteristics and partly by the individual characteristics of technology students, in terms of their self-regulated learning abilities.

Identifying Challenges and Opportunities

"Industry 4.0 and Industry 5.0 are changing the ways business operations are carried out" (Patel, Angrish, & Nadda, 2023, p. 99). Although organizations "across the sectors have been facing **challenges** in" the supply chain management of fast-moving consumer goods (FMCG) and the *automotive sector*, a cross-sector comparison of Industry 5.0 by the latter authors showed that **digital technologies** were also involved when **identifying** the **challenges and opportunities** related to Business 5.0 in **emerging** markets.

Also in the book on *Embracing Business Sustainability Through Innovation and Creativity in the Service Sector* mentioned in the previous section of this chapter, the chapter by Nadda and Pospíšilová (2023, p. 249) indicated that "Airbnb is a platform allowing a peer-to-peer accommodation option for people sharing their own extra space. As simple it sounds, there are many **challenges** behind" the implementation of Airbnb in the local neighborhood related to **innovation** vs. disruption.

In the context of a book on *Employability and Skills Development in the Sports, Events, and Hospitality Industry* edited by Nadda, Arnott, Sealy and Delaney (2022), the latter editors indicated that to "enter the sports, events, and hospitality industry, it is necessary to develop and hone certain skills to ensure competitiveness. These skills must be studied further" towards providing applicable education to the service sector. "The tourism and hospitality industry nowadays requires … graduates to have specific competencies, **problem** solving skills, critical thinking, creativity, analytical and ICT skills". The chapter in the latter book by Nadda (2022b, p. 139) therefore suggested **Problem**-Based Learning (PBL) and employability skills development for the hospitality sector. The latter is especially important, as a general estimate mentioned by Nadda (2022a, p. 25) suggested "that up to 10% of the global workforce is directly or indirectly employed in" the tourism and hospitality sectors, with these being some "of the fastest growing sectors" globally.

According to the paper presented by Singh, et al. (2023b, p. 619) at the second International Conference on Electronics and Renewable Systems (ICEARS), in the tourism and hotel realm, the use of the Internet of Things "is recognized for its potential to create new business **opportunities**. With" the "IoT, the tourism and hospitality industries can" be described in a bibliometric study using the Bibliometrix R-Tool.

Research Context

In Kenya, the Government has flagged the Konza Technology City project to launch East Africa into Global Business Process Outsourcing (BPO), by harnessing talent from a strong well-educated and highly competitive local work force. The project dubbed the Silicon Savannah of Africa, is expected to host innovators in a state-of-the-art 21st century exemplar city and provide University and Science Parks (Frischmann, 2011).

But how well are universities preparing the technology students to be able to innovate and meet the new **challenges** of the 21st skills and jobs? Hence, it remains doubtful if the current design of programs and the psychosocial factors among technology students will guarantee graduates, who can intentionally **introduce** and apply "within a job of ideas, processes, products, and procedures that are new to that job and which are designed to benefit it" (West & Farr, 1990, p. 9).

Research Design and Method

Research design was **defined** by Creswell (2009, p. 3) as the "plans and the procedures for research that span the decisions from broad assumptions to detailed methods of data collection and analysis". The choice of the proper research design is crucial to ensure that the study provides relevant information to the research objectives. The design of this research is therefore a quantitative, non-experimental, cross-sectional, explanatory (correlational) survey.

Measurement of Individual Innovative Behavior

The measure of individual innovative behavior was based on the scale of De Jong and Den Hartog (2010). The scale has twelve items that measure the four (4) sub constructs of: opportunity exploration, idea generation, championing, and **implementation**. The scale was anchored from 1 (never) to 7 (always). The revised scale consisted of 11 items, four (4) response measure of the following four (4) sub-dimensions: opportunity exploration, idea exploration, championing, and application. More on the use of similar scales can be found in Ngugi and Goosen (2019) towards smart innovation for information systems and technology students by modelling motivation, metacognition and affective aspects of learning, as well as Goosen and Ngugi (2018) on rethinking teaching and learning in the 21st century through course design characteristics towards innovative behavior.

The format utilized a Likert scale that ranged from 1 (never) to 5 (always). High scores signify high levels of innovative behavior in a technology student. Some of the items in the opportunity exploration scale included items such "look for opportunities to improve an existing process, technology, product, service", while for idea generation "find new approaches to execute information technology tasks". Similarly, examples of items for championing and **implementation** are "attempt to convince people to support an innovative idea" and "put effort into the development of new things" respectively.

In a *Handbook of Research on Technology-Supported Teaching and Research Methods for Educators*, the chapters by Goosen (2019a; 2019b) showed how e.g., students on the autism spectrum can be supported.

The questionnaire items were as indicated in Table 1.

Ethical Considerations

Since this study involved research with real people, key ethical considerations included privacy **issues** of anonymity and confidentiality as suggested by Daymon and Holloway (2010). Neuman (2006, p. 129) defined **ethics** as what is or what is not legitimate to do, or what moral research procedure are involved.

To ensure sufficient scientific rigor, the research was performed in a systematic and objective manner. Further, due diligence was given to ensure the integrity of data by taking required steps such as: care while coding data into software, checking for discrepancies, maintaining security, and maintaining regular backups (Kakabadse, Kakabadse, & Kouzmin, 2002); (Raman & Hellerstein, 2000).

Missing Data Analysis

Cohen, Cohen, West, and Aiken (1983) suggested between 5% to 10% of missing data as being acceptable and not too large. Similarly, Hair, Anderson, Babin, and Black (2010) provided a criterion of 10% for missing data.

Table 1. Questionnaire items of the innovative behavior scale

Code	Questionnaire Items
IB_OPX1	1. …look for opportunities to improve an existing process, technology, product, service
IB_OPX2	2. …recognize opportunities to make a positive difference in IT software development, project development, class, or the society at large
IB_OPX3	3. …pay attention to non-routine **issues** related to my course, class, department, or the market place for IT products
IB_IDE1	4. …search out new Information Technology methods, techniques, or instruments
IB_IDE2	5. …generate original **solutions** to Information Technology **problems**
IB_IDE3	6. …find new approaches to execute Information Technology tasks
IB_CHA1	7. …encourage key class members to be enthusiastic about innovative Information Technology ideas
IB_CHA2	8. …attempt to convince people to support an innovative idea
IB_APP1	9. …systematically introduce innovative ideas into Information Technology course practices
IB_APP2	10. …contribute to the **implementation** of new ideas
IB_APP3	11. …put effort into the development of new things

Key to Table 1:
IB_OPX Opportunity exploration
IB_IDE Idea exploration
IB_CHA Championing
IB_APP Application

Checking Multivariate Assumptions

Normality of the Data: Skewness and Kurtosis

More details on **checking multivariate assumptions**, as well as the *normality of the data* in terms of *skewness and kurtosis*, can be found in the chapter by Ngugi and Goosen (2021a) on knowledge sharing behavior mediating information technology student innovation as part of the *Handbook of Research on Modern Educational Technologies, Applications, and Management.*

Theoretically, if the absolute value of the skewness is less than three (3) times the Standard Error (SE), then the **problem** of *kurtosis* is not significant. The two items as indicated in Table 2 and the histograms in Figures 1 and 2 each had an absolute value of SE less than the absolute value of the *kurtosis*, implying a *kurtosis* **issue** with the two items. For the two items, the frequency of distribution on the Likert scale of responses were as indicated in Table 2.

Table 2. Frequency of responses for the knowledge sharing behavior scale

		Never	Rarely	Sometimes	Often	Always
KS_WC4_4	Frequency	30	57	59	48	51
	Percent	12.0	22.8	23.6	19.2	20.4
KS_CC2_7	Frequency	3	46	68	72	60
	Percent	1.2	18.4	27.2	28.8	24.0

Homoscedasticity and Linearity

The test for *homoscedasticity* involved a visual examination of the histogram of standardized residuals (Figure 3) and the normal P-P plot of regression standardized residual (Figure 4).

The histogram of standardized residuals indicated that the data contained approximately normally distributed errors, as did the normal P-P plot of standardized residuals, which showed points that were close to the line. The random pattern of scatter of the residuals indicated that the regression models was homoscedastic. Consequently, heteroscedasticity was not an **issue** in the analysis. Thus, the data met the assumptions of homogeneity of variance and *linearity*.

Figure 1. Histogram for KS_WC4_4 with large kurtosis values
Source: Author

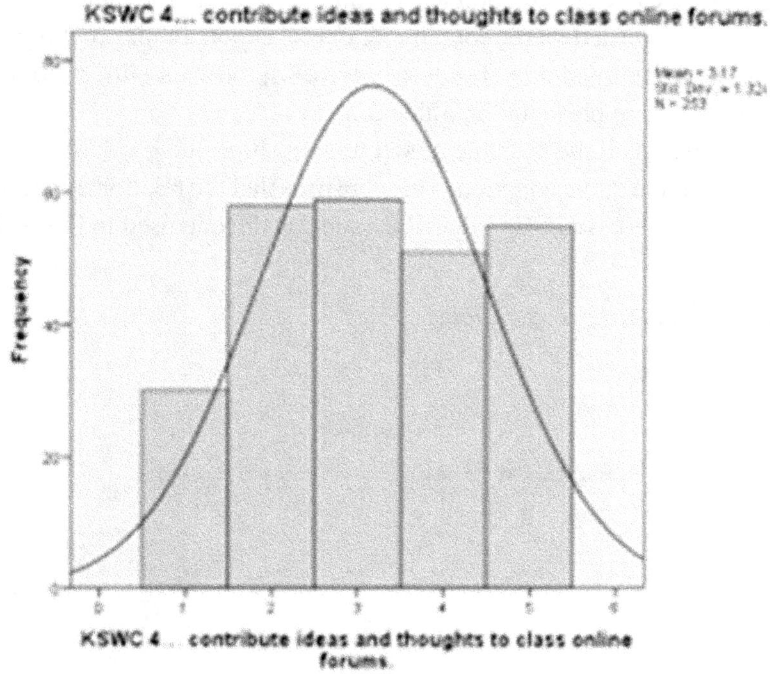

Figure 2. Histogram for KS_CC2_7 with large kurtosis values
Source: Author

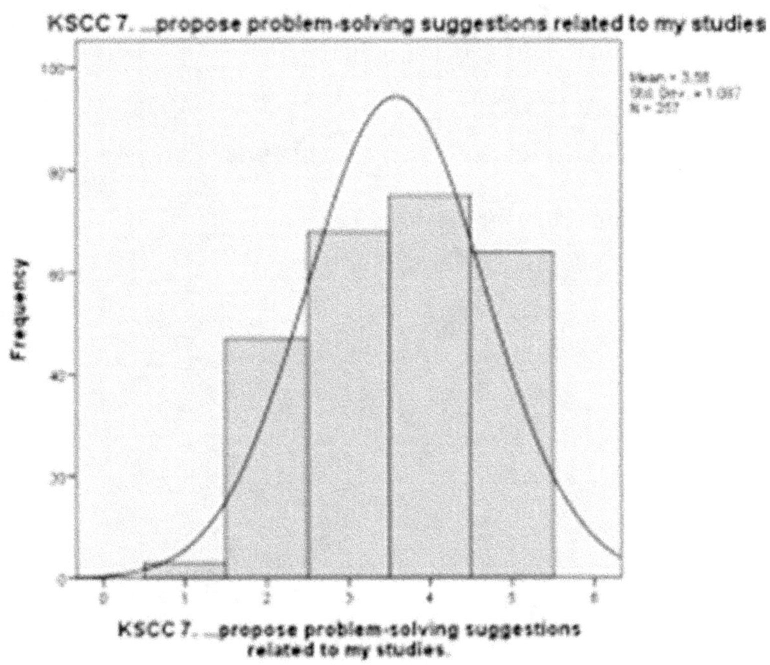

Linearity

Using SPSS 18 software, a Curve Estimation Regression (CER) was conducted for all the relationships in the model. The equations tested were: compound, cubic, exponential, growth, inverse, linear, logarithmic, logistic, power, s, and quadratic. The tests were all significant with $p < 0.05$. The F test values for each of the relationships are presented in Table 3.

The results indicate that in all the possible model relationships. the F values are largest for the linear regression and smallest for the cubic equation. This confirms that the relationships are sufficiently linear to be tested with a covariance-based SEM algorithm such as the one used in the AMOS software.

Figure 3. Histogram of standardized residuals
Source: Author

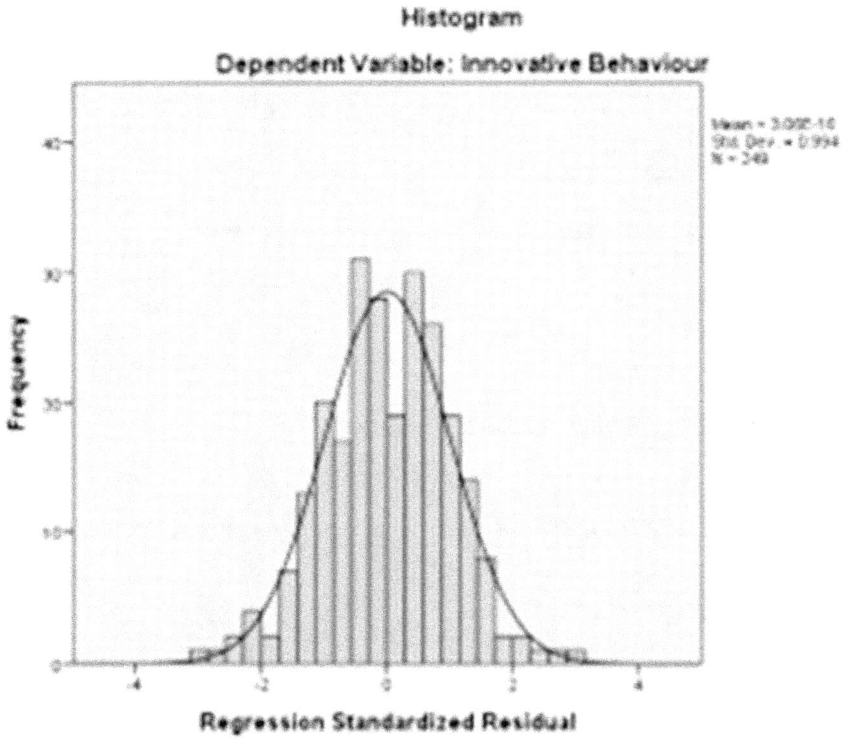

Figure 4. Normal P-P plot of regression standardized residual
Source: Author

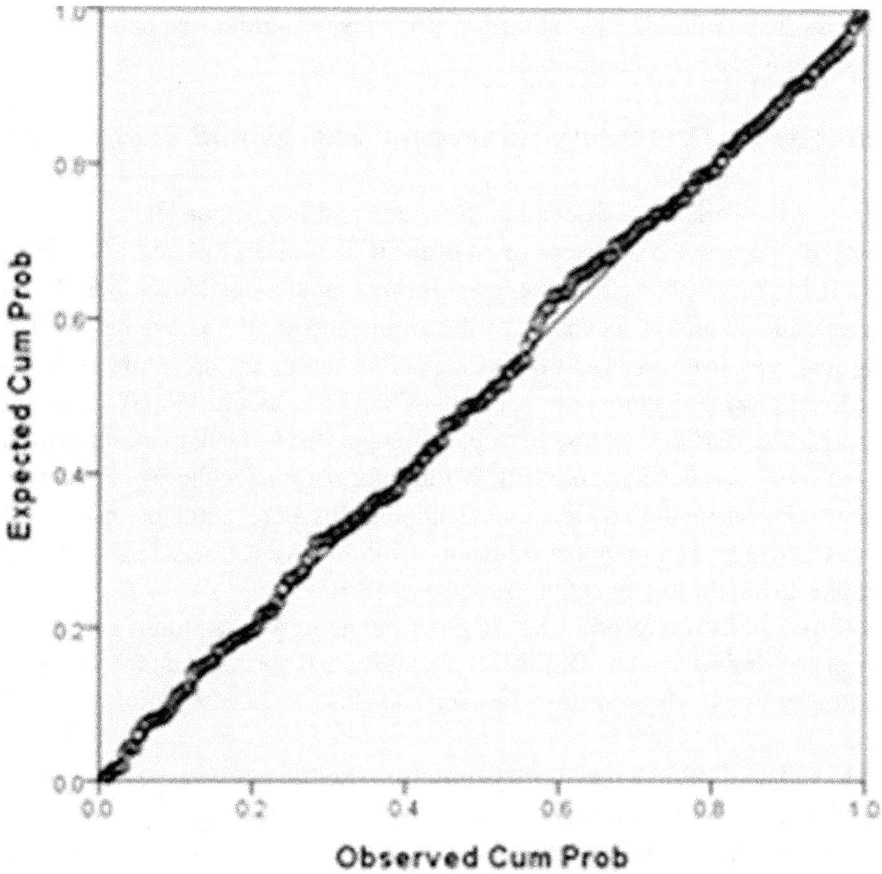

Table 3. Curve estimates for testing linearity of relationships

Equation	KS-IB	CDC-KS	SRL-KS	CDC-IB	SRL-IB	KS-IB	CDC-IB
Linear	193.368	82.360	41.249	57.883	32.211	193.368	57.883
Compound	188.518	78.368	39.025	54.805	29.378	188.518	54.805
Cubic	63.997	29.611	16.340	20.642	12.321	63.997	20.642
Exponential	188.518	78.368	39.025	54.805	29.378	188.518	54.805
Growth	188.518	78.368	39.025	54.805	29.378	188.518	54.805
Inverse	148.781	57.597	26.159	45.445	22.192	148.781	45.445
Logarithmic	180.787	71.640	34.509	53.375	27.989	180.787	53.375
Logistic	188.518	78.368	39.025	54.805	29.378	188.518	54.805
Power	189.423	69.629	32.704	51.563	25.667	189.423	51.563
Quadratic	96.372	44.596	23.767	29.529	17.668	96.372	29.529
S	167.674	57.061	24.713	44.851	20.396	167.674	44.851

SOLUTIONS AND RECOMMENDATIONS

This section of the chapter will discuss **solutions and recommendations** in dealing with the **issues** or **problems** presented in the preceding section.

Digital Solutions for Promoting Renewable Energy and Energy Efficiency

In the International Conference of Education, Research and Innovation (ICERI) proceedings, Ezema, Izobo-Martins and Owoseni (2020) were **promoting** ICTs and **digital** education in public schools in Lagos, Nigeria using affordable clean **energy solutions**, as the challenges posed by COVID-19 had "made virtual education which is dependent on the acquisition of" ICTs, and digital education, essential.

Promoting quality e-government **solutions** by applying a comprehensive information assurance model and use cases for **digital** signatures, the paper by Villalón-Fonseca, Mora-Castro, Bartels-González, Carballo-Chavarría and Marín-Raventós (2016, p. 223) suggested ICTs for **promoting** human development and protecting the environment at the 6th IFIP World Information Technology Forum (WITFOR). "This is the case when considering digital signature technology, as an essential element to" the "information assurance process to audit technological **solutions** for e-government services". The latter authors also showed "examples using **digital** signature from Costa Rica."

Wolverton (2018, p. 4) was **promoting** exercise and activity in children as **solutions** in answer to the challenges of the **digital** society. **Digital** technologies had "become an integral part of" everyone's "daily lives. In many ways", these shape "the pace and flow of society. Unfortunately," these may also shape waistlines ;).

According to Nakhoul (2019), banks are **promoting digital solutions** to cut costs.

Principals with regard to ethical data management and research integrity in the context of e-schools and community engagement, as well as ethical ICT4D **solutions** in this regard that will increase students' access to MOOCs (Goosen, 2018), were upheld in the research carried out in the study reported on in this chapter.

Independent Variable One: Course Design Characteristics

Bartlett's test of sphericity is a measure of the overall correlations between variables and tests the null hypothesis, which specifies whether the correlation matrix is an identity matrix. The Bartlett's test of sphericity value was highly significant ($p < .001$), thus confirming the existence of a relationship between the variables. All the communalities were above 0.389. The extraction of factors generated a six (6)-factor **solution**, instead of the expected 11-factor **solution** suggested by literature on the two subscales of task characteristics and course characteristics. However, the application of the scree test as indicated by Cattell (1966) suggested a four (4) factor **solution** as presented in Figure 5.

Independent Variable Two: Self-Regulated Learning

Factor analysis generated a six (6) factor **solution**, instead of the five (5) factor **solution** suggested by literature. The factor **solutions** accounted for 60.497% of the total variance for the learning strategies scale. Tests involving the scree test criterion, also generated a six (6) factor **solution**. After a series of extractions and elimination of factors with low communalities, the rotated component factor matrix that resulted was as presented in Table 4.

Mediating Variable: Knowledge Sharing Behavior

This factor analysis generated a three (3) factor **solution**, instead of the four (4) factor **solution** suggested by literature on the subscales. The factor **solutions** accounted for 60.497% of the total variance for the learning strategies scale. After a series of extractions and elimination of factors with low communalities, the rotated component factor matrix that resulted was as presented in Table 5.

Figure 5. Scree plot of components of factor analysis

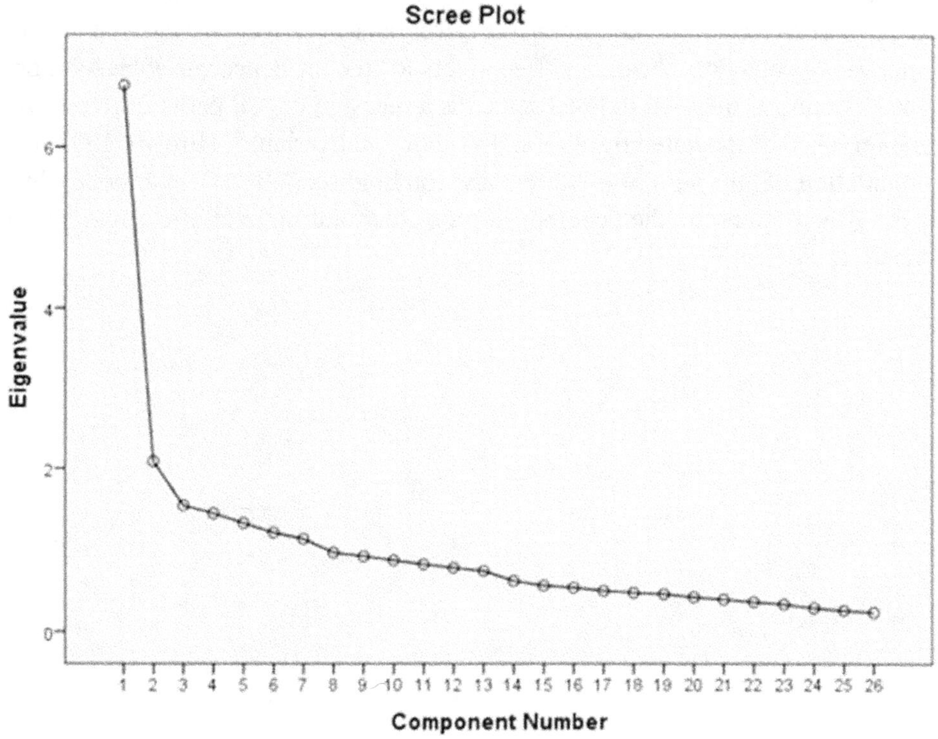

Comparative Fit Index, Normed Fit Index, Relative Fit Index

The Comparative Fit Index (CFI), Non-normed Fit Index (NFI), Relative Fit Index (RFI) and Incremental Fit Index (IFI) had maximum values of 1.00, signifying a perfect fit between the data and the model.

A statewide study of factors explaining successful completion of the probationary period of beginning teachers by Heck and Wolcott (1997) indicated that values greater than .90 signify a good fit. However, in most studies, like the replication of the confirmatory factor analysis of the end-user computing satisfaction instrument by Doll and Xia (1997), scores between .80 and .89 for the CFI, NFI and RFI suggest a reasonable fit.

In the study reported on in this chapter, the fit indexes ranged between .88 and .94, thus suggesting a reasonable to good model fit (CFI =.943, Tucker-Lewis Index (TLI)=.926, NFI=.889, IFI=.944, and Goodness-of-Fit Index (GFI)=.925).

A comparison of the fit indices for the proposed model and final model are presented in Table 4 (see Appendix 1), including chi-square ($\chi 2$) statistics and p-value, Degrees of Freedom (DF) and normed chi-square ($\chi 2/DF$), as well as values for the Adjusted Goodness of Fit Index (AGFI) and Root Mean Square Residual (RMR).

According to Cheung (2007), there are four methods for computing Confidence Intervals (CI), namely Wald CI, percentile bootstrap CI, bias-corrected bootstrap CI, and likelihood-based CI.

Direct and Indirect Effects

In line with Bollen (1987), the **direct effects, indirect** effects, and the standardized total effects values were computed in a SEM analysis to determine the effect of each exogenous variable on the endogenous variables of innovative behavior. The direct effect refers to "the influence variables have on one another in a direct linkage contrast, the total indirect effect, is a measure of "all paths from one variable to another that are intervened or mediated by at least one additional variable" (Brown, 1997, p. 5). The total effect is a computation of "the sum of the direct and total indirect effects" in a model. In addition, the specific indirect effect, refers to "the decomposition of the total indirect effect into specified indirect paths of interest".

Table 4. Rotated component matrix based on principal component analysis with varimax rotation for the self-regulated learning scale

	Components					
	1 Organization	**2 Rehearsal**	**3 Elaboration**	**4 Self-regulation**	**5 Critical Thinking**	**6 Metacognition**
METACOG5_22	.768					
ORGAN1_24	.694					
METACOG6_23	.665					
METACOG4_21	.661					
ORGAN2_25	.615	.417				
ORGAN3_26	.535					
REHERS1_28		.722				
REHERS4_31		.662				
REHERS2_29		.655				
ORGAN4_27		.655				
ELABOR1_6			.716			
ELABOR2_7			.685			
ELABOR3_8			.638			
ELABOR4_9			.594			
SREGUL1_12				.706		
ELABOR6_11				.701		
ELABOR5_10				.687		
SREGUL3_14				.548		
CTHINK3_3					.815	
CTHINK1_1					.668	
CTHINK4_4					.579	
CTHINK5_5					.471	
METACOG2_19						.736
METACOG1_18						.679
METACOG3_20						.569
No. of Items	6	4	4	4	4	3
Cronbach Alpha	.663	.801	.735	.696	.692	.660
Eigen Value	33.514	7.899	5.778	4.797	4.508	4.001
% of Variance	14.070	10.640	9.672	9.505	8.589	8.022
a. Rotation converged in 8 iterations.						

Policy Recommendations and Guidelines

According to the Republic of Kenya (2007a, p. 1), at a **policy** level, the Kenya Vision 2030 blueprint for the country's development covering 2008 -2030 seeks to transform the country 'into a newly industrializing, middle-income country providing a high-quality life to all its citizens by the year 2030". The blueprint envisages Science Technology and Innovation (ST&I) as playing a critical role in improving the quality of life and social welfare of the citizenry. The application of ST&I in education and training curricula in the country, is envisaged to lead to the creation, adoption, adaptation, and usage of knowledge (Republic of Kenya, 2007b).

Table 5. Rotated component matrix based on principal component analysis with varimax rotation for the knowledge sharing scale

	Component		
	1 Communications	2 Personal Interactions	3 Communities of Practice
KS_WC4_4	.691		
KS_WC5_5	.714		
KS_CC1_6	.729	.355	
KS_CC2_7	.730		
KS_CC3_8	.765		
KS_CC5_10	.598		
KS_PI1_11		.632	
KS_PI2_12		.669	
KS_PI3_13		.649	
KS_PI4_14		.745	
KS_PI5_15		.637	
KS_PI6_16		.613	
KS_CP1_17			.739
KS_CP2_18			.791
KS_CP3_19			.805
KS_CP4_20			.685
No. of Items	6	6	3
Cronbach Alpha	.868	.825	.758
Eigen Value	6.623	1.499	1.254
% of Variance	21.651	19.884	17.065

FUTURE RESEARCH DIRECTIONS

This section of the chapter will discuss **future** and **emerging trends** and provide insight about the **future** of the theme of **Sustainable Development Goal Advancement Through Digital Innovation in the Service Sector**, from the perspective of the chapter focus on **modelling the mediating effects of knowledge sharing behavior in the education sector** regarding **drivers of individual innovative**

behavior. The viability of a paradigm, model, implementation **issues** of proposed programs, etc., may also be included in this section. **Future research directions** within the domain of the topic will finally be suggested.

Identifying Challenges and Opportunities

Patel, et al. (2023) were identifying the challenges and opportunities related to Business 5.0 in terms of **emerging trends** across global markets.

The research reported on by Singh, et al. (2023a, p. 239) at the 5th International Conference on *Smart* Systems and Inventive Technology (ICSSIT) investigated "the number of studies conducted in the field of" green technologies "and sustainability in terms of" e.g., "annual scientific production, source, authorship", etc. in a review towards **future research directions**.

Two related publications included the journal article by Ngugi and Goosen (2019) on working towards *smart* **innovation** for information systems and technology students by modelling motivation, metacognition and affective aspects of learning, as well as the chapter by the same authors (Ngugi & Goosen, 2022) on digitalization and drivers of innovative behavior for a *smart* economy in the post-COVID-19 era in terms of technology student course design characteristics.

Digital Technologies for Enhancing Service Quality and Customer Experience

Against the background of *disruptive innovation and **emerging** technologies for business excellence in the service sector*, the aim of the chapter by Chithradevi and Nadda (2022, p. 1) was "to analyze the impact of mobile" and **digital technologies for enhancing** "the **customer** service **experience** in the" Small and Medium-sized Enterprise (SME) "hotel sector. Most of the hotels use their mobile …

CONCLUSION

This section of the chapter will provide a discussion of the overall coverage of the chapter, an overview of the findings and concluding remarks.

The first section of this chapter after the **INTRODUCTION** provided the **BACKGROUND** to the study by highlighting the need to explore the contextual and individual antecedents of innovative behavior and the possible mediating role of Knowledge Sharing Behavior (KSB) in that relationship. That section of the chapter also documented the literature reviewed on the antecedents of innovative behavior among undergraduate technology students at university. The section highlighted significant theories that informed the study, which included a review of the individual and contextual factors that act as key drivers predicting students' individual innovative behavior. Further, the literature focused on the drivers of KSB, and how KSB, in turn, is a predicator of innovative behavior. In addition, the section presented a conceptual framework that guided the study. Lastly, this section outlined the research context that informs the study.

The next section outlined the justification and **problem statement**.

The following section documented the methodology and outlined the setting, research design, population, sampling, pilot study, research measures and data collection procedure. Further, the section outlined the data analysis procedures, as well introducing the structural equation modeling techniques used to test the seven (7) hypotheses.

The subsequent section was the most important, as it presented some of the **results** of the study, by outlining the descriptive and inferential statistics. First, the data screening and cleaning procedures employed were described, followed closely by tests for multivariate assumptions, which were done as part of the preliminary pilot study. Thereafter, the reliability and validity of the instruments were explored, as well as measurement of common method bias. Then, the exploratory and confirmatory factor analysis tests were conducted. The section concluded with a test of the mediation of the hypothesized relationships between the individual and contextual antecedents of KSB and innovative behavior. Subsequently, a recap of the direct and indirect effects using bootstrap sampling was also presented.

Finally, the previous section of the chapter presented possible **future research directions**.

REFERENCES

Bollen, K. (1987). Total, direct, and indirect effects in structural equation models. In C. Clogg (Ed.), *Sociological methodology* (pp. 37–69). American Sociological Association. doi:10.2307/271028

Bolton, A. D., Goosen, L., & Kritzinger, E. (2023). Embracing Business Sustainability Through Innovation and Productivity in the Automotive Sector: Creativity, Collaboration, and Generating Savings. In P. Tyagi, V. Nadda, V. Bharti, & E. Kemer (Eds.), Embracing Business Sustainability Through Innovation and Creativity in the Service Sector (pp. 184-204). IGI Global. doi:10.4018/978-1-6684-6732-9.ch012

Brown, R. L. (1997). Assessing specific mediational effects in complex theoretical models. *Structural Equation Modeling*, *4*(2), 142–156. doi:10.1080/10705519709540067

Cattell, R. B. (1966). The scree test for the number of factors. *Multivariate Behavioral Research*, *1*(2), 245–276. doi:10.120715327906mbr0102_10 PMID:26828106

Cheung, M. W. (2007). Comparison of approaches to constructing confidence intervals for mediating effects using structural equation models. *Structural Equation Modeling*, *14*(2), 227–246. doi:10.1080/10705510709336745

Chithradevi, S. N., & Nadda, V. (2022). Impact of Mobile Technology to Enhance the Customer Service Experience in SME Hotels. In *Disruptive Innovation and Emerging Technologies for Business Excellence in the Service Sector* (pp. 1–22). IGI Global. doi:10.4018/978-1-7998-9194-9.ch001

Cohen, J., Cohen, P., West, S. G., & Aiken, L. S. (1983). *Applied regression/correlation analysis for the behavioral sciences*. Routledge.

Creswell, J. W. (2009). Qualitative procedures. In *Research Design: Qualitative, Quantitative and Mixed-Methods Approaches* (pp. 173–202). Sage Publications.

Daneva, A., & Nadda, V. (2023). Community Development Through Ecotourism: A Stakeholder Analysis of Botevgrad, Bulgaria. In Inclusive Community Development Through Tourism and Hospitality Practices (pp. 20-48). IGI Global.

Daymon, C., & Holloway, I. (2010). *Qualitative research methods in public relations and marketing communications*. Routledge. doi:10.4324/9780203846544

De Jong, J. P., & Den Hartog, D. N. (2010). Measuring innovative work behaviour. *Creativity and Innovation Management, 19*(1), 23–36. doi:10.1111/j.1467-8691.2010.00547.x

Doll, W. J., & Xia, W. (1997). Confirmatory factor analysis of the end-user computing satisfaction instrument: A replication. [JOEUC]. *Journal of Organizational and End User Computing*, *9*(2), 24–31. doi:10.4018/joeuc.1997040103

Ezema, I., Izobo-Martins, O., & Owoseni, A. (2020). Promoting ICT and Digital Education in Public Schools in Lagos, Nigeria Using Affordable Clean Energy Solutions. *13th annual International Conference of Education, Research and Innovation (ICERI) Proceedings* (pp. 9585-9590). International Academy of Technology, Education and Development (IATED). https://library.iated.org/view/EZEMA2020PRO

Forgas, J. P., Baumeister, R. F., & Tice, D. M. (2009). The psychology of self-regulation: An introductory review. In J. P. Forgas, R. F. Baumeister, & D. M. Tice (Eds.), *Psychology of Self-Regulation: Cognitive, Affective and Motivational Processes* (pp. 1–20). Psychology Press.

Frischmann, P. (2011). *Konza Technology City: Where Africa's silicon savannah begins.* Do It In Kenya. www.doitinkenya.co.ke/pdf/Konza%20Summary%20Document.pdf

Goosen, L. (2008). A Brief History of Choosing First Programming Languages. In J. Impagliazzo (Ed.), *History of Computing and Education 3* (Vol. 269, pp. 167–170). Springer. doi:10.1007/978-0-387-09657-5_11

Goosen, L. (2015a). Educational Technologies for an ICT4D MOOC in the 21st Century. In D. Nwaozuzu, & S. Mnisi (Ed.), *Proceedings of the South Africa International Conference on Educational Technologies* (pp. 37-48). Pretoria: African Academic Research Forum.

Goosen, L. (2015b). Educational Technologies for Growing Innovative e-Schools in the 21st Century: A Community Engagement Project. In D. Nwaozuzu, & S. Mnisi (Ed.), *Proceedings of the South Africa International Conference on Educational Technologies* (pp. 49-61). Pretoria: African Academic Research Forum.

Goosen, L. (2016, February 18). *"We don't need no education"? Yes, they DO want e-learning in Basic and Higher Education!* UIR. https://uir.unisa.ac.za/handle/10500/20999

Goosen, L. (2018). Students' Access to an ICT4D MOOC. In S. Kabanda, H. Suleman, & S. Jamieson (Ed.), *Proceedings of the 47th Annual Conference of the Southern African Computer Lectures' Association (SACLA 2018)* (pp. 183-201). Cape Town: University of Cape Town.

Goosen, L. (2019a). Research on Technology-Supported Teaching and Learning for Autism. In L. Makewa, B. Ngussa, & J. Kuboja (Eds.), *Technology-Supported Teaching and Research Methods for Educators* (pp. 88–110). IGI Global., doi:10.4018/978-1-5225-5915-3.ch005

Goosen, L. (2019b). Technology-Supported Teaching and Research Methods for Educators: Case Study of a Massive Open Online Course. In L. Makewa, B. Ngussa, & J. Kuboja (Eds.), *Technology-Supported Teaching and Research Methods for Educators* (pp. 128–148). IGI Global., doi:10.4018/978-1-5225-5915-3.ch007

Goosen, L., Mentz, E., & Nieuwoudt, H. (2007). Choosing the "Best" Programming Language?! In E. Cohen (Ed.), *Proceedings of the 2007 Computer Science and IT Education Conference* (pp. 269-282). Santa Rosa: Informing Science Press.

Goosen, L., & Mukasa-Lwanga, T. (2017). Educational Technologies in Distance Education: Beyond the Horizon with Qualitative Perspectives. In U. I. Ogbonnaya, & S. Simelane-Mnisi (Ed.), *Proceedings of the South Africa International Conference on Educational Technologies* (pp. 41 - 54). Pretoria: African Academic Research Forum.

Goosen, L., & Ngugi, J. K. (2018). Rethinking Teaching and Learning in the 21st Century: Course Design Characteristics towards Innovative Behaviour. In M. M. Dichaba, & M. A. Sotayo (Ed.), *Proceedings of the South Africa International Conference on Education* (pp. 376 - 394). Pretoria: African Academic Research Forum.

Goosen, L., & Ngugi, J. K. (2019a). Innovation for Computing Students Matter, of Course! In B. L. Tait & J. H. Kroeze (Eds.), *Proceedings of 48th Annual Conference of the Southern African Computer Lecturers' Association (SACLA 2019)* (pp. 19–36). University of South Africa. http://osprey.unisa.ac.za/sacla2019/SACLA2019%20Proceedings.pdf#page=31

Goosen, L., & Ngugi, J. K. (2019b). Towards Innovative Behaviour For Technology Students. In J. Kriek, A. Ferreira, K. Padayachee, S. Van Putten, D. Mogashana, W. Raucher, & M. Speight Vaughn (Ed.), *Proceedings of the 10th Institute of Science and Technology Education (ISTE) International Conference on Mathematics, Science and Technology Education* (pp. 333 - 342). Mopani Camp, Kruger National Park: UNISA. https://uir.unisa.ac.za/handle/10500/26055

Hackman, J. R., & Oldham, G. R. (1980). *Work redesign*. Addison-Wesley.

Hagger, M. S., Wood, C., Stiff, C., & Chatzisarantis, N. L. (2009). The strength model of self-regulation failure and health-related behaviour. *Health Psychology Review, 3*(2), 208–238. doi:10.1080/17437190903414387

Hair, J. F., Anderson, R. E., Babin, B. J., & Black, W. C. (2010). *Multivariate data analysis: A global perspective* (Vol. 7). Pearson.

Heck, R. H., & Wolcott, L. P. (1997). Beginning teachers: A statewide study of factors explaining successful completion of the probationary period. *Educational Policy, 11*(1), 111–133. doi:10.1177/0895904897011001005

Kakabadse, N. K., Kakabadse, A., & Kouzmin, A. (2002). Ethical considerations in management research: A truth seekers guide. *International Journal of Value-Based Management, 15*(2), 105–138. doi:10.1023/A:1015246111906

Kemer, E., & Tyagi, P. K. (2023). Application of Artificial Intelligence and Robotics in Tourism and Hospitality Marketing. In *Embracing Business Sustainability Through Innovation and Creativity in the Service Sector* (pp. 125–140). IGI Global. doi:10.4018/978-1-6684-6732-9.ch008

Lizarraga, M., Villanueva, O. A., & Baquedano, M. (2011). Self-regulation of learning supported by web 2.0 tools: An example of raising competence on creativity and innovation. In G. Dettori & D. Persico (Eds.), *Fostering self-regulated learning through ICT* (pp. 295–314). Information Science Reference. doi:10.4018/978-1-61692-901-5.ch018

Ming-Chou, L., & Ming-Hsiao, C. (2012). Investigating learner affective performance in web-based learning by using entrepreneurship as a metaphor. *Journal of Educational Technology & Society*, *15*(3), 202–213.

Moniz Vieira, R. (2022). *The tourism and lifestyle mobilities of the Madeiran community in the Channel Island of Jersey.* [PhD thesis, Edinburgh Napier University..

Nadda, V. (2022a). Employability Skills Development in Hospitality. In Employability and Skills Development in the Sports, Events, and Hospitality Industry (pp. 25-46). IGI Global. doi:10.4018/978-1-7998-7781-3.ch002

Nadda, V. (2022b). Problem-Based Learning (PBL) and Employability Skills Development in the Hospitality Sector. In Employability and Skills Development in the Sports, Events, and Hospitality Industry (pp. 139-151). IGI Global.

Nadda, V. (2023). The Role of Information and Communication Technology (ICT) in Global Higher Education Institutions (HEIs). In Knowledge Management and Research Innovation in Global Higher Education Institutions (pp. 61-74). IGI Global.

Nadda, V., Arnott, I., Sealy, W., & Delaney, E. (Eds.). (2022). *Employability and Skills Development in the Sports, Events, and Hospitality Industry*. IGI Global. https://www.igi-global.com/gateway/book/265889 doi:10.4018/978-1-7998-7781-3

Nadda, V., Gonzo, F., Batta, R., & Sharma, A. (Eds.). (2023). *Inclusive community development through tourism and hospitality practices*. IGI Global. https://www.igi-global.com/book/inclusive-community-development-through-tourism/304337 doi:10.4018/978-1-6684-6796-1

Nadda, V., & Pospíšilová, M. (2023). Airbnb in the Local Neighbourhood: Innovaiton vs. Disruption. In Embracing Business Sustainability Through Innovation and Creativity in the Service Sector (pp. 249-252). IGI Global.

Nakhoul, S. (2019). Banks are promoting digital solutions to cut costs. *Business News*. http://www.businessnews.com.lb/cms/Story/StoryDetails/7149

Neuman, L. W. (2006). *Social research methods: Qualitative and quantitative Approaches* (6th ed.). Pearson Education Inc.

Ngugi, J., & Goosen, L. (2017). The Effects of Course Design Characteristics, Self-Regulated Learning and Knowledge Sharing in Facilitating the Development of Innovative Behaviour among Technology Students at Universities. *Proceedings of the Institute of Science and Technology Education (ISTE) Conference on Mathematics, Science and Technology Education* (pp. 80-86). Mopani Camp, Kruger National Park: UNISA Press.

Ngugi, J., & Goosen, L. (2018). Modelling Course-Design Characteristics, Self-Regulated Learning and the Mediating Effect of Knowledge-Sharing Behavior as Drivers of Individual Innovative Behavior. *Eurasia Journal of Mathematics, Science and Technology Education, 14*(8). doi:10.29333/ejmste/92087

Ngugi, J., & Goosen, L. (2019, October 25). Towards Smart Innovation for Information Systems and Technology Students: Modelling Motivation, Metacognition and Affective Aspects of Learning. (Á. Rocha, & M. Serrhini, Eds.) Smart Innovation, Systems and Technologies, 111, 90-99. doi:10.1007/978-3-030-03577-8_11

Ngugi, J. K., & Goosen, L. (2021a). Knowledge Sharing Mediating Information Technology Student Innovation. In M. Khosrow-Pour (Ed.), *Handbook of Research on Modern Educational Technologies, Applications, and Management* (Vol. II, pp. 645–663). IGI Global. doi:10.4018/978-1-7998-3476-2.ch040

Ngugi, J. K., & Goosen, L. (2021b). Innovation, Entrepreneurship, and Sustainability for ICT Students Towards the Post-COVID-19 Era. In L. C. Carvalho, L. Reis, & C. Silveira (Eds.), *Handbook of Research on Entrepreneurship, Innovation, Sustainability, and ICTs in the Post-COVID-19 Era* (pp. 110–131). IGI Global. doi:10.4018/978-1-7998-6776-0.ch006

Ngugi, J. K., & Goosen, L. (2021c). Computer Science and Information Technology Students' Self-regulated Learning and Knowledge Sharing Behavior as Drivers of Individual Innovative Behavior. (R. Silhavy, Ed.) Lecture Notes in Networks and Systems, 230, 593-608. doi:10.1007/978-3-030-77442-4_50

Ngugi, J. K., & Goosen, L. (2022). Digitalization and Drivers of Innovative Behavior for a Smart Economy in the Post-COVID-19 Era: Technology Student Course Design Characteristics. In L. Reis, L. Carvalho, C. Silveira, & D. Brasil (Eds.), Digitalization as a Driver for Smart Economy in the Post-COVID-19 Era (pp. 176-197)). IGI Global. doi:10.4018/978-1-7998-9227-4.ch010

Patel, P. H., Angrish, A. K., & Nadda, V. (2023). A Cross-Sector Comparison of Industry 5.0: Digital Technologies in Supply Chain Management of FMCG and the Automotive Sector. In *Opportunities and Challenges of Business 5.0 in Emerging Markets* (pp. 99–123). IGI Global. doi:10.4018/978-1-6684-6403-8.ch006

Raman, V., & Hellerstein, J. M. (2000). *An interactive framework for data cleaning.* Digital Assets. https://digitalassets.lib.berkeley.edu/techreports/ucb/text/CSD-00-1110.pdf

Republic of Kenya. (2007a). *Kenya Vision 2030: A globally competitive and prosperous Kenya.* Government Printer.

Republic of Kenya. (2007b). Sector Plan for Science [Nairobi: Government Printer.]. *Technology and Innovation.*

Republic of Kenya. (2012). *Universities Act. Kenya Gazette Supplement No. 192 (Acts No. 42).* Nairobi: Government Printer.

Singh, A. K., Tyagi, P., Tyagi, P. K., Chanchal, H. K., Singh, A. K., & Arora, B. (2023a, January). Green Technology and Sustainability: A Review and Future Research Agenda. *5th International Conference on Smart Systems and Inventive Technology (ICSSIT)* (pp. 239-246). IEEE. 10.1109/ICSSIT55814.2023.10061015

Singh, A. K., Tyagi, P. K., Irshad, A., Singh, A. K., Tyagi, P., & Benedict, B. (2023b, March). Use of Internet of Things in the Tourism and Hospitality Realm: A Descriptive Bibliometric Study using Bibliometrix R-Tool. *Second International Conference on Electronics and Renewable Systems (ICEARS)* (pp. 619-626). IEEE. 10.1109/ICEARS56392.2023.10085341

Tyagi, P. K., Nadda, V., Bharti, V., & Kemer, E. (Eds.). (2023). *Embracing Business Sustainability Through Innovation and Creativity in the Service Sector*. IGI Global. https://www.igi-global.com/book/embracing-business-sustainability-through-innovation/303947 doi:10.4018/978-1-6684-6732-9

Tyagi, P. K., Tyagi, P., Pandey, U., Upadhyay, R., Sharma, D., & Arora, B. (2023, March). Evaluation of the Value of the Employee Tourist Interaction using Big Data Analytics. *10th International Conference on Computing for Sustainable Global Development (INDIACom)* (pp. 1289-1294). IEEE.

Villalón-Fonseca, R., Mora-Castro, A., Bartels-González, R., Carballo-Chavarría, M., & Marín-Raventós, G. (2016). Promoting quality e-government solutions by applying a comprehensive information assurance model: Use cases for digital signature. *ICT for Promoting Human Development and Protecting the Environment: 6th IFIP World Information Technology Forum (WITFOR)* (pp. 223-234). San José, Costa Rica: Springer International Publishing.

Vorster, J., & Goosen, L. (2017). A Framework for University Partnerships Promoting Continued Support of e-Schools. In J. Liebenberg (Ed.), *Proceedings of the 46th Annual Conference of the Southern African Computer Lecturers' Association (SACLA)* (pp. 118 - 126). Magaliesburg: North-West University.

West, M. A., & Farr, J. L. (1990). Innovation at work. In M. A. West & J. L. Farr (Eds.), *Innovation and creativity at work: Psychological and organizational strategies* (pp. 3–13). Wiley.

Williams, M. (2008). *Components of self-regulated learning in high school students with learning disabilities* [Unpublished Doctoral Thesis, USA: Indiana University of Pennsylvania].

Wolverton, A. (2018). Promoting Exercise and Activity in Children: Challenges and Solutions to Today's Digital Society. *Journal of Pediatric Surgical Nursing*, *7*(1), 4–5. doi:10.1097/JPS.0000000000000160

KEY TERMS AND DEFINITIONS

Class Communication: This refers to the structure means and forms of exchanges in a technology class or project group in seeking answers to ill-structured **problems**.

Communities of Practice: This refers to an informal grouping of technology students who voluntary share and communicate similar technological interests and topics.

Methods Autonomy: This refers to the degree of liberty and independence allowable to a student to choose methods and schedules while carrying out a technological assignment.

Personal Interactions: This refers to the reciprocal informal personal communication and engagements with a goal of sharing knowledge.

Rehearsal: This refers to the range of cognitive drills and dry runs that a student engages in repeatedly in the process of memorizing information and sequences required to encode technological information and procedures.

Skill Variety: This reflects the array or multifariousness of skill sets a student requires to accomplish a technological project.

Task Feedback: This refers to the level and nature of information that a student can access either directly from the project work or from peers and lecturers on the success rate or failure to perform technological task.

Chapter 4
Sustainable Supply Chain Management in Tourism:
An Understanding of the Prospective Possibilities of Environmental Performance

Badr Bentalha
https://orcid.org/0000-0003-1339-542X
National School of Business and Management, Sidi Mohammed Ben Abdellah University, Morocco

ABSTRACT

The objective of sustainable logistics management is to ensure enduring economic, environmental, and social stability, leading to long-term sustainable expansion. The global push towards sustainable development is driving the adoption of sustainable logistics practices in the management of tourism-related logistics, with a particular focus on meeting environmental performance targets. Consequently, there is an increasing amount of theoretical and practical discussion surrounding tourism logistics operations. The objective of this chapter is to examine the impact of sustainable tourism supply chain management on the environmental performance of service companies. Through a prospective analysis, the authors investigate the relationship between sustainable logistics practices in tourism and their influence on environmental performance. The findings demonstrate that coordinated, collaborative, and pooled logistics resources can enhance the efficiency of the responsible supply chain within the tourism industry.

INTRODUCTION

In today's tourism market, characterized by competition between territories, technological advances and changes in supply and demand, each destination must manage its offer, coordinate the actions of the various stakeholders and constantly evaluate and reinvent its tourism strategies to improve its appeal and performance. Tourism stakeholders are encouraged to constantly reinvent their strategies to improve the services offered and, consequently, customer satisfaction (Bentalha, 2023). This mainly involves innovating tourism and related services, spatial differentiation and improving destination visibility on national

DOI: 10.4018/979-8-3693-2065-5.ch004

and international markets (Tyagi et al., 2023). Coordinating the players involved in tourism activities is of paramount importance. The main and complementary tourist services must be arranged and coordinated to provide a successful global experience for the tourist. This coordination creates several factors of organizational complexity, and requests an appropriate management.

Tourism services therefore require a value network linking all the players involved. The logic of networks has long been omnipresent in the world of the tourism industry, so we speak of tourism logistics. Tourism Supply Chain Management is a current concept coveted by researchers and practitioners alike (Tigu & Calareţu, 2013; Szpilko, 2017). Tourism supply chain management is the process of planning, organizing and coordinating the activities required to deliver tourism services effectively and efficiently. It brings together a variety of actors, including hotels, restaurants, travel agencies, carriers, raw material suppliers, distributors and customers. It handles all the logistical flows required to ensure quality service for tourists. The tourism supply chain process begins with demand planning, which involves forecasting customers' needs for tourism services. Next, supply planning is carried out to ensure that tourism services are available to meet these needs. This stage includes supplier selection, contract negotiation and inventory management. The next phase is operations management, which involves coordinating the activities of the various service providers involved in delivering tourism services. Finally, the tourism supply chain includes the management of returns, with the aim of reusing or recycling materials, and the collection of customer feedback.

All over the world, the imperatives of sustainable development are imposing themselves on the management of tourism-related logistics flows, particularly in terms of meeting commitments to environmental performance. The sustainability of tourism logistics chains refers to their ability to maintain their effectiveness and efficiency while minimizing their environmental, social and economic impact. It is important to reduce the environmental impact of tourism activities by minimizing waste production, reducing water and energy consumption, using eco-friendly modes of transport and promoting the use of local and sustainable products (Bentalha et al., 2023). In addition, it is crucial to ensure the social sustainability of tourism supply chains by respecting workers' rights, promoting local culture and involving local communities in tourism activities. This can include creating local jobs, promoting education and citizenship. Finally, the economic sustainability of tourism supply chains needs to be transparent, ensuring the financial viability of tourism businesses and promoting a fair distribution of profits among the various stakeholders. This can include promoting fair competition, establishing sustainable partnerships between businesses and local communities, and promoting government policies that favor sustainable tourism. Tourism logistics consume energy, pollute and cause waste. Consideration of the environmental impact of the tourism logistics chain is essential to understanding its impact on environmental performance.

The aim of this paper is to analyze sustainable supply chain tourism and its effects on the environmental performance of service companies. A prospective analysis is used to study the links between sustainable supply chain tourism practices and their effects on environmental performance.

To address this issue, on the basis of a literature review on key concepts and the analysis model constructed accordingly, we introduce the theoretical and conceptual contours of the theme. Based on a prospective study of the possibilities and possible evolutions of the sustainable tourism supply chain, we will present and discuss the results of a quantitative empirical study.

THEORETICAL AND CONCEPTUAL FRAMEWORK

Sustainable Tourism Supply Chain Concepts and Approaches

The Supply Chain (SC) concept has its roots in the 1950s, with Forrester's publication (1958). According to Lambert et al (1998), a SC refers to a series of interrelated companies involved in supplying products and services to the market, encompassing not only material flows but also information and financial flows. The SC is ubiquitous across all industrial and commercial domains, including the service sector, which constitutes a distinct facet of these supply chains (Hmioui & Bentalha, 2020). Therefore, it is feasible to conduct a comprehensive analysis of a tourism supply chain.

Being a network composed of several linked actors; the Tourism Supply Chain (TSC) buys resources and transfers them to diversified services and especially to a service integrator, which provides them to tourists (Wang, 2012). According to Kaukal et al. (2000), a typical TSC consists mainly of the following elements: tourism suppliers, tour operators and travel agencies, online intermediaries and tourists, who are linked to each other in a chain. So alongside accommodation, the TSC includes transport, but also restaurants, handicrafts, food production, waste disposal and the infrastructure that supports tourism (Figure 1).

Figure 1. Tourism supply chain structure
Source: Chen, 2009, p. 310

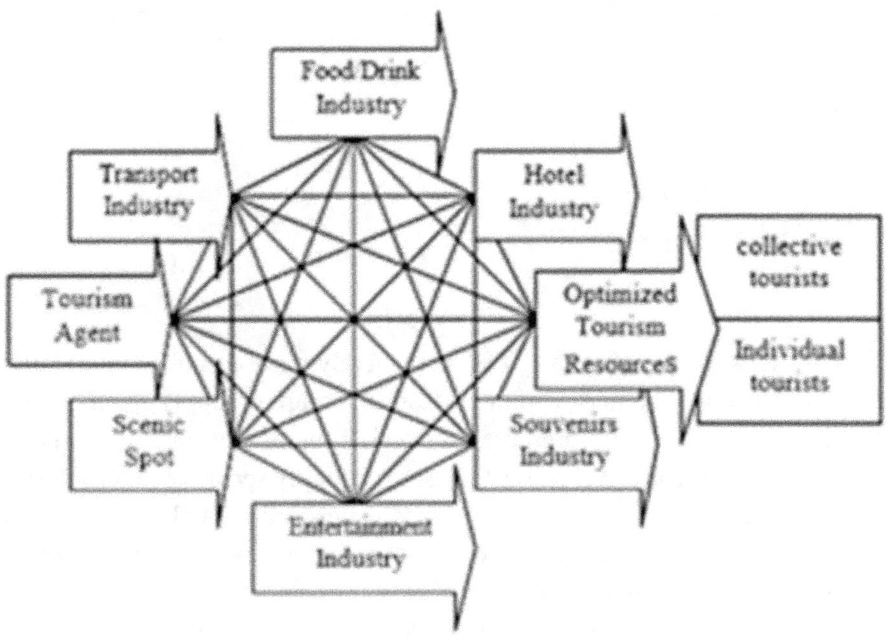

The essence of a TSC is an understanding of the nature of tourism products. Indeed, a single tourism entity cannot provide all products and services, which can only be achieved by coordinating the various businesses involved (Figure 2).

Figure 2. Tourism supply chain actors and operations
Source: Kusa, 2009, p. 135

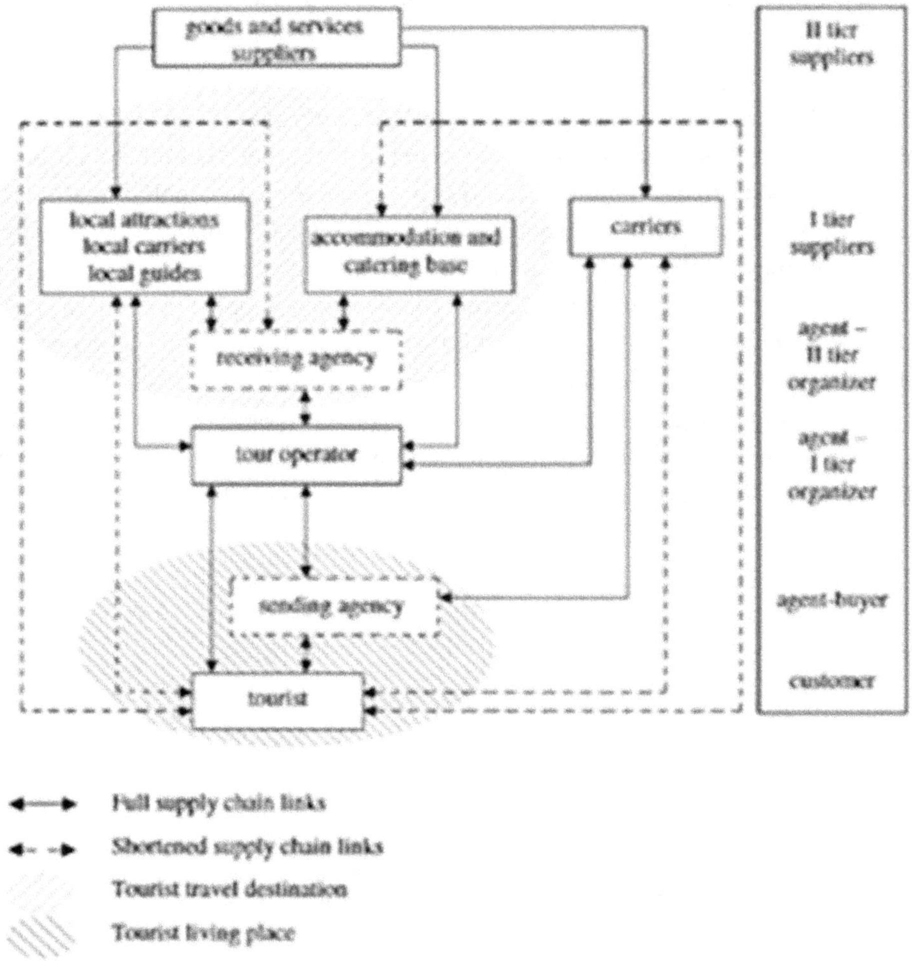

Compared to the industrial supply chain, TSC is relatively more complex, riskier and more difficult to control. Firstly, understanding tourism products leads to complex supply chain processes. The desire for homogeneity in processes leads to pressure on the coordination of quantity and quality, allocation and reasonableness of resource use. Secondly, tourism is a highly sensitive industry. Several situational or temporal factors can modify the parameters of this logistics chain. Finally, it is difficult to coordinate tourism products and control the quality of these services, as many partners are involved in creating value for the end customer (Hmioui & Bentalha, 2021).

Song et al. (2011) and Zhang et al. (2009) have developed Tourism Supply Chain models that underscore the significance of TSC management and advocate for enhanced coordination and consistency. Intojunyomg et al. (2016) have observed that Tourism Supply Chain Management (TSCM) involves a collection of strategies implemented to manage TSC operations effectively within a given destination.

The current expansion of tourism has had a number of positive effects in many countries. Nevertheless, negative effects have also been noted (Mikayilov et al., 2019). These are a series of negative impacts on the environment and society. As a result, a number of initiatives have been put in place to limit the negative effects of tourism. Numerous researchers have endeavored to specify the meaning of Sustainable Tourism Supply Chain (STSC), which pertains to logistics management aimed at fostering long-term sustainable growth by maintaining environmental, economic, and social stability (Dubey et al., 2016). The STSC concept is grounded in the notion of collaboration between companies and their suppliers. Moreover, tourists have a crucial role to play in the protection of cultural and environmental sites, promoting educational and cultural activities, fostering youth participation, and opting for more sustainable modes of transport (Bentalha, 2022).

Conception and Piloting of Environmental Performance

Environmental performance refers to the integration of environmental variables into the interpretation of a company's overall performance. "*Environmental performance is the ability of a company to responsibly and effectively manage its environmental impacts, while improving its financial performance and creating value for its stakeholders*" (Eccles & Serafeim, 2013). The importance of environmental performance is increasingly recognized in today's context of growing concern for sustainability and corporate social responsibility. Current theory accepts that environmental protection is beneficial to society. Nevertheless, the logic of environmental protection is relatively opposed to that of corporate profit maximization. At present, companies must integrate the impact of their actions on the environment and have environmental management control (Hmioui et al., 2020). Indeed, government measures, ecological regulations and pressure from civil society have introduced constraints on companies, requiring them to integrate environmental variables into their business logic.

The implication of a commitment to sustainable development thus regenerates the question of environmental performance assessment. Companies can improve their environmental performance by taking measures such as adopting sustainable resource management practices, investing in clean technologies, reducing waste, cutting greenhouse gas emissions, implementing environmental management systems, complying with environmental regulations, and so on. The various measures are complementary and can create a positive synergy over the long term.

Thus, environmental performance can only be developed on the basis of several interconnecting and coherent criteria (Bentalha et al., 2021). The problem lies in building a homogeneous model of environmental performance with relatively limited indicators and a global approach. Environmental indicators are quantities, established on the basis of observable or calculable quantities, reflecting the environmental impacts caused by a given activity (Alla et al., 2022). Companies can use environmental performance indicators to identify the areas where they have the greatest impact on the environment, and to assess the effectiveness of their sustainability initiatives. The environmental performance indicators used by companies are wide-ranging, including energy consumption, greenhouse gas emissions, water consumption, waste production, raw materials use, supplier performance and regulatory compliance. These environmental indicators, like financial indicators, are not without their critics (Hmioui et al., 2017). They can only provide partial information, as they produce a simplified view of reality, meant to reflect complex and often diffuse phenomena.

RESEARCH METHODOLOGY: THE PROSPECTIVE METHOD

The prospective approach is a methodological branch aimed at pointing out aspects that help identify possible scenarios in the future (Bentalha et al., 2019). It involves detecting several possible scenarios in order to prepare actions or plans. Using a rational, holistic approach, it aims to organize the future.

We have selected the PRODIN method, which places stakeholders and experts at the forefront of the process (Bergadaà & Thiétart, 1997). Bentalha et al. (2020) have highlighted three noteworthy aspects of this approach. Firstly, the mobilization of separate focuses groups; secondly, the engagement of diverse groups; and thirdly, the promotion of sharing results with a wider audience of researchers and practitioners. The PRODIN technique follows a series of analytical and operational stages that progressively shape the strategic prospective analysis (Figure 3).

Figure 3. Overview of the prospective approach
Source: Adapted from Bergadaà, 1999

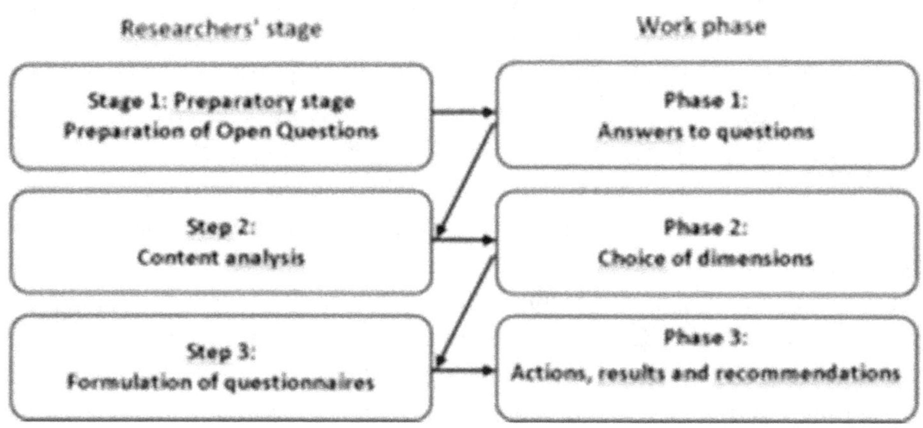

SUSTAINABLE TOURISM SUPPLY CHAIN, THE STATE OF THE ART

We conducted a review of academic and professional journals published between 2008 and 2019 and collected several articles on the topic of Sustainable Tourism Supply Chain. Font et al. (2008) suggest that tour operators can effectively contribute to sustainable tourism by implementing policies that recognize suppliers' responsibility for their impacts. Ji & Guo (2009) compare the tourism industry's development in China and other nations. They establish a framework of indices for assessing the performance of the tourism supply chain using a balanced scorecard. Zhang et al. (2009) argue that tourism products have unique characteristics. Chen (2009) notes that implementing supply chain management can help tourism companies work more closely with partners and improve their supply chain system. The author proposes that tourism supply chain innovation management should encompass a range of integrative fields.

Spasic (2012) points out that tour operators face challenges when integrating sustainable tourism into the supply chain, but a well-designed management system and long-term cooperation with suppliers can yield favorable outcomes. Vongsaroj (2013) highlights the high level of awareness among tour operators of Sustainable Tourism Supply Management and its implementation, with a significant difference between their level of knowledge and the implementation of STSM, indicating an implementation gap.

Tigu & Călărețu (2013) examine the STSC's characteristics and demand management concept in tourism, focusing on a hotel chain in Romania.

Ling (2015) proposes a new sustainable supply chain model that can facilitate the long-term sustainable development of tourism. Sanfiel-Fumero et al. (2017) analyze the role of "good" governance of a destination in the tourism network, which requires a redefinition of the relationship between government and society. Molefe et al. (2018) identify several characteristics of TSCM practices and reveal five factors related to TSCM practices. Bravo et al. (2018) find that the customer experience in a hotel has an impact on customer attitudes. Salguero et al. (2019) develop a model that empirically examines the relationship between the uses of competitive intelligence in the hospitality industry. The study provides theoretical and practical insights into the implications for helping managers develop sustainable competitive advantages through intelligence.

After this first preparatory stage, a committee of 18 experts in the field of SCM and tourism interested in the theme of sustainable tourism and SCM was formed. The theoretical study carried out enabled us to extract the main items for analyzing the relationship between the sustainability of the tourism supply chain and the environmental performance of the tourism business.

RESULTS AND DISCUSSION

Our objective was to identify the primary dimensions of the tourism supply chain and sustainability indicators through our analysis. After conducting interviews, we administered a questionnaire and analyzed the responses collected. In the initial phase of the study, we conducted a qualitative analysis using thematic and content analysis techniques with the aid of Tropes and Iramuteq software. Through this approach, we identified the essential items for the phase 2 questionnaire. Our analysis revealed several key concepts that are predominant in Sustainable Tourism Supply Chain (Table 2).

Table 2. Items most frequently used by experts in terms of sustainable tourism supply chain

Concepts	Number of items		Concepts	Number of items
Location	180		Time	31
Logistics	166		Consumption	26
Policy	106		Ecology	24
Tourism	101		Conservation	16
Transport	97		health	6
Development	79			

Source: Statistical study

The variables analyzed are related. There are many discussions about transport, politics and energy. In fact, the verbatim analyzed also evoke a large percentage of global reflection on the theme studied, of which here are some excerpts for illustration:

+ "The construction of indicators enables tourism to remain closely linked to the control of environmental and social balances."

+ “Logistics players try to go deeper into global optimization rather than local optimization.”

After analyzing the verbatim and questionnaire responses, we arrived at the following conclusions regarding the future of Sustainable Tourism Supply Chain (STSC) and the potential areas of future scenarios. Firstly, STSC’s fundamental principle is grounded in collaboration between companies and their suppliers, where they align their objectives and operational processes to create unique, international, and satisfactory resources in the market that meet customer needs and provide a competitive advantage. Secondly, companies can incorporate codes of conduct for their suppliers. Therefore, the common approach in STSC is to collect information on suppliers’ environmental compliance status, their environmental management systems’ existence and status, and the quality of materials they use. Many companies have developed their own evaluation systems or environmental management systems based on the environmental classification methodology. Companies can also arrange meetings with suppliers to exchange useful information and communicate company expectations.

At another level of analysis, consumerism plays a critical role in driving corporate operators’ social responsibility activities. We suggest that increasing customer awareness of sustainability.

On a quantitative level, there are several STSC practices identified (Table 3).

Table 3. STSC practices by item

Items	Elements	%
Hosting	• Staff employment conditions and sustainability training: This indicator assesses the working conditions of tourism employees and the availability of sustainability training programs. By evaluating these factors, stakeholders can work towards improving working conditions and promoting sustainable practices within the industry. • Employment opportunities for local community residents: This indicator evaluates the extent to which tourism businesses are providing job opportunities to local residents, particularly those who are historically marginalized or disadvantaged. By prioritizing the hiring of local residents, tourism businesses can help boost the local economy and foster community engagement. • Environmental infrastructure in the destination, particularly for solid and liquid waste management: This indicator assesses the availability and effectiveness of systems for managing solid and liquid waste in the destination, including recycling programs and wastewater treatment facilities. By promoting effective waste management practices, stakeholders can help reduce the negative impact of tourism on the environment. • Links with the local economy, particularly for food supplies, crafts and furnishings: This indicator evaluates the degree to which tourism businesses are sourcing their food supplies, crafts, and furnishings from local producers, and the impact of these purchases on the local economy. By prioritizing local sourcing, tourism businesses can help support local communities and promote sustainable economic development. • Marketing of socially and ecologically sustainable tourism packages and suppliers: This indicator evaluates the effectiveness of marketing efforts that promote socially and ecologically sustainable tourism packages and suppliers. By promoting sustainable tourism options, stakeholders can help shift consumer behavior towards more environmentally and socially responsible choices. • Select accommodations that do not conflict with local culture: This indicator assesses the extent to which accommodations are respectful of local cultural norms and customs. By prioritizing cultural sensitivity, tourism businesses can help promote cultural preservation and foster positive relationships with local communities. • Select accommodations that are environmentally friendly: This indicator evaluates the sustainability practices of accommodations, including their use of renewable energy sources, water and waste management systems, and overall carbon footprint. By promoting environmentally friendly accommodations, stakeholders can help reduce the negative impact of tourism on the environment and promote sustainable tourism practices.	**82%**
Transport	Environmental performance of ground transportation Use of airline communication to passengers on sustainability issues Plan travel itinerary with this company to minimize energy use. Select means of transport according to their carbon emissions performance	**72%**
Customer relations	Protect customer rights for tourists Request tourists' cooperation in using energy economically Inform tourists of possible negative environmental and social impacts.	**67%**
Assistance in port, excursions and activities	Local job creation Training and support for local people Marketing of sustainable and social tourism products	**49%**
Food and crafts	Environmental infrastructures	**45%**
Local food and craft producers and suppliers	Sustainable production methods	**42%**
Cooperation with stakeholders	Listen to the tourist Take action to protect the tourist destination Inform about problems or suggestions to prevent and resolve social and environmental impacts	**34%**

Source: Statistical study

At another level of our study, we consulted Supply Chain Management (SCM) managers about their future investment priorities and discovered that reducing energy consumption (67%) and utilizing more efficient and environmentally-friendly modes of transportation (53%) were the prevailing priorities (Table 4).

Table 4. STSC investment effort

Items	%
Reducing energy consumption	67%
Use of more economical and cleaner means of transport	53%
Raising awareness of tourism's impact on the environment, resource efficiency and biodiversity (communication)	41%
Protecting and highlighting cultural and natural heritage through tourism	23%
Implementation of STSC charter	22%
Make sustainability an essential condition for funding	11%
Promote sustainable tourism as a tool for poverty reduction	9%

Source: Statistical study

We also noted the low priority given to financing and poverty alleviation. Indeed, stakeholders are more concerned with energy, transport and environmental considerations. In terms of the benefits sought from the STSC, we found the following (Table 5).

Table 5. Desired benefits of STSC

Items	%
Logistics flexibility	61%
Improved quality	53%
Reduced logistics times	52%
Lower transportation expenses	46%
Lower inventories	41%
Conversion from production from stock to production to order	29%
Optimize batch sizes	22%
Fewer logistics providers	21%
Reduce supply chain management risks	19%
Lower supply chain sophistication	12%
Reduce back-office expenses	9%

Source: Statistical study

Our interviews revealed that investing in and adopting emerging technologies can provide companies with a sustainable competitive advantage. Moreover, each industry has its own unique STSC Vision grounded in industry-specific use cases of innovative technologies, which necessitates a distinct roadmap to enhance the maturity of these technologies (Bentalha, 2022).

CONCLUSION

This article has attempted to analyze the tourism supply chain, and in particular the questions of its sustainability. Our prospective study sought to forecast possible trends in tourism supply chains. The examination carried out shows the potential for rationalizing these chains, and the prospects for improving the performance of the tourism business. Indeed, whether in terms of coordination, sustainability or robotic or computerized modernization, it is clear that these logistics chains have several avenues for modernization.

Hotels can adopt sustainable practices to reduce their environmental impact, such as waste management, the use of renewable energy sources, reduced water consumption and the use of eco-friendly cleaning products. Hotels can also encourage guests to adopt eco-responsible behaviors, such as recycling and reducing water and energy consumption. In addition, companies can promote the use of electric or hybrid vehicles for transfers to hotels or excursions. Companies can raise customers' awareness of sustainable development issues by providing information on sustainable practices, encouraging them to adopt eco-responsible behavior and informing them about local sustainable development initiatives. Companies can obtain environmental certifications, such as ISO 14001 or Green Key, to demonstrate their commitment to sustainable development.

The study we have carried out is innovative in its field, and has the advantage of describing future prospects and possible avenues with the help of experts in the tourism supply chain. Nevertheless, the generalization of our findings requires a confirmatory approach, given the size of the study sample, the study period and also the localized conditions of data collection. Thus, it is possible to extend this study to other territories in a comparative approach or to other periods in a temporal perspective.

REFERENCES

Alla, L., Bentalha, B., & Bouhtati, N. (2022). Assessing Supply Chain Performance in the Covid 19 Context: A Prospective Model. In *2022 14th International Colloquium of Logistics and Supply Chain Management (LOGISTIQUA)* (pp. 1-6). IEEE.

Bentalha, B. (2022). Green Transportation Balanced Scorecard Model: A Fuzzy-Delphi Approach During COVID-19. In *Computational Intelligence Techniques for Green Smart Cities* (pp. 107–127). Springer. doi:10.1007/978-3-030-96429-0_5

Bentalha, B. (2022). Smart Technologies for a Sustainable Service Supply Chain: A Prospective Perspective. *Journal of Environmental Issues and Climate Change*, *1*(1), 77–89. doi:10.59110/jeicc.v1i1.81

Bentalha, B. (2023). Motivating Factors for Hotel Employees: A Fuzzy Logic Approach. In Strategic Human Resource Management in the Hospitality Industry: A Digitalized Economic Paradigm (pp. 159-178). IGI Global. doi:10.4018/978-1-6684-7494-5.ch008

Bentalha, B., Hmioui, A., & Alla, L. (2019). The digitalization of the supply chain management of service companies: a prospective approach. In *Proceedings of the 4th International Conference on Smart City Applications* (pp. 1-8). ACM. 10.1145/3368756.3369005

Bentalha, B., Hmioui, A., & Alla, L. (2020). Digital service supply chain management: current realities and prospective visions. In *The Proceedings of the Third International Conference on Smart City Applications* (pp. 808-822). Springer, Cham. 10.1007/978-3-030-37629-1_58

Bentalha, B., Hmioui, A., & Alla, L. (2021). The global performance of a service supply chain: a simulation-optimization under arena. In *The Proceedings of the Third International Conference on Smart City Applications* (pp. 489-502). Springer, Cham. 10.1007/978-3-030-66840-2_37

Bentalha, B., Hmioui, A., & Alla, L. (2023). Green Transportation Balanced Scorecard: A VIKOR Fuzzy Method for Evaluating Green Logistics Initiatives. In *International Conference on Digital Technologies and Applications* (pp. 916-925). Cham: Springer Nature Switzerland. 10.1007/978-3-031-29857-8_91

Bergada, À. (1997). Stradin: A strategic dynamic and interactive decision-making process. *Group Decision and Negotiation*, *6*(1), 61–75. doi:10.1023/A:1008688508836

Bergadaà, M. (1999). Strategic Decisions and Implementation: PRODIN™, a Prospective Dialectic Interpersonal Method. *Journal of Business Research*, *45*(2), 211–220. doi:10.1016/S0148-2963(97)00225-7

Bravo, R., Martinez, E., & Pina, J. M. (2019). Effects of service experience on customer responses to a hotel chain. *International Journal of Contemporary Hospitality Management*, *31*(1), 389–405. doi:10.1108/IJCHM-09-2017-0569

Casado, S. G., Manuel, Á. F. G., Fernández, I. A., & Palomo, D. R. (2019). Competitive Intelligence and Sustainable Competitive Advantage in the Hotel Industry [March.]. *Sustainability, MDPI, Open Access Journal*, *11*(6), 1–12.

Chen, D. (2009). *Innovation of Tourism Supply Chain Management. 2009 International Conference on Management of e-Commerce and e-Government*, Nanchang. 10.1109/ICMeCG.2009.79

Dubey, R., Gunasekaran, A., Papadopoulos, T., Childe, S. J., Shibin, K. T., & Wamba, S. F. (2016). Sustainable supply chain management: Framework and further research directions. *Journal of Cleaner Production*.

Eccles, R. G., & Serafeim, G. (2013). A tale of two stories: Sustainability and the quarterly earnings call. *The Bank of America Journal of Applied Corporate Finance*, *25*(3), 8–19. doi:10.1111/jacf.12023

Font, X., Tapper, R., Schwartz, K., & Kornilaki, M. (2008). Sustainable supply chain management in tourism. *Business Strategy and the Environment*, *17*(4), 260–271. doi:10.1002/bse.527

Forrester, J. (1958). Industrial Dynamics A Major Breakthrough for Decision Makers. *Harvard Business Review*, *36*, 37–66.

Hmioui, A., Alla, L., & Bentalha, B. (2017). *Pilotage de la touristicité territoriale au Maroc Proposition d'un indice de touriscticité pour la destination Fès. ntrepreneuriat, Innovation, Gouvernance et Développement territorial*. Faculté Polydisciplinaire de TAZA.

Hmioui, A., & Bentalha, B. (2020). Service Supply Chain Management et performance commerciale: Esquisse d'une synthèse théorique. *Alternatives Managériales Economiques*, *2*(2), 1–21.

Hmioui, A., & Bentalha, B. (2021). Service supply chain management: A literature review. *International Journal of Logistics Systems and Management, 40*(3), 332–353. doi:10.1504/IJLSM.2021.120253

Hmioui, A., Bentalha, B., & Alla, L. (2020). Service supply chain: A prospective analysis of sustainable management for global performance. In *2020 IEEE 13th International Colloquium of Logistics and Supply Chain Management (LOGISTIQUA)* (pp. 1-7). IEEE. 10.1109/LOGISTIQUA49782.2020.9353940

Huang, A., & George, Q. (2003). Huang, Jason S. K. LAU, K. L. Mak (2003), The impacts of sharing production information on supply chain dynamics: A review of the literature. *International Journal of Production Research, 41*(7), 1483–1517. doi:10.1080/0020754031000069625

Intojunyomg, S., Kaewkitipong, L., & Ractham, P. (2016). *Thailand's tourism industry: Demystifying the supply chain.* SMU. https://cmp.smu.edu.sg/amb/article. [Accessed 01 February 2023].

Ji, G., & Guo, B. (2009). *Study on the performance evaluation of sustainable tourism supply chain based on balanced scorecard.* 2009 6th International Conference on Service Systems and Service Management, Xiamen.

Kaukal, M., Werthner, H., & Hoepken, W. (2000). An approach to enable interoperability in electronic tourism markets. ECIS 2000 Proceedings. ACM.

Kusa, R. (2009). *Analiza łańcucha dostaw produktu turystycznego, w: Konkurencja i kooperacja w strategiach zarządzania organizacjami, red.* Jana Pyki, Towarzystwo Naukowe Organizacji i Kierownictwa. Oddział w Katowicach.

Lambert, D. M., Stock, J. R., & Ellram, L. M. (1998). *Fundamentals of Logistics Management.* Irwin/McGraw-Hill.

Ling, R. (2015). A review of Tourism Supply Chain based on the Perspective of sustainable development. *J Econ Sustain Develop, 6*, 128–13.

Mikayilov, J. I., Mukhtarov, S., Mammadov, J., & Azizov, M. (2019). Re-evaluating the environmental impacts of tourism: Does EKC exist? *Environmental Science and Pollution Research International, 26*(19), 19389–19402. doi:10.100711356-019-05269-w PMID:31073834

Molefe, P., Tauoatsoala, P., Sifolo, P., Pfarelo, S., Unathi, M., & Henama, U. (2018). The effects of tourism supply chain management practices on tourism operations in Pretoria, South Africa. *African Journal of Hospitality, Tourism and Leisure*, 7.

Preuss, L. (2005). Rhetoric and reality of corporate greening: A view from the supply chain management function. *Business Strategy and the Environment, 14*(2), 123–139. doi:10.1002/bse.435

Rao, P., & Holt, D. (2005). Do green supply chains lead to competitiveness and economic performance. *International Journal of Operations & Production Management, 25*(9), 898–916. doi:10.1108/01443570510613956

Sanfiel-Fumero, A., Armas-Cruz, Y., & González-Morales, O. (2017). Sustainability of the tourist supply chain and governance in an insular biosphere reserve destination: The perspective of tourist accommodation. *European Planning Studies, 25*(7), 1256–1274. doi:10.1080/09654313.2017.1319466

Song, D., & Xu, Y. (2011). Integrated Design of Service Supply Chain in the Perspective of Producer Service Outsourcing. *International Conference on Management and Service Science (MASS),* IEEE, pp. 1-4. 10.1109/ICMSS.2011.5998333

Song, H., Li, G., Witt, S. F., & Athanasopoulos, G. (2011). Forecasting tourist arrivals using time-varying parameter structural time series models. *International Journal of Forecasting*, *27*(3), 855–869. doi:10.1016/j.ijforecast.2010.06.001

Spasic, V. (2012). Integrating sustainable tourism in tour operators' supply chain. *Singidunum Journal of Applied Sciences.*, *9*(1), 60–66. doi:10.5937jas1201060S

Szpilko, D. (2017). Tourism Supply Chain–overview of selected literature. *Procedia Engineering*, *182*, 687–693. doi:10.1016/j.proeng.2017.03.180

Tigu, G., & Calareţu, B. (2013). Supply Chain Management Performance in Tourism. Continental Hotels Chain Case. *Amfiteatru Economic*, *15*, 103–115.

Tyagi, P. K., Nadda, V., Bharti, V., & Kemer, E. (Eds.). (2023). *Embracing Business Sustainability Through Innovation and Creativity in the Service Sector*. IGI Global. doi:10.4018/978-1-6684-6732-9

Vongsaroj, R. (2013). *Sustainable Tourism Supply Chain Management Of Tour Operator And Its Deteminants: A Case of Thailand.* Semantic Scholar.

Wang, H. Y. (2012). Value as a medical tourism driver. *Managing Service Quality*, *22*(5), 465–491. doi:10.1108/09604521211281387

Zhang, X., Song, H., & Huang, G. Q. (2009, June). Tourism Supply Chain Management: A New Research Agenda. *Tourism Management*, *30*(3), 345–358. doi:10.1016/j.tourman.2008.12.010 PMID:32287729

Chapter 5
Challenges and Prospects of Homestay in Rural Tourism: A Study of Uttarakhand

Bhola Chourasia
Assam Downtown University, Guwahati, India

ABSTRACT

This chapter examines the prospects and challenges of homestay accommodation in rural Uttarakhand, India, based on secondary data sources. Homestays are a sort of community-based tourism that provides visitors with an authentic experience of the local culture and way of life by allowing them to stay in the homes of local families. This chapter examines the potential of homestay accommodation to contribute to rural development and tourism promotion in Uttarakhand. The research is based on current literature and studies, as well as government and tourism sector data. The findings indicate that homestay accommodation has significant potential to generate income and provide alternative livelihood options for rural communities in Uttarakhand; but requires greater support and investment from the government and other stakeholders in order to address the challenges facing the homestay sector. The chapter finishes with suggestions for enhancing the viability of homestay accommodations in rural Uttarakhand, including capacity building, infrastructural improvement, and marketing assistance.

INTRODUCTION

Uttarakhand, located in northern India, is known for its natural beauty and is a popular tourist destination. The state is home to several religious and pilgrimage sites such as Haridwar, Rishikesh, Kedarnathand Badrinath, which attract millions of tourists each year. The state also offers adventure and eco-tourism activities such as trekking, skiing, river rafting, and paragliding.

As per the World Bank the global share of rural population was 57% in 1991 which decreased to 53% in 2001 and 48% in 2011. In India also condition is not any more different. The rural share of the Indian population was decrease from 74% in 1991 to 72% in 2001 and 69% in 2011. As the rural population decrease the agriculture contribution to GDP has gradually decline in past two decade. Decrease in farm-

DOI: 10.4018/979-8-3693-2065-5.ch005

ing activities may lead to food insecurity. The main problem of decreasing rural population is migration from rural to urban area. People from rural area migrate to urban area in search of better education and employment opportunity. Activities like Industries, trade and commerce, education centre in the city influence rural people to migrate from rural areas to urban areas. Pankaj, Faculty of Architecture, DIT University, Dehradun, India. Ashish Pant, Faculty of Architecture, DIT University, Dehradun, India. Migration is the movement of people from one place to another with the purposes of taking up permanent or semi-permanent residence in the new location. One of the most significant migration patterns has been rural to urban migration in search of opportunities. In the rural areas, sluggish agricultural growth and restricted development of the rural non-farm sector increases the rural poverty, unemployment and underemployment. Due to lack of employment opportunities people migrated from rural to urban areas in search of jobs. Migration results in abandonment of villages and causes congestion in the cities. Migration is not new to Uttarakhand. It reached a peak in the 1980s and fuelled the demand for a separate state, which everyone hoped would lead to economic growth and check migration. But according to census data the rate of migration from the hilly areas of the state has increased after it was formed in 2000, only the destination of migrants has changed. In fact, the migration to cities has been in such great numbers that Uttarakhand has recorded the highest increase in the share of urban population in any of the Himalayan states of the country while its rural decadal growth rate is the lowest. Difficult terrain, lack of transport, the lack of employment along with small landholding sizes and low farm incomes has fuelled large migration from rural areas of the state to the cities across the country. Migration leads to abandonment of villages which causes degradation of land, makes villages unlivable. Rural tourism can be a solution for these abandon villages of Uttarakhandto decrease migration and to generate sustainable employment opportunities in the rural areas of Uttarakhand.

The Uttarakhand state formerly known as Uttaranchal was carved out of the state of Uttar Pradesh in 2000 and became the 27th state in the country of India. Uttarakhand is situated in the central Himalayan zone extending between 77° 34' and 81° 02' E longitude and 28° 43' to 31° 27' N latitude. Uttarakhand share borders with China in the north and Nepal to the east, while its neigh boring States is Himachal Pradesh Rural Tourism a Solution for Ghost Villages of Uttarakhand Pankaj, Ashish Pant Figure 1: World & India Rural Population (%) (Source –www.Data.worldbank.org) 53 www.ijntr.org Fig. 3: Rural – Urban proportion of Uttarakhand state (2001 & 2011) to the west and Uttar Pradesh in the south. The high Himalayan ranges and glaciers form most of the northern parts of the state while the lower reaches are densely forested. The state is spread over an area of about 53,483 sq. km. out of which 86% is mountainous. Dehradun is the provisional capital of the state. The state is comprised of13 districts, of which four districts (Nainital, Haridwar, Dehradun and Udham Singh Nagar) have large areas in the plains, whereas the other nine districts comprise the hill region of the state. Figure 2: Uttarakhand state Map with its Districts (Source – www.mapsofindia.com) The Population of Uttarakhandwas 10,086,292 (census 2011), making it the 20th most populated state on 1.69% of land of India. Out of total population 69.44% (7,025,583) of the people living in 16,793 villages. The 30.55%(3,091,169) of urban population is mostly settled in the southern Terai region and the Doon valley. More than 90% of the people in the mountain districts live in rural areas. More than 82.5% of this urbanized population is concentrated in the plains of 4 districts and rests 17.5% also largely belong to the district headquarter towns of the remaining 9 districts. The density of population per sq. Km. is about 189 (census, 2011)which is fairly below than the national average of 382 per sq. Km. The state has a growth rate of about 19.17% which slightly exceeds the national growth rate of about 17.64%, is somewhat lower than the previous (1991-2001) growth rate of 20.41%. Migration in Uttarakhand is both a historical and present phenomenon.

It has started since nineties and has gradually accelerated with each passing decade. Earlier the pattern of migration was from plain to hilly areas, in the search of better environmental condition and scenic beauty. But now the direction of migration has changed visa a versa, now migration takes place from hilly rural areas to plains in search of better job, education and health. Uttarakhand state has a high rate of out-migration and majority of the population migrate from rural areas to various urban areas. Migration in the Uttarakhand hilly region is intra-regional (i.e., from remote rural locations to developed urban centres in the hills) as well as inter-regional (i.e., from the hill regions to the developed plains).Earlier the rate of out migration has accelerated due tomale-out migration in search of employment,in contrast to the earlier pattern of only men going out, now entire families are migrating form hilly rural area tourban areas in plains. Out of the 13 districts of Uttarakhand, migration has hit 9 hill districts over the last decade, this is reflected in the 2001–2011 decadal population growth data. The Garhwal (PauriGarhwal) and Almora districts witnessed negative rural population growth rates during the decade. Among the TehriGarhwal and Rudrapraya districts, population growth was near zero, and among the Chamoli, Bageshwar, and Pithoragarh regions, growth rates were low. Depopulation of the Garhwal and Almora districts and the significantly low population growth rates in other hill districts is the result of rural to urban migration of peoples. The state is also known for its scenic beauty and is home to several national parks and wildlife sanctuaries such as the Jim Corbett National Park, which is known for its tigers and elephants, and the Rajaji National Park, which is home to a wide variety of fauna and flora. The state is also home to several hill stations such as Nainital, Mussoorie and Almora, which are popular among tourists for their natural beauty and cool climate.The state government has been promoting tourism as one of the main drivers of economic growth, and has taken several measures to improve the infrastructure and facilities for tourists. The state has also been promoting sustainable tourism and encouraging tourists to experience the local culture and way of life.

Generally, the term homestay hasn't received a great deal of attention in the academic literature. However, there are similar terms that have.

Two terms that reflect the notion of using your home as a business are 'home-based enterprise' (Di Domenico & Lynch, 2007, p. 321) and 'commercial home enterprise' (CHE) (McIntosh, Lynch, & Sweeney, 2011, p. 511).

Lynch (2005); *A 'Commercial home' refers to types of accommodation where visitors or guests pay to stay in private homes, where interaction takes place with a host and/or family usually living upon the premises and with whom public space is, to a degree, shared. 'Commercial home' therefore embraces a range of accommodation types including some (small) hotels, bed and breakfasts (B&Bs), and host family accommodation, which simultaneously span private, commercial, and social settings.*

Characteristics of a homestay

Lynch (2005) goes on to identify several key characteristics of a homestay. These are;

- Family involvement
- Local community benefits
- Guest engagement with the property
- The sharing of space between guest and host
- The participation of owner-managers in the shaping of the accommodation product
- The involvement of 'lifestyle entrepreneurs'
- The importance of gender, personal networks, social values, and family life cycle

As you can see from the list above, culture and connection between host and guest is, according to Lynch, an important part of the homestay experience. However, since his works written in 2005,a lot has changed. And I would now argue that financial gain is, in most circumstances, far superior to host-guest interaction.

Homestay as a Cultural Experience

Whilst there has been a clear move away from culture being the focus and towards economic benefit, a homestay experience can be a significant cultural experience.There are many different ways that you can experience culture through a homestay, and this is largely dependent on the set up of the homestay itself.

Inevitably, if a guest is staying in the home of a local person, who regularly interacts with the guest, then they will receive a greater cultural experience than someone who is simply paying to rent a bedroom or entire property.

Some of the cultural experiences that a tourist may receive include;

- Learning a new language
- Tasting new food and learning to cook new recipes
- Learning about the local way of life
- Learning about local history
- Exposure to the local community
- Taking part in village, nature or workplace tours
- Learning about the religion and visiting religious sites
- Taking part in local events and celebrations

Homestay as a Commercial Enterprise

In recent years we have witnessed monumental growth in the so called 'sharing economy'. The sharing economy is a socio-economic ecosystem that is built around the sharing of human, physical and intellectual resources. Also known as collaborative consumption or peer-to-peer-based sharing, the sharing economy is a concept that highlights the way in which people rent or borrow goods and services rather than buying or owning them. In the context of homestay, this represents the sharing of one's home.

This notion of 'sharing' has, however, has disrupted many traditional commercial operations. Hotel occupancy rates around the world are down as tourists opt for homestay options instead of hotel rooms. In addition, the income potential for homestay has driven up real estate prices in many areas, meaning that local people are struggling to get on the property ladder and gentrification is taking place.

Homestays are a popular accommodation option in Uttarakhand, as they provide a more authentic and immersive experience for visitors by allowing them to stay with local families and learn about their culture and way of life. Homestays can also be found in rural areas, offering a chance to experience the village life and explore the natural surroundings. Homestays in Uttarakhand are also popular among tourists who are looking for budget friendly options.

An Overview of the Tourism Industry in Uttarakhand

The rural heartland of India is an unexplored treasuretrove with its diverse lifestyle concentrated on arts andcrafts, culture and natural heritage. Over the past fewdecades, the country's tourism industry has grownrapidly, but rural tourism has never been given fullattention. As per the report of International CropsResearch Institute for the Semi-Arid Tropics (ICRISAT),India's strength lies in its villages, as a large part of ourpopulation (69 per cent) lives in rural areas and the ruraleconomy contributes about 46 per cent to the nationalincome and 25-30 per cent of India's GDP. The ruralareas in India have a lot to offer to the rest of the world.

Rural tourism can be defined as an encounter thatincludes an extensive scope of attractions and activitiesthat take place in agricultural or non-urban areas. Thekey features of rural tourismcomprise of open space,low-level tourism development, and opportunities forvisitors to experience agriculture and the naturalenvironment directly. Rural tourism focuses on the visitors, actively participating in the rural lifestyle.Tourists also get an opportunity to know the traditionand culture of the region. Rural tourism is multifacetedand includes agricultural tourism, cultural tourism,nature tourism, adventure tourism and ecotourism, allof which are closely linked.India's vast geographical and rich cultural heritage makesit a unique place to tap unique tourism opportunities,with rural tourism being one of them. Rural tourism is an opportunity to promote sustainable and responsibletourism. Given that the majority of the country'spopulation still resides in rural area, the potential tocreate mutually enriching experience that benefit localcommunities as well as tourists is important. Ruraltourism has been viewed as an instrument that has thecapacity to effect socio-economic changes through the use of natural and socio- cultural economic resources.

(MoT, 2022), In the year 2021 there is an increase of 177% in domestic tourist arrival in the state with total number of domestic tourist arrival recorded in year 2021was 19434475 (19.43 mil) in comparison to 7005264 in the year 2020. During the same year state witnessed drop of 79.36% foreign tourist arrival in the year 2021 the state recorded 8532 tourists in comparison to 41339 in the year 2020.The stateranked 12th in the country with a share of 2.87% in terms of domestic tourist and ranked 15th with a share of 0.81% in terms of foreign tourist arrival.

The contribution of tourism in GSDP was 17.1% in the year 2019-20 which reduced to 0.10% in the year 2020-21.

The government have taken special initiatives and upgraded them with innovative ideas to promote livelihood generation through tourism. Presently two schemes are in enforce namely Veer Chandra Garhwali Paryatan SwarojgarYojna and DeenDayal Upadhyay GrahAwas Scheme.(UKGov, 2022), Under VCGPS Yojana the amount of subsidy for non-movable assets has been increased by 33% maximum from ₹ 15.00 lakh to ₹ 33.00 lakh in hilly areas and by 25% from ₹ 10.00 lakh to ₹ 25.00 lakh in plain areas. (UKGov, 2022). Under DDUGAS 1262 homestays were registered in the year 2019-20, 880 in 2020-2021 and 857 in year 2021-2022.

Table 1. Registered hotels, dharmshalas, guest house, and homestays

S.No.	Registered Hotels, Dharmshalas, Guest House and Homestays	
1	Registered Hotels	3976
2	Registered Dharamshala	872
3	Registered Guest House	362
4	Registered Homestays	4686

Source: https://c.gov.in/hotel-listing

Future Prospects of Tourism

(IBEF, 2022), By 2030 Uttarakhand hopes to have had 70 million more tourists. The National Highways Logistics Management Limited (NHLML) proposal to build a ropeway connecting Sonprayag, Gaurikund, and Kedarnath will be 13 km long and cost more over Rs.985 crore (US$126.77 million). With a $90.09 million investment, Empyrean Skyview Projects will build two additional ropeway systems in Mussoorie and Yamunotri. After the government loosened covid-related regulations, Dehradun and Mussoorie recorded over 11 lakh vacationers in the most recent three months from January to April 2022.The government announced intentions to create 6 city forests in August 2020 in order to boost the amount of greenery in metropolitan areas, as well as to build the first Snow Leopard Conservation Center in India in the state. Anand Van, a sizable urban forest, was officially opened in Doon Valley City in September 2020. By building a green landscape, the park will help to alleviate congestion and regulate air pollution in the city. 7.32 lakh of the 27.81 lakh pilgrims who entered the state for the Chardham Yatra in 2018 travelled to Kedarnath. In an effort to increase tourism, the centre introduced the "*Udan*" regional connection programme in January 2018. This programme will make it easier for people in low-income groups to travel for reasonable plane prices.Hello Uttarakhand, a public service mobile app, was introduced in December 2019 and offers tourists the ability to engage with locals in multiple languages. To draw tourists, the Uttarakhand government will provide mobile caravans or motor homes outfitted with all of a home's amenities. Tourism has played an important role in providing economic benefitsto the farmers in the hilly areas. The development oftourism markets in rural mountainous regions canincrease demand for the maintenance and promotion oflocal services, diversify activities in the rural economy,and preserve natural landscape (Jaffar et al., 2013).Therefore, it is important to identify the rural tourismopportunities in the state and assess the challengeshindering the sustainable rural development.

Homestay

A form of affordable lodging that allows visitors to stay with a local family rather than a hotel or hostel, homestays are hosted by individuals or families in their private residences. Staying with a local family is a great method for tourists to get a feel for the local culture and get some much-needed language practise.

Homestay Origin (Global)

The first known homestay programmes were established in Europe in the 1940s by language schools catering to international students. These courses are meant to introduce students to the local language and culture in an all-encompassing way. Homestay programmes eventually made their way to other regions of the world, such as North America and Asia.

Homestays gained popularity in the 1960s and 1970s as more people began to go overseas for vacation and cultural experiences. Homestays emerged as a low-cost alternative to hotels, facilitating in-depth cultural exchange between visitors and natives.

Homestay Origin (India)

In India, homestays are a popular kind of tourism, particularly in rural areas where visitors can experience the local culture and way of life. The origins of the concept of homestays in India lie in the tradition of extending hospitality to guests. People used to offer their homes to travellers as a place to stay in ancient times. This custom was known as "atithi devo bhava," which translates to "the guest is akin to god." This mentality is still prominent in many regions of India, where residents greet travellers with open arms. Throughout the 1980s and 1990s, however, the current notion of homestays in India gained prominence. It was initially spurred by the need to supply guests with economical and genuine lodging, especially in rural areas where traditional hotels and resorts did not exist.

Advancement in Homestay Business:

Significant developments have taken place in the homestay business as a result of the proliferation of sharing economies and online booking platforms. Airbnb, Homestay.com, and Booking.com are just a few of the many homestay booking systems that exist today, making it simple for tourists to search and book homestays anywhere in the globe. These sites have also made it less of a hassle for people to rent out their extra rooms or even their entire houses to strangers.

OBJECTIVES

- To explore prospects of developing homestay in Uttarakhand
- To understand the challenges of developing homestay in Uttarakhand

RESEARCH METHODOLOGY

The purpose of this exploratory study is to see whether there is room for additional research in this area. The data has been gathered from secondary sources, such as journals, newspapers, and public and unpublished government agency reports.

LITERATURE REVIEW

The origins of the homestay concept in Uttarakhand may be traced back to the state's rural tourism initiatives, which began in the late 1990s. Along with a number of non-governmental organisations (NGOs), the state government began supporting community-based tourism programmes as a means of generating income for local people and protecting the region's natural and cultural legacy.It was determined that homestays may provide guests with a genuine cultural experience while giving local families with an additional source of income. Together with NGOs and local groups, the state government began creating homestay infrastructure in isolated villages and rural areas of the state.The state of Uttarakhand is renowned for its own culture, traditions, and language; it is a microcosm of the nation's rich cultural diversity. The total area of Uttarakhand is 53,483 km2, with a rural area of 52,581.08 km2 and an urban area of 901.92 km2(*List of Districts of Uttarakhand (UT) | Villageinfo.In*, n.d.). Local fair and festivals not only for the joy for locals but they show the way to experience ones local culture(Bairwa, 2021).

Prospects:

Homestay accommodation has gained popularity in recent years as an alternative form of accommodation for travellers seeking a more authentic and immersive experience. Uttarakhand, located in the northern part of India, is a popular tourist destination due to its natural beauty and cultural heritage. This literature review aims to examine the existing literature on the prospects of homestay accommodation in Uttarakhand.

Authentic Cultural Experience: Homestays in Uttarakhand give travellers with an authentic cultural experience, which is one of the most essential advantages. Several studies have demonstrated that tourists who stay in homestays gain a deeper appreciation for the local culture, customs, and traditions(Chakraborty, 2019; Dey et al., 2020; Imran &Ngyuen, 2018). Homestays in Uttarakhand offer tourists an opportunity to interact with local people, taste local food, and participate in cultural activities, which adds value to their travel experience.

Cultural Exchange: Tourists get the opportunity to mingle with locals and discover their culture, traditions, and way of life through homestay accommodations(Krepps, 2018). Such experiences foster cross-cultural understanding, which is vital for tourist sustainability.

Economic Development: In Uttarakhand, homestay accommodations have the potential to foster economic growth. Several studies have demonstrated that homestays produce money and employment prospects for local populations (Jayara, 2017; Kala et al., 2018; Macek, 2012; Maheshwari, 2020). Furthermore, homestays help to diversify the tourism product in Uttarakhand, which is currently dominated by conventional hotel accommodation (Binita Chakraborty, 2020). This diversification can lead to the development of new tourism markets and increase the overall economic impact of tourism in the region.

Environmental Sustainability: Homestay accommodation in Uttarakhand can contribute to environmental sustainability by promoting eco-friendly practices. Several studies have emphasized that homestays have a lower carbon footprint than hotels (Jayara, 2018; Prajapati et al., 2018; Sati, 2020). Furthermore, homestays promote the use of locally sourced products, which reduces the carbon footprint associated with transportation and packaging.

PersonalisedExperience: Homestay accommodations provide travellers a customised travel experience, as they can tailor their itinerary to their specific interests and preferences(Bhalla et al., 2016; Chauhan et al., 2022). The ability of homestay owners to inform visitors about local sights, activities, and cultures enriches the whole trip experience

CHALLENGESFOR RURAL TOURISM IN THE STUDY AREA

Transportation

Many Rural Areas are still facing the problem of Road connectivity. Kacha roads become unserviceable during the monsoon and interior villages get isolated. It's almost 15 years after becoming a separate state but the connectivity to Uttarakhand is still not as well developed as in other states like Himachal Pradesh. In order to attract the rural tourism in the middle and lower income brackets, it needs to concentrate on improving the road and rail connectivity.

Cultural Beliefs

Rural population are bounded by the traditional values and customs. Their culture, religion, superstition have a strong influence on their attitudes and behaviours. The thinking and believes of the rural area differs from Urban. Sometime cultural believes can also be a constraint for outsider (tourist) to get involve in their tradition and rituals. Restrictions for women in the temple complex still exist in some of the areas.

Poor Infrastructure Facility

The infrastructure facilities is one of the major challenge for the rural tourism. Proper infrastructure facilities like health, water supply, electricity, road and telecommunications in the region are not adequate. Summer are very tough for hill area in Uttarakhand as ground water level goes down all natural portable water sources dry ups and residents have to collect water from other sources.

Natural Calamity

Harsh weather condition too much cold and heavy rain results in land slide and cloud bursting. Certain areas of the hills even become inaccessible in winter due to extremities of climate causing prolonged snowfall. The tourism business in Uttarakhand witness a 70% fall during 2014-15 due to 2013 flood in Kedarnath valley.

Seasonal Tourism

Most Tourist spots in Uttarakhand is very much influence by seasonal tourism. Tourism has mainly been confined to the three months in summers (April –June), when people form the neighbouring states come to get relief from the heat in the plains. In the summer chardhamKapaat (door) is also open for the pilgrimage between the months of May to July. In winter tourist visit Uttarakhand to see Snow fall between the months of December – February.Tourism in Uttarakhand is a seasonal tourism confined to three months in summer and three months in winter.

Lack of Financial Aid

People in rural Uttarakhand are not financially strong to develop rural tourism in their villages without the help of government bodies or NGO's. Sufficient financial support is required for essential developments like human resource, enforcement of rules and regulations, building of physical infrastructures, and land use management. Lack of financial aid is a major challenge to develop rural tourism in Uttarakhand.

Lack of Trained Manpower

Youth from the hilly area of state migrate to urban areas in plains in search of better education and job. After getting education, they stetted down in the urban centres and does not want to come back to the hills as there are lack of opportunity and resources in the hills. Due to this there is lack of trained manpower in the hills.

Public Awareness

Currently, most of the tourists visit Uttarakhand only for religious purposes.As per current scenario tourists are aware of only some demarcated tourist places, pilgrims and heritage sites, such as chardhamyatra, Mussoorie and Nainital.

Challenges of Homestay

Homestay accommodations have become increasingly popular in Uttarakhand due to the state's natural beauty and cultural heritage. However, these accommodations also come with a range of challenges that can impact the experience of both guests and hosts. In this literature review, we will explore some of the key challenges facing homestay accommodations in Uttarakhand.

Limited Infrastructure: One of the major challenges faced by homestay accommodations in Uttarakhand is the lack of basic infrastructure(Kala et al., n.d.). Many homestays lack access to basic amenities like electricity, water, and sanitation facilities(Kapil et al., n.d.). This can make it difficult for guests to enjoy their stay and can also impact the health and safety of both guests and hosts.

Seasonal Tourism: Uttarakhand experiences a significant influx of tourists during the peak season, which typically lasts from April to June and September to November(Kala et al., n.d.; Kumar et al., 2017). However, the rest of the year sees relatively few tourists, making it difficult for homestay accommodations to sustain their businesses. This can result in a lack of income for hosts and can also impact the quality of service offered to guests.

Limited Marketing and Promotion: Another challenge faced by homestay accommodations in Uttarakhand is a lack of marketing and promotion. Many homestays are not listed on popular booking websites and may not have an online presence, making it difficult for potential guests to find them(Semwal, 2022). This can result in a lack of bookings and can also limit the potential for growth and expansion.

Cultural Differences: Uttarakhand is a diverse state with a range of cultures and traditions. This can create challenges for both hosts and guests, particularly when it comes to communication and understanding of cultural norms(Anup & Fernandez, 2022; Pal & Environmental, n.d.). Hosts may struggle to communicate effectively with guests who speak different languages or come from different cultural backgrounds, while guests may find it difficult to adapt to local customs and practices.

Environmental Sustainability: Uttarakhand is known for its pristine natural environment, but this can also create challenges for homestay accommodations(Ghosh, 2021). Hosts may struggle to manage waste and sanitation in a way that is environmentally sustainable, while guests may not be aware of the impact of their activities on the local ecosystem(Payal et al., 2021).

Quality Standards: It is crucial for homestay accommodations to uphold quality standards like cleanliness, hygiene, and safety. Inadequate training and oversight might result in variable quality and service standards(Lynch, 1999). The proprietors of homestays require training in providing excellent services and upholding hygienic requirements.

SUGGESTIONS

a) In Uttarakhand, the Uttarakhand Tourist Development Board (UTDB) encourages homestay tourism. The effort intends to allow visitors to enjoy the state's natural beauty, culture, and hospitality. But as of now there is no SOP for the functioning of Homestay.

b) The government of Uttarakhand is providing financial assistance to residents of the state through the Deen Dayal Upadhyaya Homestay Scheme and the Veer Chandra Singh Garhwali Yojana, but financial assistance alone is insufficient; additional training for homestay owners is required on a regular basis from time to time by which they can learning new skills and upgrade the existing learned skills.

c) Further special centres at block level need to be established for promotion and development Homestay accommodation in rural areas of Uttarakhand.

d) Promoting synergy between homestays and local attractions in terms of culture, art, and local people is necessary so that homestays are not limited to merely housing tourists but also offer local cuisine and sightseeing.

e) Proper guest registers need to be maintained at existing homestays and data should be collected by the district tourism offices of UTDB. As of now UTDB have no data regarding the number of tourists stayed in homestay.

f) The tourist who are visiting the rural areas of Uttarakhand must take the pledge to be a responsible tourism.

g) At village level the Pradhan of the village should act as the Village tourist representative. His/her proper training and grooming should be the responsibility of the District Tourism office.

h) The state tourism board should provide additional funds for celebrating regional festivals at block level which will provide unique experience to tourist and will also provide additional activities for tourist. Similarly, the event sections can be created on the theme of Utsav.gov.in an Ministry of Tourism initiative where the tourist will get details of the local fair and festivals.

i)The state tourism board and local authorities should organise Local Food Festival quarterly with in the region at popular tourist destination. Special recognition must be given to restaurants and homestays for providing local cuisine.

CONCLUSION

This study identifies the opportunities and obstacles associated with establishing homestays in rural Uttarakhand. The study examined how the homestay idea can assist to the growth of tourism in Uttarakhand, a state with enormous tourism potential. Several points of interest for tourists are located in rural areas of Uttarakhand, but they are only visited for a few hours due to a lack of accommodations. The promise of having homestays to increase the economy and tourism is highly promising. If there is information and availability of hotel facilities, these tourists' stay could be extended by a few days. The study has launched research to address the problem of low tourism by proposing homestays as a means of providing lodging for visiting visitors and a source of income for locals. Lack of training and awareness for providing accommodation through homestays, New financial schemes to boost tourism activities, lack of basic infrastructure such as electricity, healthcare, and internet connectivity, and extreme winter weather conditions in the high altitude rural region are the challenges identified based on secondary data available through journals, newspapers, and published and unpublished reports by government agencies. The study's limitations include its exploratory nature and its exclusive focus on rural region of Uttarakhand, as well as its reliance on secondary sources for data collection.

REFERENCES

Anup, K. C., & Fernandez, M. (2022). Tourism and Himalayan Indigenous Communities. *Tourism and Development in the Himalaya*, 149–169. https://doi.org/ doi:10.4324/9781003030126-12/TOURISM-HIMALAYAN-INDIGENOUS-COMMUNITIES-ANUP-MARIELA-FERNANDEZ

Bairwa, M. K. (2021). Festivals for Sustainable Tourism Development: A case study of Marwar Region of Rajasthan. In *Local Food and Community Empowerment through Tourism* (*Vol. 1,* pp. 82–96). Eureka Publication. https://www.researchgate.net/publication/354061838_Festivals_for_Sustainable_Tourism_Development_A_case_study_of_Marwar_Region_of_Rajasthan

Bhalla, P., Coghlan, A., & Recreation, P. B.-T. (2016). Homestays' contribution to community-based ecotourism in the Himalayan region of India. *Taylor & Francis, 41*(2), 213–228. doi:10.1080/02508281.2016.1178474

Binita, C. (2020). Homestay as a reliable promotional tool for Cultural Tourism and Security in Indian context. *IJSSTH, 21*(5). https://dialnet.unirioja.es/servlet/articulo?codigo=7962192

Chakraborty, B. (2019). Homestay And Women Empowerment: A Case Study Of Women Managed Tourism Product In Kasar Devi, Uttarakhand, India. *Tourism International Scientific Conference Vrnjačka Banja - TISC, 4*(1), 202–216. https://www.tisc.rs/proceedings/index.php/hitmc/article/view/252

Chauhan, H. & Jain, V. (2022). *Destination branding as new tool for economic development: a qualitative approach with reference to JaunsarBawar Region, Uttarakhand.* Taylor & Francis. doi:10.1080/24721735.2022.2115331

Dey, B., Mathew, J., & Chee-Hua, C. (2020). Influence of destination attractiveness factors and travel motivations on rural homestay choice: The moderating role of need for uniqueness. *International Journal of Culture, Tourism and Hospitality Research, 14*(4), 639–666. doi:10.1108/IJCTHR-08-2019-0138

Ghosh, P. (2021). Model Village Development in Indian Himalayan Region: An Overview of Initiatives and Activities. *International Journal of Social Sciences Citation*, 315–328. doi:10.46852/2249-6637.04.2021.4

IBEF. (2022). *Uttarakhand State Report*. Delhi: India Brand Equity Foundation (IBEF). https://www.ibef.org/states/uttarakhand

Imran, M. M., & Ngyuen, N. (2018). A Community Response to Tourism, Focusing on the Home-stay Program in K Village in Nainital. *Journal of Urban and Rgional Studies on Contemporary India*, *4*(2), 55–62. https://home.hiroshima-u.ac.jp/hindas/index.html

Jayara, J. (2017). *Home-Stay Tourism in Uttarakhand: Opportunities and Challenges*. Researchgate.Net. https://www.researchgate.net/profile/Jaswant-Jayara/publication/354143118_Home_Stay_Tourism_In_Uttarakhand-_Opportunities_Challenges/links/61272bd72b40ec7d8bc4677c/Home-Stay-Tourism-In-Uttarakhand-Opportunities-Challenges.pdf

Jayara, J. (2018). *Home-Stay Tourism in Uttarakhand: Opportunities and Challenges*. Researchgate.Net. https://www.researchgate.net/profile/Jaswant-Jayara/publication/354143118_Home_Stay_Tourism_In_Uttarakhand-_Opportunities_Challenges/links/61272bd72b40ec7d8bc4677c/Home-Stay-Tourism-In-Uttarakhand-Opportunities-Challenges.pdf

Kala, D. (2018). Barriers to local community participation in tourism development: Evidence from mountainous state Uttarakhand, India. *Hrcak.Srce.Hr, 66*(3). https://hrcak.srce.hr/clanak/303072

Kapil, S., & Planning, B. V. T. (n.d.). *Territorial Planning Models in Homestays: An Indian Context*. IGI Global. https://www.igi-global.com/chapter/territorial-planning-models-in-homestays/317827

Krepps, K. (2018). *An Appalachia Abroad: Connecting to International Mountain Cultures in India's Uttarakhand*. MDS. https://mds.marshall.edu/asa_conference/2018/accepted_proposals/145/

Kumar, S., Rana, G., & Mairaj, H. (2017). *Status and Scenario of Tourism Industry in India-A Case Study of Uttarakhand*. Academia. https://www.academia.edu/download/52174384/STATUS_AND_SCENARIO_OF_TOURISM_INDUSTRY_IN_INDIA_-_A_CASE_STUDY_OF_UTTARAKHAND.pdf

Lynch, P. A. (1999). Host attitudes towards guests in the homestay sector. *Tourism and Hospitality Research, 1*(2), 119–144. doi:10.1177/146735849900100203

Macek, I. C. (2012). *Homestays as livelihood strategies in rural economies: The case of Johar Valley, Uttarakhand, India*. Proquest. https://search.proquest.com/openview/60d93a96583095eaa262583a4ab60097/1?pq-origsite=gscholar&cbl=18750

Maheshwari, A. (2020). Attitude and Perception of the Local Community Towards Community based Tourism Development in Har Ki Dun Valley Uttarakhand. *EM International, 27*(1), 2021–2115. http://www.envirobiotechjournals.com/EEC/v27i121/EEC-16.pdf

MoT. (2022). INDIA TOURISM STATISTICS. Delhi: Market Research Division, Ministry of Tourism, Government of India. https://tourism.gov.in/sites/default/files/2023-01/India%20Tourism%20Statistics%20English%202022%20%28Revise%29.pdf

Pal, A. (n.d.). Potential and Planning for Ecotourism Development in Dehradun District (Uttarakhand). *Essence-Journal*. https://essence-journal.com/wp-content/uploads/Archives/Volume_VII/Issue_1/Potential-and-Planning-for-Ecotourism-Development-in-Dehradun-District-Uttarakhand.pdf

Payal, M. (2021). *Overview of tourist behavior with respect to environmental sustainability of tourism in the context of a developing economy-a case study of Mussoorie, India*. Researchgate.Net. https://tinyurl.com/kuffa2dn

Prajapati, V., Dhodi, R., & Journal, R. D.-I. (2018). *Women Empowerment Through Participation In Homestay In Sari Village Of Uttarakhand*. Researchgate.Net. https://tinyurl.com/2zxpzvyk

Sati, V. P. (2020). A Sustainable Homestay Tourism and Its Prospects. In *Sustainable Tourism Development in the Himalaya: Constraints and Prospects*. Springer. https://link.springer.com/chapter/10.1007/978-3-030-58854-0_9

Semwal, R. (2022). Preserving and Marketing Rural Cultural Heritage through Homestays of Uttarakhand State. In *Recent Trends in Tourism and Hospitality* (1st ed., Vol. 1, pp. 85–97). Eureka Publications., https://www.researchgate.net/publication/365635848_Preserving_and_Marketing_Rural_Cultural_Heritage_through_Homestays_of_Uttarakhand_State

UKGov. (2022). *Economic Survey 2021-22 (Vol-1)*. Dehradun: DIRECTORATE OF ECONOMICS & STATISTICS. https://des.uk.gov.in/pages/display/177-economic-survey-2021-22

Vikuk, A. L. (2021). *Handbook of Sustainable Development andLeisur e Services*. Springer Science and Business Media LLC. doi:10.1007/978-3-030-59820-4

Chapter 6
Responsible Practices by Tour Guides Promoting Sustainable Tourism

Sandeep Paatlan
https://orcid.org/0000-0002-8746-3133
Chandigarh University, India

Jayati Ranga
Department of Business Administration, Amity University, Mohali, India

ABSTRACT

In the context of sustainable tourism, the part that tour guides play in influencing visitors' experiences and views has drawn a lot of attention. This study explores the crucial function of tour operators as advocates for ethical behavior in the field of sustainable tourism. The research examines how tour guides operate as change agents, encouraging sustainable practices among tourists, in light of growing concerns regarding the environmental, sociocultural, and economic implications of tourism. This chapter investigates the many duties of tour guides in sharing knowledge about sustainable tourism practices. It does so by drawing on a thorough review of academic literature and case studies. It emphasizes the significance of tour guides' capacity to persuade various tourist groups to adhere to responsible tourism's core values. Tour guides can encourage tourists to adopt more responsible behaviour by raising understanding about the local ecosystems, cultures, and social norms through engaging storytelling.

INTRODUCTION

The dynamic and significant industry of tourism has the ability to influence the future of ecosystems and communities all around the world. The importance of tour guides in encouraging ethical and sustainable behavior has grown as the world's understanding of environmental and cultural preservation broadens.(Pu et al., 2023) These intelligent and dynamic leaders are working hard to turn tourism from a potentially destructive force into a force for good. Tour guides play a crucial role in promoting and demonstrating

DOI: 10.4018/979-8-3693-2065-5.ch006

sustainable tourism practices at destinations, emphasizing their crucial role in maintaining the natural beauties and various cultures of our globe(Weiler & Kim, 2011). The idea of sustainable tourism has gained popularity recently and aims to create a healthy balance between the positive economic effects of travel and its possible drawbacks. In this quest, tour guides become essential change agents since they serve as interpreters and instructors(McGrath, 2007). Beyond their outward appeal, breathtaking landscapes and exotic cultures have the power to motivate and educate visitors about the value of making ethical travel decisions. Tour guides encourage a deeper awareness of the complex interactions between human activity and the environment by conveying knowledge about the local ecosystems, wildlife, and cultural quirks. Responsible behavior on the part of tour guides takes many different forms. As tour guides inform guests about delicate ecosystems, endangered animals, and the effects of reckless behavior, environmental consciousness takes center stage(Christie & Mason, 2010). For example, in coastal areas where sea turtles breed, a tour guide's description of the lifecycle of these animals and the significance of maintaining their habitats can discourage visitors from disrupting nests or leaving dangerous debris behind.

Sustainable tourism is based on cultural sensitivity. Tour guides are conduits for cultural knowledge, explaining the practices, traditions, and social mores that influence the community's way of life(Li et al., 2022). Guides provide meaningful discussions that celebrate variety and dispel cultural stereotypes by promoting respectful interactions between tourists and host communities. In a traditional village, a guide's knowledge of the customs and traditions could inspire visitors to interact respectfully, promoting respect and understanding amongst them.

Additionally, tour guides might inspire tourists to make sustainable purchasing decisions. Supporting community-based activities and emphasizing local product purchases helps local economies and lessens the detrimental effects of tourism. Visitors can become conscious consumers who directly improve the quality of destination communities by understanding the power of their purchasing decisions under the supervision of an informed tour guide.

Tour guides are essential in fostering appropriate conduct in the area of wildlife. Guides make sure that visitors can admire the beauty of creatures without doing them harm by promoting moral wildlife interactions and the preservation of natural environments. With their leadership, a stroll in the forest can develop into an educational experience that teaches participants to keep their distance from animals and resist the urge to harm their ecosystems.(Boakye Agyeman et al., 2022) Waste minimization is becoming increasingly important as we move into a time where environmental awareness is in fashion. Inspiring tourists to reduce their use of single-use plastics and switch to a sustainable method of trash disposal can be a key role for tour guides. By taking such straightforward but significant steps, tour guides lessen the harm that tourism-related garbage does to regional ecosystems(Bauske et al., n.d.). The search for sustainability also heavily weighs the modes of transportation used by tourists. Tour guides can influence tourists to choose environmentally friendly modes of transportation by encouraging them to bike, walk, or take public transportation. By doing this, guides help to lower carbon emissions, reduce traffic, and improve the destination's general environmental health.

The objective of the tour guide still places a strong emphasis on education. A profound connection between visitors and the locations they travel to is fostered by guides by providing rich narratives about a destination's history, culture, and sustainability initiatives. Tourists are given insight into community initiatives to preserve their history and environment through the stories of locals(Bryon, 2012). Last but not least, travel operators encourage civic involvement. A mutually beneficial connection between tourists and the local communities is made possible by guides through well-planned exchanges, such as cultural seminars, homestays, and volunteer opportunities. Through these encounters, visitors can go beyond the status of an observer and make a beneficial impact on the places they travel to. The path towards sustainable tourism depends on the tour guides' ethical behavior(Bansal et al., n.d.). These tour operators act as change agents, paving the way to a future where travel enhances rather than depletes the environment as they strike a delicate balance between instruction, enjoyment, and moral duty. Their initiatives serve as a testament to how tourism has the capacity to contribute to environmental and cultural preservation, preserving the world's treasures for future generations.

LITERATURE REVIEW

When interacting with tourists, tour guides may experience role conflicts due to the many roles they play. (Zhu & Xu, 2021) It is argued that the tour guide plays a crucial role in directing the adventure and, as a result, in upholding western local traditions(Beedie, 2011). Variables that have an impact on the satisfaction of tourists and the quality of service provided by tour guides. Tour guides were found to have four qualities. These variables include behavior, moral character, employment, and safety and security in public spaces(ALmasoodi & Rahman, 2023). One of the most important contributors to the industry's ability for travel companies to operate sustainably is the role of tour guides. They are crucial in creating visitor satisfaction and revisit intention(Syakier & Hanafiah, 2021). Front-line participants in the tourist sector is the tour guide. They have the power to turn a tourist's visit from a tour into an experience by their understanding and interpretation of a destination's attractions and culture, as well as through their communication and service skills (Ap & Wong, 2001) . The mentor and the pathfinder are the two sources of the modern tourist guide. These serve as the leadership and mediating realms in the position of the guide, respectively. Four main elements of the function are identified since each has an inner and an exterior directed aspect: the instrumental, social, interactionary, and communicative. (Cohen, 1985). The sustainable tourism strategy is the best way to guarantee the growth and protection of a location. Due to the close relationships that exist between the tourist and the place, tour guides may assist in the management of the destination's resources, as well as its economic and sociocultural effect. (Güzel, n.d.). Stakeholders Due to the importance of the tourist industry, tour operators have significant influence in guaranteeing coordination and motivation among supply and demand items. Tour operators possess a significant sectoral position, but ensure also actively directs the involvement of all stakeholders in the sustainability process. (ARICA, n.d.) The tour operators have a key role in the supply chain for vacation packages and a strong distribution network, which gives them some control over market development and could be used to inform and motivate buyers and sellers to engage in more responsible tourism practices.(Budeanu, 2005) The importance of tour guides in giving guests a top-notch experience cannot be overstated. Visitors generate positive opinions through website when they have a quality experience, which would increase their pleasure and subsequently encourage sustainable behavior. This offers a more thorough justification of the significance of tour guides in encouraging sustainable behavior.(Alazaizeh et al., 2019) .

Advantages of Tour Guiding

The promotion of sustainable practices at a location is greatly aided by tour guides who inform and persuade visitors to make thoughtful decisions that have the least possible negative effects on the local environment, culture, and communities. Here are some examples of how tour guides might encourage environmentally friendly practices:

Figure 1. Tour guides

a) Travelers can learn about local ecosystems, plants, and fauna from tour guides, who can also emphasize the value of conservation. They can stifle practices like littering and destroying natural habitats that are harmful to the environment.
   Example- A tour guide in a coastal location can give an example of the importance of maintaining sea turtle breeding grounds and urge visitors to refrain from littering the beach or upsetting turtle nests. Cultural Respect:
b) Respect for regional cultures, traditions, and legacy can be encouraged through tour guides. They can give visitors knowledge of the region's traditions, morals, and social mores, enticing them to behave sensibly and respectfully when interacting with residents. Example: A tour guide in a traditional village, for instance, might explain the significance of particular rituals or ceremonies

and give advice to visitors on how to conduct themselves and how to dress in a way that respects the culture

c) Promoting Local Economies: Tour guides should stress the value of patronizing locally produced goods and nonprofit organizations. This lessens the economic leakage frequently linked to mass tourism and aids in funding local communities. Example: In a handicraft fair, a tour guide may discuss the importance of buying goods directly from regional craftspeople to support the local economy and ensure that the money goes to the creators.

d) Respectful Wildlife Interaction: Tour guides can inform visitors on respectful wildlife watching and dissuade them from engaging in actions that endanger or disturb animals. They can stress how crucial it is to keep a safe distance and refrain from damaging wildlife habitats. Example: As an illustration, a tour guide at a national park could inform guests on the value of keeping distance from and refraining from feeding wild animals in order to preserve the animals' natural habits.

e) Waste reduction: Tour guides can inform visitors about local recycling and waste reduction initiatives. They can nudge visitors to reduce single-use plastic consumption and practice responsible waste disposal. Example: A tour guide can advise hikers to carry out all trail rubbish and to bring refillable water bottles rather than single-use ones.

f) Sustainable Transportation: To lessen carbon emissions and traffic in the destination, tour guides might encourage eco-friendly transportation methods like walking, cycling, or using the bus. Example: Instead of depending on private vehicles or taxis, a tour guide in a city can advise using electric scooters or public transportation to explore the area.

g) Educational Interpretation: Tour guides can tell engaging stories about the history, ecology, and sustainability initiatives of the site, promoting a greater understanding and appreciation among visitors. Example: A tour guide could convey the idea of ecotourism while leading a nature excursion, describing how the neighborhood has come together to safeguard the area's habitat and fauna.

h) Community Engagement: Through responsible and genuine connections, such as cultural seminars, homestays, or volunteer opportunities, tour guides can introduce tourists to local communities. Example: A tour operator could arrange for tourists to attend a local resident's traditional cooking lesson, resulting in a meaningful exchange that benefits both the tourists and the neighbourhood.

Responsible Tourism Activities

Responsible tourism is a type of travel that lessens its detrimental effects on a destination's environment, society, and culture. It strives to increase the sustainability of tourism and make it advantageous to both visitors and local communities.

The following are some of the fundamental tenets of responsible tourism:

a) Sustainability: By minimizing waste, preserving resources, and safeguarding delicate ecosystems, responsible tourism aims to have the least possible negative effects on the environment.

b) Economic and social advantages to local communities are sought after by responsible tourism, which also supports local companies, employs locals, and honors regional cultures and traditions.

c) Authenticity: The goal of responsible tourism is to connect visitors to the ecology and culture of the destination by offering genuine and meaningful experiences.

d) Education: The goal of responsible tourism is to inform visitors about the value of eco-friendly travel and the effects of their decisions on the location.

Here are some actions that visitors can do to engage in responsible tourism:

a) Pick a vacation spot that values sustainable tourism. The World Tourism Organization (UNWTO) and the Sustainable Tourism Stewardship Council (STSC) are two examples of the organizations that accredit travel destinations as sustainable.
b) Book environmentally friendly lodging. Many hotels, resorts, and guesthouses have received eco-friendly certification from groups like Green Globe and Earth Check.
c) Eat foods grown nearby. Consuming local food lessens the environmental impact of food transportation while also assisting neighborhood farmers and businesses.
d) Take the bus or another sustainable mode of transportation. Air pollution and traffic congestion are reduced by using public transportation and environmentally friendly modes of mobility like bicycles and walking.
e) Get to know the traditions and culture of the area. Tourists should respect local traditions and culture and refrain from engaging in actions that are deemed offensive or disrespectful.
f) Treat the environment with respect. By minimizing waste, conserving water, and refraining from littering, tourists can lessen their negative environmental effects.
g) Assist regional companies. By using local guides and drivers, eating at local eateries, and shopping at local markets, tourists may help local businesses.
h) Properly dispose of garbage. Tourists must properly dispose of their waste and abstain from leaving behind litter.
i) Set a positive example for other people. Tourists should lead by example by engaging in responsible travel.

STR Cycle

Figure 2. STR cycle

Although tourism contributes significantly to the world economy, its effects on the environment, culture, and local populations have prompted an increasing focus on ethical and sustainable behaviour. In their capacity as liaisons between travellers and their locations, tour guides have a significant impact on the perceptions and actions of travellers. This study examines the critical connection between tour guides, ethical behavior, and sustainable tourism, emphasizing the function of tour guides in promoting travel that is both socially and environmentally responsible.

Tour guides interpret the place by sharing knowledge about its history, culture, and environmental value. Their stories and knowledge have the power to shape tourists' perceptions and actions, which has an effect on how long tourism-related businesses can exist.

(Korstanje, 2012)The Theory and Practice of Dark Tourism, or the Travel's Darker Side. Publications by Channel View. This edited book examines several facets of tourism, including the function of tour guides in interpreting delicate and troubling locations, highlighting the influence that guides have on visitors' worldview

Tour Guides Facilitating Responsible Practices

Tour guides are essential in advising visitors on responsible conduct and promoting activities that lessen their negative effects on the area. Tour guides help ensure that tourism is sustained over the long run by encouraging a sense of responsibility.

(Gössling et al., 2015)The Tourism and Water. Publications by Channel View. This book explores the connection between tourism and water resources, highlighting how ethical travel habits, supported by tour operators and guides, can aid in the preservation of essential water resources.

Sensitivity Towards Local Culture

Travelers are introduced to regional cultures and traditions through tour guides, who serve as cultural mediators. Their advice can guarantee that visitors interact with host communities in a respectful manner, protecting cultural assets and fostering intercultural understanding.

(Richards, n.d.)Gastronomy and tourism. Routledge. This edited book examines the relationship between gastronomy and tourism, placing special emphasis on the function of tour operators in creating genuine culinary encounters that support cultural preservation.

Interpreting the Environment and Conservation

A destination's ecological worth is highlighted through effective tour guides' environmental interpretation. Guides can encourage tourists to value and conserve natural resources by telling instructive stories.

("Ecotourism Policy and Planning," 2003)The Eco-Tourism policy or Planning. CABI. The role of knowledgeable tour guides in promoting ecological ideas and sustainable habits is emphasized in this book's insights into ecotourism planning and policy.

CONCLUSION

It is impossible to exaggerate how important tour guides are in promoting ethical and environmentally friendly tourist activities. Tour guides hold a unique and powerful position to influence tourists' experiences and actions since they act as liaisons between tourists and the places they travel to. The power of tour guides to inform, motivate, and sway visitors holds enormous promise for reducing the negative effects of tourism and fostering constructive contributions to host areas. Tour guides have the ability to establish a sense of cultural sensitivity and preservation among tourists through their insightful narratives. Tour guides build an environment where visitors interact with host communities in ways that preserve and celebrate their cultural identity by telling tales about local customs, traditions, and legacy. This promotes cross-cultural understanding and respect. A third way in which tour guides contribute to the preservation of regional cultures and traditions is by promoting authentic gourmet experiences. It is important to equip tour guides with the required information, skills, and ethics because of their crucial role in sustainable tourism. It is crucial to provide tour guides with thorough training that covers both factual information and ethical considerations. This makes it possible for them to persuade visitors to travel responsibly, promoting a culture of conscientious and thoughtful tourism. Tour guides are viewed as agents of change in a world where tourism's effects are being examined more closely. They have the key to transforming the tourism industry into one that is more responsible, respectful, and sustainable because of their capacity to engage, educate, and inspire. It is crucial that all parties involved in the tourism sector, such as tour operators, educational institutions, and governing authorities, work together to give tour guides the resources they need to promote responsible travel. By doing this, we open the door to a time when tourism not only improves the lives of tourists but also has a beneficial and long-lasting impact on the places they visit.

REFERENCES

Alazaizeh, M. M., Jamaliah, M. M., Mgonja, J. T., & Ababneh, A. (2019). Tour guide performance and sustainable visitor behavior at cultural heritage sites. *Journal of Sustainable Tourism*, *27*(11), 1708–1724. doi:10.1080/09669582.2019.1658766

ALmasoodi, M. F., & Rahman, S. (2023). International Tourists' Satisfaction with Tour Guide's Service Quality at Babylon Archaeological Site. *International Journal of Sustainable Development and Planning*, *18*(1), 17–28. doi:10.18280/ijsdp.180102

Ap, J., & Wong, K. K. F. (2001). Case study on tour guiding: Professionalism, issues and problems. *Tourism Management*, *22*(5), 551–563. doi:10.1016/S0261-5177(01)00013-9

Arica, R. (n.d.). *A Review of Barriers of Tour Operators Sustainable Tourism Activities*. Academia. https://www.academia.edu/31115290/A_Review_of_Barriers_of_Tour_Operators_Sustainable_Tourism_Activities

Bansal, S. P., Gautam, P. K., & Kulshreestha, S. (n.d.). *THE DEVELOPMENT TEAM Principal Investigator Co-Principal Investigator Paper Coordinator Content Reviewer*.

Bauske, D. (n.d.). *B., von Münchhausen, M., Plitharas, A., Tsoukalas, K., Bauer, U., Köberich, T., WWF Deutschland, & WWF Deutschland*. Stoppt die Plastikflut Wirksame Maßnahmen zur Vermeidung von Einwegplastik und Verpackung im Hotel.

Beedie, P. (2011). Mountain guiding and adventure tourism: reflections on the choreography of the experience. L*eisure Studies*, *22*(2), 147–167. doi:10.1080/026143603200068991

Boakye Agyeman, Y., Boaa Antwi-Bosiako, N., Box, P. O., & Wong, J. (2022). Visitor perceptions of the roles of tour guides in Kakum National Park in Ghana. *Cogent Social Sciences*, *8*(1), 2052403. doi:10.1080/23311886.2022.2052403

Bryon, J. (2012). Tour Guides as Storytellers – From Selling to Sharing. *Scandinavian Journal of Hospitality and Tourism*, *12*(1), 27–43. doi:10.1080/15022250.2012.656922

Budeanu, A. (2005). Impacts and responsibilities for sustainable tourism: A tour operator's perspective. *Journal of Cleaner Production*, *13*(2), 89–97. https://www.academia.edu/8505736/Impacts_and_responsibilities_for_sustainable_tourism_a_tour_operators_perspective. doi:10.1016/j.jclepro.2003.12.024 PMID:32288344

Christie, M. F., & Mason, P. A. (2010). Transformative Tour Guiding: Training Tour Guides to be Critically. *Journal of Ecotourism*, *2*(1), 1–16. Https://Doi.Org/10.1080/14724040308668130. doi:10.1080/14724040308668130

Cohen, E. (1985). The tourist guide: The origins, structure and dynamics of a role. *Annals of Tourism Research*, *12*(1), 5–29. doi:10.1016/0160-7383(85)90037-4

Ecotourism policy and planning. (2003). *Ecotourism Policy and Planning*. Ecotourism policy and Planning. doi:10.1079/9780851996097.0000

Gössling, S., Hall, C. M., & Scott, D. (2015). *Tourism and Water*. Academia. https://www.academia.edu/9394033/Tourism_and_Water

Güzel, Ö. (n.d.). *Sustainable Tourism and The Roles of Tour Guides in Destinations: A Qualitative Case Study in Turkey*. Academia. https://www.academia.edu/44606413/Sustainable_Tourism_and_The_Roles_of_Tour_Guides_in_Destinations_A_Qualitative_Case_Study_in_Turkey

Korstanje, M. E. (2012). The Darker Side of Travel: The Theory and Practice of Dark Tourism. *International Journal of Contemporary Hospitality Management*, *24*(1), 160–162. doi:10.1108/09596111211197854

Li, J., Lee, T. J., Chen, N., & Park, K. S. (2022). Pro-environmental behaviour of the residents in sensitive tourism destinations. *Sage, 29*(2), 291–308. doi:10.1177/13567667221101406

McGrath, G. (2007). *Towards developing tour guides as interpreters of cultural heritage: The case of Cusco*. Quality Assurance and Certification in Ecotourism., doi:10.1079/9781845932374.0364

Pu, P., Cheng, L., Samarathunga, W. H. M. S., & Wall, G. (2023). Tour guides' sustainable tourism practices in host-guest interactions: When Tibet meets the west. *Tourism Review*, *78*(3), 808–833. doi:10.1108/TR-04-2022-0182

Richards, G. (n.d.). *Cultural tourism : global and local perspectives*. Routledge. https://www.routledge.com/Cultural-Tourism-Global-and-Local-Perspectives/Richards/p/book/9780789031174

Syakier, W. A., & Hanafiah, M. H. (2021). Tour Guide Performances, Tourist Satisfaction And Behavioural Intentions: A Study On Tours In Kuala Lumpur City Centre. *Journal of Quality Assurance in Hospitality and Tourism, 23*(3), 597–614. doi:10.1080/1528008X.2021.1891599

Weiler, B., & Kim, A. K. (2011). Tour guides as agents of sustainability: Rhetoric, reality and implications for research. *Tourism Recreation Research*, *36*(2), 113–125. doi:10.1080/02508281.2011.11081313

Zhu, D., & Xu, H. (2021). Guides' handling of multiple roles in interactions with tourists: The prism of impression management. *Tourism Management*, *85*, 104306. doi:10.1016/j.tourman.2021.104306

Chapter 7
Sustainable Tourism Perspective in the Sustainable Development Goals:
A Case Study of Heritage Sites in Uttarakhand

Sujay Vikram Singh
https://orcid.org/0000-0002-7113-2698
Banaras Hindu University, India

Rashmi Jha
Banaras Hindu University, India

Ajit Kumar Singh
University Institute of Tourism and Hospitality Management, India

Rajeev Ranjan
Mangalayatan University, India

Sachin Pandey
Banaras Hindu University, India

ABSTRACT

The present study attempts to make a meaningful contribution to both the academic dialogue and the practical comprehension of how the Sustainable Development Goals can be utilised as a catalyst for profound change within the distinct socio-cultural and environmental context of Uttarakhand. Three heritage sites have been discussed in this context: Natural (Nanda Devi National Park), Built (Kedarnath), and Riverscape (Har ki pauri).The study discovers significant insights that will resonate with policymakers, practitioners, and communities all around the world by conducting an exhaustive study of the complexities of sustainable development in this particular region.

DOI: 10.4018/979-8-3693-2065-5.ch007

INTRODUCTION

The idea of sustainable development has recently emerged as a potentially useful strategy for attaining a harmonious cohabitation between the progression of humanity and the responsible management of the environment, with the end goal of benefiting both the current generation and those to come in the foreseeable future. The Sustainable Development Goals (SDGs) are an all-encompassing worldwide framework that envisions a future in which economic prosperity, social equity, and ecological conservation are intertwined. These goals are at the center of the dramatic shift that is taking place. Despite their universal nature as a roadmap for nations around the world, the success of the Sustainable Development Goals (SDGs) is inextricably tied to its contextual implementation and applicability at regional and local levels.

The Indian state of Uttarakhand is distinguished for the vast socio-cultural diversity that it possesses as well as its picture-perfect landscapes. However, the fact that the operations of development and conservation are being carried out in this region simultaneously creates a unique and difficult situation. This northern state is encircled by the gorgeous Himalayan highlands, and it serves as an excellent example of the delicate balance that must be struck between the need of human populations and the protection of the natural environment in their surrounds. In view of the engagement of the international community with the Sustainable Development Goals (SDGs), it is essential to have a solid understanding of the complex interaction that exists between these goals and the one-of-a-kind circumstances, opportunities, and challenges that Uttarakhand faces.

The Sustainable Development Goals (SDGs) and the state of Uttarakhand have a convoluted and multifaceted relationship, which the purpose of this research study is to analyse. The purpose of this research is to investigate the interrelationships between economic growth, social justice, and environmental resiliency, with a particular emphasis on gaining an understanding of how the global aims of the Sustainable Development aims (SDGs) correspond with the regional setting of Uttarakhand. Specifically, the research will look at how the SDGs can be achieved in the state of Uttarakhand. As we investigate the many facets of sustainable development, our primary purpose is to pinpoint the strategies, activities, and perspectives that have the potential to accelerate Uttarakhand's population towards a future that is both more equitable and environmentally sound.

The primary objective of this research project is to conduct an in-depth investigation on the essential components of the Sustainable Development Goals (SDGs) and how they correspond to the particular characteristics of Uttarakhand. The first part of the study is dedicated to providing a comprehensive analysis of the socioeconomic and environmental conditions that exist within the state, with an emphasis on the state's most significant characteristics, challenges, and aspirations. Following this, the current study will investigate the relationship between the Sustainable Development Goals (SDGs) and the state's top developmental goals, shedding light on the interconnections that exist between global aspirations and local prerequisites. In addition, the current policies, activities, and collaborations that serve as examples of Uttarakhand's dedication to achieving the Sustainable Development Goals (SDGs) will be subjected to a critical analysis during the course of this study. In addition to this, the study investigates potential paths, developments, and collaborations that can make it easier to achieve sustainable advancement within the region.

AN OVERVIEW OF THE SUSTAINABLE DEVELOPMENT GOALS

The Sustainable Development Goals (SDGs) are a set of targets established by the United Nations in 2015 inclusion in the 2030 Agenda for Sustainable Development. These goals are a comprehensive set of 17 goals that have been set at the global level. These objectives provide a framework that is both comprehensive and integrative for solving a wide variety of social, economic, and environmental concerns that are faced on a worldwide scale. The main aim of the Sustainable Development Goals (SDGs) is to advance sustainable development by achieving a harmonious equilibrium between economic progress, social inclusivity, and environmental preservation, while concurrently guaranteeing that no individual or group is marginalised or excluded.

The 17 Sustainable Development Goals (SDGs) encompass distinct dimensions of development and well-being, and are complemented by a comprehensive collection of 169 objectives and a corresponding set of indicators to assess and monitor advancements in these areas. The Sustainable Development Goals (SDGs) encompass a diverse range of interrelated subjects, such as poverty reduction, food security, public health, education, gender equality, access to clean water and sanitation, affordable and sustainable energy, decent employment opportunities, sustainable consumption patterns, and climate change mitigation. The aforementioned objectives were formulated in the year 2015 with the aim of providing direction to international endeavours in the realm of development until the year 2030. The Sustainable Development Goals (SDGs) represent a worldwide pledge to collectively address pressing issues, including poverty, inequality, environmental degradation, and climate change, via cooperation and collaboration. These challenges have been recognised as being among the most significant on a global scale. The authors highlight the interrelated nature of these difficulties and underscore the necessity of comprehensive solutions that foster both short-term and long-term welfare.

The Notion of Sustainable Tourism Development

The notion of sustainable tourism is relatively recent, and our understanding of it is still in its nascent stages. The notion of sustainable development, which was first articulated in the Brundtland Report of 1987, garnered global acceptance at the Rio Summit in 1992 with the endorsement of the Agenda 21 principles by the worldwide community. Following this, the topic was further discussed and examined during the World Summit on Sustainable Development (WSSD) held in Johannesburg in 2002. Since then, sustainable development has been a subject of extensive discussion and analysis in various UN and international forums, as well as among academics, scientists, non-governmental organisations (NGOs), public sector development agencies, and private businesses. The concept of sustainable development encompasses a wide range of concerns, encompassing both social and physical aspects. However, there has been a particular emphasis on environmental sustainability, as tourism often surpasses the capacity of a destination and depletes its natural resources. The concept of sustainable tourism was defined and elucidated by the World Conservation Union in 1996. It refers to a form of travel and visitation to natural areas that is characterised by environmental responsibility. The primary objective is to enable individuals to enjoy and appreciate nature while simultaneously promoting conservation efforts. This type of tourism emphasises minimising the impact on the environment and actively involving local communities in socio-economic activities. The three components of sustainable tourism can be elucidated as three fundamental elements, commonly known as the “triple bottom line” notions, which were formulated by the International Ecotourism Society in 2004. These components are as follows:

From an environmental perspective, sustainable tourism aims to minimise its impact on natural resources and, ideally, seeks to contribute positively to the environment.

From a social and cultural perspective, the presence of this entity within the community does not have any detrimental effects on its social structure or cultural fabric. Moreover, it demonstrates reverence towards indigenous cultures and customs.

From an economic standpoint, it plays a crucial role in enhancing the financial prosperity of the community by creating income that is both sustainable and equitable for the local populace. A tourism firm that adheres to these three criteria will achieve success through ethical and sustainable practises.

The notion of sustainable tourism pertains to a kind of tourism that endeavours to mitigate adverse effects on the environment, society, and economy.

As per the definition put forward by the United Nations World Tourism Organisation (UNWTO), sustainable tourism pertains to the implementation of strategies and policies aimed at effectively managing the tourist industry, taking into consideration its present and future impacts on society, economy, and the environment. This approach involves considering the desires and requirements of visitors, as well as the environmental concerns of the industry and the local communities hosting the tourism activities.

The World Summit on Sustainable Development (2002) defines sustainable tourism as a type of tourism that encompasses both the present and future aspects of tourism and its accompanying infrastructure.

The acknowledgement of the significant impact that individuals, cultural practises, ways of life, and local communities make towards enhancing the overall tourism experience.

- It is imperative to utilise nature and its natural resources in an optimal manner, ensuring their regeneration for the benefit of future generations. This necessitates the adoption of a cyclic process for resource utilization. - The engagement of the local community residing in the host area is crucial for its development, as it enables the generation of revenue both directly and indirectly.

Therefore, it is evident that sustainable tourism endeavours to fulfil the immediate requirements of both tourists and host regions while safeguarding and improving the tourism offering for future generations.

In their study, Ramirez and Rangel (2018) conducted an analysis on the economic activity of tourism and its interaction with the environment. They found that tourism has both good and bad consequences. On the positive side, it contributes to the enhancement of economic competitiveness. However, on the negative side, it leads to issues such as overcrowding in tourist destinations and deterioration of the places where tourism is practised. Hence, it is evident from the aforementioned arguments that inadequate management has the potential to undermine the integrity of tourism assets.

According to Alday and Ara (2012), tourism is a significant economic activity that is characterised by its ability to generate money and jobs. Additionally, it has a substantial impact on several sectors, which further emphasises its strategic importance.

In their study, Altinay and Hussain (2005) aimed to investigate the perspectives of tourist experts regarding the environmental impact of hotel investment in the Bafra, Karpaz region. An environmental impact model is employed to assess the impact of tourism, revealing a significant correlation between waste disposal and the environmental consequences of this industry. The primary focus of this study was on the untapped region of North Cyprus, which has garnered significant interest from investors seeking to allocate their resources.

According to Hall (2013), tourism has been demonstrated to have a beneficial impact on the advancement of various public services and infrastructure at both regional and local levels. This is achieved through the facilitation of unrestricted tourist movement, the introduction of other cultures and customs, and the promotion of social connections among individuals.

The term "Sustainable Development Goals" (often abbreviated "SDGs") refers to a set of global objectives formulated by the United Nations (UN) to resolve a variety of socioeconomic and environmental challenges that are currently being encountered. The United Nations General Assembly's 70th session, which began on September 25, 2015, resulted in the adoption of a document with the title "Transforming Our World: The 2030 Agenda for Sustainable Development." The formulation of a comprehensive sustainable development strategy has resulted in the establishment of a set of 17 goals and 169 targets, which are intended to be accomplished during the next 15 years or by the year 2030. The primary objectives of these goals are to eradicate poverty, safeguard the environment, and promote inclusive prosperity for all individuals. There is a consensus among stakeholders that the 17 Sustainable Development Goals (SDGs) are interconnected and indivisible, and that their applicability extends globally. The objectives have been formulated with the intention of adhering to national policies and goals, but also considering the diverse national circumstances, capabilities, and levels of progress. Furthermore, the Sustainable Development Goals (SDGs) are linked to a total of 169 interrelated objectives. 'Transforming our world: The 2030 Agenda for Sustainable Development' is a seminal document that outlines a comprehensive and integrated approach to address the multifaceted challenges confronting our planet. It aims to foster the welfare of its people while simultaneously fostering sustainable economic growth. The aforementioned paper can be accessed at the following location. The 17 Sustainable Development Goals (SDGs) and their corresponding 169 goals exemplify the extensive scope and ambitious character of the recently established global Agenda. Efforts are being made to prioritise the Millennium Development Goals and address the outstanding objectives that have not yet been attained, both presently and in the foreseeable future. The various components of sustainable development are effectively harmonised through the integration of economic, social, and environmental factors.

Uttarakhand and Sustainable Development Goals

Uttarakhand, situated in the northern region of India, presents a distinct set of challenges and opportunities within the framework of the Sustainable Development Goals (SDGs). These SDGs offer a holistic platform for addressing a diverse array of social, economic, and environmental concerns. Here's a detailed overview of how the SDGs relate to Uttarakhand:

1. **No Poverty (SDG 1):** Uttarakhand, despite its natural beauty and resources, still grapples with pockets of poverty, especially in remote and hilly areas. Initiatives are needed to ensure equitable economic growth, create livelihood opportunities, and provide social safety nets for vulnerable populations.
2. **Zero Hunger (SDG 2):** Ensuring food security and promoting sustainable agriculture is crucial in Uttarakhand, where agriculture is a significant sector. Encouraging practices like organic farming and improving access to markets for local farmers can contribute to this goal.
3. **Good Health and Well-being (SDG 3):** While Uttarakhand has made progress in healthcare, there are challenges related to healthcare access in remote areas. Improving healthcare infrastructure, maternal and child health, and addressing non-communicable diseases are important aspects.
4. **Quality Education (SDG 4):** Improving the quality of education and reducing dropout rates, especially among marginalized communities, is a priority in Uttarakhand. Ensuring access to education in hilly and remote regions is also a challenge.

5. **Gender Equality (SDG 5):** While the state has made progress in gender equality, there are still issues of gender-based violence and discrimination. Promoting women's participation in decision-making and economic activities is important.
6. **Clean Water and Sanitation (SDG 6):** Uttarakhand faces both water scarcity and water quality issues. Ensuring access to clean and safe drinking water, especially in rural areas, and promoting sustainable water management practices are critical.
7. **Affordable and Clean Energy (SDG 7):** The state's hilly terrain offers opportunities for renewable energy sources like hydroelectric power. Expanding renewable energy infrastructure can contribute to sustainable development while reducing reliance on fossil fuels.
8. **Decent Work and Economic Growth (SDG 8):** Encouraging industries that are in harmony with the environment and promoting tourism can create jobs while preserving the state's natural beauty.
9. **Industry, Innovation, and Infrastructure (SDG 9):** Developing sustainable infrastructure, including road networks and connectivity to remote areas, is crucial for balanced economic development.
10. **Reduced Inequality (SDG 10):** Addressing inequalities between urban and rural areas, as well as among different socioeconomic groups, are essential for inclusive development in Uttarakhand.
11. **Sustainable Cities and Communities (SDG 11):** Balancing urbanization with environmental conservation is a challenge. Ensuring sustainable urban planning, waste management, and disaster preparedness are important in Uttarakhand's context.
12. **Responsible Consumption and Production (SDG 12):** Promoting sustainable tourism, reducing waste generation, and encouraging eco-friendly practices can contribute to responsible consumption and production.
13. **Climate Action (SDG 13):** Uttarakhand is vulnerable to the impacts of climate change, including erratic weather patterns and natural disasters. Mitigation and adaptation strategies are essential to protect communities and ecosystems.
14. **Life Below Water (SDG 14) and 15. Life on Land (SDG 15):** Uttarakhand's rich biodiversity and ecosystems need protection. Addressing deforestation, promoting sustainable forest management, and conserving water bodies are vital.
16. **Peace and Justice Strong Institutions (SDG 16):** Ensuring effective governance, access to justice, and reducing crime rates contribute to peace and justice in the state.
17. **Partnerships to achieve the Goal (SDG 17):** Collaborative efforts involving government, civil society, businesses, and international organizations are essential to address the diverse challenges and opportunities in Uttarakhand.

Need of Implementing Sustainable Tourism Goals and Practices

The tourism sector, especially post-pandemic, has been marred with an increasing need for sustainable practices that minimize environmental burden and increase socio-economic benefits. For the state of Uttarakhand, tourism is a big driving factor in benefitting the socio-economic circuit. The tourism sector has the capacity to produce income from foreign sources, foster job opportunities, stimulate development across different regions, mitigate economic inequalities between areas, enhance connections among various sectors in both the national and state economies, and contribute to poverty reduction. The foundation of sustainable tourism development lies in the obligation of governments and all participants in the tourism industry to safeguard the well-being of future generations and guarantee their long-term prosperity without compromising their quality of life. A few heritage tourist sites have been discussed to exemplify how sustainable tourism is crucial.

Nanda Devi National Park (Natural Heritage)

Nanda Devi National Park, situated in the Uttarakhand state of India, represents an unspoiled and captivating expanse of wildness that embodies the magnificence of the Himalayan region. The site was officially established in the year 1982 and subsequently recognized as a UNESCO World Heritage Site in 1988. This designation was primarily attributed to its remarkable natural aesthetics, distinctive biodiversity, and cultural importance.

The sanctuary is widely recognized for its abundant biodiversity, encompassing a variety of endangered animals like the snow leopard, Himalayan tahr, and musk deer. The location is highly favorable for birdwatching enthusiasts, as it offers a diverse array of avian species, including notable examples such as the Himalayan monal and other types of pheasants, which can be observed in flight.

The Nanda Devi National Park possesses cultural value for the indigenous populations residing in the area. Villages such as Lata and Tolma have effectively maintained their ancient way of life, exhibiting robust connections to the encompassing natural environment. Figure 1 presents Nanda Devi National Park presenting challenging trekking routes, and an unparalleled sense of serenity.

Figure 1. The trek at Nanda Devi National Park
Source: The economic times [et] (2017).

- **Conservation of Biodiversity:** Nanda Devi National Park is a UNESCO World Heritage site and "one of the most ecologically sensitive areas in the world" (UNESCO, 2018). It is home to a wide variety of flora and fauna, including many endangered species. Sustainable tourism helps minimize the impact of human activities on this fragile ecosystem, ensuring the long-term conservation of biodiversity.
- **Protection of the Nanda Devi Sanctuary:** The park includes the Nanda Devi Sanctuary, which is off-limits to tourists to protect its pristine environment. Sustainable tourism practices ensure that visitors stay within designated areas and do not encroach upon sensitive zones, preserving the sanctuary's natural beauty and ecological balance.
- **Economic Benefits:** Sustainable tourism can provide a source of income for local communities living around the park. This can reduce their dependence on activities that may harm the environment, such as illegal logging or poaching, and promote conservation efforts by offering alternative livelihoods.
- **Cultural Preservation:** Nanda Devi National Park is not only a natural treasure but also has cultural significance for the local communities, including the Bhotia, Johar, and Shauka tribes (UNESCO, 2018). Sustainable tourism can help preserve their traditions, as well as educate visitors about the rich cultural heritage of the region.
- **Awareness and Education:** Responsible tourism practices involve educating visitors about the importance of conservation and sustainable living. Tourists can become ambassadors for environmental protection and biodiversity conservation, spreading awareness when they return home.
- **Regulation of Visitor Numbers:** Sustainable tourism often involves setting limits on the number of visitors allowed in the park at any given time. This helps prevent overcrowding and minimizes the environmental impact of tourism activities.
- **Infrastructure Development:** Sustainable tourism can lead to the development of eco-friendly infrastructure, such as low-impact accommodation and waste management systems, which can benefit both tourists and the environment.
- **Research Opportunities:** Tourism can provide funding and support for scientific research and monitoring efforts in the park. This research is vital for understanding the ecosystem and developing effective conservation strategies.
- **Long-term Viability:** By adopting sustainable practices, Nanda Devi National Park can continue to attract tourists while protecting its natural and cultural assets for future generations.

Sustainable tourism at Nanda Devi National Park (Fig. 1) is essential to strike a balance between conservation and tourism, ensuring the protection of its unique biodiversity, culture, and natural beauty while providing economic benefits to local communities and promoting environmental awareness.

Kedarnath Temple (Built Heritage)

The Kedarnath Temple, an exemplary illustration of constructed cultural legacy, is a revered Hindu sanctuary situated in the Garhwal Himalayas in Uttarakhand, India. The ancient temple, dedicated to Lord Shiva, is estimated to have been constructed more than a millennium ago, utilizing large stone slabs that were beautifully carved. The architectural configuration of the edifice is distinguished by a roof in the shape of a pyramid and elaborate stone engravings, which serve as a tribute to the enduring craftsmanship and artistic prowess of the indigenous artisans in the area. The Kedarnath Temple stands as a testament to the steadfast devotion and architectural prowess of its builders, even in the face of natural calamities and adverse weather conditions. The temple is widely regarded as a significant spiritual and architectural achievement. It stands as a prominent representation of India's abundant religious and architectural legacy. Figure 2 presents Kedarnath temple and its built heritage.

Figure 2. Kedarnath temple
Source: Kumar (2019), CC BY-SA 4.0

Diversifying our set of examples with a tangible heritage site, it is important to illustrate the sustainable tourism steps that are required at the Kedarnath Temple:

- **Eco-friendly Infrastructure:** Sustainable tourism efforts focus on developing eco-friendly infrastructure around the temple. This includes using sustainable building materials, energy-efficient technologies, and waste management systems to minimize the environmental footprint of tourism-related developments.
- **Waste Management:** Managing solid waste and sewage is a significant challenge in places with high tourist footfalls. Sustainable tourism initiatives aim to implement proper waste disposal and recycling systems to keep the area clean and prevent pollution of the nearby Mandakini River and surrounding ecosystems.
- **Controlled Visitor Numbers:** To prevent overcrowding and environmental degradation, there may be restrictions on the number of pilgrims allowed to visit the temple each day. This helps maintain the sanctity of the site and minimizes the impact on the fragile mountain environment.

- **Biodiversity Conservation:** The Kedarnath region is rich in biodiversity, with diverse flora and fauna. Sustainable tourism seeks to protect and preserve this natural heritage by enforcing rules against deforestation, illegal hunting, and other harmful activities.
- **Sustainable Transportation:** Encouraging eco-friendly transportation options, such as electric or hybrid vehicles, and improving pedestrian pathways can reduce the carbon footprint associated with travel to Kedarnath.
- **Cultural Preservation:** Sustainable tourism also focuses on preserving the cultural heritage of the region. This includes supporting local artisans and craftsmen, as well as promoting traditional practices and rituals associated with the temple.
- **Education and Awareness:** Tourists and pilgrims are educated about responsible and respectful behavior when visiting the temple and its surroundings. This includes guidelines on waste disposal, conservation, and cultural sensitivity.
- **Disaster Preparedness:** Given the region's susceptibility to natural disasters, including avalanches and flash floods, sustainable tourism efforts also include disaster preparedness and response plans to ensure the safety of visitors and residents.
- **Community Involvement:** Engaging local communities in tourism management and sharing the economic benefits of tourism with them can foster a sense of ownership and responsibility among the residents, leading to better preservation efforts.
- **Monitoring and Research:** Regular monitoring of the environmental and cultural impact of tourism is essential to adapt and improve sustainable practices continually. Scientific research can provide valuable insights into the region's ecology and ways to protect it.

In essence, sustainable tourism at Kedarnath Temple seeks to strike a balance between religious and cultural significance and environmental preservation, ensuring that the site remains spiritually significant while protecting its fragile mountain ecosystem for future generations.

Haridwar and Rishikesh (Riverscape Heritage)

Har Ki Pauri, situated in the city of Haridwar, India, is a revered and emblematic riverscape historic site situated along the banks of the Ganges River. This esteemed ghat is purported to be the location where Lord Shiva imprinted his foot, rendering it a momentous place of pilgrimage for adherents of the Hindu faith. The riverscape legacy of Har Ki Pauri encompasses the customary practice of Ganga Aarti, a captivating ceremonial event in which priests engage in prayer and illuminate lamps, resulting in a remarkable display that attracts a multitude of devotees and tourists. Har Ki Pauri is a site of great historical and cultural importance, renowned for its breathtaking natural location on the banks of the Ganges. It stands as an enduring emblem of spiritual devotion and deep reverence towards the sacred river. Figure 3 presents Har ki Pauri Ghat, Haridwar.

Figure 3. Har Ki Pauri Ghat, Haridwar
Source: Singh (2021).

- **Waste Management:** Proper waste management is a significant concern in both Haridwar and Rishikesh due to the large number of pilgrims and tourists who visit. Sustainable tourism initiatives focus on waste segregation, recycling, and minimizing littering to keep the Ganges River and surrounding areas clean.
- **Eco-friendly Infrastructure:** Sustainable development includes the construction of eco-friendly infrastructure, such as hotels and restaurants that use renewable energy sources, energy-efficient appliances, and sustainable building materials to reduce their environmental impact.
- **River Conservation:** The Ganges River is sacred in Hinduism, and sustainable tourism efforts aim to protect its water quality and ecosystems. Measures include restrictions on activities like sand mining and promoting awareness about the importance of clean water.
- **Traffic Management:** Both cities can get congested with traffic, particularly during peak tourist seasons. Sustainable tourism efforts may involve promoting public transportation, cycling, and pedestrian-friendly infrastructure to reduce pollution and congestion.
- **Cultural Preservation:** Sustainable tourism supports and preserves the cultural heritage of the region. This includes promoting traditional festivals, rituals, and practices while discouraging any activities that may harm cultural sites or artifacts.
- **Adventure Tourism:** Rishikesh is known for adventure tourism activities such as white-water rafting and trekking. Sustainable tourism ensures that these activities are conducted responsibly and do not harm the natural environment or endanger visitors.
- **Community Engagement:** Involving local communities in tourism management and providing economic opportunities to residents can help them benefit from tourism while fostering a sense of responsibility for preserving their heritage and environment.
- **Education and Awareness:** Tourists are educated about responsible behavior, such as not polluting the river, respecting local customs, and not disturbing wildlife. This helps ensure that visitors are aware of and adhere to sustainable tourism practices.
- **Yoga and Wellness Tourism:** Rishikesh is a hub for yoga and wellness tourism. Sustainable initiatives focus on promoting holistic health practices, supporting local yoga schools, and ensuring that yoga retreats and wellness centers adhere to eco-friendly principles.

- **Regulation and Monitoring:** Government bodies and local authorities play a crucial role in regulating tourism activities and monitoring their impact on the environment and culture. Regular assessments and adjustments to policies are essential for sustainable tourism management.

Sustainable tourism in Haridwar (Figure 3) and Rishikesh aims to strike a balance between the spiritual and natural significance of the region and the need for responsible and eco-friendly tourism. By implementing these measures, these cities can continue to attract visitors while preserving their unique cultural and environmental assets for future generations.

Rural Tourism in Uttarakhand

Rural tourism has gained popularity as a sustainable and community-driven form of tourism. It offers tourists an opportunity to explore the rustic charm of rural life, experience local cultures and traditions, and contribute to the economic development of rural communities.

- **Binsar Village:** Binsar, a picturesque village in Uttarakhand, has embraced rural tourism. Travelers can stay in eco-friendly cottages and enjoy nature walks, bird-watching, and trekking in the Binsar Wildlife Sanctuary. Local villagers often serve as guides and share their knowledge of the flora and fauna.
- **Kasar Devi:** Kasar Devi, near Almora, is known for its serene environment and the Kasar Devi Temple. Visitors can stay in village homestays, engage in organic farming, and participate in cultural activities with local residents. The Kasar Devi Mountain Festival promotes eco-friendly and sustainable practices.
- **Khirsu:** Khirsu is a tranquil village in the Pauri Garhwal district of Uttarakhand. It offers panoramic views of the Himalayas. Travelers can stay in rustic homestays, explore the village, and enjoy local Garhwali cuisine. The village's eco-friendly initiatives aim to minimize the environmental impact of tourism.
- **Sarmoli Village:** Located in the Munsiyari region, Sarmoli Village has been a pioneer in community-based tourism. Visitors can experience traditional village life, interact with local women's groups, and purchase handmade products like woolens and natural cosmetics. The village also promotes responsible waste management.
- **Munsiyari:** Munsiyari is a gateway to the Johar Valley and offers stunning Himalayan vistas. Tourists can participate in treks, bird-watching, and cultural exchanges. Many guesthouses in Munsiyari are owned and operated by locals, providing income to the community.
- **Chopta:** Chopta is known for its breathtaking meadows and proximity to the Tungnath Temple. Travelers can camp or stay in eco-friendly lodges. The area is a popular destination for trekking, and local guides often accompany visitors on treks to educate them about the region's flora and fauna.
- **Binsar Wildlife Sanctuary:** The Binsar Wildlife Sanctuary itself is a model for sustainable tourism. It restricts the number of tourists allowed to enter the park each day to minimize environmental impact and ensure a peaceful experience for visitors. The sanctuary is a haven for bird-watchers and nature enthusiasts.

- **Lansdowne:** Lansdowne is a quiet hill station known for its colonial architecture and pristine surroundings. Travelers can stay in heritage properties or eco-friendly resorts, hike in the nearby forests, and visit local markets to support artisans and craftspersons.

These examples vividly showcase the wide-ranging possibilities for rural tourism in Uttarakhand. Here, travelers have the chance to fully engage with the region's pristine natural landscapes and rich cultural heritage. Simultaneously, they play a pivotal role in bolstering the prosperity of local communities and advancing the sustainable growth of the area.

Pro-Poor Tourism at Uttarakhand

"The Millennium Declaration" of the United Nations emphasises the prioritisation of poverty on the agenda for international development. This implies that the scope of sustainable tourism development should prioritise the alleviation of poverty over the sheer advancement of global socioeconomic progress. The shift in emphasis is in line with a recommendation from the 7th session of the "Commission on Sustainable Development", which emphasised the need for governments to use tourism to alleviate poverty. This can be accomplished by implementing appropriate strategies in partnership with key stakeholders, such as significant groups, indigenous communities, and local populations (Ahmed, 2013).

The Pro-Poor tourism (PPT) approach can be distinguished from other sustainable tourism initiatives, such as ecotourism, by its unique emphasis on providing tangible benefits to disadvantaged populations. Although there may be overlapping goals between PPT (Pro-Poor Tourism) and ecotourism, it is essential to note that the primary focus of the PPT method is poverty alleviation, while environmental sustainability is typically a secondary factor. Despite the fact that PPT recognises the significance of environmental preservation, it is merely a component of a more comprehensive strategy for alleviating poverty.

There are additional arguments in support of the notion that the expansion of tourism could be a viable strategy for reducing poverty. Beginning with rural and urban areas, the tourism industry offers significant employment opportunities to individuals without specialized talents. In addition, it frequently includes women from low-income households. In addition, there are strong ties to the informal sector, which have the potential to generate multiplier effects that benefit marginalized populations that rely on this sector as their primary source of income. Furthermore, it is important to note that tourism generally focuses on the preservation of natural resources, such as animals, picturesque landscapes, and cultural heritage. According to a 2013 study, these resources are frequently possessed by individuals with limited financial means.

There is a growing awareness of the significance of involving local communities in the process of tourism growth. This approach not only increases the motivation to preserve natural resources, but also promotes a more equitable distribution of benefits and a greater capacity for reducing poverty. PPT distinguishes itself by incorporating explicit tools to increase participation and provide opportunities for socioeconomically disadvantaged groups, whereas both ecotourism and PPT share the objective of promoting community involvement.

The PPT strategy comprises three fundamental components:

a) Its primary objective is to increase the accessibility of the economic benefits associated with tourism. This is accomplished by expanding employment and business opportunities for those from low-income origins. In addition, they are provided with the appropriate training to equip them with the skills and knowledge required to effectively capitalise on these opportunities.

b) Implementing strategies to mitigate the social and ecological impacts of tourism development, with a concentration on issues such as social exploitation, overexploitation of natural resources, the formation of pollution, and the degradation of ecosystems.

c) Policy reform is a fundamental component of the PPT's strategy. This involves increasing the participation of economically disadvantaged groups in the planning, development, and oversight of tourism activities that directly affect them. In addition, it entails the elimination of barriers that impede the increased participation of individuals from low-income backgrounds, as well as the cultivation of partnerships between government entities or private businesses and impoverished individuals, with the aim of producing novel tourism offerings and amenities. The purpose of this policy reform is to cultivate a tourism industry that is characterised by inclusivity and equity, with the intention of benefiting all segments of society, especially those living in poverty.

Relating Tourism and Sustainable Economic Investment

Figure 4. Flow chart of a conceptual framework linking tourism with sustainable tourism policies
Courtesy: Khan et al. (2020)

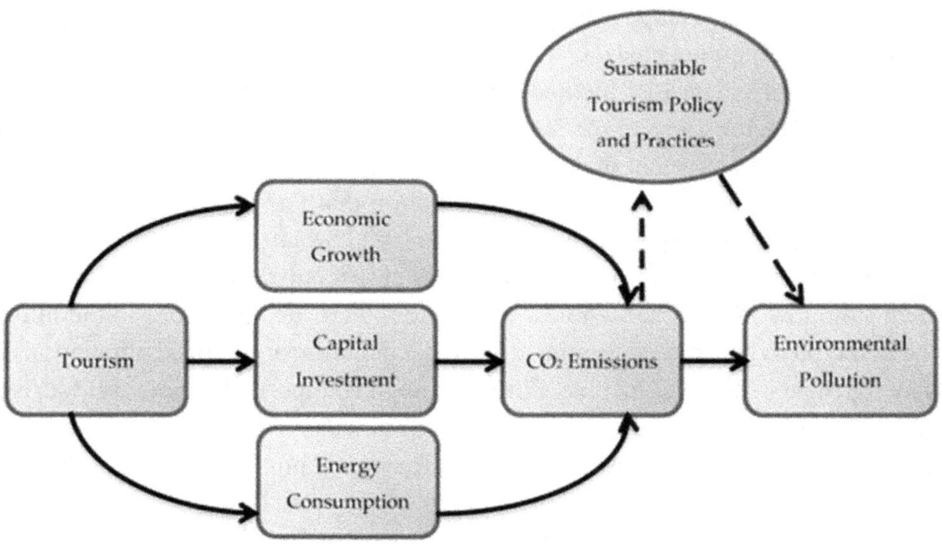

Tourism has been identified as a factor influencing foreign direct investment (FDI) based on a conceptual framework by Khan et al. (2020), as shown in Figure 4. Foreign Direct Investment (FDI) indeed plays a crucial role in the development of the tourism industry. It can have a significant impact on tourism-related infrastructure, services, and overall growth. In the context of globalization, these elements—tourism, FDI, economic expansion, and environmental pollution—are intricately interconnected. The liberalisation transition has increased the volume of FDI in the services sector. Observations indicate that the increase in foreign direct investment (FDI) has led to an increase in carbon dioxide (CO2) emissions in developing economies, primarily as a result of lackadaisical environmental regulations. It is asserted that tourism holds substantial influence as a location-specific determinant of FDI (Khan *et al.*, 2020). The current body of literature highlights a notable gap in research regarding the causal relationship between capital formation and tourist arrivals within a time-series framework. This suggests that there is limited prior investigation into the dynamic interplay between these two critical factors in the context of tourism. Drawing from these trends, two conclusions have been drawn- that tourism exerts an influence on capital investment; and capital investment has an impact on tourism. The results indicated that economic growth results in a notable rise in tourist arrivals, providing support for the conclusions that economic growth drives tourism.

Theoretical Implications of Sustainable Tourism for Heritage Sites in Uttarakhand

The 1992 UN Conference on "Environment and Development" in Rio de Janeiro changed sustainable tourist development. Since then, sustainable tourism (ST) has become a global economic, social, and environmental challenge (Roblek, 2021). ST is extremely useful when studying tourism and hospitality. These include assessing socioeconomic implications, conserving natural and cultural assets, managing water and energy resources, and creating environmentally and locally sustainable tourism policy.

The 2015 UN 2030 Agenda for Sustainable Tourism was a crucial step towards socioeconomic and environmental progress that advanced sustainable tourism. The 17 Sustainable Development Goals (SDGs) for ST are the focus of this agenda to ensure corporate sustainability.

Tourism drives economic growth in many countries, especially emerging ones. These regions rely on tourism and hospitality to provide jobs and raise living standards (Roblek, 2021). Countries with lower environmental standards are often prone to the negative environmental effects of tourism, including pollution and direct environmental harm like sewage discharge into the sea and natural environment damage from overcrowding and transportation emissions. This emphasises the need for regional and national decision-makers to follow the 2030 Agenda to "protect tourism businesses and services and promote sustainable development".

Tourism is the world's largest service business, and more visitors mean more environmental damage. New tourism concepts and categories have emerged from mass tourism. As an extra benefit, various tourist plans and policies encourage ecological principles, tailored tourism services, and authentic places. In the literature, economic success is typically cited as a key component in sustainable behaviour. We believe this component is becoming more significant for tourism destination growth (Roblek, 2021). Thus, stakeholders must do in-depth, long-term study to understand the intricate relationship between business success and long-term community benefits.

Organizational Implications of Sustainable Tourism for Heritage Sites in Uttarakhand

A critical concern for owners, investors, managers, and policymakers in the tourism sector, both locally and nationally, is to re-engage tourism during the current post-pandemic era by embracing sustainable and resilient tourism approaches. This can include supporting initiatives to transform city centers into greener spaces with restricted vehicular access, aligning them with well-being objectives. Embracing cost-effective operations in the tourism industry necessitates the integration of digitalization, along with the restructuring and optimization of operations. A key aspect of this transformation involves phasing out outdated and unsustainable practices, including environmentally dismissive hotel land usage and infrastructures in tourist destinations, particularly as sustainable land usage by hotels in urban and rural areas can ultimately lower costs for the property owner.

Sustainability extends beyond satisfying consumer needs, and benefits the hotel over long-term applicability (Nathaniel 2020). The primary goal of such sustainability projects will be to enhance efficiency, often through energy and resource savings, leveraging renewable resources, and waste reduction. Implementing these initiatives correctly and consistently can result in significant and enduring savings for a hotel by lowering operating costs and minimizing waste. While the initial capital investment for such projects can be high, the subsequent savings over time can more than compensate for the initial outlay. Additionally, there is a growing availability of government-supported, low-cost financial options that can assist in retrofitting and sustainable investments, reducing the hurdle of the initial cost.

Individual tourism often flourishes in settings that prioritize boutique, small-scale, and independent accommodations such as hotels and camps. These establishments are typically locally owned and operated, which creates opportunities for direct and meaningful interactions between tourists and the local traditions and culture. Sustainability in the hospitality industry extends far beyond the provision of eco-friendly hotel services. It involves the creation of a sustainability hub within the community, leveraging local goods, products, materials, and food sources. Embracing a strong sustainability tendency can have several tangible and intangible benefits.

CONCLUSION

The SDGs are meant to be universal, with applicability across all countries and stages of development. This global scope inspires cooperation between national governments, non-governmental organisations, and private sector firms to realise these objectives by the year 2030. The SDGs are a road map for countries to design their policies, plans, and actions in accordance with these global objectives and represent a shared vision for a more egalitarian, sustainable, and prosperous world. As we get started on this effort, aim is for this scholarly article to make a meaningful contribution to both the academic dialogue and the practical comprehension of how the Sustainable Development Goals can be utilised as a catalyst for profound change within the distinct socio-cultural and environmental context of Uttarakhand. The present study discovers significant insights that will resonate with policymakers, practitioners, and communities all around the world by conducting an exhaustive study of the complexities of sustainable development in this particular region.

This attempt aims to foster a more profound awareness of how global goals can effectively manifest as actual and positive reforms at the local level by focusing on the benefits of such changes. In the context of this initiative, our goal is to emphasise the inherent capacity of Uttarakhand as a typical example of sustainable development and to promote techniques that may be copied globally, with the final goal of fostering a future that is both sustainable and equitable for all parties involved.

REFERENCES

Ahmed, N. (2013). Sustainable Tourism Development in Uttarakhand Region of India. *International Journal of Management and Social Sciences Research, 2*(4).

Altinay, M., & Hussain, K. (2005). Sustainable tourism development: A case study of North Cyprus. *International Journal of Contemporary Hospitality Management, 17*(3), 272–280. doi:10.1108/09596110510591963

Alvarez Alday, M., & Fernández-Villaran, A. (2012). Economic Impact of Leisure in the 21st Century. *Arbor, 188*(754), 351–363. doi:10.3989/arbor.2012.754n2008

Hall, C. M. (2013). *Green growth and tourism for a sustainable future: "We just need to put the right policies in place", or, the lunatics have taken over the asylum.* Presented at International Critical Tourism Studies, Canterbury, NZ. http://canterbury-nz.academia.edu/CMichaelHall

Khan, A., Bibi, S., Ardito, L., Lyu, J., Hayat, H., & Arif, A. M. (2020). Revisiting the Dynamics of Tourism, Economic Growth, and Environmental Pollutants in the Emerging Economies—Sustainable Tourism Policy Implications. *Sustainability (Basel), 12*(6), 2533. doi:10.3390u12062533

Kumar, S. (2019). *Kedarnath temple in Rainy season.* OpenVerse. https://openverse.org/image/78936110-af1e-4549-9a39-98c690268c5c?q=kedarnath%20temple.

Nathaniel, S. P., & Adedoyin, F. F. (2020). Tourism development, natural resource abundance, and environmental sustainability: Another look at the ten most visited destinations. *Journal of Public Affairs*, 25–53.

Ramirez, C., & Rangel, J. (2018). Sustainable Tourism:The New Engine for the Economic Development of the 21st Century in APEC. *International Journal of Sustainable Economies Management, 7*(4), 29–36. doi:10.4018/IJSEM.2018100103

Robertson, V. J. (2021). *UNESCO Statement for the World Summit on Ecotourism.* UNESCO. http://www.unep.fr/shared/publications/cdrom/WEBx0139xPA/statmnts/pdfs/rouneef

Roblek, V., Drpić, D., Meško, M., & Milojica, V. (2021). Evolution of Sustainable Tourism Concepts. *Sustainability (Basel), 13*(22), 12829. doi:10.3390u132212829

United Nations. (2021). *Rio+20. Report on the UN Conference on Sustainable Development.* UN. https://www.uncsd2012.org/content/documents/814UNCSD%20REPORT%20final%20revs.pdf

UNWTO—United Nations World Tourism Organisation. (2021). *The Guidebook "Sustainable Tourism for Development" Brussels.* UNWTO. http://icr.unwto.org/content/guidebook-sustainable-tourism-development

World Summit on Sustainable Development. (2002). *Tourism and the Earth Summit, World Summit on Sustainable Development.* Tourism Concern UK. www.tourismconcern.org.uk

Chapter 8
Rural Tourism and Supply Chain:
Features and Components and the Contribution Towards Sustainable Development Goals in the Indian Context

Swati Shah
Kumaun University, Nainital, India

Devendra Krishana Bhatt
https://orcid.org/0000-0002-5203-1699
Kumaun University, Nainital, India

Ashok Kumar
Kumaun University, Nainital, India

ABSTRACT

Rural tourism, increasingly recognized as a driver of economic growth in rural areas, acts as a catalyst for local development and sustainability. The purpose of this study is to explore the dynamic interplay between rural tourism supply chains and the sustainable development goals (SDGs), and also gain a deeper understanding of Rural tourism's components important from the prospect of India, its supply chain, and stakeholders in the supply process and potential of rural tourism in its contribution to SDG. By fostering economic growth, preserving cultural heritage, and promoting responsible supply chains, rural tourism can be a catalyst for sustainable development, bringing us closer to achieving the global goals of prosperity, social equity, and environmental sustainability. The study advocates for a holistic approach to rural tourism development that prioritizes sustainability, inclusivity, and social responsibility to maximize its positive impact on the SDGs.

DOI: 10.4018/979-8-3693-2065-5.ch008

INTRODUCTION

Tourism is the smokeless yet largest industry with a contribution of around 10% to the world's gross Domestic Product outcome. Tourism in India is the most rapidly growing business phenomenon which is increasing acceptance because of its business potential, representation in GDP employment generation infrastructure development forex generation, and tax collections. Tourism has proven to be the most profitable business entity and has continuously proven a substantial record of earning foreign exchange. This industry is the largest in the country having a contribution of 9.2% in the total economy and generation of USD 247.3 in GDP. Tourism is the third-largest foreign exchange earner for the country. (FICCI, April 2019). Real India lives in villages as said by "Mahatma Gandi". To experience the true, entice of India visit villages. The authenticity of the people, the green fields, respect and pride for culture, the varied cuisine, and the clean air and water will keep you mesmerized. The rural villages have so much to offer to the tourists, that national and international tourists are drawn towards it.

Ministry of Tourism- Government of India (2011) defined Rural tourism as "Any form of tourism that showcases the rural life, art, culture, and heritage at rural locations, thereby benefiting the local community economically and socially as well as enabling interaction between the tourists and the locals for a more enriching tourism experience can be termed as rural tourism" (Ray, Nilanjan et Al. 2020).

The tourism supply chain is a network model of suppliers where a good sense of sources is involved in delivering tourism products to the end-users (Tapper & Font, 2004). We consider that the end user will consume a travel package in tourism products. The main supply chain for this product consists of intermediaries that exist between the user and the service provider are the travel agency and ground tour operator. Where the role of an agency is to sell a package and the role of an operator is to execute the services promised. (Page,2014; Buhalis & Laws, 2001; Baloglu & Mangaloglu, 2001).

Rural tourism supply chains can make a meaningful contribution to Sustainable Development Goals by enhancing economic development, alleviating poverty and inequality, promoting cultural and natural heritage, and fostering sustainable practices in rural areas. Lately, it's essential to ensure that rural tourism is enacted responsibly and sustainably to optimize its positive impact on these SDGs.

Objective of the Study

- To understand Rural tourism, its components, and its benefits and cost
- To understand the basics of the Rural Tourism supply chain structure (RSTC)
- To study the link between Rural tourism supply chain stakeholders and SDG

RESEARCH METHODOLOGY

This article is based on the review of research papers & articles and compilations of information gathered from all secondary sources such as academic writings and information from various institutes. The content written in this paper is a conceptual offering aiming to share its contribution to the discussion and debate of the development of the tourism supply chain and addressing the potentials of Rural tourism and its supply chain process and its contribution towards SDG. Studying from secondary data is less time-consuming and easy to gather information but it requires more focus in interpretation.

Rural Tourism: A Sustainable Tourism

Tourism is considered a world-changing domain for the global community in which one should use a sustainable approach to generate, increase business & establish a long-term livelihood. Due to the problems posed by rapid industrialization and urbanization, the concept of sustainable development gained prominence in the 19th century amid industrialization. (Choi & Sirakaya, 2005). Sustainable development is defined by the World Commission on Environment and Development (WCED) as a kind of development that "Meets the need of the present without compromising the ability of future generations to meet their own need." (WCED 1987 page 43). Tourism as an industry, is expected to develop the economy in a way it favors both economic development along with the development of depressed or underdeveloped areas at the same time. It is also expected that by any act of tourism, no harm will be delivered to any destination's resources. In total, we can say as an industry we are expecting to develop as a long-term employment and resource generation, without destroying natural resources. Rural tourism in a sustainable way is a kind of tourism that emphasizes nature's nature-related environment and benefits with cultural connections. Rural tourism can be described as affordable tourism which is based on local heritage run by local communities with an aspect of the culture and craftsmanship the tradition and offer the essence of nature to the guests for the entire stay duration (Ivona, Antonietta et. Al 2006). Some examples of sustainable tourism across the globe: "Pibija Lodge: Conservation and Community Development through Ecotourism Project" in Colombia; "Rural Tourism in Gmina Muszyna: Development of new and existing trails, rest areas and signposting system" in Poland; "Rural hosting system in the Cserhát region" in Hungary (WTO, 2001). Various estimates suggest that tourism in rural areas makes up 10 to 20% of all tourism activity, and a Eurobarometer survey reported that 23% of European holidaymakers choose the countryside or rural areas as a destination every year. (Tourismnotes,18 March 2021)

Rural tourism is in actual commodification of local culture, history, heritage, local stakeholders, and social bonding between community contributors and the natural environment kept in a geographical boundary and shaped by historical trajectories of relations of the contributors. (Panyik et al., 2011). The forms of tourism that show village life, their Heritage, their locations, the local stakeholder's opportunity to get a livelihood, local community's social and economic values, which enable the communication between guests and tourists which help to enrich a business form can be termed as Rural Tourism (Nagarjuna, L.G et Al 2014). Culture tourism, heritage tourism, rural tourism, Ecotourism, etc. all forms of tourism are very new to the Indian tourism industry if we compare with other developed countries. (National Tourism Policy 2002) gave impetus to tourism in Rural form and coined the rural tourism industry. Rural tourism and another popular form of possible tourism business practices in different parts of the blue with the increasing demand for or a different segmentation in the tourism market (Negi, 1990; Zurick 1992). With the help of certain logistics and supply chain procedures and tourist inflow, rural tourism becomes an essential activity that takes place in villages for remote site areas. Sustainability in Tourism is emphasized by the use of different names like eco-tourism, green tourism Agri-tourism, farm tourism, alternative tourism, etc. (Kapoor S, 2016). In total, we can say rural tourism could be a frontline self-sustained unit for the economy, for the people, for the infrastructure, and for the country as a whole.

Components of Rural Tourism

Rural Tourism is a unique concept where an economic activity offers us a way to encash nature sustainably. In Rural tourism developed villages, or the small business units and people staying in the village as primary stakeholders of this business. They cater & present their village as the product and its sub-products as the environment, the heritage, and the surroundings in front of visitors. Most often villages near natural attractions can be turned into a major attraction for such tourism by developing infrastructure and accessibility from far and near cities. Such development should be sustainable which will help the rural community to evolve as a strong basic business unit in the long run and will empower the entire economy's GDP and generate employment it also compensates to the low-income groups.

Figure 1. The rural tourism concept
(Source: Nutly, 2004,13)

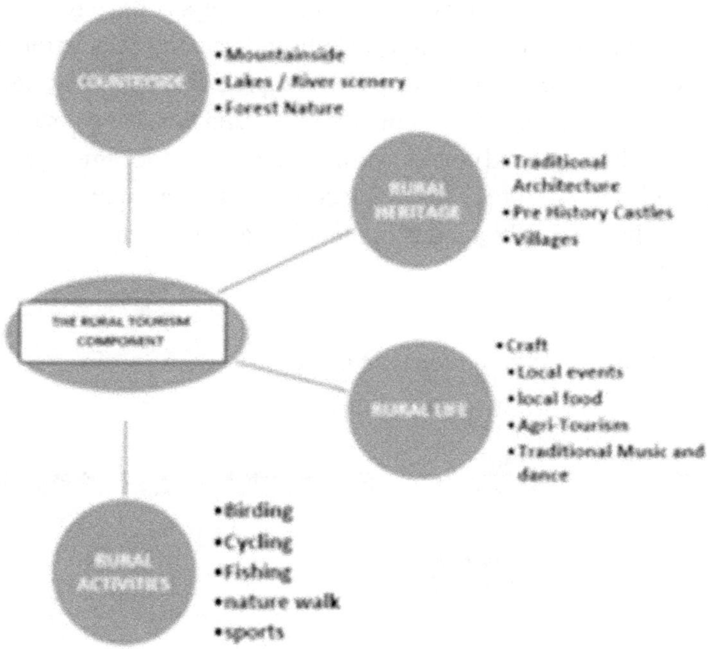

Table 1. The benefits and costs of rural tourism

DIMENSIONS	POTENTIAL BENEFITS	POTENTIAL COSTS
ECONOMIC	• Employment creation (Direct, indirect, and induced) • Improvement of Balance of Payment • Income generation • Entrepreneurship opportunities • Benefits to local government through taxes and rates	• Inflation – increase in prices of resources like land and goods • Pressure on public services • The opportunity cost of developing tourism at the expense of other activities. • High dependency on tourism can be risky • Seasonality is also a major disadvantage of tourism • Leakage of money earned to MNC
SOCIAL	• Support for local services • Infrastructure creations • Maintenance of museums, restaurants • Cultural exchange • The revitalization of traditions, customs, and crafts	• Congestion • Overcrowding • Health issues • Crime
ENVIRONMENTAL	• Conservation of redundant and historic buildings for alternative uses. • Protection of wildlife • Enhancement of the local environment	• Inappropriate development • Pollution of the natural environment • Loss of habitat – reduce ground vegetation cover • Waste creation • Traffic congestion • Loss of spirit of destination

Tourism Supply Chain

The current supply chain management has its roots from the start of the 20th century as that time it was primarily used for the military's Logistic goals of "getting the right people and the appropriate supplies to the right place at the right time and in the proper condition" (U.S. Department of the Army, 1949; Gibson B, et al, 2013). Supply chain origins from the logistics, the flow of materials and flow of information from origin to end customer, the journey of material handling, information flow, and other moment functions in the organization, The complete procedure in total makes a chain of supply of materials (Baddeley & Font, 2011).

The tourism industry runs on a large supply chain system because of its dynamic nature, This sector requires an efficient supply chain system that can give the business edge to the enterprises and maintain a competitive advantage to enable quick decision-making and according to actions allowing meeting the never-ending customers' expectations. Because of the complex distribution system, the tourism supply chain model always faces the challenges of design innovation and the change in demands. Strong coordination & cooperation through a clear and concise communication model among the various stakeholders and tourism supply chain is the key predictor of successful business operation. Right services, by the right people, and at the right time is the modus operandi of a tourism supply chain (Tadić et al., 2012; Muhcina & Popovici, 2008).

Figure 2. The evolution of supply chain management
(Jean-Paul Rodrigue, 2020)

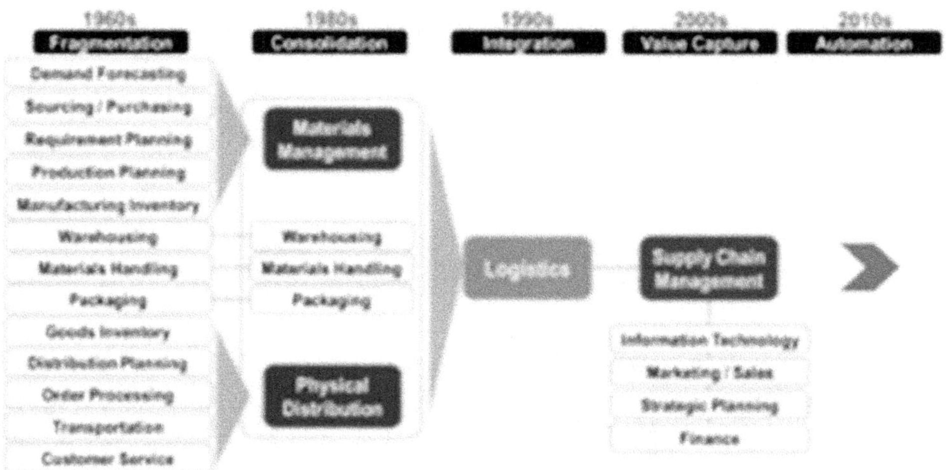

According to (Zhang et Al. 2009) the tourism supply chain is the network of multiple tourism entities where all are indulging in any series of diversified actions such as flights, accommodation, sightseeing, and local transportation, with the end of the final tourism product. This network has a wide range of contributors from both the public and private sectors in the development of sales package promotion and promotion of the destination. Due to the growing number of tourists every year and also because of global acceptance of tourism as a major employment and economic contributor the supply chain in tourism becoming more predominant accordingly.

The tourism supply chain's success can be achieved only by correct information flow, timely delivery of services & good supplier relationship management. To achieve a good supply chain system, supplier selection is also equally important. Well-defined & managed supplier relationships in the Tourism service supply chain will always help a business achieve competitive advantages Besides it also helps in improving the quality of the services offered at a lesser cost. **(Danuta Szpilko, 2017).**

Figure 3. Framework for the supplier selection problem
(Silva et al., 2009)

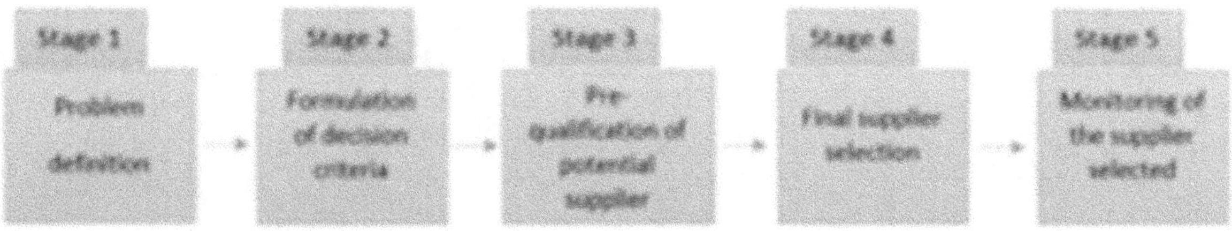

Rural Tourism Supply Chain Structure (RTSC)

The tourism services and activities which is executed in rural areas don't have any urban flavor, these activities are purely meant to be executed in the rural environment without changing the nature of performance constituted as rural tourism **(Lane, 1994).** In rural tourism, we consider only those areas that have certain characteristics of low settlement areas, natural environment, agriculture, and Forestry land use with very few populations **(Lane, 1994).** The basic elements of Rural or Agritourism are accommodation, food, and entertainment **(Ciolac et al., 2019).** In a standard rural tourism supply chain model as defined by **(Tadić et al., 2012)** the tour operator plays a crucial role. The front-line suppliers receive supply from the second-line supplier and the second-line supplier receives supply from the third-line suppliers. In many cases, second and third-line suppliers do collective supply to the direct suppliers of tourism services. Here we also have another kind of supplier called indirect suppliers i.e., Food, energy, power, equipment manufacturer, craft & culture related suppliers, etc. **(Tadić et al., 2012)**

Rural Supply chain is quite different from a regular supply chain model because of non-identical characteristics from a regular business model. Supply chains we have different characteristics as per the degree of development of the area. **(Tadić, Snežana et. Al 2020).** We can use different supply chain structures for rural tourism purposes by observing and analyzing the requirements and the destinations as per the topography.

We could have the simplest form of this model where a rural tourism product (for example: Staying in an area with farming experience) is sold to a visitor of a nearby City. In this product supply chain, the household that gets the tourist is the sole owner of the execution part. The household alone offers the accommodation, and experience to the guest as a tourist service. Here we can categorize such service experiences into two parts: tangible & intangible. Tangible experience: is the housing unit where the Guest gets accommodation, food & beverages, and the intangible experience: is the services, skills, and knowledge shown to the guest. Since in this model the household is the sole independent organizer of the tourism services, if this household is not able to meet adequate expectations of the guest, may create a negative impact on the development of tourism for the future at that particular destination. In the absence of, a lack of connections with possible other tourism entities and is not a part of the supply chain this unit may have not accessed professional kitchen services, training, and education centers, transport services sales and marketing setups, etc. This model shows the absence of a supply chain in rural areas which can have a pessimistic impact on the future development of rural tourism **(Tadić, Snežana et al. 2020).**

Figure 4. An example of a complex RTSC
Source: revised (Tadić et al., 2012)

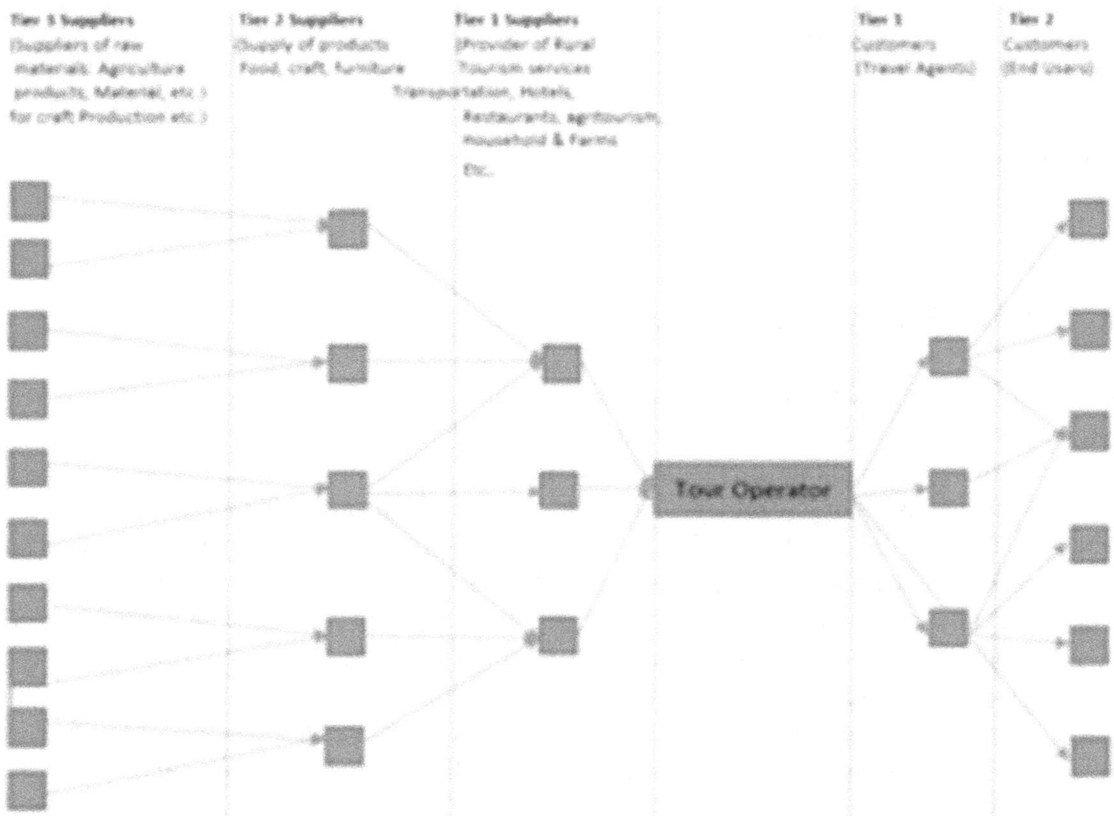

Rural Tourism Supply Chain and Its Stakeholders

The tourism supply chain (TSC) is a network of multiple tourism organisations participating with different capacities and service levels example stay, accommodation, land transport, and flights for the distribution and marketing of the final tourism products. **(Song et al. 2012).** The Term Tourism Service Supply Chain Management (TSCM) refers to a set of processes and activities related to tourism (viz. distribution activities including, promotional and marketing activities, supply networks involving inter-firm relationships and product development), facilitated by a network of tourism organizations to serve specific tourism destination while optimizing the value chain **(Zhang et al., 2009)**. An effective Tourism Supply Chain Management (TSCM) should ensure to supply of best-of-the-breed tourism products to consumers while involving a wide range of participants **(Tapper and Font, 2004).** In rural tourism, we have multiple kinds of stakeholders and they play a significant role. Success lies in the 3 C's of the work process: cooperation, coordination, and communication.

Table 2. Rural tourism development: stakeholders, roles, benefits and its linkages to SDG

Stakeholder Group (Supply chain)	Roles	Rural Tourism benefits	SDG
• Local communities	• Service provider • Cultural Preservation and Awareness • Say in tourism planning and development	• Income generation, • Jobs opportunities • New skills and training • Livelihood from tourism • Improved quality of life • Culture as a source of attraction	• SDG 1: No Poverty • SDG 2: Zero Hunger • SDG 8: Decent Work and Economic Growth
• Local entrepreneur	• Service upgradation	• Support for local business • Market access (artisans, producers) • Prevents migration	• SDG 2: Zero Hunger • SDG 8: Decent Work and Economic Growth • SDG 9: Industry, Innovation, and Infrastructure
• Tourists	• Service consumer	• Natural beauty and connection with nature • Culture immersion • Authentic experience • Peace and tranquillity	• SDG 12: Responsible Consumption and Production
• State governments	• Policy formulation and support	• Compliance to policy • Infrastructure development (Roads, Sanitation, transportation, utilities) • Equitable Distribution of benefits	• SDG 9: Industry, Innovation, and Infrastructure • SDG 16: Peace, Justice, and Strong Institutions
• Local governments	• Monitoring, evaluation, and recommendation	• Wholistic rural development • Preservation of historical or cultural sites • Equitable Distribution of benefits	• SDG 9: Industry, Innovation, and Infrastructure • SDG 16: Peace, Justice, and Strong Institutions
• Environmental Agencies at various levels	• Environment impact assessment	• Environmental conservation • Sustainable Practices • Waste Management	• SDG 15: Life on Land:
• Tourism authorities	• Marketing • Communications	• Popularity of destination	• SDG 11: Sustainable Cities and Communities
• Not-for-profit Organisations	• Initial funding, research • and capacity building	• Local empowerment, livelihood creation, boost entrepreneurship	• SDG 17: Partnerships for the Goals
• Tour operators	• Tourists' acquisition	• Returns on their investment	• SDG 1: No Poverty • SDG 8: Decent Work and Economic Growth

Contribution of Rural Tourism Supply Chain in Attainment of SDG

SDG 1: No Poverty: Rural tourism can create job opportunities and generate income for people in rural areas, reducing poverty and promoting economic development. Rural tourism offers an interesting job creation path for local youths. Local stakeholders not only get employment and financial stability but also help them to increase their standard of life, reduce migration, and contribute significantly to the country's GDP.

SDG 2: Zero Hunger: Tourism can boost agricultural and food-related businesses in rural areas, providing income for farmers and improving food security. Many rural tourism initiatives promote sustainable farming practices, such as organic farming or agro, ecotourism. These practices can enhance agricultural productivity while preserving natural resources, contributing to long-term food security. Rural tourism can provide additional sources of income for local communities. This additional income can help rural households afford a more diverse and nutritious diet, reducing the risk of hunger and malnutrition

SDG 8: Decent Work and Economic Growth: The development of rural tourism can lead to the creation of sustainable jobs and stimulate economic growth in rural **communities. Tourism** is the sector in our economic system that can develop into a sustainable business model with the help of stakeholders in the area, which will aid the development process for the local economy and improve infrastructure structure without harming nature. (Relate it with SDG). rural tourism has the potential to positively impact supply chains, especially in rural areas. By connecting local producers and artisans with tourism-related businesses, such as hotels, restaurants, and souvenir shops, supply chains can be strengthened, leading to increased income and employment opportunities for rural communities.

SDG 9: Industry, Innovation, and Infrastructure: Developing rural tourism often requires infrastructure improvements, which can enhance transportation and connectivity in these areas, contributing to economic growth and development. Infrastructure development is one of the most important aspects of rural tourism as such business activity tends to promote the manifold development of infrastructure benefits to the host community. Such development includes a good rail and road network, a market for daily livelihood things, health and hygiene facilities, development authorities or Municipal authorities, and the development of a vast network of education and training schools in & nearby areas.

SDG 11: Sustainable Cities and Communities: Promoting rural tourism can help distribute economic benefits more evenly between urban and rural areas, reducing urban migration and supporting sustainable rural communities. Rural tourism the entire business system is based on community support so all stakeholders are connected with a common goal. (**Yourarticlelibrary, 18 March 2021).** Rural tourism not only stimulates economic activity in rural areas but also promotes the preservation of local culture and heritage. By engaging tourists in authentic rural experiences, we can foster a greater appreciation for traditional practices and craftsmanship, ultimately contributing to the preservation of indigenous knowledge and cultural diversity.

SDG 12: Responsible Consumption and Production: Rural tourism can encourage sustainable practices in the production and consumption of local goods and services, promoting responsible tourism. Food and beverages play a significant role in promoting any destination and also in presenting the lifestyle and cultural heritage of a destination. According to **UNTWTO 2012,** gastronomy plays an important role in the choice of destination tourism consumption. Also, food and beverages involve a considerable part of the total tourist spending on any destination. In rural destinations, it means it offers an opportunity for promoting farm products and local products such as Dairy, vegetables, fruits & mouth-watering local dishes & cuisine. (**Herrer F, et al, 2012).** The main characteristic of community art is community participation where local artisans and actors are involved, Visitors do visit remote areas for community tourism and they enjoy the artistic forms during their stay, they also purchase these arts and handicraft items at Souvenirs while going back.

SDG 15: Life on Land: Rural tourism can promote the conservation of natural landscapes, biodiversity, and traditional land use practices, contributing to the preservation of ecosystems. Sustainable rural tourism practices, which prioritize environmental conservation and responsible resource management. Through eco-friendly initiatives, such as promoting organic farming, reducing waste, and conserving biodiversity, rural tourism can mitigate its environmental footprint while promoting sustainable agriculture and protecting natural ecosystems.

SDG 16: Peace, Justice, and Strong Institutions: Tourism can support the development of strong institutions and governance structures in rural areas, helping to maintain peace and stability. Encouraging participation from local communities in the development and management of rural tourism initiatives promotes inclusivity and empowers rural residents to have a say in decision-making processes. This aligns to promote effective, accountable, and inclusive institutions at all levels.

SDG 17: Partnerships for the Goals: Collaboration between governments, businesses, and local communities is essential for the sustainable development of rural tourism, emphasizing the importance of partnerships. Even if tourism is targeted towards the development of the rural sector, without local cooperation, it may turn out to be an impossible mission as many local tribes, may not be tourist-friendly and familiar with tourism practices. (Radhika V, 2020) and may radically oppose development. So, a partnership between the government and locals is essential to understand the community sentiment and foster sustainable development. Stakeholders in remote destinations can manage the development of rural tourism (Ezeuduji, 2015). The stakeholders of this Rural tourism business, do ensure the sustainability and revenue generation within the rural system and also work for future growth with the help of community support thus contributing towards SDG. A well-managed successful rural tourism model shows cooperation, coordination, and communication among stakeholders **(Ayazlar Gökhan et al, 2015)** and leads to a self-sustaining rural life.

The individual Organizer of Rural Tourism Services: Example of Rural Homestays in Uttarakhand

Rural tourism homestays are community-based accommodation that is meant to provide a comfortable hygienic stay to preserve the environment development of economics and promotion of the destination. (Martha, 1999; Kiss, 2004) These practices are promoted as a low-impact environmentally sensitive way to travel (Jones, 2005; Nelson, 2007).

Figure 5. Basic model of self-arranged supply chain system by household

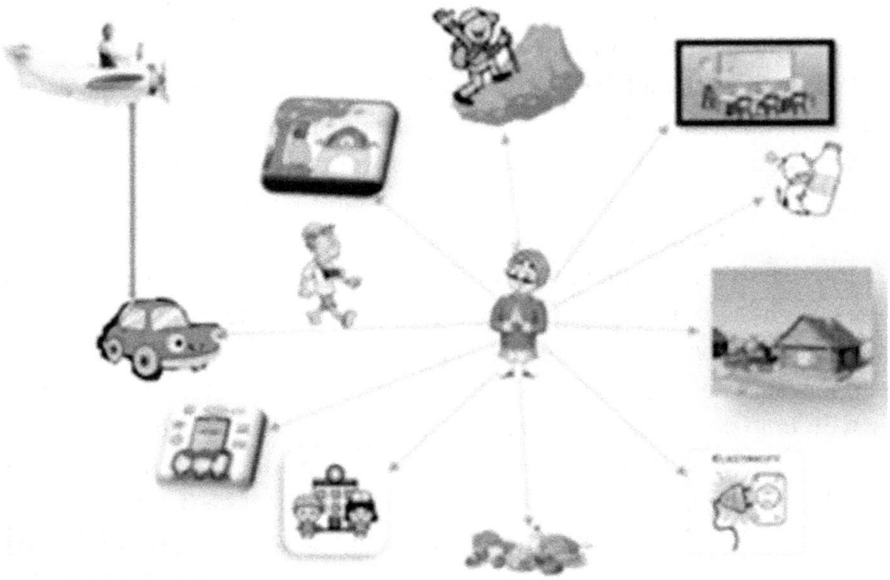

Though this is a practice that is in continuation in many rural homestays, with the help of tourism supply chain management we can make such individual household tourism service provider practices more efficient and eliminate the possible waste in the chain example: Waiting for time, inventory, and production of non-requested products. A quality supply chain will help them to offer efficient and latest hospitality-related knowledge sharing & pieces of training, enable the management of inventories with the latest software system, easy Logistic and transportation, better communication between different stakeholders of the tourism chain, and ultimately a good sales marketing and distribution system to sell their tourism product and by-products also (**UKEssays, November 2018).** It will also help to improve the quality of customer services which will lead to more profit generation

CONCLUSION

The paper explores the basics of supply chain structure practiced in the rural tourism industry. The findings of this study are valuable in practice and f, to understand the basic structure of rural tourism and its supply chain. The paper will be helpful for both scholars and tourism practitioners. The findings of this paper can help rural tourism practitioners understand the community rules and requirements for this business and also improve community participation and create employment possibilities in rural areas. This paper also highlights on possibilities of homestays as a business in rural areas and also can be operated by individual stakeholders without any support of tourism players or major government stakeholders. Rural tourism has become a new form of tourist activity that can give a competitive advantage to any business firm and also to the rural community with less imitable and rare resources. This tourism structure is completely based on community-based participation with intangible resources such as experience to the tool using the humble nature courteous community environment unique rural landscape and regional culture and heritage flavour.

In conclusion, rural tourism, supply chains, and the Sustainable Development Goals (SDGs) are interconnected in a way that holds significant promise for sustainable development and positive societal impacts. Rural tourism can play a pivotal role in achieving several SDGs, particularly those related to economic growth, poverty reduction, sustainable agriculture, and responsible consumption and production.

In practice, its most significant feature is gender empowerment which is rarely noticed by any previous research. The active participation by women and rural community tourism practices example cooking meals, dairy-related jobs, all housekeeping jobs, and also welcoming their host with their docile caring and humble behaviour makes this business workable for them. Good cooperation among the community, knowledge about the environment, awareness, learning, and development, growing interest in heritage, and also by educating tourists visiting them.

In conclusion, rural tourism is not only a means to boost rural economies but also a powerful tool for advancing the SDGs. By fostering economic growth, preserving cultural heritage, and promoting responsible supply chains, rural tourism can be a catalyst for sustainable development, bringing us closer to achieving the global goals of prosperity, social equity, and environmental sustainability. To fully harness this potential, governments, businesses, and communities must work together to implement policies and practices that prioritize both rural tourism and the SDGs. This interconnectedness not only boosts incomes and employment in rural areas but also fosters cultural preservation, environmental stewardship, and social well-being. By nurturing this link, we not only drive economic progress but also advance the broader goals of sustainable development, ultimately benefiting both the local communities and the global pursuit of a more prosperous and equitable world.

REFERENCES

Aref, F., & Gill, S. S. (2009). Rural tourism development through rural cooperatives. *Nature and Science*, *7*(10), 68–73.

Ayazlar, G. & Ayazlar, R. (2015). *Rural Tourism: A Conceptual Approach*. Research Gate.

Baddeley, J., & Font, X. (2011). Barriers to tour operator sustainable supply chain management. *Tourism Recreation Research*, *36*(3), 4. doi:10.1080/02508281.2011.11081667

Baloglu, S., & Mangaloglu, M. (2001). Tourism destination images of Turkey, Egypt, Greece, and Italy as perceived by US-based tour operators and travel agents. *Tourism Management*, *22*(1), 1–9. doi:10.1016/S0261-5177(00)00030-3

Gibsen, B. (2013). *Definitive Guide to Integrated Supply Chain Management*. Pearson.

Buhalis, D., & Laws, D. (2001). Tourism distribution channels: Practices, issues and transformations. London: Continuum International Publishing Group.

Chakraborty, B. (2019). *Homestay and women empowerment: A case study of women managed tourism product in Kasar Devi*. Uttarakhand.

Chen, J., Guan, J., Xu, J., & Clergeau, C. (2018). Constructing the Green Supply Chain for Rural Tourism, in China: Perspective of Front–Back Stage Decoupling. *Sustainability (Basel), 10*(11), 4276–4293. doi:10.3390u10114276

Choi, H.-S. C., & Sirakaya, E. (2005). Measuring residents. attitude toward sustainable tourism: Development of sustainable tourism attitude scale. *Journal of Travel Research, 43*(4), 380–394. doi:10.1177/0047287505274651

Ciolac, R., Adamov, T., Iancu, T., Popescu, G., Lile, R., Rujescu, C., & Marin, D. (2019). Agritourism - A Sustainable Development Factor for Improving the "Health" of Rural Settlements. Case Study Apuseni Mountains Area. *Sustainability (Basel), 11*(5), 1467–1490. doi:10.3390u11051467

DroliM.OstiL. (2013). Developing health tourism in healthier rural areas: the role of matrix-resources. doi:10.13140/2.1.4023.9685

Ebrahimi, M. & Eizad, E. (2018). *Effects of rural tourism: A case study of Iran*. Isfahan University of Technology.

Ezeuduji, I. O. (2015). Strategic event-based rural tourism development for sub-Saharan Africa. *Current Issues in Tourism, 18*(3), 212–228. doi:10.1080/13683500.2013.787049

Hall, M. C., Sharples, L., Mitchell, R., Macionis, N., & Cambourne, B. (2003). *Food Tourism around the World*. Development, Management and Markets, Elsevier Butterworth-Heinemann.

Heckmann, P., Shorten, D., & Engel, H. (2003). *Supply Chain Management at 21*. Chief Logistics Officer.

Herrera, F. & Blanco, C. (2012). Gastronomy's importance in the development of tourism destinations in the world. *Ref. Revista: Global Report on Food Tourism.* [UNWTO]. *World Tourism Organization.*

Ivona, A., Claval, P., Pagnini, P. & Scaini, M. (2006). *Farm tourism and rural development. a successful combination? a local experience*. OpenStarTs.

Rodrigue, J. (2020). *The Geography of Transport Systems.* Routledge.

Jones, S. (2005). Community-Based Ecotourism the Significance of Social Capital. *Annals of Tourism Research, 32*(2), 303–324. doi:10.1016/j.annals.2004.06.007

Kapoor, S. (2016) Rural Tourism In India: Relevance, Prospects And Promotional Strategies. *International Journal of Tourism and Travel, 9*(1, 2).

Kiss, A. (2004). Is community-based ecotourism a good use of biodiversity conservation funds? *Trends in Ecology & Evolution, 19*(5), 232–237. doi:10.1016/j.tree.2004.03.010 PMID:16701261

Martha, H. (1999). *Ecotourism and sustainable development: Who owns paradise?* Washington, D.C.: Trove.

Mehdi, S. A. (2018), Sustainable Supply Chain Management in Pithoragarh: Prospects of Rural Tourism. *The IUP Journal of Supply Chain Management*. https://ssrn.com/abstract=3191710

Lateef Ahmad, M. (2014). An Economic Evaluation of Indian Tourism Industry. *International Journal of Scientific and Research Publications, 4*(12).

Misra, L. (2012). *Role of Homestay in the Promotion of Rural Tourism in India.*

Nagaraju, L. G., & Chandrashekara, B. (2014). Rural Tourism and Rural Development in India. [IJIMS]. *International Journal of Interdisciplinary and Multidisciplinary Studies, 1*(6), 42–48.

Nair, V., Munikrishnan, U. T., Rajaratnam, S. D., & King, N. (2015). Redefining rural tourism in Malaysia: A conceptual perspective. *Asia Pacific Journal of Tourism Research, 23*(3), 314–337. doi:10.1080/10941665.2014.889026

National tourism policy. (2002) Tourism.gov. https://tourism.gov.in/sites/default/files/2019-11/National_tourism_Policy_2002.pdf

Negi, J. M. (1990). *Tourism development and nature conservation.* Metropolitan Publishers.

Nelson, F. (2007). *Emergent or illusory? Community wildlife management in Tanzania.* Russell Press.

Nulty, P. M. (2004). *Keynote Presentation: Establishing the Principles for Sustainable Rural Tourism, Rural Tourism in Europe: Experiences, Development, and Perspectives.* WTO.

Önder, E., & Kabadayi, N. (2015). Supplier Selection in Hospitality Industry Using ANP. *International Journal of Academic Research in Business & Social Sciences, 5*(1). Advance online publication. doi:10.6007/IJARBSS/v5-i1/1417

Page, S. J. (2014). *Tourism management: Managing for change.* Routledge. doi:10.4324/9781315768267

Page, S. J., & Connell, J. (2014). *Tourism: A Modern Synthesis* (4th ed.). Thomson Learning.

Pankaj. (2016). Rural Tourism a Solution for Ghost Villages of Uttarakhand. *International Journal of New Technology and Research, 2*(6).

Panyik, E., Costa, C., & Rátz, T. (2011). Panyik. E., Costa, c., and Rátz, T, (2011). Implementing integrated rural tourism: An event-based approach. *Tourism Management, 32*(6), 1352–1363. doi:10.1016/j.tourman.2011.01.009

Pearcy, H. D., Gorodina, D., & Lester, J. (2011). *Using the Resource-Based View to Explore the Jamaican Health Tourism Sector as a Service: A Preliminary Examination.* 2011 Las Vegas International Academic Conference Conference Proceedings. Caesars Palace, Las Vegas.

Pechlaner, H., & Fischer, E. (2006). Alpine Wellness: A Resource-based View. *Tourism Recreation Research, 31*(1), 67–77. doi:10.1080/02508281.2006.11081248

Radhika, V. (2020). RURAL TOURISM – Features, Components and Key drivers for its Growth. *IJCRT, 8*(10).

Ray, N. & Das, D. (2020). *Relationship among Influencing Factors of Tourism Infrastructure: An Empirical Assessment at Kamarpukur, India.* IGI Global. . doi:10.4018/978-1-7998-2469-5.ch039

Reichel, A., Lowengart, O., & Milman, A. (2000). Rural tourism in Israel: Service quality and orientation. *Tourism Management, 21*(5), 451–459. doi:10.1016/S0261-5177(99)00099-0

Sidola, A., Kumar, P., & Kumar, D. (2012). System dynamics investigation of information technology in small and medium enterprise supply chain. *Journal of Advances in Management Research, 9*(2), 199–207. doi:10.1108/09727981211271940

Silva, A. S., Nascimento, L. P., Ribeiro, J. R., & Belderrain, M. C. N. (2009). ANP and ratings model applied to supplier selection problem. *Proceedings of the International Symposium on the Analytic Hierarchy Process.* Semantic Scholar.

Song, H., Liu, J., & Chen, G. (2012). Tourism Value Chain Governance. *Review and Prospects Journal of Travel Research, 2012*, 96–107.

Szpilko, D. (2017), Tourism Supply Chain–Overview of Selected Literature. *Procedia Engineering, 182*.

Tadić, S., & Veljović, M. (2020). LOGISTICS OF RURAL TOURISM. *International Journal for Traffic and Transport Engineering, 10*(3), 323–350. doi:10.7708/ijtte.2020.10(3).06

Tadić, S., Zečević, S., & Krstić, M. (2012). Logistics and Supply Chain Management in tourism: Present state and limitations. *Tehnika, 67*(6), 1018–1025.

Tapper, R., & Font, X. (2004). *Tourism supply chains: Report of a desk research project for the travel foundation.* Leeds Metropolitan University, Environment Business & Development Group. http://www.lmu.ac.uk/lsif/the/Tourism-Supply-Chains.pdf

UKEssays. (2018). *Supply Chain Management in Tourism.* UKEssays. https://www.ukessays.com/essays/business/supply-chain-in-tourism-services.php?vref=1

WCED. (1987). *Our Common Future.* WCED.

WTO. (2001). Sustainable Development of Tourism. A Compilation of Good Practices. WTO.

Zhang, X., Song, H., & Huang, G. Q. (2009). Tourism supply chain management: A new research agenda. [Websites]. *Tourism Management, 30*(3), 345–358. doi:10.1016/j.tourman.2008.12.010 PMID:32287729

Zurick, D. N. (1992). Adventure travel and sustainable tourism in the peripheral economy of Nepal. *Annals of the Association of American Geographers, 82*(4), 606–628. doi:10.1111/j.1467-8306.1992.tb01720.x

Chapter 9
Understanding the Dynamics of Blockchain Technology and Its Impact on Environmental Sustainability in the Hospitality Industry

Sunita Jatav
https://orcid.org/0000-0002-7946-4638
School Of Business, MIT World Peace University, Pune, India

Rupali Gupta
School of Business, MIT World Peace University, Pune, India

Vijeta Singh
Ramcharan School of Leadership, MIT World Peace University, Pune, India

ABSTRACT

This research examines the possible contributions that blockchain technology could make to overcoming a variety of obstacles and accomplishing the objectives of sustainable tourism. Blockchain technology shows promise for the development of sustainable tourism that is aligned with the Sustainable Development Goals (SDGs). Blockchain technology has the potential to disrupt existing tourism operations, boost local economies, manage food supply chains, reduce food waste, improve tourists' satisfaction, influence sustainable behaviour, and address awareness-related concerns. In addition, this study makes suggestions for new lines of research that could be pursued in order to investigate the full potential of blockchain technology as it relates to sustainable tourism. This study covered Indian and International Cases of Multinational and Indian Companies with challenges and opportunities.

DOI: 10.4018/979-8-3693-2065-5.ch009

INTRODUCTION

The United Nations' 2030 Agenda includes seventeen sustainable development goals (SDGs) aimed at ending global poverty, safeguarding the planet's natural resources, and boosting economic opportunity for all people. The tourist industry is mentioned three times in the United Nations 2030 Agenda for Sustainable Development, but it nonetheless has ramifications in terms of employment opportunity, sustainable production, utilization of goods and services, and sustainable use of natural resources. If tourism is done in a sustainable manner, it can have positive effects on the economy, society, and environment. Responsible management of the tourism industry's financial, ecological, and social impacts is a hallmark of sustainable travel.This type of tourism also considers the requirements of all stakeholders involved. In general, for tourism to be sustainable, it must cater to the tourists and tourism destinations needs and requirements but without harming nature. This must be done while also making room for opportunities for the industry's continued growth and ensuring that its cultural and natural landmarks, ecosystems, and life-supporting mechanisms are preserved (UNEP and UNWTO 2005; Pan et al 2018).

Economic sustainability, social sustainability, and environmental sustainability are the three pillars upon which the notion of sustainable development. Economic sustainability refers to the effectiveness of a company's operations over the course of time; social responsibility refers to the provision of equal opportunities, the respect of diverse cultures, the reduction of poverty and discrimination; and environmental sustainability refers to the appropriate management of scarce resources, particularly those that are not renewable (Kuhn, 2007; Tanguay, 2013). The blockchain technology possesses exceptional qualities and has the potential to exert a significant influence on the operations of businesses as well as an entire sector's worth of industries. High energy consumption, greenhouse gas emissions, incorrect waste management and treatment, and the loss of biodiversity are some of the obstacles in the way of the growth of sustainable tourism.

Furthermore, tourism causes a decline in communication channels and restricts access to informational resources, as well as contributing to the deterioration of natural ecosystems and endangers heritage management and the authenticity of cultural traditions. Two ways to start dealing with these problems are to look into how blockchain technology could be used to solve some of them and to talk about how this new technology could possibly help other parts of sustainable tourism. The areas of sustainable tourism in which the implementation of blockchain technology might have a favourable impact on the respective fields (Treiblmaier, 2019).

Overview of Indian Hospitality Industry

Indian hospitality is based on the ancient convention of "Atithi Devo Bhava" which means "the Guest is God". India is popular with people from all over the world because it has different cultures and ethnic groups. Additionally, India has gained recognition as a destination for spiritual tourism, attracting both domestic and international travellers. The Indian hospitality industry falls within the spectrum of travel and tourism. According to the World Tourism Organization of the United Nations, tourism is "a social, cultural, and economic phenomenon that involves the movement of people to countries or places outside of their usual environment for personal or business or professional purposes". The hospitality industry sets the very foundation for travel and tourism which means providing services to customers in terms of food & beverages, accommodation, travel and tourism and entertainment and recreation. The tourism and hospitality industry is not only the most populous service industry in India, but also a major source of employment for the country's workforce.

The contribution of Travel and Tourism to India's GDP accounted for about 5.19% (both direct and indirect) in 2019 creating 69.44 million jobs through direct and indirect employment. The Indian tourism and hospitality business brings in the third most money outside for the country. India is placed 34 rank on the TTCI (Travel and Tourism Competitive Index) out of a total of 140 countries, according to the Ministry of Tourism, Government of India's Annual Report.

Covid-19 Pandemic and Hospitality Industry

Hospitality industry has been one of the hardest hit industries by the COVID-19 pandemic (Gursoy & Chi, Citation2020). Lockdowns and travel restrictions implemented worldwide because of the Covid-19 outbreak wreaked havoc on the global economy by bringing a halt to trade and travel. The number of international visitors to the world fell by 74% in 2020, from 1.5 billion in 2019 to 381 million. This number is on par with that seen in 1990. An estimated $1.3 trillion was lost by countries in 2020, 11 times greater than the loss incurred during the Global Financial Crisis of 2009. By 2020, the tourism industry has already lost between 100 and 120 million jobs.

India witnessed a decline by 59% in the Air Passenger Traffic having a 71% decline in the International Air Passenger Traffic and 56% decline in the Domestic Air Passenger Traffic. Foreign Travel Arrivals also fell down by 76% yoy in 2020. The covid 19 impact on the Indian Hotel Sector was seen with an estimated total revenue loss of 900 Billion INR. Approximately 40-50% of employees working in the organized hotel sector in India have been laid off, while an equivalent number have been affected by salary reductions. The hospitality industry in India was still reeling from the devastating impacts of the pandemic's second wave in the third quarter of 2021. However, in the third quarter of 2022, the Indian hospitality sector showed a significant year-on-year growth in performance, mostly attributable to corporate travel. Because of this, the 89.6% YoY increase in RevPAR from Q3 2021 to Q3 2022 is extremely high [1].

According to the Ministry of Tourism Annual Report 2022-2023, Foreign Tourist Arrivals (FTAs) in 2022 were 6.19 million (Provisional), up 305.4% from 2021. India received 5.48 million NRIs in 2021. UNWTO considers FTAs and NRI arrivals ITAs. India has 7,000,000 FTAs in 2021. FEEs increased 106.77% to Rs. 1,34,543 crores in 2022 (provisional projections). 2022 FEE was US$ 16.926 billion, up 92.41% from the previous year. Indian National Departures (INDs) increased 146.7 percent to 21.09 million (Provisional) in 2022. The Ministry of Tourism estimated that there were 677.63 million domestic tourist visits (DTVs) and 10.55 million foreign tourist visits (FTVs) throughout the country.

Technology in Hospitality Industry

The industrial revolution began in Europe in the 1800s and spread to other countries through the use of different technologies. Changes in all areas have been caused by changes in the field of communication and in the field of information technology. The first three of the previous industrial revolutions are called mechanisation, use of electrical energy and automation and electronics respectively (Lasi et al., 2014). Today's economies are turning to the fourth industrial revolution defined by the use of cyber systems, smart factories and innovations in the service sector (Shamim et al., 2016; Lee et al., 2014). Industry 4.0 can also be called as a subcomponent of digital transformation in existing business and processes

(Porter and Heppelmann, 2014). Changes in all areas have been caused by changes in the field of communication and in the field of information technology. Peceny et al. (2019) discussed Tourism 4.0 as a new tourism paradigm that emerged to reveal the potential for innovation in the entire tourism sector. It is believed that the Internet of Things (IoT), Big Data, Chained Disabilities, Artificial Intelligence, Virtual Reality, and Augmented Reality could all have potential uses in the tourism business. These technologies are all part of business 4.0. Business 4.0 technologies have quickly found a home in the tourism sector since the tourism business is dynamic and rapidly adapts to innovations and technologies. Some researchers have defined Industry 4.0 in tourism or Tourism 4.0 as smart or intelligent tourism (Buhalis & Amaranggana, 2013; Gretzel et al., 2015a; Hunter et al., 2015; Gretzel et al., 2015b; Schwab, 2016; Verevka, 2018; Lebedev et al., 2018). The tourist industry is affected by technological advancements in communication, internet of things, cloud and cognitive computing, internet and mobile banking, and national and international money transfer. (Figure 1)

The Internet of Things, artificial intelligence, blockchain, robotics, big data analytics, digital twins, augmented reality, and virtual reality are all examples of digital technologies with the potential to impact hotel management and the value chain (Anser et al., 2020). Experiencing the dip due to Covid 19 Pandemic, there have been major shifts in the functionality of the hospitality industry wherein adoption of digital technologies are no more a choice but a necessity.

Figure 1. Industry 4.0 for tourism
Source: Handbook on research on Smart Technological Applications in Tourism Industry, IGI Global. Pp. 209.

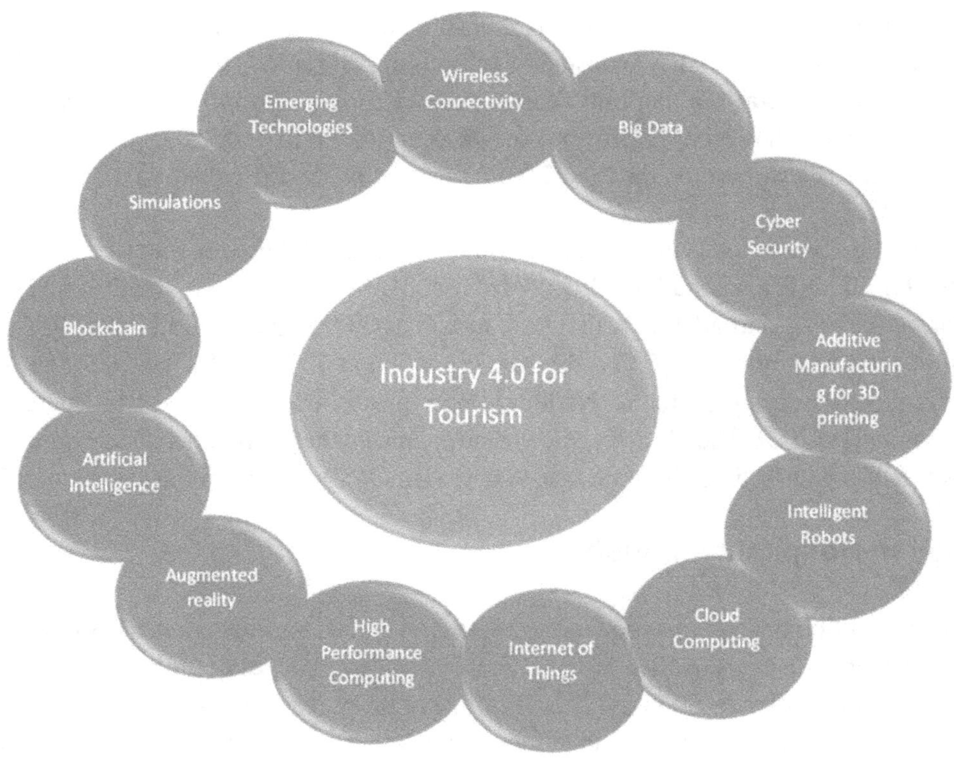

Hotels across the world (including India) have been focusing in providing contactless services which is possible by adapting to technological innovations. Post pandemic revolution in hospitality sector in terms of contactless customer service, sales, contactless check-ins, QR based menus, multichannel communications, virtual property tours (3D tour), user friendly apps for real time communication and feedback, instant reservations, lodging, etc. is all possible due to the adaptation of digital technologies and technological innovations.

Strengthening customer relationship demands not only easy access and visibility but also increased security and reduced risks. Timely and accurate measurement of different quality attributes such as weather, traffic, route changes, modifying operations etc. is significant to achieve such an objective. Data analytics has simplified the tasks of data analysis to a considerable level.

Monitoring current booking, room revenues, analysing occupancy rates, ascertaining strengths and weaknesses, noticing similarities, trends and differences, identifying opportunities and targeted promotions is all possible by Big Data making it extremely helpful in managing sales by delivering information to clients in a better way than it has ever before.

The removal of financial intermediaries has been made possible by the usage of blockchain technology, which has made it possible to share digital databases, verify visitors using fingerprints, and give direct payment to merchants. The information will no longer be collected or deleted by cybercriminals who increase customer traffic.

LITERATURE REVIEW

Sustainable Tourism

Sustainable tourism is defined as tourism that assumes full responsibility for the current and future economic, environmental, and social impacts it has. This type of tourism also takes into account the requirements of the industry, the environment, tourists, and the communities that they visit.To be sustainable, tourism must first cater to the requirements of existing travelers and tourist sites, while also creating openings for the industry's continued growth and safeguarding the planet's cultural and natural treasures, as well as the ecosystems and species that depend on them for their very survival (Pan et al., 2018). Scholars in the tourist industry have taken an avid interest in sustainability and sustainable development since the 1980s. The economic, social, and environmental pillars form the basis of sustainable tourism. Environmental sustainability refers to the efficient long-term use of scarce and especially nonrenewable resources; social responsibility to the provision of equal opportunities, respect for diverse cultures, and the reduction of poverty and discrimination; and economic sustainability to the long-term viability of a company's operations UNEP and UNWTO (2005). Many academics share the view that sustainable tourism is best understood as the interplay between the industry's bottom line, society at large, and the natural world. A sustainable location is one that meets the criteria of being livable, equitable, and economically viable (Kuhn, 2007; Tanguay et al., 2013). However, much emphasis is placed on strong sustainability, and some studies have interpreted the intersection of these three aspects of tourism as evidence of the opposite. The three-pillar idea of sustainability has been expanded by some scholars to include organizational growth as a fourth pillar (Laririt, 2011; Pomering et al., 2011). Recent studies highlight the most widely studied issues in the field, including tourism's impact, sustainability assessment, development, visitors' attitudes, and planning; they also look into gamification techniques and applications that can be used to achieve sustainable tourism; and they propose a multilevel approach to understanding sustainable tourism development (Negrusa et al., 2015; Roxas et al., 2020; Buckley 2012). Although the influence of IT on the tourism industry has been widely acknowledged, sustainable tourism studies have paid less attention to disruptive IT.

Blockchain

A blockchain is a distributed digital ledger in which blocks include individual transaction data. These components cannot be easily changed once they have been integrated into a sophisticated decentralized procedure. Changing anything would be extremely difficult because altering a single block would need altering all subsequent blocks (Nakamoto, 2008).The blockchain is not administered by any one entity; rather, it is distributed over a network of computers called "nodes," each of which stores a complete copy of the blockchain.The individuals referred to as miners take part in the process of adding new records and verifying those entries. They first have to solve a computationally challenging problem in order to add and validate the data, and then they are compensated for providing the resources that they have (Narayanan et al., 2016). To provide more precision in data monitoring and security, each new block in the chain is assigned a hash based on the hashes of the blocks that came before it (Seffinga et al., 2017). Smart contracts are implemented across a variety of blockchain-based platforms to facilitate the secure completion of online agreements between untrusted third parties (Giancaspro, 2017).

Objective

This conceptual paper aims to contribute to the literature and case base analysis on the impacts of blockchain technology and its application on the environmental sustainability in the hospitality industry, through the research it presents. The proposed study discusses national and international cases that are exposed to blockchain technology in sustainable tourism and so a better, evidence based and pragmatic approach and second objective is based on PESTEL analysis. There lies an immense potential disruptive technology like blockchain in bringing about transformational change in environmentally conscious tourism and hospitality industry.

Research Methodology

In terms of methodological assessment the study will have two fold approaches - 1) case study 2) PESTEL analysis. The wider adoption of blockchain technology in tourism and hospitality would require comprehensive assessment of the factors that impact appropriation of novel technologies like blockchain - also understanding relative strength and weakness. The effort also lies in building models that describe the structural framework for inclusion of blockchain technology.

Cases of Multinational and Indian Companies

The tourism industry has just one of several that might be upended by the rise of digital currency and smart contracts. There is a possibility that digital currencies and smart contracts will disrupt many other businesses, including the tourism industry. The following statement details important aspects of

blockchain technology, with the potential connections between those aspects and sustainable tourism.
Blockchain based companies with sustainable tourism practices

Disintermediation: Blockchain technology, due to its distributed and peer-to-peer nature, cannot have a single, overarching governing body. The internet has made it feasible for travelers, service providers, and hosts to all communicate directly with one another.

Trust: All involved can feel safe dealing directly with one another. Travelers have an open forum for discussing and rating their interactions with various tour operators.

Costs: The removal of intermediaries allows for savings. Money-saving opportunities for travellers and service providers alike.

Traceability: The history and provenance of each given transaction may be verified with this system. Verify that the environmental friendliness claims made for seafood, lumber, and other items are accurate.

Integration of coins or tokens: The coins or tokens facilitate a more efficient method of trade, loyalty program participation, and the distribution of review incentives. Sustainable tourism practices can yield monetary rewards for both visitors and the local community.

Access to high quality data to everyone: Accurate, timely, consistent, and comprehensive information shall be available to all parties involved in a transaction. When all parties are aware of the costs associated with a certain travel service or product, they can treat all customers fairly.

The travel sector is a major investor in blockchain-based businesses. TUI is one example of a company operating within the travel sector that has embraced blockchain technology and integrated it into its online booking, reservation, and payment processes. Bitcoin is one of many cryptocurrencies that can be used as a means of payment on a number of the industry's most prominent online travel booking platforms, including CheapAir, Expedia, One Shot Hotels, and Webjet, to name just a few. Only a tiny number of academic studies have investigated blockchain technology's possible applications in the tourism sector. The majority of the literature on blockchain's potential effects thus far has focused on broad, industry-wide implications for the tourism, hotel, restaurant, and airline industries.Certain articles also address the topic of blockchain implementation in smart tourism. Some authors suggest a set of blockchain fundamentals against which DApps can be evaluated (Dogru et al, 2018; Udegbe, 2017;Baralla et al, 2018; Nam et al., 2019;Ozdemir et al).

However, there is a shortage of research examining how this innovative technology can contribute to the tourism industry's sustainable growth. It appears that specialists are accelerating their efforts to achieve the SDGs by promoting sustainable tourism practices. Businesses based on blockchain technology in India and abroad that implement sustainable tourism practices:

DeskBellChain: The tourists have the opportunity to earn prizes for activities such as recycling, participating in Beach Cleanups, and Using Bicycles Instead of Cars.

Provenance: Tracks yellowfin and skipjack tuna from the time it is caught until it is purchased by customers and uses digital technology to highlight the benefits of Soil Association Organic certification.This is a London based company and they worked on Tracks yellowfin and skipjack tuna from the time it is caught until it is purchased by customers and uses digital technology to highlight the benefits of Soil Association Organic certification.

IDGO: Intends to improve both the indigenous people's sense of autonomy and their ethnic identity. Discounts on locally produced goods are available to tourists. The money will be given back to the community so that it may be used for things like education and maintaining cultural traditions and the environment. The objective is to strengthen the independence and cultural identity of indigenous communities. Discounts will be offered to tourists on things that are manufactured in the community, and the money saved from these sales will go back into the community to assist local initiatives for the preservation of cultural traditions, the environment, and educational opportunities.

Tranexus: Helpful agents offering assistance booking trips that minimize their impact on the environment.A travel assistant will be made available to provide assistance with various travel services, as well as providing solutions that are kind to the environment and have a minimal carbon footprint.

NatureCoin App: Users get money for their efforts to recycle plastic. After some time has passed, they will be able to trade the coins for regional goods.

Winding Tree: Connects travelers directly with service providers through the use of smart contracts and ERC827 standards, resulting in the best savings possible for the travel industry as well as a reduction in the fees associated with the booking process.Winding Tree has formed partnerships and collaborated with large travel organizations, who have quite distinct requirements compared to those of small and medium-sized businesses. Simard is a commercial organization that was established so that it may guide you through the various integrations and implementations that are necessary in order to benefit from the Winding Tree ecosystem and protocol.

Sandblock: The goal is to improve consumer loyalty programs by developing a flexible token that can be used by any firms in the travel industry. The target is a general improvement in the effectiveness of loyalty programs.

Accenture: To speed up the process of verifying documents at airports, a new system called the Traveler Digital Identity System is being adopted. The main goal is to streamline the procedure so that passenger wait times are minimized.

Travelchain: It has been decided to build an open-source database management system with the intention of using it to manage traveler information. Users of the system will be rewarded with tokens in exchange for sharing their personal information, and the system will monitor and protect all of the data that is linked to traveling.

Trippki:Plans to create improved methods for maintaining consumer loyalty.

ShoCard and SITA: Intends to improve overall management of identities within the tourism industry.

Lockchain: Allows hotels and airlines to participate in a direct marketplace; employs a decentralized system for payment, property management, and booking procedures.

SoftProdigy System Solutions: This Indian startup works in NFTs, Crypto Exchanges, Smart Contracts, Blockchain Security, Blockchain Logistics, and Ledgers. SoftProdigy is the next-generation IT solutions provider and digital innovation hub. Tech enthusiasts, committed computer programmers, and marketing specialists aim to change digital companies.

PESTEL Analysis

Political: The implementation of policies and efforts that conserve the natural resources of India, including the country's lakes, rivers, biodiversity, forests, and wildlife, is necessary for the growth of tourism in India to be carried out in a sustainable manner. The Ministry of Environment, which drafts environmental and forest rules and regulations, may greatly aid in the development of ecotourism by providing essential leadership in the conservation of natural resources.

Economic: This effort intends to build economically sustainable enterprises that provide job and income opportunities, social services, and poverty reduction for local communities. Additionally, this initiative aims to ensure stability and distribute benefits fairly among all stakeholders.

Socio Cultural: Incorporate and maintain the one-of-a-kind sociocultural characteristics of the host communities, safeguard their cultural and historical legacy, and encourage intercultural understanding and acceptance.

Technological: To increase everyone's awareness, understanding, and acceptance of sustainable tourism, a well-planned Information, Education, and Communication (IEC) campaign is essential. The federal government should spearhead this initiative with help from state and regional governments, as well as businesses, conservation groups, and citizens. The overall IEC content will be developed by the Ministry of Tourism with the assistance of technical specialists, and then adapted by State Governments to meet their individual requirements. The content will be made available via multiple channels, including websites and social media, and will be made available in both digital and print formats.

Environmental: The Ministry of Tourism acknowledges that environmental sustainability is a key component of environmentally responsible tourism, and one of its primary goals is to maximize the efficiency with which environmental resources are utilized for the growth of the tourism industry, all the while ensuring that vital ecological processes, natural heritage, and biological diversity are preserved. This is in accordance with the UNWTO's principles for the development of sustainable tourism.

Legal: Legal considerations refer to the rules and policies that are pertinent to the trade, including labor and capital, whereas environmental elements are concerned with maintaining ecological balance, adhering to environmental regulations, and ensuring sustainability.

CONCLUSION

The purpose of this article is to begin up a discussion in academic circles on the possible effects that blockchain technology could have on the tourist sector, particularly in relation to sustainable tourism. The number of academic publications devoted to blockchain technology is rising in tandem with the widespread interest in the technology's potential applications. Despite this, study of blockchain's potential impact on the travel industry is just getting started.

Within the framework of the United Nations Agenda for Sustainable Development and its Sustainable Development Goals, this research makes a significant addition to the ongoing conversation about environmentally responsible tourism. In this study, we conceptualize blockchain technology and its potential role in promoting eco-friendly vacations. The writers have discussed the PESTEL study of sustainable tourism as well as the Indian and worldwide situations. Because of its potential to improve local economies, increase visitor happiness, and inspire more sustainable behaviors, blockchain technology has the potential to contribute to the achievement of numerous SDGs. However, blockchain technology may not be sustainable because it consumes too much energy during the block creation process.

The study also provided specifics on how to put blockchain technology into action. Potential applications of blockchain technology considered include cryptocurrencies, smart contracts, and decentralized applications. This article has some shortcomings, chief among them being the limited scope the authors examined on how blockchain technology might affect sustainable tourism. Neither the negative effects of blockchain implementation on sustainability nor the obstacles to its adoption in the tourism industry were identified or elaborated upon in the research. Therefore, it is crucial to conduct experiments to back up the claims made in this work.

REFERENCES

Anser, M. K., Yousaf, Z., Usman, M., & Yousaf, S. (2020). Towards Strategic Business Performance of the Hospitality Sector: Nexus of ICT, E- Marketing and Organisational Readiness. *Sustainability (Basel), 12*(4), 1346. doi:10.3390u12041346

Baralla, G., Ibba, S., Marchesi, M., Tonelli, R., & Missineo, S. (2018) A blockchain based system to ensure transparency and reliability in food supply chain. In: *European conference on parallel processing*. Springer, Cham, pp 379–391

Buckley, R. (2012). Sustainable tourism: Research and reality. *Annals of Tourism Research, 39*(2), 528–546. doi:10.1016/j.annals.2012.02.003

Buhalis, D., & Amaranggana, A. (2013). *Smart tourism destinations. Information and Communication Technologies in Tourism 2014*. Springer International Publishing.

Dogru, T., Mody, M., & Leonardi, C. (2018). *Blockchain technology & its implications for the hospitality industry*. Boston University.

Giancaspro, M. (2017). Is a 'smart contract' really a smart idea? Insights from a legal perspective. *Computer Law & Security Report, S026736491730167X*(6), 825–835. https://www.sciencedirect.com/science/article/pii/. doi:10.1016/j.clsr.2017.05.007

Gretzel, U., Sigala, M., Xiang, Z., & Koo, C. (2015a). Smart tourism: Foundations and developments. *Electronic Markets, 25*(3), 179–188. doi:10.100712525-015-0196-8

Gretzel, U., Werthner, H., Koo, C., & Lamsfus, C. (2015b). Conceptual foundations for understanding smart tourism ecosystems. *Computers in Human Behavior, 50*, 558–563. doi:10.1016/j.chb.2015.03.043

Gursoy, D., & Chi, C. G. (2021). Celebrating 30 years of excellence amid the COVID-19 pandemic — An update on the effects of COVID-19 pandemic and COVID-19 vaccines on hospitality industry: Overview of the current situation and a research agenda. *Journal of Hospitality Marketing & Management, 30*(3), 277–281. doi:10.1080/19368623.2021.1902052

Hunter, W. C., Chung, N., Gretzel, U., & Koo, C. (2015). Constructivist research in smart tourism. *Asia Pacific Journal of Information Systems, 25*(1), 105–120. doi:10.14329/apjis.2015.25.1.105

Kuhn, L. (2007). Sustainable tourism as emergent discourse. *World Futures, 63*(3–4), 286–297. doi:10.1080/02604020601174950

Kuhn, L. (2007). Sustainable tourism as emergent discourse. *World Futures, 63*(3–4), 286–297. doi:10.1080/02604020601174950

Laririt, M. R. I. (2011) *Sustainable tourism for biodiversity conservation - case study: El Nido Resorts, Palawan, Philippines*. Ten Knots Group. https://environment.elnidoresorts.com/2012/01/05/ sustainable-tourism-for-biodiversity-conservation/

Lasi, H., Fettke, P., Kemper, H. G., Feld, T., & Hoffmann, M. (2014). Industry 4.0. *Business & Information Systems Engineering, 6*(4), 239–242. doi:10.100712599-014-0334-4

Lebedev, O. T., Mokeeva, T. V., & Rodionov, D. G. (2018) Matrix Structures of Science and Technology Innovations Development and Implementation Trajectory. In *Proc. of the 31st Int. Business Information Management Association Conf.* IOP Science.

Lee, J., Kao, H. A., & Yang, S. (2014). Service innovation and smart analytics for industry 4.0 and big data environment. *Procedia CIRP*, *16*, 3–8. doi:10.1016/j.procir.2014.02.001

Nakamoto, S. (2008). *Bitcoin: a peer-to-peer electronic cash system.* Bitcoin.org. https:// bitcoin.org/ bitcoin.pdf

Nam, K., Dutt, C. S., Chathoth, P., & Khan, M. S. (2019). Blockchain technology for smart city and smart tourism: Latest trends and challenges. *Asia Pacific Journal of Tourism Research*, *60*, 1–15.

Narayanan, A., Bonneau, J., Felten, E., Miller, A., & Goldfeder, S. (2016). *Bitcoin and cryptocurrency technologies: a comprehensive introduction.* Princeton University Press.

Negruşa, A. L., Toader, V., Sofică, A., Tutunea, M. F., & Rus, R. V. (2015). Exploring gamification techniques and applications for sustainable tourism. *Sustainability (Basel)*, *7*(8), 11160–11189. doi:10.3390u70811160

Ozdemir, A. I., Ar, I. M., & Erol, I. (2019). Assessment of blockchain applications in travel and tourism industry. *Quality & Quantity*, *54*, 1–15.

Pan, S. Y., Gao, M., Kim, H., Shah, K. J., Pei, S. L., & Chiang, P. C. (2018). Advances and challenges in sustainable tourism toward a green economy. *The Science of the Total Environment*, *635*, 452–469. doi:10.1016/j.scitotenv.2018.04.134 PMID:29677671

Peceny, U. S., Urbančič, J., Mokorel, S., Kuralt, V., & Ilijaš, T. (2019). Tourism 4.0: Challenges in Marketing a Paradigm Shift. In Consumer Behavior and Marketing. IntechOpen.

Point 1. website: https://travel.economictimes.indiatimes.com/news/research-and-statistics/figures/ indian-hospitality-sector-witnessed-90-yoy-revpar-growth-in-q3-2022-jll/95375678

Pomering, A., Noble, G., & Lester, W.J. (2011). Conceptualising a contemporary marketing mix for sustainable tourism. *J Sustain Tour 19*(8), 953–969. https://doi.org/. 584625 doi:10.1080/09669582.2011

Porter, M. E., & Heppelmann, J. E. (2014). How smart, connected products are transforming competition. *Harvard Business Review*, *92*(11), 64–88.

Roxas, F. M. Y., Rivera, J. P. R., & Gutierrez, E. L. M. (2020). Framework for creating sustainable tourism using systems thinking. *Current Issues in Tourism*, *23*(3), 280–296. doi:10.1080/13683500.2018.1534805

Schwab, K. (2016) *The Fourth Industrial Revolution: what it means, how to respond.* World Economic Forum. https://www.weforum.org/agenda/2 016/01/the-fourth-industrial revolution- what it- means-and-how to- respond/

Seffinga, J., Lyons, L., & Bachman, A. (2017). *The blockchain (r)evolution - the Swiss perspective.* Deloitte.

Shamim, S., Cang, S., Yu, H., & Li, Y. (2016). Management approaches for Industry 4.0: A human resource management perspective. In *2016 IEEE Congress on Evolutionary Computation (CEC)* (pp. 5309-5316). IEEE. 10.1109/CEC.2016.7748365

Tanguay, G. A., Rajaonson, J., & Therrien, M. C. (2013). Sustainable tourism indicators: Selection criteria for policy implementation and scientific recognition. *Journal of Sustainable Tourism*, *21*(6), 862–879. doi:10.1080/09669582.2012.742531

Treiblmaier, H. (2019) Toward more rigorous blockchain research: recommendations for writing blockchain case studies. *Front Blockchain*, *2*(3), 1–15. https://doi.org/. 2019.00003 doi:10.3389/fbloc

Udegbe, S. (2017). E: impact of blockchain technology in enhancing customer loyalty programs in airline business. *Int J Innov Res Adv Stud*, *4*(6), 257–263.

UNEP and UNWTO. (2005). *Making tourism more sustainable - a guide for policy makers*. UN.http://www.unep.fr/shared/publications/pdf/DTIx0592xPA-TourismPolicyEN.pdf

Verevka, T. (2018). Key performance indicators of high-tech enterprises. *The Convergence of Digital and Physical Worlds: Technological, Economic, and Social Challenges (CC-TESC2018).* EDP Sciences.

Chapter 10
Dimensional Role of the Latest Trends in Sustainability at Religious Places in Rural Rajasthan

Umang Bhartwal
Suresh Gyan Vihar University, Jaipur, India

Naveen Sharma
Suresh Gyan Vihar University, Jaipur, India

Monika
UITHM, Chandigarh University, Mohali, India

Deep Mathur
Suresh Gyan Vihar University, Jaipur, India

Ravi Kumar Tiwari
S. S. Jain Subodh Girls P.G. College, Jaipur, India

Sandeep Saxena
Suresh Gyan Vihar University, Jaipur, India

ABSTRACT

Religious tourism is the blissful and mindful action of a human being. Much of the evidence is present by way of the printed manuscript in the written form of articles in the journal, and news newspapers along with physical evidence from Temples, Mosques, Gurudawaras, and many other places in the world. In earlier ages, some of these temples and mosques were in isolated places or away from society which helped to make them in "DHYAN" (spending time in concentration for GOD). Later some of these places became urban and rural in regions of the world. Rajasthan is the province of India which is known for its colorful culture, rich tradition, royalness, and religious places all over the world. Religious places present in regions of Rajasthan are famous names such as Dargah Sharif Ajmer, Khatu Shyam Ji Ringus, Salasar Balazi Sikar, Karni Mata Mandir, Bikaner, Mahandipur Balazi Karauli, and so on.

INTRODUCTION

Human being visits from one place to another for different purposes, and religion is one of the main purposes mainly concerned with beliefs, faith and mindfulness. There is much evidence present in many

DOI: 10.4018/979-8-3693-2065-5.ch010

manuscripts about these religious practices coming from the past till today. It is correct to say that the oldest form of tourism activity. RT can be referred to as on type of tourism in which people move to religious places either in individuals or groups with motives of missionary, leisure, or pilgrimage. Rajasthan is a region of India that is known to the world for its colorful culture, tradition, and rich heritage apart from harsh weather conditions. Moreover, it is also correct to say that this region has many places that are famous for their pilgrimage concern most of the religious people belong HINDU, MUSLIM, and CHRISTAN. India is known in the world for harmony among Indian citizens with different religious beliefs. Many places in Rajasthan are one of the best illustrations like Daharagh Sharique Ajmer, Khatu Shyam ji Skiar, Shree Salasar Balaji Sikar, Mahandipur Balaji Karuli, Karni Mata Mandir Bikaner, and many other famous pilgrimages. A huge number of people devote use to visit from the rest part of India and the world to this region every year.

The latest trends in religious tourism can have a significant impact on the industry. These trends often reflect changes in the preferences and behaviors of religious travelers. Some of the roles that the latest trends can play in religious tourism include:

Diversification of destinations: Travelers are now seeking out new and unique religious destinations beyond the traditional pilgrimage sites. This trend has led to the emergence of lesser-known religious sites gaining popularity.

Integration of technology: The latest trend in religious tourism involves the integration of technology to enhance the visitors' experience. This can include the use of virtual reality, augmented reality, and mobile applications to provide informational and immersive experiences.

Sustainable and responsible tourism: There is a growing emphasis on sustainable and responsible tourism practices in religious tourism. Travelers are increasingly interested in visiting destinations that prioritize environmental conservation, cultural preservation, and community involvement.

Wellness and spiritual retreats: Another trend in religious tourism is the rise of wellness and spiritual retreats. Many travelers are seeking opportunities to relax, rejuvenate, and connect with their spirituality in peaceful and natural settings.

Figure 1.
Source: Author

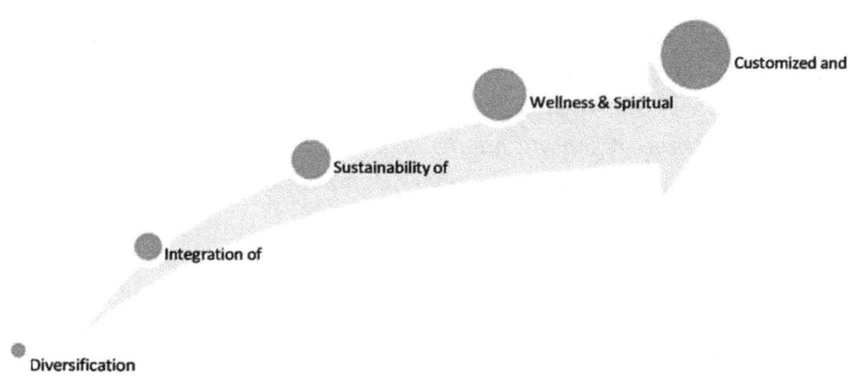

Customized and personalized experiences: Travelers are now looking for more personalized and customized experiences in religious tourism. This can include tailor- made itineraries, personalized activities, and opportunities for meaningful interactions with local communities.

Overall, the latest trends in religious tourism are shaping the industry by offering a wider range of destinations, incorporating technology, promoting sustainability, and catering to the evolving needs and preferences of religious travelers.

DAHARAGH SHAIQUE: Also known as Khwaja Gharib Nawaz Dargah Sharif, this is one of the world's best-known pilgrimage places for Muslims as well as other followers of other religions. This one is situated in Ajmer, which is approximately 130 kilometres away from Jaipur, the capital of Rajasthan, India. This religious place is popular with tourists throughout the year, both international and national. This religious place has a Sufi Tomb, regarded as *"SUFI SAINT MOINUDDIN CHISHTI"*. Every year, Ajmer hosts the URS fair, which is in regard to the death anniversary of Sufi Moinuddin Chaishti and is celebrated for six days. Pushkar is also one of the famous religious places, famous for the "BHARMA JI TEMPLE," just 17–20 kilometres away from Ajmer. This is the only temple in the world for BHARMA Ji, who is regarded as one of the three creators of the "BHARMAN" (world environment) as per Hindu believers. This place hosts the camel and animal fair every year, which is a very famous event among international and national tourists for 7-10 days.

KHATU SHYAM JI: Khatu Shyam Ji is one of the religious sites that gained popularity among Hindu followers in the late 1990s. As this place is in the Sikar district of Rajasthan, it falls under the rural region of Rajasthan. Many festivals and fairs are celebrated at this place, which helps to improve the revenue and living standards of the host society due to huge footfalls over the years.

SHREE SALASAR BALAJI: One of the significant pilgrimages in the Hindu religion due to the strong belief in Hanuman Ji This place attracts pilgrims and tourists throughout the year, despite fairs and festivals. Many domestic people like to visit this place for wishes and peace. As for concern in the region, this place falls into the rural region of Rajasthan in Sikar district. This is the only reason for many tourists to visit this place and feel pleasure.

MAHANDIPUR BALAJI: Mahandipur Balaji is the temple that has the most significant place in religious Rajasthan tourism in all of India as well as the world. The visitors of the places used to visit with the particular motive of mental health. This place is in Dausa, near Jaipur. Here, the maximum number of followers of Hanuman ji comes around the year.

KARNI MATA MANDIR: Karni Mata Mandir is one of the world's best-known religious places, located near Bikaner district (between Noka and Bikaner) an isolated place in Rajasthan. This Temple accomplishes the desires and wants of Hindi Followers who used to visit around the year with strong belief and faith. This temple is full of Rats and the eagle flies on the premises and on the top of the Temple respectively.

Contribution of Religious Tourism local region: After having interactions with the host region of these five parts in a few numbers they have presented the views that are concerned about the basics, wants, and desired amenities. As per them, in this paper, different elements are inculcated into three basics, want, and desired. The below presentation state that the basic, desire and wants of the host are related to amenities, which improves the standards of living in the local regions.

As per the above-mentioned sources, religious tourism contributes to three dimensions of life that are related to basic amenities such as drinking water, sanitization and hygiene, electricity, and other aspects of life that are needed as of now. Apart from that, some essential desires like banking services, telephonic services, and so on Whereas, wants amenities include more components in regards to leisure

Figure 2.
Source: Author

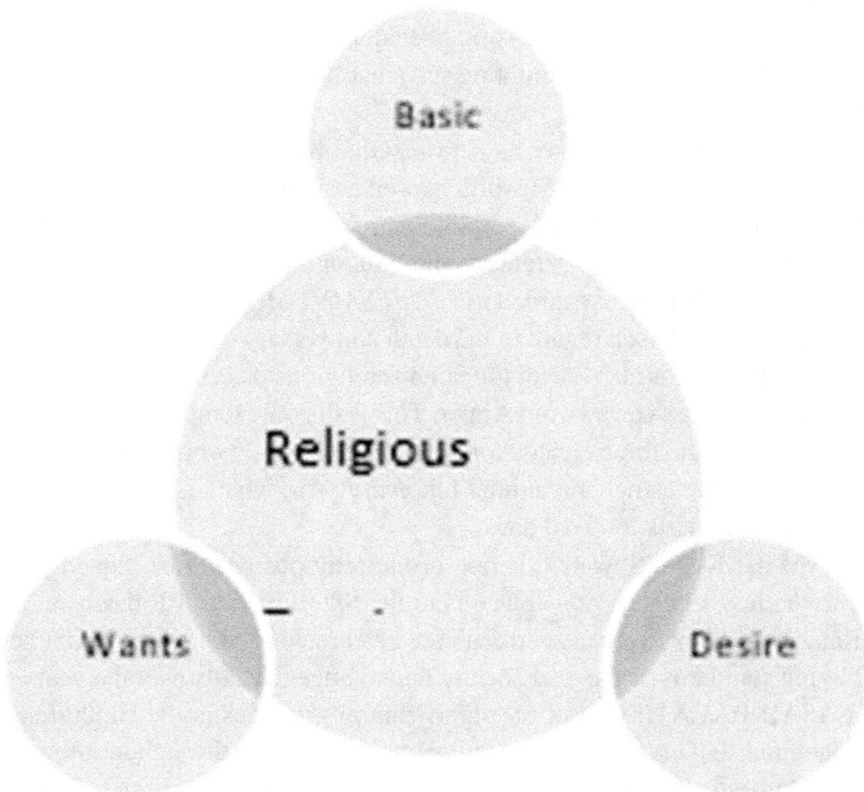

and luxury aspects of life, mainly one touch screen that mainly concerns pendings with the internet and time to gain memorable movement and experience.

LITERATURE REVIEWS

Many authors presented their important views in articles in regards to religious tourism. This study considers a few articles in fruitful ways to form the objectives and hypotheses for this research. As per the author's views, many of the religious places offer opportunities to participate in fairs and festivals in host regions. He conducted his study at Tuba in Senegal, which is one of the biggest religious events in the Muslim community. This study considers and analyses the spiritual connection that contributes to the creation of the different facilities during the religious event in the host region and evaluates the social as well as economic impact on the local society, especially the MURIDS community (Abbou, 2022). According to the author's study, which analyses the latest trends and future of religious tourism after COVID-19, this study concerns the Orthodox segment present in Greece. As per the author, many international bodies are also putting their rightful efforts towards the growth of religious tourism, such as UNESCO, to preserve the heritage of religious tourism. (Tsironis, 2022). This study contains information about the behaviour of children and youth in terms of religious tourism practises such as physical, emotional, and chronological order, This study was conducted in Ireland (Quinn & Quinn, 2022). The literature mentions the ethnographic element with anti-ethnography, considering the natural climbing practices of religious tourism, which help preserve the natural aspect of the host destination. (Shultz & Shultz, 2022)

The study reveals the transformation of religious tourism into the present or upgrade as per the latest trend, which helps to identify the segmentation by taking into account the multidisciplinary approach and in-depth evaluation of this religious tourism in terms of alternative and mass tourism. Considering leisure tourism, business and professional tourism, VFR, and health tourism due to the horizontal and vertical dimensions of tourism, they have a remarkable impact on the host region. (Iliev, 2020) The study was conducted at the pilgrimage site of Mecca with the objective of finding out the dimension of demand for religious tourism through the identification of segments and the establishment of relationships between segments and socio-demographic variables via satisfaction and loyalty. (Hassan et al., 2022) This paper focuses on the role of guide at religious places like temples and other man-made scriptures by collecting the views through structured and semi-structured interviews from the concerned authorities and personnel of the temple of Japan in aspects of sphere, outer-directed role, and inner-directed role, focusing on leadership, mediation, resource management, and economic sphere, while outer-directed roles like instrumental social motivators, gatekeepers, and promoters are considered, along with inner-directed roles such as interactional, communicative, interpreter, heritage interpreter, and philanthropist (Progano & Progano, 2022). According to the author, immigration was a normal practice in the olden days of human life. As per the author, many of the people live in their place for many reasons, but as per him, the first factor is visiting the pilgrimage site in Africa with the concern of a missionary. (Mcintosh & Mcintosh, 2022). In the study, the author explains the role of miracles happening in religious tourism, whereas in the present day, it's completely opposite to the science world, and these miracles have some concern with addressing medical and health issues. Therefore, as per the author, this is also one of the motives for tourists to visit religious places, which also contributes to the development of accommodation units of different sizes and dimensions. (Haller, 2022). As per the study of the author, some of the religious places also offer medical facilities to address health issues, and many of the medical professionals offers their services at these sites, such as doctors, nurses, chemists, and other related personnel from the medical domain (Km & Munro, 2022).

This study adds to the patriotic emotion at the border of pilgrimage. For the study, the author visits the Atari-Wagha border, which offers a strong argument in favour of the verbal aspect. This place is at the border of India and Pakistan, where the border security forces of India and Pakistani Rangers show aggressive designs and symbols to each other, which are enjoyed by both nationalities. This creates lots of employment in hospitality and allied services. (Bochkovskaya & Bochkovskaya, 2022). As per the author, tourism is an aspect of the exchange of values, understanding the culture, and generating revenue for the host society, along with contributing to peace at the international level, which helps in the overall development of the society. (Robinson & Picard, 2011). This study focused on the awareness of religious places via marketing and the correct segmentation of believers who have a strong faith in Gautam Buddha in terms of the formation of marketing strategies and promotional plans among religious tourists (Gurung, 2016). The author examines the challenges of pilgrimage with the help of imperial studies, focusing mainly on the commercial activities in religious places. (Balle, 2022). This article elaborated on the gastronomic practices of the host region, considering the religious places, which are known as maha prasada, a food of "God. (Sorokina, 2016).

Therefore, considering the literature review section helps form the objectives and hypotheses for the paper, which mainly focus on the role of religious tourism in the host region.

The digital transformation of destinations refers to the integration and utilisation of digital technologies to enhance the overall experience for tourists, residents, and businesses within a specific location. It involves leveraging technology to improve the efficiency of tourism, services, and infrastructure, as well as creating new and innovative ways to engage with visitors.

Here are some key aspects and examples of how digital transformation can impact destinations:

Digital Marketing and Promotion: Destinations can use social media, websites, mobile apps, and virtual reality experiences to attract potential visitors and showcase their unique offerings. Personalised marketing strategies can be employed based on user data and preferences to target specific demographics effectively.

Data Analytics and Insights: Collecting and analysing data from various sources, such as mobile devices, social media, and sensors, can provide valuable insights into visitor behaviour, preferences, and trends. This information can be used to make informed decisions about infrastructure improvements, crowd management, and resource allocation.

Smart Infrastructure: Implementing smart technologies, such as IoT (Internet of Things) devices, can improve the management of resources like water, energy, and waste. Smart traffic systems can optimise transportation flows, reducing congestion and improving the overall travel experience.

Contactless Solutions: In the post-COVID-19 era, contactless solutions have become even more critical. Digital payment options, self-check-in processes, and touchless information kiosks can help provide a safer and more convenient experience for visitors.

Augmented Reality (AR) and Virtual Reality (VR): AR and VR can be used to enhance tourists' experiences by offering virtual tours, interactive guides, and immersive storytelling. This technology allows visitors to explore historical sites or experience attractions remotely.

Online Booking and Reservation Systems: Digital platforms and mobile apps that facilitate easy booking of accommodations, activities, and tours can streamline the planning process for travellers and encourage more bookings.

Smart Tourism Apps: Destination-specific apps can provide real-time information about local events, attractions, and services, offering visitors a comprehensive guide in their pocket.

Digital Cultural Heritage Preservation: Technology can aid in the preservation of cultural heritage through digitization efforts, making historical artefacts and documents accessible to a broader audience through virtual museums and archives.

Sustainability Initiatives: Digital tools can help destinations monitor and manage environmental impacts, promoting sustainable practices and responsible tourism.

Collaborative Platforms: Destination stakeholders, such as local businesses, governments, and tourism organisations, can use digital platforms to collaborate, share information, and coordinate efforts to improve the overall tourism experience.

Successful digital transformation requires a strong commitment from all stakeholders, adequate investment in technology infrastructure, and a clear vision of the destination's goals and priorities. When implemented effectively, digital transformation can lead to increased tourism revenues, improved visitor experiences, and enhanced destination competitiveness in the global tourism market.

THE DIGITAL TRANSFORMATION OF RELIGIOUS PLACES

The digital transformation of religious places in Rajasthan, India, can bring numerous benefits to both the pilgrims and the authorities managing these sacred sites.

Rajasthan is known for its rich cultural heritage and historical significance, making digital initiatives particularly valuable in preserving and promoting religious tourism in the region. Here are some potential areas where digital transformation can be implemented:

Figure 3. Digital transformation

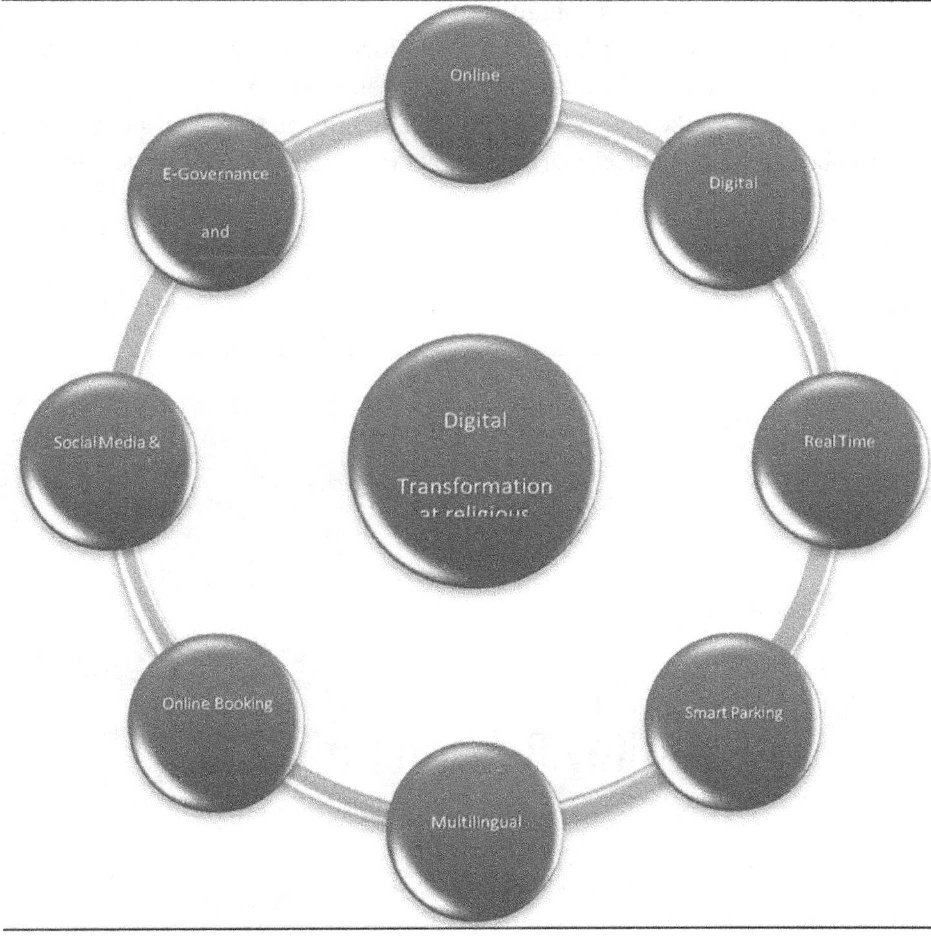

ONLINE INFORMATION AND VIRTUAL TOURS

Creating user-friendly websites and mobile apps that provide detailed information about religious places, their historical background, significance, timings, and facilities can help pilgrims plan their visits better. Virtual tours can give a glimpse of the temples, mosques, and other religious sites, enticing potential visitors and helping them make informed decisions.

Digital Payments and Donations: Implementing digital payment solutions and donation platforms can simplify the process of offering contributions to religious institutions. This can include setting up online payment gateways or using QR codes for contactless donations.

Real-time Crowd Monitoring: Utilising sensors and data analytics to monitor crowd density can help manage and prevent overcrowding at popular religious sites. This ensures the safety and comfort of pilgrims and helps preserve the sanctity of the sites.

Smart Parking Solutions: Implementing digital systems for parking management can help pilgrims find parking spaces easily, reducing congestion and traffic-related issues.

Multilingual Audio Guides and Augmented Reality: Developing multilingual audio guides and augmented reality experiences within the religious sites can enhance the visitor's understanding and appreciation of their cultural and historical significance.

Online Booking of Accommodations: Integrating with local hotels and guesthouses to offer online booking options can ease the process of finding suitable accommodations for pilgrims.

Social Media and Content Marketing: Leveraging social media platforms to share inspiring stories, pictures, and videos about religious places can help attract more tourists and promote religious tourism in Rajasthan.

Figure 4. Key reasons

Digital Preservation of Art and Artefacts: Digitising and archiving the art, artefacts, and manuscripts present in these religious places can aid in their preservation and provide access to a wider audience, even those who cannot physically visit.

E-Governance and Administrative Efficiency: Implementing e-governance solutions for managing permissions, permits, and other administrative tasks can streamline operations for the authorities responsible for religious sites.

Digital Safety and Security Measures: Installing surveillance cameras and implementing digital security measures can enhance safety and deter any potential threats to religious places and their visitors.

The successful digital transformation of religious places in Rajasthan requires collaboration among various stakeholders, including the government, local authorities, religious institutions, technology providers, and tourism organizations. By embracing digital technologies, Rajasthan's religious sites can not only preserve their cultural heritage but also create more meaningful and engaging experiences for pilgrims and visitors from around the world.

Digital transformation is of paramount importance in the tourism industry due to the significant impact it can have on various aspects of the sector. Embracing digital technologies can revolutionise how tourism businesses operate, how tourists plan and experience their trips, and how destinations market themselves. Here are some key reasons why digital transformation is essential in tourism:

ENHANCED RELIGIOUS TOURIST EXPERIENCE

Digital tools enable personalised analysis and seamless customer experiences. From online booking platforms to mobile apps that provide real-time information and virtual tours, tourists can access the information they need and tailor their travel plans according to their preferences.

Improved Efficiency and Productivity of Religious Places: Automation and digitalization of processes can streamline operations for tourism businesses, reducing manual work and improving efficiency. This can lead to cost savings, better resource management, and faster service delivery.

Data-Driven Decision Makin religious destination: Digital technologies provide access to vast amounts of data. Analysing this data allows businesses and destinations to gain insights into customer behaviour, preferences, and trends. Data-driven decision-making enables them to target specific markets, optimise pricing, and enhance services.

Global Reach and Marketing of Religious Destinations: Digital platforms offer the opportunity to reach a global audience. Through social media, websites, and online advertising, destinations can showcase their unique offerings to potential travellers worldwide, leading to increased tourist arrivals.

Innovation and Competitive Advantage: Embracing digital transformation encourages tourism businesses and destinations to innovate and stay ahead of their competitors.

Adopting new technologies and approaches can differentiate them from others in the industry.

SUSTAINABLE TOURISM PRACTICES

Digital technologies can aid in promoting sustainable tourism practices. By using smart technologies to manage resources efficiently and offering eco-friendly alternatives, destinations can reduce their environmental impact.

Contactless Solutions and Safety: In light of the COVID-19 pandemic, contactless solutions have become more critical than ever. Digital platforms for reservations, mobile check-ins, and virtual experiences can enhance safety and reassure travellers.

Real-Time Communication: Digital transformation allows businesses and destinations to communicate with tourists in real time, addressing their concerns, providing updates, and offering assistance when needed.

Crisis Management and Recovery: During times of crises, such as natural disasters or pandemics, digital tools can facilitate communication and coordination among tourism stakeholders. They also play a crucial role in promoting recovery and rebuilding after a crisis.

Cultural Preservation and Education: Digital platforms can be used to preserve and showcase cultural heritage, offering tourists valuable insights into local traditions, art, and history. Virtual museums and interactive experiences can promote cultural education.

Overall, digital transformation in tourism is not only about adopting technology but also about embracing a new mindset and leveraging digital tools to enhance every stage of the tourist journey. By doing so, the tourism industry can become more resilient, sustainable, and responsive to the evolving needs of travellers.

CONCLUSION

The main consideration of the study was to observe the host community's feelings in regards to religious tourism in terms of the contribution of the basics, desire, and wants elements, which cover all the important dimensions of life that are required by anyone in order to live the life in regions of Rajasthan, while some other means of earning are also available to the lively hood, like agriculture, production units for handicrafts, and other ways. For the validation of the study, hypotheses were designed, and accordingly, hypothesis tests were carried out to offer the result with valid consideration of the host respondent.

As for the concern of limitation, this chapter covers only the religious religion of Rajasthan for research that is also five in number and comes under the urban and rural regions.

REFERENCES

Abbou, T. (2022). The Pilgrimage to the Grand Magal in Ṭūbā, Senegal. International Journal of Religious Tourism and Pilgrimage, 10(4).

Balle, M. (2022). The Social and Organisational Life of a Nocturnalilgr image in Mallorca From Palma to Lluc. *International Journal of Religious Tourism and Pilgrimage, 10*(4).

Bochkovskaya, A. V, & Bochkovskaya, A. (2022). Emotions at the Border : Verbal Aspects of the Attari-Wagah Patriotic Pilgrimage. *International Journal of Religious Tourism and Pilgrimage, 10*(4).

Gurung, R. K. (2016). *Marketing Religious Tourism Destination, Case study: The Birthplace of Gautama Buddha, Lumbini, Nepal*. Research Gate.

Haller, S. F., & Haller, S. (2022). A Changed Understanding of Miracles in Religious Tourism A Changed Understanding of Miracles in Religious Tourism. *International Journal of Religious Tourism and Pilgrimage, 10*(4).

Hassan, T., Carvache-Franco, M., Carvache-Franco, W., & Carvache-Franco, O. (2022). Segmentation of Religious Tourism by Motivations: A Study of the Pilgrimage to the City of Mecca. *Sustainability (Basel), 14*(13), 1–19. doi:10.3390u14137861

Iliev, D. (2020, December). The evolution of religious tourism: Concept, segmentation and development of new identities. *Journal of Hospitality and Tourism Management, 45*, 131–140. doi:10.1016/j.jhtm.2020.07.012

Km, D. M., & Munro, D. (2022). A Semi-autoethnographical Account of the Order of Malta ' s Annual Pilgrimage to Lourdes. *International Journal of Religious Tourism and Pilgrimage, 10*(4).

Mcintosh, I. S., & Mcintosh, I. S. (2022). Working Paper Part 1 : The Very First Pilgrimage - An Inspired Trajectory Out of Africa Working Paper Part 1. *International Journal of Religious Tourism and Pilgrimage, 10*(4).

Progano, R. N., & Progano, R. N. (2022). Roles of Religious Guides in Tourism : A Qualitative Study from Japan Roles of Religious Guides in Tourism. *International Journal of Religious Tourism and Pilgrimage, 10*(4).

Quinn, E. M., & Quinn, E. M. (2022). Making History Visible : Ireland ' s National Famine Way Told Through Models and Interactive Digital Narratives Making History Visible. *International Journal of Religious Tourism and Pilgrimage, 10*(4).

Robinson, M., & Picard, D. (2011). Tourism, Culture and Sustainable Development. *Sustainable Development, 54*(1&2), 97.

Shultz, J., & Shultz, J. A. (2022). The Epic Pilgrimage : The Way of the Ascetics of El Capitan. *International Journal of Religious Tourism and Pilgrimage, 10*(4).

Sorokina, A. (2016)... *Typology of Gastronomy Tourists and Tourism.*, (January), 99.

Tsironis, C. N. (2022). Pilgrimage and Religious Tourism in Society, in the Wake of the COVID-19 Pandemic: A Paradigmatic Focus on 'St. Paul's Route' in the Central Macedonia Region, Greece. *Religions, 13*(10), 887. doi:10.3390/rel13100887

Chapter 11
A Theory-Based Approach to Understanding Social Sustainability in Tourism

Shivam Bhartiya
https://orcid.org/0000-0001-5532-2283
Centre for Distance and Online Education, Jain University, India

Vaibhav Bhatt
https://orcid.org/0000-0003-2859-7913
Central University of Tamil Nadu, India

Afsheen H. Rathore
Superior University, Pakistan

Tasleem Khanam
G.D. Goenka University, India

ABSTRACT

The current study aims to determine how social sustainability and tourism are related, and how social sustainability can benefit all parties involved in the tourism industry. The qualitative study employed a theory-based methodology to ascertain the solutions to the question: How can we establish and preserve an economically sustainable tourism system that contributes favourably to social sustainability? How can we use social resources in the tourism industry without increasing them but instead by fostering their development? How do we ensure that the tourism-related mechanisms that promote social sustainability continue to work? The study came to the conclusion that social sustainability through tourism focuses on the core elements of social sustainability, namely improving infrastructure and working conditions, ensuring that men and women have equal access to job opportunities and security, and establishing more secure supply chains.

DOI: 10.4018/979-8-3693-2065-5.ch011

INTRODUCTION

The highly competitive character of the tourism sector prompted the stakeholders to look for strategies that would lead to the development of sustainable new products, which would open up a wealth of potential for the country's economic growth and pave the way for comprehensive social improvement. When it comes to tourism, sustainability is preserving the diversity of the industry's resources so that their use doesn't deplete them but instead gives future generations an equal chance to profit from them. We talk about sustainability in the context of social systems in this study. In order to address sustainability in a social system, all of its constituent parts must be taken into consideration. Concurrent development of the economic, environmental, cultural, and social resources used in the tourism industry is necessary for sustainability. A social system that is sustainable can function in its surroundings and accomplish its objectives. Through skill/work-based learning, growth, and well-being, host communities' capacity to meet the demands of the visitors increases in a sustainable social system. Through fair and open dialogue between the many tourist stakeholders, which improves mutual understanding and increases the capacity for collaboration, the rise of social sustainability is ensured. This research focused on determining the answers to the following questions: How can we develop and sustain an economically viable tourist system that benefits social sustainability? How can we make use of social resources in the tourism industry without increasing them but instead by fostering their development? How do we make sure that the tourism-related mechanisms that promote social sustainability continue to work?

We view the diversity and abundance of tourism resources as a significant contributor to and a significant outcome of social sustainability. Diverse communities, as well as real and intangible resources, make up a tourist system. We are able to respond to societal possibilities and difficulties in a flexible, innovative way because of the diverse tourist system. A tourist system is therefore not in a static or steady state; rather, during its life cycle, it changes continuously. The tourism industry works to reach new heights of development and undergoes a radical change. With its focus on resource regeneration rather than resource consumption for future processes, social sustainability means that the existence of a tourist system has established a foundation for the existence of tourism systems and processes in the future.

To sum up, the following are some guidelines for a sustainable tourist system:

- A tourist system's functioning attempts to replenish its social, cultural, and environmental resources.
- In addition, developing one kind of resource does not use up resources of other kinds.
- A sustainable tourism system "gives back" to society as opposed to merely utilizing the resources that the natural and social environment has to offer.
- We require more complex tools to comprehend what a tourism system is and how it works since it must be able to renew resources of all types and take into account the legitimate needs of many stakeholders.

LITERATURE REVIEW

Sustainability

Sustainability is described as "the combination of environmental health, social fairness, and economic vitality to produce flourishing, healthy, diversified, and resilient communities for this generation and generations to come" in the charter for the UCLA Sustainability Committee. The practice of sustainability acknowledges the connections between these problems and the need for a systems approach and an appreciation of complexity. Before the increase in environmental awareness in the 1960s and 1970s, which was commonly credited as a major factor in the invention of the term "Sustainable development," the concept of sustainable development has existed for a number of years (Bramwell & Lane, 1993; Dovers & Handmer, 1993; Hall, 1998; Wilbanks, 1994). Prior to being an economic theory, sustainable development was initially a conservationist vision, followed by a communal vision. According to the Brundtland Commission, often known as WCED, sustainable development is a process that secures resources for future generations while enabling current generations to meet their own requirements.

The phrase "sustainable development" was approved as a global need, a need for Our Common Future, in 1989 at the G-7 Economic Conference in Paris. The Brundtland Report was investigated, the foundations of sustainable development were created, and the scope of sustainable development was expanded at the much-discussed Earth Summit, also known as the United Nations Conference on Environment and Development (UNCED), which took place in 1992. In fact, the idea came into existence at a time when issues in science, business, socio-culture, and the environment were all intertwined.

Social Sustainability

Human, Social, Economic, and Environmental are the four pillars of sustainability (See Table 1), which are often known as "People, Profit, and Planet." A community's health and vitality depend on social sustainability. The social component of sustainability has generally been disregarded in favor of an economic stability strategy to promote it. Attention must be paid to investigating a tourist destination's social infrastructure via the prism of the built environment (Dempsey et al.,2009). Scientists prioritize economic and environmental sustainability over social sustainability, ignoring it, which has led to a dearth of literature on social sustainability and unrest in local communities as tourism activities have increased (Eizenberg and Jabareen, 2017).

Table 1. Four pillars of sustainability

Human Sustainability	Aims to preserve and enhance society's human capital. Major financial commitments to the health and education systems. Services, nourishment, education, and skill access. Balanced development and growth in relation to a limited area and natural resources. The growth of human capacity and skills to support regional sustainability. Enhancing community and societal well-being.
Social Sustainability	By making investments and building social institutions and services, seeks to protect social capital. Allowing for a broader understanding of the world in terms of communities, cultures, and globalization. Focuses on preserving and enhancing interpersonal honesty, reciprocity, and societal cohesion. In accordance with the objectives of sustainable development, and supported by laws, knowledge, and concepts that are widely held. Addressing social and economic improvement that promotes equality, the economy, and the ecological system while protecting the environment.
Economic Sustainability	Is to raise the standard of living while protecting capital. Incorporating social and environmental factors into the economic model. Reducing the danger of damaging natural and human systems.
Environmental Sustainability	Aims to increase human welfare by safeguarding natural resources (land, air, water, minerals etc.). To ensure that the needs of the population are addressed without jeopardizing those of future generations, implement ecologically sustainable strategies. Emphasize finding green businesses to concentrate on. Putting strategic decisions into practice will help the policies and procedures effectively adopt a sustainable approach.

Source: Adapted from "The Four Pillar of Sustainability", RMIT University (2017)

Polese and Stren's (2000) comprehensive definition of social sustainability is as follows:

"Development that is compatible with the peaceful evolution of civil society, fostering a setting favorable to the peaceful coexistence of culturally and socially diverse groups while at the same time encouraging social integration, with improvements in the standard of living for all segments of the population"

Because fostering engagement from diverse stakeholders is essential for the development of a sustainable tourist business, social sustainability aims to assure local community knowledge, participation, equity, and social cohesion (Murphy, 2012). Moreover, Hall (2008) has developed a novel strategy that emphasizes efficiency, investment return, and improved stakeholder involvement. All parties involved in tourism destinations, including the government, are expected to work closely together to outline the advantages of tourism for residents, raising the standard of living in the neighborhood.

Sustainable Tourism

The most recent area of research to emerge is sustainable tourism. When we talk about sustainable tourism, we're talking about the social, economic, and environmental aspects of the sector, which include the requirements of guests, the economy, the environment, and host communities (UNEP and UNWTO 2005, p. 12). In order to advance the principles of sustainable tourism development, it is necessary to plan and implement a number of initiatives for the protection of sensitive areas [33,34]. Formally, Our Common Future (WCED, 1987) outlined six common issues and suggested solutions, including conservation outside of protected areas, wildlife-based travel, and, in the Australian edition, the importance of small-scale, culturally and environmentally conscious travel involving Aboriginal communities.

Due to the involvement of people, sustainable tourism and its associated mien are highly complex in nature. Several researchers have contributed to our understanding of issues including the environment, equity, and life quality (Wall, 1997; Butler, 1999; Hunter, 1997; Collins, 1999; Farrell & Twining Ward, 2004). In order to assess its linkages to ecological, social, and economic aspects at multiple scales and historical periods in a meaningful and critical manner, it is further argued that sustainable tourism needs to be understood more thoroughly. (McKercher, 1999; Farrell & Twining-Ward, 2004). Because of this, the best way to understand sustainability tourism is either as an "adaptive paradigm" (Hunter, 1997) or as an "adaptive management" (Farrell & Twining Ward, 2004), which deals with issues like the unpredictable nature of events, doubts about how they will turn out, and challenges of scale and time.

Social Sustainability and Host Population

Residents play a significant role in creating a competitive brand for their area and are arguably the biggest and most influential stakeholders of destination brands. The importance of the community or local community in the development of tourism was also addressed by Arida & Sunarta (2017), who emphasized that the performance or success of the tourism sector over the long term is significantly influenced by the degree of acceptance and support from the local community. A tourism model based on sustainable tourism is seen as one of the best solutions to overcome the negative effects of mass tourism while also making this model a strategy to ensure that the majority of the benefits of tourism return to the local community given the involvement of the community in planning, organizing, and developing tourist areas (Widari, 2020).

Social Sustainability and Destination Image Building

From a governance standpoint, it's critical to include local stakeholders in a more sustainable place development, which is a community-based participatory approach (Kavaratzis & Hatch, 2013). A participatory branding strategy, destination branding is thought to be a co-creation process where stakeholders are the co-creators, engaged in discourse to co-construct the location as a brand (Kavaratzis, 2012). As destinations are "a network of interdependent diverse stakeholders," Waligo et al. (2013, p. 342) underline that effective stakeholder participation is crucial for sustainable tourism. Although bottom-up and top-down techniques are not mutually exclusive, this bottom-up strategy promotes the mobilization of local resources for the development process more successfully than top-down marketing strategies. As a result, top-down strategies from national or regional authorities can be complemented by bottom-up community-led strategies (Zago et al., 2014).

A top-down method called local tourism branding has the ability to "bring together a network of grassroots initiatives" (Woodland & Acott, 2007, p.719). This approach is especially important in rural areas, where micro/small-sized businesses, which typically have few resources and less experience, make up the majority of the tourism industry. As a result, collaboration, resource sharing, and information exchange between operators are key components of small-scale, community-based rural tourist development (Ying et al., 2015). According to Idziak et al. (2015), local participation has been acknowledged as facilitating the redistribution of power and empowering local communities, enhancing social capital, and strengthening local identity. It also builds capacity and increases the efficiency and effectiveness of implemented sustainable development projects.

Table 2. Domains of sustainability

Domain	Principle	Policy and Operational Implications
Material	Limit entropy and make sure that the economy's resource flow is as close to non-declining as is permitted by physical laws.	Attempt to maximize resource productivity Use renewable energy sources and consistently recycle non-renewable materials. Increasing performances with each use cycle Influence the uninterrupted, closed-loop flow of matter and energy in the entire planetary industrial infrastructure. Control leaks and prevent stagnation, erroneous concentrations, or random chemical element diffusion during use cycles. Promote the management of durable items with a service- and performance-leasing emphasis.
Economic	Develop an accounting framework that is suitable for economic management, entirely compatible with natural processes on the globe, and accurately reflects biospheric pricing.	Use a holistic view of wealth that takes into account the simultaneous development of five major types of capital: natural, human, social, manufactured, and financial. Connect the global economy with the capacity of nature to regenerate and include essential "externalities" in all cost and benefits accounts. Include a metric for happiness and human growth in economic calculations. Develop regulation and taxation measures to emphasize positive effects and minimize negative ones, so maximizing the whole. Depend on transparent, accurately calibrated market procedures for capital asset allocation.
Life	Assure the preservation of the fundamental diversity of all forms of life in the biosphere.	Take on guardianship of the biosphere on our planet. Only harvest species that can regenerate. Keep the variety of the current gene pool. Create land use patterns that promote biological diversity and minimize human encroachment on other species in places that are home to humans.
Social	maximizing everyone's capacity for self-realization and independence while preventing any one person or organization from negatively harming others.	As the foundation of social interactions, promote tolerance. Enshrine universal rights within a global citizenship framework Ensure inclusiveness and effective democracy in the political process Provide fair access to resources that support life Create a foundation of cooperation to manage global concerns and the planetary commons Ban the commerce in weapons technologies and put an end to war Encourage environmental literacy through all levels of school Integrate sustainability-enhancing ideas into a strong global legal framework.
Spiritual	Recognize the seamless, dynamic continuum of mystery, wisdom, love, energy, and matter that unites the solar system, our planet, and its biosphere, which includes all humans, with our internal metabolic systems and their externalized technology extensions; embody this recognition in universal ethics to direct human behavior.	Recognize the supreme mystery that underlies reality. Investigate and fulfil the special roles that humankind plays in the cosmos. Honor the earth's complex ecology, of which people are an essential component. Encourage compassion and all-encompassing, inclusive viewpoints in the underlying purpose, driving force, and practical application of human endeavors. Establish a connection between personal transformation and social collective change to establish the groundwork for the emergence of a new global awareness.

Source: Adapted from The Sustainability Laboratory, Michael Ben-Eli (2015)

Social Sustainability and Tourism

Understanding how tourism affects people and society from the standpoint of tourism is key to social sustainability. Social sustainability is important in the tourist industry since it has an impact on the standard of the industry and how stakeholders are treated. The value chain system, local communities, tourists, and employees are all managed and identified proactively. Social sustainability is crucial for tourism organizations and their companies as well as for society as a whole. In the tourism industry, there are two types of stakeholders: those who are part of the company itself (the supply or value chain), including employees, suppliers, and customers, and those who are not, like the neighborhood and even society at large. Equity, variety, social cohesiveness, and quality of life are the four characteristics of social sustainability as outlined by Amartya Sen in his book "A study of sustainable development: social and economic components." It is possible to tell whether a project or the tourism industry as a whole is socially sustainable by taking these factors into account. Developing inclusive and resilient societies where the populace has a voice and legislative authorities respond is key to achieving social sustainability through tourism. From the perspective of social inclusion, tourism fosters equitable opportunity and confronts pervasive systemic disparities. The main goal of tourism has been to allow local communities to design their own strategies for economic growth and poverty alleviation. Enhancing community services and infrastructure benefits the host people, especially the most disadvantaged, by enabling them to realize their potential and build a living. By generating socioeconomic opportunities, tourism builds resilience in those who live in the most difficult environments. Additionally, it supports targeted initiatives to lessen interpersonal disputes as well as monitoring, participatory service delivery, peacebuilding, and reconciliation processes. The management of social risks plays an important role in the growth of the tourism industry. The tourism and social sustainability framework strengthen environmental and human rights protections, expands the capacity of destinations, and makes substantial strides in areas like transparency.

It is crucial to link social cooperation and tourist enterprises through sustainable tourism projects where it represents the trust between the tourism system and the societies in order to realize the goal of social sustainability through tourism. To create a constant fit between the demands of the community and the tourism industry, the following guidelines may be helpful:

Figure 1.
Source: Adapted from Sustainable Committee, ACCIONA (2018)

CONCLUSION

It is crucial to proactively manage consequences since host communities and other related social dimensions at the destination are impacted by tourism development, either directly or indirectly. Lack of social development, such as poverty, inequality, and bad governance, might impede the expansion of the tourism industry. Businesses in the tourism industry can take additional measures to promote social sustainability:

- Provide chances for employment, commodities and services to meet basic necessities, and a more inclusive value chain structure as approaches to enhance people's lives.
- Promote socially sustainable policies and make thoughtful social investments.
- forming alliances with other companies and building on strengths to have a more positive influence.

To retain brand and product quality, tourism businesses must create and support solid social sustainability initiatives. Better infrastructure and working conditions, equal job opportunities and security for men and women, and the development of a more secure supply chain are all essential components of social sustainability. Informed and involved consumers and host communities are more prevalent today. They are worried about how tourism-related products may affect society and the environment. In order to be more transparent, make their operations and supply chains more socially and environmentally responsible, and better understand human behavior, the tourism industry is now working with social sustainability organizations. Innovating new product or service lines, retaining business partners, increasing morale and employee involvement, improvising risk management measures, and reducing company-community conflicts are all benefits of aiming for social sustainability in the tourism industry.

REFERENCES

Arida, N. S. N. S., & Sunarta, N. (2017). *Pariwisata berkelanjutan*. Pariwisata Berkelanjutan.

Ben-Eli, M. (2015). *Sustainability: The Five Core Principles–A New Framework*. Buckminster Fuller Institute. http://bfi-internal. org/sustainability/principles.

Bramwell, B., & Lane, B. (2012). Towards Innovation in Sustainable Tourism Research? *Journal of Sustainable Tourism*, *20*(1), 1–7. doi:10.1080/09669582.2011.641559

Butler, R. W. (1999). Sustainable Tourism: A State-of-the-Art Review. *Tourism Geographies*, *1*(1), 7–25. doi:10.1080/14616689908721291

Byrd, E. T. (2007). Stakeholders in Sustainable Tourism Development and Their Roles: Applying Stakeholder Theory to Sustainable Tourism Development. *Tourism Review*, *62*(2), 6–13. doi:10.1108/16605370780000309

Byrd, E. T., Bosley, H. E., & Dronberger, M. G. (2009). Comparisons of Stakeholder Perceptions of Tourism Impacts in Rural Eastern North Carolina. *Tourism Management*, *30*(5), 693–703. doi:10.1016/j.tourman.2008.10.021

Clarkson, M. B. E. (1995). A Stakeholder Framework for Analyzing and Evaluating Corporate Social Performance. *Academy of Management Review*, *20*(1), 92–117. doi:10.2307/258888

Currie, R. R., Seaton, S., & Wesley, F. (2009). Determining Stakeholders for Feasibility Analysis. *Annals of Tourism Research*, *36*(1), 41–63. doi:10.1016/j.annals.2008.10.002

Dempsey, N., Bramley, G., Power, S., & Brown, C. (2009). The social dimension of sustainable development: Defining urban social sustainability. *Sustainable Development (Bradford)*, *19*(5), 289–300. doi:10.1002d.417

Eizenberg, E., & Jabareen, Z. (2017). Social sustainability: A new conceptual framework. *Sustainability (Basel)*, *9*(1), 68–82. doi:10.3390u9010068

Freeman, R. E. (1984). *Strategic Management: A Stakeholder Approach*. Pitman.

Hawkins, D., & Cunningham, J. (1996). It Is 'Never-Never Land' When Interest Groups Prevail: Disney's America Project, Prince William County, Virginia, USA. In L. Harrison & W. Husbands (Eds.), *Practicing Responsible Tourism: International Case Studies in Tourism Planning, Policy and Development* (pp. 350–365). John Wiley.

Hunter, C. (1997). Sustainable Tourism as an Adaptive Paradigm. *Annals of Tourism Research*, *24*(4), 850–867. doi:10.1016/S0160-7383(97)00036-4

Hunter, C. J. (1995). On the need to re-conceptualise sustainable tourism development. [Google Scholar] [CrossRef]. *Journal of Sustainable Tourism*, *3*(3), 155–165. doi:10.1080/09669589509510720

Imran, S., Alam, K., & Beaumont, N. (2014). Environmental Orientations and Environmental Behaviour: Perceptions of Protected Area Tourism Stakeholders. *Tourism Management*, *40*, 290–299. doi:10.1016/j.tourman.2013.07.003

Jamal, T., & Stronza, A. (2009). Collaboration Theory and Tourism Practice in Protected Areas: Stakeholders, Structuring and Sustainability. *Journal of Sustainable Tourism*, *17*(2), 169–189. doi:10.1080/09669580802495741

Kavaratzis, M. (2012). From "necessary evil" to necessity: Stakeholders' involvement in place branding. *Journal of Place Management and Development*, *5*(1), 7–19. doi:10.1108/17538331211209013

Kavaratzis, M., & Hatch, M. J. (2013). The dynamics of place brands: An identity-based approach to place branding theory. *Marketing Theory*, *13*(1), 69–86. doi:10.1177/1470593112467268

Ko, T. G. (2005). Development of a Tourism Sustainability Assessment Procedure: A Conceptual Approach. *Tourism Management*, *26*(3), 431–445. doi:10.1016/j.tourman.2003.12.003

Line, N. D., & Wang, Y. (2017). A multi-stakeholder market oriented approach to destination marketing. J. Destin. [CrossRef]. *Mark. Manag.*, *6*, 84–93.

Lu, J., & Nepal, S. K. (2009). Sustainable Tourism Research: An Analysis of Papers Published in the Journal of Sustainable Tourism. *Journal of Sustainable Tourism*, *17*(1), 5–16. doi:10.1080/09669580802582480

Murphy, P. E. (1983). Perceptions and Attitudes of Decisionmaking Groups in Tourism Centers. *Journal of Travel Research*, *21*(3), 8–12. doi:10.1177/004728758302100302

Nyaupane, G. P., & Poudel, S. (2011). Linkages among Biodiversity, Livelihood, and Tourism. *Annals of Tourism Research*, *38*(4), 1344–1366. doi:10.1016/j.annals.2011.03.006

Polese, M., & Stren, R. (2000). *The Social Sustainability of Cities: Diversity and the Management of Change*. University of Toronto Press. doi:10.3138/9781442682399

Rowley, T. J. (1997). Moving Beyond Dyadic Ties: A Network Theory of Stakeholder Influences. *Academy of Management Review*, *22*(4), 887–910. doi:10.2307/259248

Sautter, E. T., & Leisen, B. (1999). Managing Stakeholders a Tourism Planning Model. *Annals of Tourism Research*, *26*(2), 312–328. doi:10.1016/S0160-7383(98)00097-8

Sautter, E. T., & Leisen, B. (1999). Managing Stakeholders a Tourism Planning Model. *Annals of Tourism Research*, *26*(2), 312–328. doi:10.1016/S0160-7383(98)00097-8

Sen, A. (2013). *A survey of sustainable development: social and economic dimensions* (Vol. 6). Island Press.

Seyedabolghasemi, M. A., Kilic, H., Avci, T., Eluwole, K. K., & Lasisi, T. T. (2022). Residents' perceptions of sustainable tourism destination recovery: The case of Northern Cyprus. [CrossRef]. *Land (Basel), 11*(1), 94. doi:10.3390/land11010094

(Social Sustainability I UN Global Compact) https://www.sustain.ucla.edu/wp-content/uploads/UCLA-Sustainability-Charter.pdf

Stoddard, J. E., Pollard, C. E., & Evans, M. R. (2012). The Triple Bottom Line: A Framework for Sustainable Tourism Development. *International Journal of Hospitality & Tourism Administration, 13*(3), 233–258. doi:10.1080/15256480.2012.698173

Triši'c, I., Šteti'c, S., Privitera, D., Petrovi'c, M. D., Maksin, M., Vujovi'c, S., Jovanovi'c, Z., & Kalini'c, M. Perspectives on sustainable tourism development in the hotel industry—A case study from Southern Europe. Sustainability, 13, 5563.

UNEP & UNWTO. (2005). *Making Tourism More Sustainable: A Guide for Policy Makers*. UNEP and UNWTO.

Waligo, V. M., Clarke, J., & Hawkins, R. (2013). Implementing sustainable tourism: A multi-stakeholder involvement management framework. *Tourism Management, 36*, 342–353. doi:10.1016/j.tourman.2012.10.008

Waligo, V. M., Clarke, J., & Hawkins, R. (2013). Implementing Sustainable Tourism: A Multi-Stakeholder Involvement Management Framework. *Tourism Management, 36*, 342–353. doi:10.1016/j.tourman.2012.10.008

Wassler, P., Wang, L., & Hung, K. (2019). Identity and destination branding among residents: How does brand self-congruity influence brand attitude and ambassadorial behavior? [CrossRef]. *International Journal of Tourism Research, 21*(4), 437–446. doi:10.1002/jtr.2271

Widari, D. A. D. S. (2020). Kebijakan Pengembangan Pariwisata Berkelanjutan: Kajian Teoretis dan Empiris. *Jurnal Kajian Dan Terapan Pariwisata, 1*(1), 1–11. doi:10.53356/diparojs.v1i1.12

Zago, R., Block, T., Dessein, J., & Brunori, G. (2014). Participatory democracy in integrated rural development: the case of LEADER programme: towards Europe 2020 and community-led local development. In *ILVP Winter school 'Place base approaches in regional development'. Proceedings.* Universiteit Gent. https://biblio.ugent.be/publication/6845538

Chapter 12
Outcome-Based Education: A Transformational Outlook on Quality and Mobility of Hospitality Education in India

Gaurav Bathla
Lovely Professional University, India

Ashish Raina
https://orcid.org/0000-0001-5812-5920
CT University, India

Varinder Singh Rana
https://orcid.org/0000-0001-6158-9195
City University, Ajman, UAE

Aman Kumar
Chandigarh University, India

ABSTRACT

Education opens numerous revenues to register economic expansion all around the world with specific reference to developing nations. Advancement of India in education indicators has been severely lacking during the previous decades. Decreased financing along with inefficiency in budget expenditure, plus weak management system, have crippled the education sector ensuing poor educational outcomes. Outcome based education (OBE) is widely recognized as a prominent benchmark within contemporary educational system and has recently gained much attention in India as it proposes an influential and interesting option of transforming and organizing hospitality education. OBE is used in hospitality education because it clearly focuses and organizes everything in an educational system around what is necessary for all students to be able to do at the end of their learning. The purpose of this chapter is to look into the extent of quality and mobility of outcome-based education in hospitality education.

DOI: 10.4018/979-8-3693-2065-5.ch012

INTRODUCTION

The internationalisation of education has brought up various difficulties and innovations that necessitate attention and response from academic institutions to ensure their alignment with established norms. Some of the problems encompass the task of generating graduates who possess employable skills relevant to the demands of the 21st century, adhering to international benchmarks, and designing curricula that align with industry needs in order to meet workplace expectations. This necessitates educators to critically evaluate their instructional approaches and adapt to the advancements in pedagogy and educational practices. The adoption of outcomes-based teaching and learning (OBTL) is a notable solution to the aforementioned challenges.

During the early nineteenth century, the significance of investing in human resources was relatively low across nations. Expenditures allocated towards education, ongoing professional development, and other associated investment categories were of negligible significance. The transformation of this trend began in the present century with the incorporation of technology and scientific advancements in the manufacture of cutting-edge equipment and more sophisticated methods of manufacturing in Britain, then adopted by other nations. The development and economic success of a nation are currently contingent upon the educational attainment, competence, knowledge, and efficiency of its populace. Currently, the present era can also be referred to as the Age of Capital due to the significant influence of a nation's standard of living on its utilisation of skills, practical knowledge, and competencies (Ozturk, 2008). Education plays a key role in facilitating economic growth and development, particularly in underdeveloped countries. According to Rahman (2013) empirical evidence from worldwide data indicates a positive and consistent relationship between education and economic growth. Education possesses the capacity to facilitate the emergence of creativity and innovation within a given society. Hence, it is imperative for developing nations such as India to undertake a significant endeavor in equipping its young population with essential attributes such as knowledge, creativity, vision, critical thinking, and leadership skills. This would enable them to make informed decisions for their own growth, contribute positively to their nation, and fulfil their responsibilities as active citizens. In order to effectively handle obstacles within the education system, it is imperative to possess a comprehensive understanding of the issues at hand. This necessitates the acquisition of precise and unambiguous information, which can then inform the development of relevant strategies and approaches. The progress made by many developing countries including India in terms of education metrics has been notably inadequate during the past few decades. The nation faces a deficiency in highly educated and proficient human capital capable of actively contributing to the country's development. The education sector has been severely impacted by a combination of reduced funding, ineffective budget allocation, and a deficient management system, resulting in subpar educational achievements (Ali & Jabeen, 2015). The government is making persistent efforts to enhance both the quantity and quality of education through the provision of sufficient educational facilities. In the past, emerging nations such as India encountered challenges in achieving their educational objectives due to the inability to implement necessary reforms within the education sector. The current objective of the government is to align with the Sustainable Development Goals (SDGs), specifically focusing on ensuring inclusive and equitable quality education and promoting lifelong learning opportunities for all. This is to be achieved through significant enhancements in the education sector (Nazar, Chaudhry, Ali, & Faheem, 2018).

According to Woo, Kim and Lim (2017) the allocation of resources towards educational initiatives, such as the integration of innovative pedagogical approaches, emerging technologies, revised instructional methods, and the establishment of clear educational objectives, has the potential to foster economic advancement. This, in turn, can lead to the evolution of the educational system and subsequent economic growth. When examining the various degrees of education, it becomes evident that their influence on economic growth varies. Higher education is associated with increased economic expansion and growth. According to Lin (2004) empirical evidence from Taiwan spanning the period of 1985 to 2003 indicates a positive relationship between an additional year of education and a 0.15% rise in outcomes.

Nevertheless, the present education system in India exhibits a greater emphasis on inputs rather than outputs. The educational system provided students with exposure to a certain portion of the curriculum within a designated timeframe. Upon the conclusion of the instructional period, a comprehensive assessment is administered to evaluate the students' performance, notwithstanding the fact that all students have achieved a high level of proficiency in the acquired knowledge and skills. The current perspective and methodology of the school system necessitates a significant overhaul. The concept of "outputs" in education encompasses more than just achieving favorable outcomes. It entails the establishment of a well-structured and coherent educational framework that identifies the essential skills and competencies that all students should possess upon completing their learning journey. Outcome Based Education (OBE) has emerged as a prominent approach to educational reform in the United States. According to Zakaria and Yusoff (2010) contemporary students display a desire to not only acquire theoretical knowledge, but also to engage in an educational framework that emphasizes future employability. Over time, this method has garnered increasing support from other governments. The OBE approach was chosen and implemented in South Africa due to its emphasis on curricular elements such as problem-solving, idea production, and skill acquisition, which are intended to foster critical thinking and the development of capable individuals (Botha, 2002). The shift from traditional teaching methods to a greater emphasis on student learning outcomes is becoming increasingly significant in Malaysia (Mohayidin, Suandi, Mustapha, & Konting, 2008).

Outcome-based Education (OBE) has emerged as a prominent focus of interest within the educational landscape of India in recent times. The utilisation of Outcome-Based Education (OBE) in the field of education is motivated by its ability to effectively concentrate and structure all components within an educational system towards the attainment of essential learning outcomes for all students (Spady, 1994). Educators have long demonstrated a keen interest in comprehending the fundamental elements that influence student learning outcomes. This interest centers on the effective dissemination of knowledge and skills, ensuring their seamless integration into both the public sphere and the economy. Educators worldwide have come to the realization that learning encompasses more than the mere transmission of knowledge. This pertains to the engagement of cognitive processes in the formation of knowledge, which is significantly shaped by cultural, sociological, and emotional aspects. The educational system in developing nations, such as India, continues to be primarily characterized by the traditional approach to teaching, wherein a predetermined curriculum is imparted to pupils through conventional instructional techniques (Portnov-Neeman & Barak, 2013). The transition from the conventional teacher-centered model to the current student-centered model is a significant global trend in higher education. This movement is widely recognised as a crucial development occurring in numerous nations across the globe (Tam, 2014). The contemporary demands of the 21st century encompass not only economic, political, and socio-economic considerations, but also place significant emphasis on educational paradigms. These paradigms pertain to various aspects such as teaching and learning activities, as well as evaluation methods, across different disciplines and the development of specific personal abilities. In contemporary times, the possession of individual potential and skillfulness has emerged as a crucial prerequisite for graduates seeking employment and acceptance within the market. Due to this rationale, numerous countries are undergoing a transformation in their educational paradigm in order to conform to the contemporary demands of the present century. OBE is used in hospitality education because it clearly focuses and organizes everything in an educational system around what is necessary for all students to be able to do at the end of their learning. As outcome based education is trending in India and there is intense need to evaluate factors that impact student learning outcomes. Therefore, the purpose of this chapter is to look in the extent of quality and mobility of outcome based education in hospitality education.

Outcome Based Education: Background and Rationale

Spady (2020) Outcome Based Education (OBE) is a pedagogical approach that involves the conception, development, delivery, and documentation of teaching with a focus on its intended goals and outcomes. Hence, the curriculum is designed based on the desired results that we aim for students to exhibit, rather than establishing objectives for the existing curriculum. In summary, Outcome-Based Education (OBE) provides a manageable approach to instruct, assess, and monitor the essential engineering competencies necessary for the successful career development of students. Hence, Outcome-Based Education (OBE) represents a significant movement in the academic process and practices, departing from the conventional approach known as Traditional Education (TE). The TE refers to an educational approach that emphasizes input-focused learning, with material serving as the primary focus. Assessment in this approach is predominantly reliant on traditional tests, and any outcome is embraced with satisfaction. The primary objective of acquiring knowledge ultimately narrows down to achieving favorable academic performance and obtaining a high cumulative grade point average (CGPA) upon completion of the educational programme (Jasim Mohammad, 2021). Hence, the current educational system places significant emphasis on the Cumulative Grade Point Average (CGPA) as a primary metric for evaluating students. However, this approach is criticised for its limited ability to comprehensively assess a student's strengths and flaws. The implementation of Outcome-Based Education (OBE) allows for the systematic assessment of students' strengths and shortcomings, supported by empirical evidence. This approach enables educators to develop targeted strategies to enhance students' academic progress.

Definition of Operational Terms

Outcome Based Education (OBE) is an educational framework that is centered around the learner and is implemented at the institutional level. It aims to determine the specific results that students are expected to attain by the time they complete their education. Outcomes Based Teaching and Learning (OBTL) refers to the implementation of outcomes-based education at the classroom level. This element is considered to be a constituent of Outcome-Based Education (OBE). The instructional strategies employed in the classroom setting for professional courses encompass teaching, learning, and assessment methodologies. Teaching and learning practices refer to the instructional and assessment procedures employed by educators to facilitate student learning.

Literature Review

The concept of Outcomes-Based Teaching and Learning (OBTL) refers to an educational approach that focuses on the desired outcomes or learning objectives of a course or programme. Outcome-based

Teaching and Learning (OBTL) is based on the Outcomes-Based Education (OBE) framework, which is grounded in three fundamental principles. These principles include the belief that all students have the ability to learn and achieve, the understanding that success leads to further success, and the recognition that schools have the ability to influence the factors that contribute to success (Killen, 2000 as cited by Castillo, 2014). The OBTL framework refers to the application of the Outcome-Based Education (OBE) approach at the classroom or subject level. The OBTL framework necessitates a precise articulation of the intended educational outcome resulting from instruction. The statement delineates the expected abilities or competencies that the learner or student should possess, as per the specified learning objectives. Teaching and Learning Activities (TLA) necessitate that students engage in tasks that they are expected to demonstrate proficiency in at the conclusion of the course. The Three-Letter Acronyms (TLAs) are formulated to facilitate the achievement of the overarching objectives at both the programmatic and institutional levels. The present study aims to explore the optimal strategies and methodologies employed in outcomes-based teaching and learning (OBTL). Mejia et al. (2014) examined the optimal strategies employed in the collaboration between Dusit Thani College and Lyceum of the Philippines University, with the aim of enhancing programme competitiveness. The findings of the study indicated that this partnership yielded improved prospects for students' on-the-job training and internships, as well as opportunities for faculty immersion, both at the local and international levels. The study additionally discussed the significance of the curriculum design and the collaborative relationship between two educational institutions in achieving local and international accolades and acknowledgements. The findings underscored the significance of educational endeavors such as simulations, excursions, laboratory exercises, internships, and participation in contests. Awwad (2010) pointed that the University's accolades and acknowledgments were a result of implementing the outcomes-based approach. The study emphasised that a significant measure of the effectiveness of their outcomes-based curriculum design and implementation was the high employability of their graduates, as evidenced by an employment rate of 80 percent. The best practices implemented by Philadelphia University encompassed many strategies aimed at enhancing the quality of instruction. These strategies involved the organisation and facilitation of seminars and workshops focused on teaching and research. Additionally, collaborative efforts were made with faculties to enhance programme structure, delivery, evaluation, and change. According to a report by the Information Management Programme at the University of Hong Kong, one of their effective practises is establishing desired objectives at many levels, including the programme, course, and general levels. Chu et al (2010) shown that the students successfully attained the learning outcomes for the generic academic skills, namely in the areas of information management, technology, and information literacy. At the programme level, it was seen that two out of the six outcomes were achieved. The study proposed that additional research be conducted in order to gain a deeper understanding of the factors contributing to the students' failure to achieve the desired learning outcomes. This may be accomplished through the use of focus group discussions and individual interviews. The Chinese University of Hong Kong, another esteemed institution of higher education in the region, has undertaken the task of identifying and disseminating its exemplary practises in Outcome-Based Teaching and Learning (OBTL). The optimal strategies are centered on the domains of intended objectives, curriculum design, cultivation of desired outcomes, evaluation and feedback for assessment purposes. The study incorporated the most effective strategies identified in the narratives of highly acclaimed educators and the depictions of instructional and learning contexts provided by students across various programmes.

The Pacific Policy Research Centre (2010) provided a comprehensive summary of the definitions of 21st century learning skills and OBTL. According to the Educational Testing Service (ETS), 21st century learning skills encompass several key abilities. These include the capacity to gather and retrieve information, effectively organise and manage information, critically assess the quality, relevance, and usefulness of information, and produce accurate information by utilizing available resources. The North Central Regional Educational Laboratory (NCREL) has identified a set of comprehensive 21st century skills, which encompass the attainment of 21st century learning through the development of digital age literacy, innovative thinking, proficient communication, and enhanced productivity. The Partnership for 21st Century Skills has outlined six fundamental components that are crucial for promoting 21st century learning. These elements include:

1. prioritizing core subjects.
2. emphasising the development of learning skills.
3. utilizing modern tools to cultivate these learning skills.
4. engaging in teaching and learning within a 21st century context.
5. incorporating 21st century content into the curriculum.
6. employing assessments that effectively measure 21st century skills.

The aforementioned study delineated the optimal strategies for acquiring the 21st century abilities among both students and educators. The attainment of specific targets was also addressed. The optimal strategies encompassed outcomes-based methodologies such as cooperation, problem-based pedagogy, project-based instruction, technology integration, fostering a conducive learning environment, and the acquisition of foreign languages.

Outcome-Based Education (OBE) Framework

Figure 1. Outcome based education framework

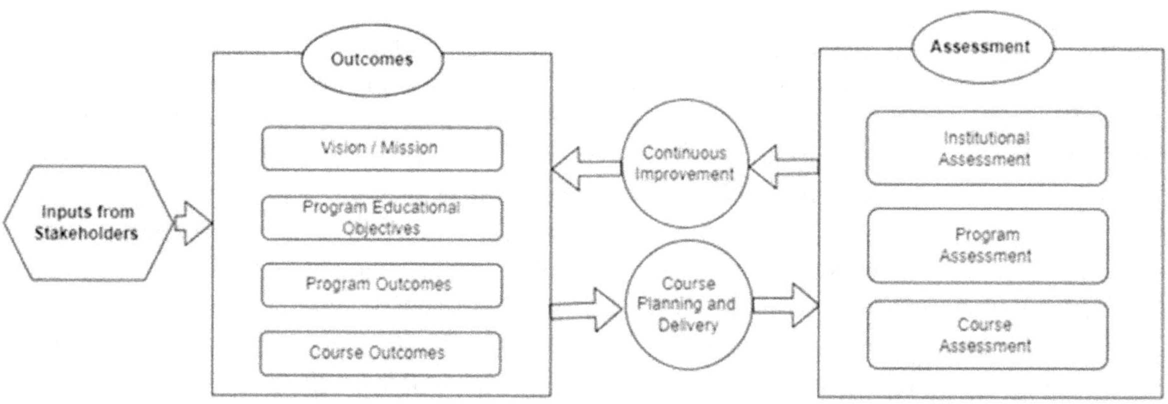

Outcome-Based Education (OBE) is an educational methodology that centers around the pursuit of predetermined learning outcomes for each individual student. An outcome-based approach to learning comprises three essential components. Firstly, it involves a clear and explicit articulation of the desired learning objectives, which should align with the broader educational goals, purposes, and values. Secondly, it entails the implementation of appropriate methods and strategies to facilitate and assess the intended learning outcomes, encompassing elements such as curriculum design, teaching methodologies, learning activities, assessment techniques, and support and guidance mechanisms. Lastly, it necessitates the establishment of criteria for evaluating and measuring the attainment of the desired learning outcomes, ensuring alignment between the assessment criteria and the intended educational objectives.

The outputs of the educational institute are defined by the Vision and Mission Statements, as well as the inputs from many stakeholders.

The program's educational objectives refer to the desired outcomes of a particular educational programme. These objectives outline the knowledge, skills, and abilities that students are expected to acquire upon completion

Programme Educational Objectives encompass overarching declarations that delineate the career and professional achievements that the programme endeavours to equip its graduates to attain within a span of three to five years subsequent to their completion of studies.

The programme outcomes refer to the specific goals and objectives that a programme aims to achieve. These outcomes are often defined by the program's

Programme Outcomes, also known as Student Outcomes, encompass concise statements that delineate the specific knowledge and skills that students are anticipated to possess and demonstrate upon completion of an academic programme. These pertain to the cognitive, psychomotor, and emotional domains of knowledge, skills, and behavior that students learn during the programme.

The course outcomes refer to the specific knowledge, skills, and abilities that students are expected to acquire and demonstrate upon completion of a course

Course Outcomes (COs) refer to declarative statements that delineate the knowledge or abilities that students are expected to gain upon completion of a certain assignment, class, course, or programme. These outcomes serve the purpose of elucidating to students the practical relevance and use of the aforementioned knowledge and skills. The acquisition of both technical and soft skills is necessary for every student prior to the successful completion of a certain course, which is taught within a given subject. The purpose of CO is to provide support and be capable of being measured in relation to PO. The specificity of CO varies depending on the particular course for each individual. Castillo (2014) developed an institutional framework which was introduced as per the directive of the Commission on Higher Education in the Philippines for the implementation of Outcome-Based Education (OBE). The framework comprises various components namely

1. Mission and Vision
2. Program Educational Objectives (PEOs)
3. Program Outcomes
4. Matrix of Courses with Program Outcomes (Curriculum Map)
5. Outcomes-Based Teaching and Learning Delivery Processes,
6. Program Assessment and Evaluation Process
7. Continuing Quality Improvement Program

DISCUSSION

Outcome based education is a student centric learning approach and has been nominated with many other names as well from the earlier decennary such as Competency based education, Transformation education, Results based education and Performance based education (Gieseen-Hood, 1999; Harden, 2002). It is now one of the most widely accepted and successful educational systems in many countries like united states, united kingdom, New Zealand, Malaysia, Australia, South Africa, Philippines and totally it is currently incorporated in over 47 countries around the globe (Baguio, 2019; Midraj, 2018; Rao, 2015; Tam, 2014). OBE is used in hospitality education because it clearly focuses and organizes everything in an educational system around what is necessary for all students to be able to do at the end of their learning.

As outcome based education is trending in India and there is intense need to evaluate factors that impact student learning outcomes. Present chapter aimed to look in the extent of quality and mobility of outcome based education in hospitality education. OBE in hospitality education is still partial implemented both at institutional and classroom level

It is imperative to thoroughly examine the alignment of objectives with anticipated outcomes, as well as the assignment of responsibility in relation to the implementation and monitoring of Outcome-Based Education (OBE). Additionally, careful attention should be given to the transmission of information, the attainment of course outcomes, and the motivation of students. This suggests the necessity of a comprehensive orientation on Outcome-Based Teaching and Learning (OBTL) for both educators and learners. Borsoto et al. (2014) argue that effective identification and dissemination of students' requirements require coordination among teachers, students, and relevant authorities. The predominant instructional methodologies employed in educational settings were lecture, group work, and case study. In order to cultivate the anticipated results, Kember (2005) posited that the teaching and learning environment is a crucial determinant. Additionally, he underscored the importance of offering active learning opportunities to foster the development of students' talents. The need of teamwork was also highlighted through the use of group activities. The relevance of instructional practises such as demonstration, hotel immersion, and field visits also need to be improved. Both instructors and students exhibit consistency in their use of the top three evaluation modalities, namely written tests, assignments, and projects. it is evident that both educators and students exhibit a lack of familiarity with OBTL, despite its partial implementation within the classroom setting. The process of disseminating information will involve providing orientation to relevant stakeholders and conducting a comprehensive information campaign on Outcome-Based Education (OBE) and Outcome-Based Teaching and Learning (OBTL). The necessity for alignment is apparent in this investigation. The establishment of constructive alignment between learning objectives, teaching and learning activities, and assessment instruments is crucial for the development of a conducive learning environment that facilitates outcomes-based teaching and learning

Outcome-Based Teaching and Learning (OBTL) recognized several key factors that contribute to the establishment of an effective educational environment, including the importance of a nurturing atmosphere, the integration of teaching and learning processes, the alignment of curricular components, the cultivation of positive student-student interactions, and the development of strong teacher-student connections. The process of disseminating information will involve providing orientation to relevant stakeholders and conducting a comprehensive information campaign on Outcome-Based Education (OBE) and Outcome-Based Teaching and Learning (OBTL). The necessity for alignment is apparent in this investigation. The establishment of constructive alignment between learning objectives, teaching and learning activities, and assessment instruments is crucial for the development of a conducive learning environment that facilitates outcomes-based teaching and learning. The institution should conduct a comprehensive evaluation and, if necessary, implement measures to assess the outcomes at both the institutional level and the course or subject level. Emphasis should be placed on the development of capacity. It is imperative for instructors to undergo orientation, training, and/or refresher courses on Three-Letter Acronyms (TLAs). Likewise, it is imperative for students to possess adequate preparation in order to effectively engage in an Outcome-Based Teaching and Learning (OBTL) recognised several key factors that contribute to the establishment of an effective educational environment, including the importance of a nurturing atmosphere, the integration of teaching and learning processes, the alignment of curricular components, the cultivation of positive student-student interactions, and the development of strong teacher-student connections. The learning objectives currently in place needs to be revisited to make them more outcomes-based. It appears that while some OBTL practices are in place, OBE and OBTL awareness and delegation, implementation, and monitoring need to be reinforced among hospitality education faculty and students in India.

REFERENCES

Ali, H., & Jabeen, A. (2015). Effects of Education on Economic Growth: Evidence from Pakistan. American Journal of Economics. *Financial Management, 1*(6), 579–585.

Baguio, J. B. (2019). Outcomes-based education: Teachers' attitude and implementation. *University of Bohol Multidisciplinary Research Journal, 7*(1), 110–127. doi:10.15631/ubmrj.v7i1.113

Borsoto, et al. (2014). Status of implementation and usefulness of outcomes-based education in the engineering department of an Asian university. *International Journal of Multidisciplinary Academic Research,* 14-25

Botha, R. J. (2002). Outcomes-based education and educational reform in South Africa. *International Journal of Leadership in Education, 5*(4), 361–371. doi:10.1080/13603120110118831

Castillo, R. (2014). A paradigm shift to outcomes-based higher education: Policies, principles and preparations. [R]. *International Journal of Sciences, Basic and Applied Research*, 174–186.

Castillo, R. (2014). A paradigm shift to outcomes-based higher education: Policies, principles and preparations. *International Journal of Sciences, Basic and Applied Research*, 174–186.

Chu, S. (2010). *Applying outcomes-based teaching and learning framework in the BSc Information Management Program in the Faculty of Education. Centre for information Technology in Education.* The University of Hong Kong.

Giessen-Hood, C. (1999). *Teacher'sattitudes towards the implementation of outcomes based education (OBE) in South Africa* [Doctoral dissertation University of the Witwatersrand].

Harden, R. M. (2002). Developments in outcome-based education. *Medical Teacher, 24*(2), 117–120. doi:10.1080/01421590220120669 PMID:12098427

Jasim, M. M. (2021). Universities to adopt outcome-based education system. *The Business Standard*. https://www.tbsnews.net/bangladesh/education/universities-adopt-outcome-based-education-system-215209

Kember, D., & Leung, D. (2005). The Influence of the Teaching and Learning Environment on the Development of Generic Capabilities Needed for a Knowledge-Based Society. *Learning Environments Research*, *8*(3), 245–266. doi:10.100710984-005-1566-5

Lin, T.-C. (2004). The role of higher education in economic development: An empirical study of Taiwan case. *Journal of Asian Economics*, *15*(2), 355–371. doi:10.1016/j.asieco.2004.02.006

Midraj, S. (2018). Outcome-Based Education (OBE). The TESOL Encyclopedia of English Language Teaching, 1-7.

Mohayidin, M. G., Suandi, T., Mustapha, G., Konting, M., Kamaruddin, N., Man, N. A., Adam, A., & Abdullah, S. N. (2008). Implementation of Outcome-Based Education in Universiti Putra Malaysia: A Focus on Students' Learning Outcomes. *International Education Studies*, *1*(4), 147–160. doi:10.5539/ies.v1n4p147

Nazar, R., Chaudhry, I. S., Ali, S., & Faheem, M. (2018). Role Of Quality Education For Sustainable Development Goals (SDGS). PEOPLE. *The International Journal of Social Sciences (Islamabad)*, *4*(2), 486–501. doi:10.20319/pijss.2018.42.486501

OzturkI. (2008). The role of education in economic development: a theoretical perspective. *SSRN*. doi:10.2139/ssrn.1137541

Pacific Policy Research Center. (2010). *21st Century Skills for Students and Teachers. Honolulu: Kamehameha Schools, Research & Evaluation Division*. Resource Center. http://resourcecentre.foodrisc.org/surveys_32.html

Portnov-Neeman, Y., & Barak, M. (2013). Exploring Students' Perceptions about Learning in School: An Activity Theory Based Study. *Journal of Education and Learning*, *2*(3), 9–25. doi:10.5539/jel.v2n3p9

Rahman, M. S. (2013). Relationship among GDP, per capita GDP, literacy rate and unemployment rate. *British Journal of Arts and Social Sciences*, *14*(2), 169–177.

Rao, N. J. (2020). Outcome-based education: An outline. *Higher Education for the Future*, *7*(1), 5–21. doi:10.1177/2347631119886418

Spady, W. (2020). *Outcome-Based Education's Empowering Essence*. Mason Works Press. https://williamspady.com/index.php/products/

Spady, W. G. (1994). *Outcome-based education: Critical issues and answers*. American Association of School Administrators.

Tam, M. (2014). Outcomes-based approach to quality assessment and curriculum improvement in higher education. *Quality Assurance in Education*, *22*(2), 158–168. doi:10.1108/QAE-09-2011-0059

Woo, Y., Kim, E., & Lim, J. (2017). The impact of education and R&D investment on regional economic growth. *Sustainability (Basel)*, *9*(5), 676. doi:10.3390u9050676

Zakaria, S., & Yusoff, W. W. (2010). Outcome-based education in a private HIL: Perceptions of students. *Advances in Management*, *3*, 31.

Chapter 13
Determinants of Consumer Preference for Traditional Indian Cooking Practices:
A Perspective Towards Healthy Food

Mayanka Chhonker
De Montfort University, UK

Dilip Kumar
Manipal Academy of Higher Education, India

Abhinav Kumar Shandilya
BIT Mesra, India

ABSTRACT

Food plays a vital role in the growth and development of human beings and helps fight many diseases, shaping consumers' intentions and actual behaviour. Consumers prefer a healthy lifestyle in the current COVID-19 situation, where immunity is one of the most critical factors in fighting the deadly coronavirus. The constructs of the health belief model (HBM) and the theory of planned behaviour (TPB) plays an essential role in shaping consumers' preferences for food. To identify the determinants of consumers' choice for traditional Indian cooking practices, a mixed-method approach was followed in the study. Qualitative research prepared the base for quantitative research. First, an open-ended personal interview of 12 respondents was conducted to develop a questionnaire used for the quantitative survey. Exploratory factor analysis results helped identify the seven factors, i.e., behaviour, cues in action, social influence, perceived benefits, self-efficacy, perceived susceptibility, and readiness, as determinants of consumers' preference for traditional Indian cooking practices.

DOI: 10.4018/979-8-3693-2065-5.ch013

1. INTRODUCTION

Consumers prefer a healthy lifestyle in the current COVID-19 situation, where immunity is one of the most critical factors in fighting the deadly coronavirus; healthy food is at the core of the healthy lifestyle concept in traditional Indian cooking practices. (Kone & Samayamanthula, 2021) found that detox drink keeps a person refreshed and active, and protein-rich food in breakfast increases the basal metabolic rate in the context of traditional Indian food as an immune booster. Also, local and seasonal food has a better influence on health. The stock of spices with medicinal benefits has been an important section of the Indian kitchen pantry. However, the presence of the fast-food industry across India serving foods with hedonic attributes cannot be denied. Hedonic hunger leads to increased overeating, snacking frequency, and palatable food intake without less self-control (Horwath et al., 2020). According to (Bakaloudi et al., 2021), lockdowns imposed during COVID-19 have increased snacking habits. Food in which the amount of salt, sugar, or fat is high is considered harmful to health (Ares et al., 2015).

(Barrett et al., 2020) reported that there needs to be more awareness about the benefits of whole grains among consumers, resulting in less fibre intake. Some food items like fruits, vegetables, milk, and milk products are considered suitable for health. Non-vegetarians feel fish, shellfish, and some meat products are good (Ares et al., 2015). Well-being about eating healthy food is linked with good physical health (Ares et al., 2014). Health-conscious eating behaviour emphasises local and regional foods, includes seasonal fruits and vegetables in their diet, takes a balanced diet, and avoids processed items (Jung et al., 2020; Kokkoris & Stavrova, 2021).

We have not found any research highlighting the psychological factors associated with diners for Indian Traditional food. Hence, we took the present study to explore the psychological factors of consumers' preference for traditional Indian cooking and food.

2. THEORETICAL BACKGROUND AND RESEARCH QUESTIONS

Food plays a vital role in the growth and development of human beings and helps fight many diseases, shaping consumers' intentions and actual behaviour. The theory of planned behaviour (TPB) establishes the relationship between consumers' preferences and food habits. The variables of TPB, i.e., attitude, perceived behaviour control, and subjective norms, have a strong to medium association with intention and behaviour of dietary patterns (McDermott et al., 2015; Yadav & Pathak, 2016). Perceived behavioural control has the strongest predictive power of purchasing healthy or well-being food (Ates, 2019; Lim & An, 2021).

The strength of relationships of variables of TPB with intention may vary in other geographical locations. (Boobalan et al., 2021) noted attitude as a predictor of intent to adopt organic food in the United States, whereas subjective norms in India. Further, (Voon et al., 2011) explained that attitude and subjective norms are positively related to willingness to pay in the case of organic food, and affordability has no impact. The choice of healthy food behaviour largely depends on friends' and family members' opinions (Samoggia & Riedel, 2020).

The health belief model (HBM) is used to predict health-related intention and behaviour of consumers by using the six constructs - perceived susceptibility (PSc), perceived severity (PS), perceived benefits (PB), perceived barriers (PBa), cues to actions (CA), and self-efficacy (CE) (Champion & Skinner, 2008; Le et al., 2021; Wang et al., 2021). TPB and HBM are good theories for predicting consumer preference, and in a specific sense, constructs of HMB are better predictors (Ataei et al., 2021). (Huang et al., 2020; Qiao et al., 2021) the healthy eating intention and behaviour are better explained by combining constructs of TPB and HBM, and perceived susceptibility, perceived severity, and perceived benefit affect the attitude of consumers. Individuals' health concerns affect their preference for well-being food consumption (Apaolaza et al., 2018). (Chang et al., 2020) reported that cues to actions and self-efficacy are not significant predictors of purchase intention in the case of students' preference for functional beverages.

Hence, the constructs of TPB and HBM should be explored to determine the factors responsible for diners' preference to adopt Indian traditional cooking practices post-COVID-19, and we propose the following research questions based on the above backdrop.

2.1 Which psychosocial factors are associated with diners' preference to adopt traditional Indian cooking practices post-COVID-19?

3. RESEARCH DESIGN AND DATA COLLECTION

The present study explores the factors responsible for practising traditional Indian cooking, which can help build their immunity. There is no established instrument to measure diners' preference for food; hence, the study adopted a mixed-method approach.

In phase I, a qualitative research technique was used to understand the underlying variables that shape the factors responsible for diner's preference for traditional Indian cooking practices post-COVID-19. Open-ended, In-depth personal interviews were conducted based on the constructs of TPB (Ajzen, 1991) and HBM (Hochbaum et al., 1952). A cross-sectional study was preferred over a longitudinal study. It was conducted through open-ended, semi-structured interviews (qualitative study) (George, 2022), which can also help minimise uncertainty about a robust and well-established concept (Sofaer, 1999). This dynamic approach enabled the team to explore new ideas in interviews (Creswell & Poth, 2016). The recording of the interviews was further analysed to develop the instrument for phase II.

In phase II, the structured questionnaire developed in phase I was used to collect the data from potential respondents. The instrument consists of 36 items consisting of seven possible dimensions, namely *perceived susceptibility, perceived benefits, cues in action, self-efficacy, readiness to act, social influence and behaviour* were measured using a 5-point Likert scale (Strongly disagree to Strongly agree); the survey also included the demographics gender, age, and number of family members. The study used careful consideration to reach the potential cases who have preliminary knowledge of Indian traditional cooking methods/processes, ingredients and equipment and are actively engaged in cooking at home or possess thorough knowledge about generational cooking methods and recipes.

The collection of data was done by utilising the convenience sampling method by the team. Further, to identify the other potential respondents, a network or snowball sampling technique was used as selection criteria for the study, where each informant was asked to refer a potential respondent who could be suitable for the study from their respective social circle. Out of 153 total collected responses, 16 responses were removed from the collected data due to incomplete responses. Data from 137 usable responses were included in the final data set after excluding missing responses.

Finally, SPSS software version 27 was used to do statistical analysis for respondents' profiles and establish sample adequacy of the data set, computation of factors by exploratory factor analysis and reliability of the measured items in the instrument.

4 DATA ANALYSIS AND DISCUSSION

4.1 Phase One: Qualitative Research

4.1.1 Sample Characteristics of Open-Ended Interview

Firstly, a qualitative research method (Open-ended interview) was conducted on 12 respondents between June and July 2022. They all were working professionals and belonged to different states (Rajasthan, Uttar Pradesh, Gujarat, Goa, Maharashtra, Bengal, Punjab, Haryana, Delhi, Kerala, and Jammu) and were found in the age group of 30-54. The average age of the respondents was found as 42 years mentioned in **Table 1**. Twenty-five minutes was the average time the respondents took to answer all the questions related to the study.

Table 1. Details of the respondents'

Gender	Number	Average Age
Female	9	40.88
Male	3	45.33

75% of the participants were female (working), directly or indirectly involved in cooking. At the same time, 25% of the participants were men (working) and involved fully or partially in cooking following traditional recipes/practices. Respondents' characteristics are exhibited in **Table 2**.

Table 2. Participant's information involved in a qualitative study

Participant No.	Gender	Age	State	Profession
P1	Male	45	Goa	Working
P2	Female	42	Maharashtra	Working
P3	Female	45	Kerala	Working
P4	Male	48	Delhi	Working
P5	Male	43	Maharashtra	Working
P6	Female	45	Haryana	Working
P7	Female	54	Jammu	Working
P8	Female	42	UP & Rajasthan	Working
P9	Female	35	Gujarat	Working
P10	Female	38	Rajasthan	Working
P11	Female	37	Bengal	Working
P12	Female	30	Punjab, Gujarat, Madhya Pradesh	Working

4.1.2 Phase One: Personal Interview

Various factors were considered while selecting the participants, such as cooking knowledge, involvement in cooking, location, education, profession, and age. At the beginning of the interview, they were informed about the interview's purpose, and we obtained their consent. The responses collected are exhibited in **Table 3**. Participants often refer to the same notion using a variety of phrases and idioms when completing qualitative activities. That is why grouping responses into specific and exclusive categories is typically used to analyse reactions to qualitative tasks (Krippendorff, 2018).

While exploring the participants' interviews, different terms with similar meanings were merged according to all three researchers' interpretations and mutual consent. After critically analysing and reviewing all the interviews and combining words with similar meanings, a final questionnaire (research instrument) was designed for quantitative research. Output, statement, and keywords generated during the semi-structured interview prepared a base for conducting a quantitative study through a questionnaire and developing items based on the construct. Variables are essential in justifying the construct's relevance and importance in understanding the participant's opinion and mindset.

Table 3. Responses of the participants obtained during open-ended interviews

Questions	Responses
"Do you practice Indian traditional cooking techniques/methods in your kitchen?"	"Yes" or "to some extent."
"Do you think Indian traditional food practices are beneficial to or help build immunity. If yes, why?" (PB)	"Yes" as it was used by our ancestors and used as a home remedy.
"Do you think not practising Indian traditional food practices causes health problems? If yes, why?" Perceived threats (PT)	"yes" to "cannot comment" responses were given by the participants.
"Have you started practising traditional methods of Indian cooking (because of COVID-19). If yes, why?" (PT)	A mixed reaction (Yes, partially agree, no)
"Do you believe that practising Indian traditional cooking methods *(because of COVID-19)* will reduce health problems. If yes, why?" (PT)	"Yes"
"Do you cook food at home using traditional recipes passed on from the previous generation. If yes, why?" (PT)	"Somewhat to yes and already practising."
"Do you share your belief and value system about Indian traditional cooking practices in your social circle that could be beneficial in fighting *COVID-19.* If yes, why?" (PB)	Mixed reactions varied from "no to yes." 80% of participants agreed on "yes,"
"What kind of challenges or difficulties do you face in practising the Indian traditional cooking methods?"	Less/no dependency on organic food, too many uses of pesticides, time constraints, lack of authentic materials (raw materials and equipment), lack of knowledge and awareness, mindset, diversified eating habits, cleaning, and maintenance of equipment.
"Efforts taken by the individual to follow the traditional Indian cooking methods since COVID-19."	Increased intake of hot water, more dependency on fresh food and vegetables, use of authentic recipes, more workouts, consumption of locally grown fruits and vegetables, timely eating, and increased fluid intake in the diet.
"Efforts have taken due to the external influence (illness in family/friends/ workplace) to continue to allow the Indian traditional methods of cooking since COVID–19."	Feel surrounded by healthy people who kept them informed about the benefits of traditional cooking practices in building immunity.
"Does your social circle? *Influence* your efforts to follow the Indian traditional cooking practices since COVID-19. If yes, how?" (Perceived norms)	60% of participants said "yes," whereas 25% said that others get influenced by them, and the remaining 5% said "no." "not much."

Table 4 depicts various keywords that appeared during the interview were segregated into various categories, and category-related keywords were arranged. Such as, ingredients category-related words have the maximum appearance, i.e., 21 shows the participant's inclination to try various components, mainly traditional ingredients that can help build immunity. Utensils-related keywords (appeared ten times) and lifestyle-related keywords (appeared nine times) insist on the uses of utensils in following Indian traditional cooking practices and changes required in the lifestyle to adopt it in our daily routine. Although various categories were identified as impactful as above mentioned three categories, finally, 36 items were identified for the next stage of questionnaire preparation and quantitative survey.

Table 4. Category-wise appearance of keywords

Category	Category related words	Number of appearances
Traditional	Going traditional, traditional ingredients, medicinal effect.	3
Habits	Eating habits, food consumption, psychology, emotionally.	4
Ayurveda	Virudha aahar, ayurvedic tablet.	2
Culture	Rich cooking culture, perception, mindset, workplace culture.	4
Cooking practices	Cooking techniques, cooking habits, generation to generation.	3
Ingredients	Ghee, khada masala (whole spices), jaggery, carom seeds, cinnamon powder, Tulsi (Basil), turmeric, pulses, Ginger, Garlic, seasonal vegetables, blend of spices, detox water, Vitamin-C, Honey, Dalia, Coconut milk, organic food, availability of ingredients, boiled vegetables, citrus fruits.	21
Utensils	Chulha, copper utensils, non-stick pan, grinding stone, desi-tawa, earthenware, water purifier, brass, cast iron vessel, kulhar.	10
Lifestyle	Obesity, practices are forgotten, stopped melamine crockery, Satvik food, microwave uses, practising before preaching, consistency, timely eating, changed lifestyle.	9
Immunity	More consumption of hot water, avoiding buying readymade food, increased fluid intake in the diet, more physical workout.	4
Attention	More time is given to cooking, and more alert and cautious, about pesticide uses, utensils washing, knowledge, reading good books, reduced refrigerator inventory, and more focus on local food.	8
Balanced food	Proper food combination, consumption of more proteinaceous food, supplement, Khichadi	4
Awareness	Conscious, more emphasis on local food, adulteration, unwanted chemical uses	4
Health problem	Gastric, acidity	2

4.2 Stage Two: Quantitative Research

4.2.1 Sample Characteristics

Table 5. Profile of respondents

Characteristics	Frequency	Percentage
Gender		
Male	59	43.1%
Female	78	56.9%
Total	**137**	
Family Members		
1-2	14	10.2%
3-4	87	63.5%
5-6	29	21.2%
7 or more	7	5.1%
Total	**137**	
Age group		
18 - 29	42	30.66
30 - 39	38	27.74
40 - 49	45	32.85
50 - 59	10	7.30
60 above	2	1.46
Total	**137**	
Occupation		
Working professionals (expert/skilled)	60	43.80
Academician	28	20.44
Homemaker	24	17.52
Student	14	10.22
Business	8	5.84
Doctor	3	2.19
Total	**137**	

The characteristics of the respondents were identified with the help of demographic profiles collected during data collection. Of 137 respondents, 43.1% (59) were males, and 56.9% (78) were females. Further, 63.5% (87) were reported to have 3-4 family members, 21.2% (29) consisted of 5-6 family members, 10.2% (14) reported to have 1-2, and lastly, 5.1% (7) were reported to have more than seven members in their family. 32.85% (45) of 137 respondents belonged to the age category of 40-49, followed by 30.66% (42) between 18-29, 27.74% (38) between 30-39, 7.3% (10) between 50-59 and 1.46% (2) above 60 years of age. Lastly, the study also collected the occupation of the respondents. It was reported that

43.8% (60) respondents were working professionals, followed by 20.44% (28) academicians (professors, research scholars, independent researchers), 17.52% (24) homemakers, 10.2% (14) students, 5.84% (8) either self-employed or entrepreneurs and lastly 2.19% (3) medical doctors.

4.2.2 Factor Analysis

The data was analysed on 36 items (25 items taken in EFA, 11 dropped) using exploratory factor analysis with the help of SPSS version 27 to identify the underlying factors in the dataset. To check whether the sample was adequate for the study Kaiser – Meyer – Olkin test was analysed. Values above 0.7 are suitable for good sample adequacy, and it was reported within the acceptable range, KMO 0.773 (Field, 2009). Hence, based on the results, it was indicated that the sample was adequate to run the factor analysis. Similarly, Bartlett's test of Sphericity, Chi-Square (1322.958) $p < 0.001$, reported that there was a correlation between the items to run the factor analysis. (Refer to **Table 6**)

Table 6. KMO and Bartlett's test

		.773
Bartlett's Test of Sphericity	Approx. Chi- Square	1322.958
	Df	300
	Significance	.000

Firstly, to identify components, the data was analysed to obtain eigen values. **Figure 1** shows the scree plot curve, which indicates the decline after seven components. The results reported seven components that explained 65.72% of the variance. The scree plot curve indicated the decline after seven retained components which were considered for further final analysis.

Figure 1. Plot curve

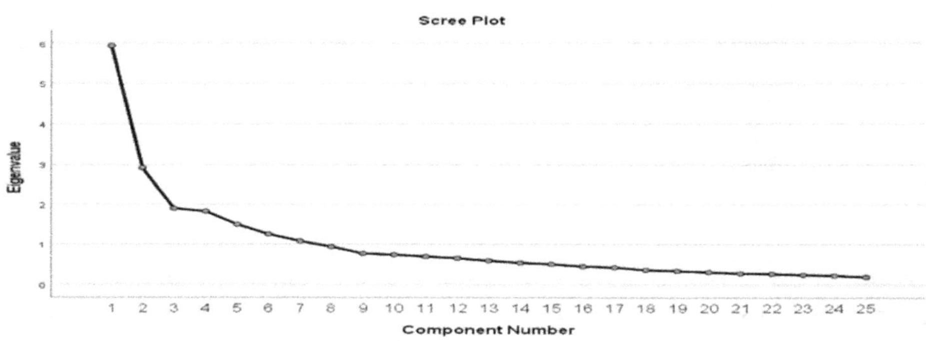

The last criterion to identify the number of factors was to group the measured items into their corresponding variables exploratory factor analysis (EFA) was conducted to extract from 36 items. **Table 8**, given below, shows the rotated factor matrix *(factor loadings)*. Items clustered together with less than 0.4-factor loading are suppressed. The table displays a 7-factor solution (Field, 2009). A 7-factor solution ranging from 0.571 to 0.859 satisfies the recommended factor loading criterion in the rotated pattern matrix.

However, due to poor factor loadings, a few items were dropped, i.e. PS1 *(practising Indian traditional cooking methods, helps in overall health problems (diabetes, obesity, gut health etc.),* RA1 (more uses of local and seasonal material/consistently avoiding things, which are not local), RA3 *(I put extra efforts in cooking),* RA4 *(I focus on more physical workout), RA6 (Use of authentic spices),* PB1 *(more than techniques and application, ingredients also have connection with immunity),* PB3 *(I use ghee to build immunity),* SI2 (my family - grandparents and parents, influence on my diet and lifestyle), CA2 (lack of authentic, organic, and unadulterated raw materials), SE2 *(increased the consumption of fruits, vegetables, and fresh products), and* B1 *(I will continue to put conscious & responsible effort).*

Post factors extraction, the requirement is to identify whether the items loaded to corresponding components are reliable. **Table 7** shows the overall reliability of the scale in the instrument. The results reported that all seven components' Cronbach's alpha values were within acceptable range from 0.70 to 0.81, greater than 0.70 (Cronbach, 1951; Field, 2009).

Table 7. Construct Reliability and Validity

	Construct	Cronbach's Alpha
Factor score 1	Behaviour	0.819
Factor score 2	Cues in action	0.817
Factor score 3	Social Influence	0.712
Factor score 4	Perceived Benefits	0.735
Factor score 5	Self-efficacy	0.70
Factor score 6	Perceived susceptibility	0.761
Factor score 7	Readiness to act	0.801

The details of each factor extracted are as follows:

***Component 1*: Behaviour:** This computed factor indicates the respondent's overall behaviour in practicing traditional Indian cooking methods. Five items adopted from phase 1 i.e., B1 was dropped due to poor factor loading (<0.4) and rest four items were loaded above the recommended value 0.5, the Factor Loading for this factor was 0.798 (B4), 0.763 (B5) 0.625 (B2) and 0.563 (B3) exhibited in **Table 8**. Amongst four items the highest factor loading was on item B4 and B5 which indicated that respondents believe in practicing Indian traditional cooking methods that leads to good health followed by their conscious effort in urging others also to follow it.

1. For me, Indian traditional cooking practices leads to good health, I will always follow.
2. I follow myself and urge others to follow.
3. I will try to follow Indian traditional cooking practices.
4. I will continue to follow Indian traditional cooking practices as COVID was an eye-opener towards healthy living and food/cooking practice.

***Component 2*: Cues in action:** This computed factor indicates the profile of the respondents, it has reported the behaviour which prompted their decision making towards practicing traditional Indian cooking methods. The factor shows the significance of how lack of awareness & knowledge towards traditional cooking is observed in the last few years. Further, the diminished practices from generation to generation, regional & climatic impact on traditional methods of cooking. Lastly, the mindset to cook due to the laborious process and lack of traditional equipment. Out of six items identified based on the in-depth interviews five items were loaded above the recommended value 0.5, the Factor Loading for this factor was 0.725 (CA3), 0.722 (CA4), 0.674 (CA6), 0.58 (CA5), 0.571 (CA1) exhibited in **Table 8** except CA2.

1. Lack of awareness & knowledge
2. Practices getting diluted diminished from generation to generation.
3. Climate and region impact practicing the traditional methods of cooking.
4. Mindset to cook due to its laborious process of cooking (efforts in cooking)
5. Lack of traditional equipment

***Component 3*: Social Influence:** This computed factor indicates the respondent's perception towards the influence of social circle judgements, opinions and what they think of them in terms of practicing traditional Indian cooking methods. Five items adopted from phase 1 i.e., SI2 was dropped due to poor factor loading (<0.4) and rest four items were loaded above the recommended value 0.5, the Factor Loading for this factor was 0.797 (SI3), 0.738 (SI4), 0.659 (SI1) and 0.649 (SI5) exhibited in **Table 8** except SI2.

Amongst four items the highest factor loading was on item SI3 and SI4 which indicates that post covid individuals do extensive discussion on traditional cooking methods of Indian cuisines in their social circle. They share family/generational recipes and appreciates each other to boost their morale in sustaining traditional ways of cooking food (family, friends, or colleagues).

1. I surround myself at my workplace with people having healthy lifestyle and positive attitude.
2. My friends influence diet and lifestyle.
3. People I am surrounded with do extensive discussion regarding Indian traditional cooking practices.
4. People I am surrounded with recognise, appreciate and they contribute by sharing their recipe.

***Component 4*: Perceived benefits:** This computed factor indicates the profile of the respondents which reported their perceived behaviour of benefits they get practicing traditional Indian cooking methods. The factor shows the significance of specific herb usage especially post Covid 19 such as home remedies, use of ginger, Tulsi (Indian basil) and preference over seasonal vegetables to avoid long food miles. Out of five items identified based on the in-depth interviews three items were loaded above the recommended value 0.5, the Factor Loading for this factor was 0.859 (PB2), 0.835 (PB4), 0.764 (PB5) exhibited in **Table 8** except PB1 and PB3.

1. Indian kitchen has so many remedial medicine
2. Ginger, Garlic, and Tulsi found more beneficial post COVID.
3. I use seasonal vegetables.

***Component 5*: Readiness to act:** This computed factor indicates the profile of the respondents which reported their readiness to act in practicing traditional Indian cooking methods. The factor shows the significant impact of COVID on respondent's due to which individuals have begun to put efforts in innovative and healthy alternatives, realisation of wrong food combinations and active initiatives towards healthy lifestyle. Out of seven items identified based on the in-depth interviews three items were loaded above the recommended value 0.5, the Factor loading for this factor was 0.84 (RA2), 0.70 (RA5), 0.678 (RA7) exhibited in **Table 8** except RA1, RA3, RA4, RA6.

1. COVID forced me to think of creative and innovative healthy options.
2. I am careful now about combination of wrong food.
3. I have observed changed lifestyle post-COVID.

***Component 6*: Perceived susceptibility (PS):** This computed factor indicates the profile of the respondents which informs about their susceptible behaviour if they don't practice traditional Indian cooking methods. The factor shows not practicing will cause health problems, loss of immunity and affects their mental health in terms of nutritional value traditional Indian cooking methods retained in the food. Out of four items identified based on the in-depth interviews three items were loaded above the recommended value 0.5, the Factor loading for this factor was 0.855 (PS3), 0.828 (PS4), 0.804 (PS2) exhibited in **Table 8** except PS1. It revealed that loss of immunity is a major concern for the respondents if they don't cook food by traditional methods.

1. Due to lifestyle change *(automation, gadgets)* if I don't practice Indian traditional cooking methods it will cause health problems.
2. If I don't practice Indian traditional cooking methods, it causes loss of immunity.
3. If I don't Indian traditional cooking methods, it affects my mental health (such as focus, concentration).

***Component 7*: Self-efficacy:** This computed factor indicates the profile of the respondents which reported efficiency of respondents in practicing traditional Indian cooking methods. Four items adopted from phase 1 i.e., in-depth interview, out of which SE2 was dropped due to poor factor loading (<0.4) and rest three items were loaded above the recommended value 0.5, the Factor loading for this factor was 0.764 (SE4), 0.761 (SE1) and 0.571 (SE3) exhibited in **Table 8** except SE 2.

1. I able to follow traditional methods the way learnt from family.
2. I am confident that I will continue to follow traditional methods.
3. Overall, I am confident I can cook traditional recipes.

Table 8. Rotated component matrix

	Components						
	1	2	3	4	5	6	7
Q7_4	**0.798**						
Q7_5	**0.763**						
Q7_2	**0.625**						
Q7_3	**0.563**						
Q3_3		**0.725**					
Q3_4		**0.722**					
Q3_6		**0.674**					
Q3_5		**0.58**					
Q3_1		**0.571**					
Q6_3			**0.797**				
Q6_4			**0.738**				
Q6_1			**0.659**				
Q6_5			**0.649**				
Q2_2				**0.859**			
Q2_4				**0.835**			
Q2_5				**0.764**			
Q4_2					**0.84**		
Q4_5					**0.70**		
Q4_7					**0.678**		
Q1_3						**0.855**	
Q1_4						**0.828**	
Q1_2						**0.804**	
Q5_4							**0.764**
Q5_1							**0.761**
Q5_3							**0.571**

5. CONCLUSION

The present study adopted a qualitative and quantitative mixed approach and found the determinants of consumer preference for traditional Indian cooking practices. The seven factors were identified: behaviour, cues in action, social influence, perceived benefits, self-efficacy, perceived susceptibility, and readiness to act. These factors are supported by previous studies done on constructs of HBM and TPB together (Huang et al., 2020; Qiao et al., 2021) and HMB only (Champion & Skinner, 2008; Le et al., 2021; Wang et al., 2021) in similar contexts. The results indicate that constructs of HBM play an essential role in determining consumers liking for traditional Indian cooking practices.

There was no specific study wherein determinants of consumer preference for traditional Indian cooking practices were found. Also, scale development was not done to measure the constructs. Hence, we generated, tested and revised the items for the potential constructs (Streiner et al., 2015), and then reliability (Saville & MacIver, 2017) and validity studies (Dimitrov, 2014) were done to fill the research gap. Annexure 1 depicts the items of constructs identified, i.e., behaviour (4 items), cues in action (5 items), social influence (4 items), perceived benefits (3 items), self-efficacy (3 items), perceived susceptibility (3 items) and readiness to act (3 items). The scale is reliable and valid and can measure real-world cases precisely.

As opposed to the previous finding that cues in actions and self-efficacy are not the determinants of purchase intention in the case of students' preference for functional beverages (Chang et al., 2020), this study conceptualised that these factors are vital in shaping the consumer preference for traditional Indian cooking practices.

6. IMPLICATIONS

The finding of the seven determinants of consumer preference for traditional Indian cooking practices adds theoretical knowledge to the present literature. These determinants and the measurement scale developed can be used as a starting point for future studies in the field of consumer preferences for traditional Indian cooking practices.

The practical implications of this study have a meaningful impact on marketing strategies. Eating joints can be more successful by focusing on the identified determinants of consumer preference for traditional Indian cooking. Including more conventional Indian food and cooking techniques with available local ingredients as part of the catering policy and highlighting them in the advertising strategy shall help attract health-conscious diners. Even if the impact of COVID-19 ends, the threat of similar viral diseases will prevail in society, and health-conscious people will look forward towards healthy food and cooking practices to develop their natural immunity.

7. LIMITATION AND FUTURE SCOPE OF THE STUDY

Scale development and standardisation is not a one-step conclusive work. The present study used exploratory factor analysis to identify the factors determining consumer preferences for traditional Indian cooking practices. Further research can be done to examine the relationship between the identified determinants and their strengths. Moreover, a similar study can also be conducted on a larger sample size and diverse population group to test and retest the scale developed in the present study.

REFERENCES:

Ajzen, I. (1991). The theory of planned behavior. *Organizational Behavior and Human Decision Processes*, *50*(2), 179–211. doi:10.1016/0749-5978(91)90020-T

Apaolaza, V., Hartmann, P., D'Souza, C., & López, C. M. (2018). Eat organic – Feel good? The relationship between organic food consumption, health concern and subjective wellbeing. *Food Quality and Preference*, *63*, 51–62. doi:10.1016/j.foodqual.2017.07.011

Ares, G., de Saldamando, L., Giménez, A., Claret, A., Cunha, L. M., Guerrero, L., de Moura, A. P., Oliveira, D. C. R., Symoneaux, R., & Deliza, R. (2015). Consumers' associations with wellbeing in a food-related context: A cross-cultural study. *Food Quality and Preference, 40*(PB), 304–315. doi:10.1016/j.foodqual.2014.06.001

Ares, G., De Saldamando, L., Giménez, A., & Deliza, R. (2014). Food and wellbeing. Towards a consumer-based approach. *Appetite*, *74*, 61–69. doi:10.1016/j.appet.2013.11.017 PMID:24295927

Ataei, P., Gholamrezai, S., Movahedi, R., & Aliabadi, V. (2021). An analysis of farmers' intention to use green pesticides: The application of the extended theory of planned behavior and health belief model. *Journal of Rural Studies*, *81*, 374–384. doi:10.1016/j.jrurstud.2020.11.003

Ates, H. (2019). Elementary school teachers' behavioral intentions for healthy nutrition: Extending theory of planned behavior. *Health Education*, *119*(2), 133–149. doi:10.1108/HE-11-2018-0056

Bakaloudi, D. R., Jeyakumar, D. T., Jayawardena, R., & Chourdakis, M. (2021). The impact of COVID-19 lockdown on snacking habits, fast-food and alcohol consumption: A systematic review of the evidence. *Clinical Nutrition (Edinburgh, Lothian)*. doi:10.1016/j.clnu.2021.04.020 PMID:34049747

Barrett, E. M., Foster, S. I., & Beck, E. J. (2020). Whole grain and high-fibre grain foods: How do knowledge, perceptions and attitudes affect food choice? *Appetite*, *149*, 104630. doi:10.1016/j.appet.2020.104630 PMID:32057840

Boobalan, K., & Nawaz, N., M, H. R., & Gajenderan, V. (. (2021). Influence of Altruistic Motives on Organic Food Purchase: Theory of Planned Behavior. *Sustainability*, *13*. doi:10.3390u13116023

Champion, V. L., & Skinner, C. S. (2008). The health belief model. *Health Behavior and Health Education: Theory, Research, and Practice*, *4*, 45–65.

Chang, H. P., Ma, C. C., & Chen, H. S. (2020). The impacts of young consumers' health values on functional beverages purchase intentions. *International Journal of Environmental Research and Public Health*, *17*(10), 3479. doi:10.3390/ijerph17103479 PMID:32429409

Creswell, J. W., & Poth, C. N. (2016). *Qualitative inquiry and research design: Choosing among five approaches*. Sage publications.

Cronbach, L. J. (1951). Coefficient alpha and the internal structure of tests. *Psychometrika*, *16*(3), 297–334. doi:10.1007/BF02310555

Dimitrov, D. M. (2014). *Statistical methods for validation of assessment scale data in counseling and related fields*. John Wiley & Sons.

Field, A. (2009). *Discovering Statistics Using SPSS (Introducing Statistical Methods)*. Sage Publications Ltd.

George, T. (2022). *Semi-Structured Interview*. Scribbr. https://www.scribbr.com/methodology/semi-structured-interview/

Hochbaum, G., Rosenstock, I., & Kegels, S. (1952). Health belief model. United States Public Health Service, 1.

Horwath, C. C., Hagmann, D., & Hartmann, C. (2020). The Power of Food: Self-control moderates the association of hedonic hunger with overeating, snacking frequency and palatable food intake. *Eating Behaviors*, *38*, 101393. doi:10.1016/j.eatbeh.2020.101393 PMID:32497904

Huang, X., Dai, S., & Xu, H. (2020). Predicting tourists' health risk preventative behaviour and travelling satisfaction in Tibet: Combining the theory of planned behaviour and health belief model. *Tourism Management Perspectives*, *33*, 100589. doi:10.1016/j.tmp.2019.100589

Jung, S. E., Shin, Y. H., & Dougherty, R. (2020). A Multi Theory–Based Investigation of College Students' Underlying Beliefs About Local Food Consumption. *Journal of Nutrition Education and Behavior*, *52*(10), 907–917. doi:10.1016/j.jneb.2020.07.002 PMID:32859527

Kokkoris, M. D., & Stavrova, O. (2021). Meaning of food and consumer eating behaviors. *Food Quality and Preference*, *94*, 104343. doi:10.1016/j.foodqual.2021.104343

Kone, M. L., & Samayamanthula, D. R. (2021). Significance of conventional Indian foods acting as immune boosters to overcome COVID-19. *Environmental Resilience and Transformation in Times of COVID-19*, *385*. doi:10.1016/B978-0-323-85512-9.00034-6

Krippendorff, K. (2018). *Content analysis: An introduction to its methodology*. Sage publications.

Le, H. T. C. H., Dang, T. N., Ware, R., Phung, D., Thai, P. K., Sly, P. D., & Le An, P. (2021). Using the health beliefs model to explore children's attitudes and beliefs on air pollution. *Public Health*, *196*, 4–9. doi:10.1016/j.puhe.2021.04.026 PMID:34126559

Lim, H. R., & An, S. (2021). Intention to purchase wellbeing food among Korean consumers: An application of the Theory of Planned Behavior. *Food Quality and Preference*, *88*, 104101. doi:10.1016/j.foodqual.2020.104101 PMID:33071469

McDermott, M. S., Oliver, M., Simnadis, T., Beck, E. J., Coltman, T., Iverson, D., Caputi, P., & Sharma, R. (2015). The Theory of Planned Behaviour and dietary patterns: A systematic review and meta-analysis. *Preventive Medicine*, *81*, 150–156. doi:10.1016/j.ypmed.2015.08.020 PMID:26348455

Qiao, X., Ji, L., Jin, Y., Si, H., Bian, Y., Wang, W., & Wang, C. (2021). Development and validation of an instrument to measure beliefs in physical activity among (pre)frail older adults: An integration of the Health Belief Model and the Theory of Planned Behavior. *Patient Education and Counseling*, *104*(10), 2544–2551. doi:10.1016/j.pec.2021.03.009 PMID:33722429

Samoggia, A., & Riedel, B. (2020). Assessment of nutrition-focused mobile apps' influence on consumers' healthy food behaviour and nutrition knowledge. *Food Research International*, *128*, 108766. doi:10.1016/j.foodres.2019.108766 PMID:31955740

Saville, P., & MacIver, R. (2017). A very good question. *Psychometric Testing: Critical Perspectives*, 29–42.

Sofaer, S. (1999). Qualitative methods: What are they and why use them? *Health Services Research*, *34*(5 Pt 2), 1101–1118. http://www.ncbi.nlm.nih.gov/pubmed/10591275%0Ahttp://www.pubmedcentral.nih.gov/articlerender.fcgi?artid=PMC1089055 PMID:10591275

Streiner, D. L., Norman, G. R., & Cairney, J. (2015). *Health measurement scales: a practical guide to their development and use*. Oxford University Press. doi:10.1093/med/9780199685219.001.0001

Voon, J. P., Sing Ngui, K., & Agrawal, A. (2011). Determinants of Willingness to Purchase Organic Food: An Exploratory Study Using Structural Equation Modeling. *Agribusiness Management Review, 14*(2).

Wang, M., Huang, L., Pan, C., & Bai, L. (2021). Adopt proper food-handling intention: An application of the health belief model. *Food Control*, *127*, 108169. doi:10.1016/j.foodcont.2021.108169

Yadav, R., & Pathak, G. S. (2016). Intention to purchase organic food among young consumers: Evidences from a developing nation. *Appetite*, *96*, 122–128. doi:10.1016/j.appet.2015.09.017 PMID:26386300

ANNEXURE

Table 9. Factors and items

Factors	Items
Perceived Susceptibility	
Q1_2	Due to lifestyle change (automation, gadgets) if I don't practice Indian traditional cooking methods it will cause health problems
Q1_3	If I don't practice Indian traditional cooking methods, it causes loss of immunity
Q1_4	If I don't Indian traditional cooking methods, it affects my mental health (such as focus, concentration)
Perceived benefits	
Q2_2	Indian kitchen has so many remedial medicine
Q2_4	Ginger, Garlic, and Tulsi found more beneficial post COVID
Q2_5	I use seasonal vegetables
Cues in action	
Q3_3	Lack of awareness & knowledge
Q3_4	Practices getting diluted diminished from generation to generation
Q3_6	Climate and region impact practicing the traditional methods of cooking
Q3_5	Mindset to cook due to its laborious process of cooking (efforts in cooking)
Q3_ 1	Lack of traditional equipment
Self-efficacy	
Q5_1	I able to follow traditional methods the way learnt from family
Q5_3	I am confident that I will continue to follow traditional methods
Q5_4	Overall, I am confident I can cook traditional recipes
Readiness to act	
Q4_2	COVID forced me to think of creative and innovative healthy options
Q4_5	I am careful now about combination of wrong food
Q4_7	I have observed changed lifestyle post covid
Social Influence	
Q6_1	I surround myself at workplace with people having healthy lifestyle and positive attitude
Q6_3	My friends influence on diet and lifestyle
Q6_4	People I am surrounded with do extensive discussion regarding Indian traditional cooking practices
Q6_5	People I am surrounded with recognise, appreciate and they contribute by sharing their recipe
Behaviour	
Q7_4	For me, Indian traditional cooking practices leads to good health, I will always follow
Q7_5	I follow myself and urge others to follow
Q7_2	I will try to follow Indian traditional cooking practices
Q7_3	I will continue to follow Indian traditional cooking practices as COVID was an eye-opener towards healthy living and food/cooking practice

Table 10. Dropped items due to poor loading

	Statements
Q7_1	B1_I will continue to put conscious & responsible effort
Q6_2	SI2_My family (grandparents and parents) influence on my diet and lifestyle
Q1_1	P. Sus1_Practicing Indian traditional cooking methods, helps in overall health problems (diabetes, obesity, gut health etc.)
Q2_1, 3	PB1_More than techniques and application, ingredients also have connection with immunity. PB3_I use Ghee to build immunity
Q3_2	CA2_Lack of authentic, organic, and unadulterated raw materials
Q5_2	SE2_Increased the consumption of fruits, vegetables, and fresh products
Q4_1, 3, 4, 6	ReA1_More uses of local and seasonal material/Consistently avoiding things, which are not local. ReA3_ I put extra efforts in cooking. ReA4_I Focus on more physical workout. ReA6_Use of authentic spices

Chapter 14
The Role of Social Media Towards Ensuring Good Health and the Well-Being of Tourists by Promoting Wellness Tourism

Buddhini Dilanthika Hennadige
University of Sunderland in London, UK

ABSTRACT

This book chapter will explore the role of social media towards promoting wellness tourism to achieve good health and the well-being of the tourists. The first section of the chapter will describe what is social media by providing a few definitions provided by various authors and giving an insight to the evolution of social media. Further, it will present the types of social media and the benefits of using social media. The next section will explain the fundamentals of social media marketing along with definitions, dimension scales, benefits, and the usage of social media according to the recent statistics. It will be followed by one of the popular social media marketing theories, technology acceptance model, analyzing its sub-constructs and its relationships to social media marketing. The subsequent section will explore the sustainability development goal three, which is ensuring good health and well-being for all at all ages listing the targets that they wish to achieve by 2030.

INTRODUCTION

The behavior of internet users has significantly changed since the introduction of Web 2.0 which led business organizations to engage and interact with their customers through social media. Social media is an online platform and a tool which provides social interaction among its users via text, photos, and videos. Moreover, it allows two-way communication enabling interactive and interconnected communication among individuals, companies, and other stakeholders. It has brought many advantages for the businesses as well as the consumers, for instance searching for products and services, finding information regarding products and services, and checking peer reviews regarding several brands etc. Some of the

DOI: 10.4018/979-8-3693-2065-5.ch014

examples for popular social media platforms are Facebook, Instagram, YouTube, LinkedIn, and Twitter etc. However, accepting and adopting these new social technologies greatly depend on the perceptions, attitudes, and beliefs of the users towards the technology. Among many technology acceptance models "Technology Acceptance Model" (TAM) developed by Davis 1989, is a psychology based simple model which has been frequently used in various contexts within the research.

Wellness tourism is one of the rapidly growing tourism segments according to the reports issued by the Global Wellness Institute (2019). This growth has directed the wellness tourism industry to offer both active and passive tourism activities within the hotels and retreats, wellness resorts and customized travel packages since it is considered as one of the niche markets for the tourists with high affordability. On the other hand, tourism service providers have started using the internet for their marketing activities, especially social media marketing over the past decade. Accordingly, the wellness tourism industry has also started using social media marketing strategies to a greater extent. In addition, it can be identified that the wellness tourism is directly linked to the Sustainable Development Goal 3 which is "Ensuring good health and well=being for all at all ages" since the main purpose of wellness tourism is to improve physical and mental health of the tourists.

What is Social Media?

Social media is one of the latest developments of Web 2.0 which enabled the users to interact with each other unlike traditional media channels (Zerman, 2022). Kaplan & Haenlein (2010) defined social media as,

"A group of internet-based applications that build on the ideological and technological foundations of Web 2.0, and that allow the creation and exchange of user generated content."

Furthermore, Tuten (2020) described social media as,

"The new way to create a connection not only business to business, but also business to consumer, and consumers to consumers, and even consumers to machines."

The organization for Economic Co-operation and Development has further highlighted that this user generated content should be published on either a public website or a social networking site and be creative. Further, it is required to be exempt from the professional purposes which excludes e-mails, instant messages, copying an existing article, and business-related content (OECD, 2006).

The history of social media goes back to 1979, when Tom Truscott and Jim Ellis created an international discussion system named "Usenet" which enabled the internet users to post public messages. Another development of social media is the invention of "Open Diary" by Bruce and Susan Abelson which connected the online diary writers together which led to the concept of blogging. Subsequently, the rapid expansion of internet facilities has led to the creation of further social media platforms such as "Myspace" and "Facebook" until the most recent addition which is "virtual worlds" (Kaplan & Haenlein, 2010). However, the most popular social media platforms are blogs and microblogs such as Twitter, social networks such as LinkedIn, Facebook and Instagram, media sharing domains such as YouTube, review sites such as Yelp and TripAdvisor, and forums (Zerman, 2022). In addition, there are many types of social media networks available at present.

- ❖ Enterprise social media (Internal organizational communication tool)
- ❖ Mobile social media
- ❖ Bought media (E.g., Advertisements)
- ❖ Owned media (E.g., Websites)
- ❖ Earned media (E.g., Review sites)
- ❖ Personal social media (E.g., Facebook)
- ❖ Public social media

Social media allows many advantages to its users where some of them are listed below.

- ❖ Interactive and interconnected communication.
- ❖ Cost effectiveness.
- ❖ Ability to create and share content.
- ❖ Learning opportunities.
- ❖ Marketing activities
- ❖ Create electronic Word of Mouth.
- ❖ Easy access to connected devices.

Social Media Marketing

Nevertheless, the companies nowadays are using social media for their marketing purposes since it allows them to communicate, connect, collaborate, and socialize with the customers, create and share content, and sell their products and services directly in a cost-effective manner (Tuten, 2020). Yadav & Rahman (2017) have defined social media marketing as,

"A process by which companies create, communicate and deliver online marketing offerings via social media platforms to build and maintain stakeholder relationships that enhance stakeholders' value by facilitating interaction, information sharing, offering personalized purchase recommendations, and word of mouth creation among stakeholders about existing and trending products and services."

Table 1. Various scholars have identified different dimension scales for social media which are presented below

Author	Dimension
Yadav and Rahman 2017	Interactivity, Informativeness, Word-of-mouth, Trendiness, Personalization
Kim and Ko 2012	Entertainment, Interaction, Trendiness, Customization, Word-of-mouth
Ebrahim 2020	Trendiness, Customization, Word-of-mouth

The marketers consider social media as one of the most influential marketing instruments due to the rapid increase of the social media users during the last decade (Ali et al., 2022). For instance, the number of social media users around the world has increased from 2.73 billion in 2017 to 4.59 billion in 2022 and expected to boost up to approximately 6 billion in 2027 (Statista, 2023). In addition, social media marketing channels allow the organizations to create "online brand communities" connecting the customers who have experiences with their brand and enable them to share their experiences, seek support and spread word-of mouth via ratings, reviews, referrals, and testimonials etc. (Yadav & Rahman, 2017). However, an over addiction to social media can create a society which lives in a digital world and lacks human interaction (Kaplan & Haenlein, 2010).

Benefits of social media marketing

- Ability to engage and communicate with the customers.
- Consumers can interact with the brand.
- Opportunity to discover brands and products.
- Searching for information about a brand or a product.
- Ability to gather suggestions from peers about a brand or a product.
- Can exchange information with each other.
- Enhancing electronic word of mouth.

SOCIAL MEDIA MARKETING THEORIES

Technology Acceptance Model

"Technology Acceptance Model" (TAM) was developed by Davis (1989) to theorize the usage behavior of computer technology comprising the general and capable computer acceptance measurements which explain the user behavior of computer technologies and user population. The model identified two constructs; "perceived usefulness" and "perceived ease of use" that can be adopted for social media as well (Rauniar et al., 2014). This theory explores the external factors affecting perceived usefulness and perceived ease of use of social media. Figure 1 shows the framework used for this theory and assumed relationships between the two external variables (informativeness and service functionality) influencing "perceived usefulness" and "perceived ease of use" which affect "behavioral intention to use" social media marketing.

Figure 1. The conceptual framework

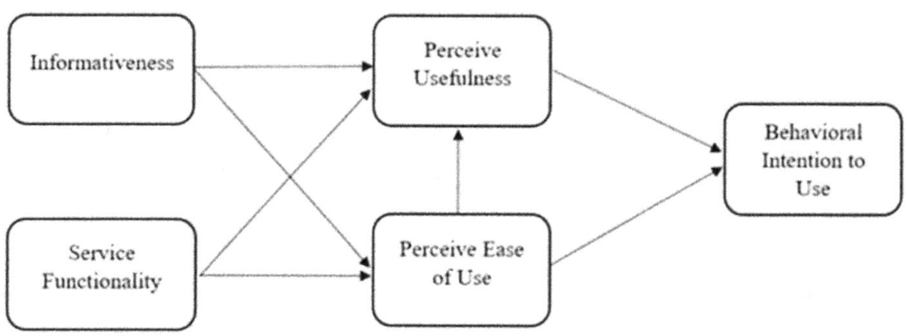

Davis (1989) have defined perceived ease of as,

"The degree to which a person believes that using a particular system would be free of effort."

In fact, social media users are likely to find it more useful if it requires minimum effort to understand, learn and use the site (Rauniar et al., 2014). Additionally, a study conducted by Lane & Coleman (2012) concluded that the perceived ease of use has positively influenced the intention to use social media as well. Therefore, the wellness tourism service providers have integrated their social media platforms to make it easy to use for their users (Lagrosen & Grundén, 2014).

Perceived usefulness was defined by Davis (1989) as,

"The degree to which a person believes that using a particular system would enhance his or her job performance."

Simultaneously, Bandura (1982, cited in Davis, 1989) has highlighted that the perceived usefulness is one of the basic determinants of the user behavior according to the research on self-efficacy. Moreover, Fishbein and Ajzen (1975, cited in Rauniar et al., 2014) identified the intention to use social media as the continuous intent to involve in the social media activities and the user's willingness to use the social media in real life. Nevertheless, in the context of wellness tourists the intention to travel is depending on the perceived expertise, health consciousness and the perceived benefits (Anannukul & Yoopetch, 2022).

Ducoffe (1996, cited in Agarwal et al., 2020) defined the informativeness of advertisements as,

"The ability of advertising to inform consumers of product alternatives so that purchases yielding the greatest possible satisfaction can be made."

In fact, the social media platforms allow the tourism companies to share information regarding their products and services while the user generated content can be considered as additional information (Chu, 2009). Moreover, research conducted by Anannukul & Yoopetch (2022) discovered that the wellness tourists are likely to obtain electronic word of mouth when selecting their travel destinations. They further concluded that the informativeness will influence the perceived usefulness and perceived ease of use of social media.

Delone & Mclean (2003) noted that the service functionality of the end user computing in mid 1980 is to provide information and supporting services to the end users. However, several scholars identify the service functionality as the ability of social media marketing strategies to provide facilitating services such as purchasing via social media (Saravanakumar & Suganthalakshmi, 2012). For instance, the wellness tourists tend to obtain travel advise and a professional level service (Anannukul & Yoopetch, 2022). In addition, it will affect perceived usefulness and perceived ease of use since if the search process is complex the user is likely to quit (Ho & Lee, 2007).

Sustainable Development Goal Three: Good Health and Well-Being

Sustainable development goals (SDG) were introduced by the 2030 Agenda for Sustainable Development adopted by the United Nations General Assembly in September 2015 and put into practice since January 2016 with the main objective of creating a broad and inclusive framework for ending poverty around the world in the next 15 years (United Nation, 2023). Further, it is the central UN platform for achieving an integrated and invisible SDGs under three categories which are social, environmental, and economic. It comprises of 17 SDGs and 169 targets which require the dedication of all sectors in the society in regional and national level. Among the 17 SDGs, the 3rd SDG is "ensure healthy lives and promote well-being for all at all ages". Health and well-being are essential for achieving all three pillars of sustainable development and it is an outcome of the successful sustainable development (Nunes et al., 2016).

The World Health Organization (WHO) has defined health as,

"A state of complete physical, mental, and social well-being and not merely the absence of disease or infirmity."

Health and well-being are directly linked to sustainable development since it is significantly determined by economic, social, and environmental circumstances such as poverty, gender equality, education, and growth. Therefore, it is vital to achieve the other SDGs, rather than considering it as a separate SDG (Nunes et al., 2016). Following are a few benefits of sustainable development towards achieving health and wellbeing.

- Poverty reduction
- Sustainable energy sources
- Safe drinking water
- Adequate sanitation
- Sustainable food production and distribution
- Urban planning

Figure 2. SDG three overview

Under the SDG 3 there are 13 targets to achieve by 2030.

- ❖ Reduce the global maternal mortality ratio to less than 70 per 100,000 live births.
- ❖ End preventable deaths of newborns and children under 5 years of age, with all countries aiming to reduce neonatal mortality to at least as low as 12 per 1000 live births and under-5 mortality to at least as low as 25 per 1000 live births.

- End the epidemics of Aids, Tuberculosis, Malaria and neglected tropical diseases and combat Hepatitis, water-borne diseases, and other communicable diseases.
- Reduce by one third premature mortality from non-communicable diseases through prevention and treatment and promote mental health and well-being.
- Strengthen the prevention and treatment of substance abuse, including narcotic drug abuse and harmful use of alcohol.
- Halve the number of global deaths and injuries from road traffic accidents.
- Ensure universal access to sexual and re-productive health care services, including for family planning, information and education, and the integration of reproductive health into national strategies and programs.
- Achieve universal health coverage, including financial risk protection, access to quality essential health-care services and access to safe, effective, quality, and affordable essential medicines and vaccines for all.
- Substantially reduce the number of deaths and illnesses from hazardous chemicals and air, water and soil pollution and contamination.
- Strengthen the implementation of the World Health Organization Framework Convention on Tobacco Control in all countries, as appropriate.
- Support the research and development of vaccines and medicines for the communicable and non-communicable diseases that primarily affect developing countries, provide access to affordable essential medicines and vaccines, in accordance with the Doha Declaration on the TRIPS Agreement and Public Health, which affirms the right of developing countries to use to the full the provisions in the Agreement on Trade-Related Aspects of Intellectual Property Rights regarding flexibilities to protect public health, and in particular provide access to medicines for all.
- Substantially increase health financing and the recruitment, development, training and retention of the health workforce in developing countries, especially in least developed countries and small Island developing states.
- Strengthen the capacity of all countries, in particular developing countries, for early warning, risk reduction and management of national and global health risks.

Wellness Tourism

Wellness tourism is one of the rapidly growing tourism segments around the world which accounted US$720 billion global wellness tourism income in 2020 and it is predicted to be increased up to US$1.1 trillion in 2025 (Global Wellness Institute, 2021). Brown et al. (2011) defined wellness tourism as,

"The sum of all the relationships resulting from a journey by people whose motive, in whole or in part, is to maintain or promote their health and well-being, and who stay at least one night at a facility that is specially designed to enable and enhance people's physical, psychological, spiritual and/or social well-being."

Smith & Puczko (2014) further noted that the wellness tourism contains at least one of the dimensions of self-sufficiency, esthetics, healthy nutrition, relaxation, meditation, education, and environmental awareness other than the above. Moreover, it encourages identifying the authenticity and the happiness of the life as a whole (Global Wellness Institute, 2021).

Several scholars have noted that the demand for wellness tourism has increased due to the Covid-19 pandemic (Wen et al., 2021). In addition, the contemporary perceptions regarding the health and wellness, the busy lifestyles of the modern society, the predictions of tourism and the affiliation between co-construction and well-being of workforces through tourism experience are few other reasons for the rising popularity of the wellness tourism industry (Dini & Pencarelli, 2022). The primary services offered by wellness service providers are accommodation, wellness activities, nutritious menus, and wellness activities (Okumus & Linton-Kelly, 2022). For instance, wellness retreats, yoga and meditation sessions, spa facilities, and private wellness concierge are some common offerings (Global Wellness Institute, 2021). On the other hand, it might not be affordable to everyone since it mainly targets on the high-end niche market as the wellness products and services are unique (Dillette et al., 2021).

Social Media Marketing on Wellness Tourism

Social media has become a widespread marketing tool in the tourism industry for the small and medium enterprises to create awareness and interact with their existing and potential customers and for national and international companies to facilitate their integrated marketing strategies at a low cost (Zerman, 2022). Moreover, Chiappa (2011) stated that it enables Word of Mouth communication which is vital for the hospitality sector since the tourism products cannot be evaluated prior actual consumption due to the intangibility nature and it needs high involvement when buying since it is not a routine purchase. On the other hand, the travelers use social media channels to search, plan and organize their tours, and share and interpret their travel experiences with other users (Leung et al., 2013). Therefore, modern tourists are mostly inspired by the content shared on social media platforms and taking unique travel photographs (Songur & Turktarhan, 2022).

However, the application of social media marketing strategies in the context of wellness tourism has a limited availability within the existing literature. One of the reasons is that they have given less prominence to this marketing approach by considering it as a part of the other marketing activities but not as an entire strategy (Lagrosen & Grundén, 2014). Lagrosen & Grundén (2014) further noted that social media marketing plans should be flexible and short term since the technology and social media are rapidly developing. According to research conducted by Shen & Bissell (2013) regarding the use of Facebook in marketing and branding the wellness tourism businesses and high-end department store beauty brands, it was finalized that both industries prefer to share the information of their brands through Facebook. Facebook is the most used platform among many wellness resorts where some of their official websites are directly connected to its Facebook page as well (Lagrosen & Grundén, 2014).

Social Media Marketing in Post Covid-19

Many cities and countries around the world had to close their borders declaring lockdowns which limited the travel of individuals and encouraged them to keep social distancing and stay at home due to Covid-19 (Donthu & Gustafsson, 2020). As a result, there was a rapid increase in the usage of internet and social media which made it as the fundamental medium of communicating and socializing with others (Necka et al., 2017). For instance, the average time spent by Americans on social media has increased up to 65 minutes per day in 2020 which was 54 minutes per day in 2019 and the most used social media platform around the world was TikTok recording 38% growth of monthly active users followed by Pinterest recording 32% advance of monthly active users from 2019 to 2021 (Statista, 2022). This trend has positively influenced the businesses to improve their customer experiences, building brand engagement and brand equity, creating positive brand perception and online presence by interacting with them via social media channels (Dubbelink et al., 2021).

Technology and internet-based businesses, especially social media marketing strategies have gained rising popularity due to Covid-19 since most of the customers have shifted towards online shopping over the past few years (Donthu & Gustafsson, 2020). Therefore, Donthu & Gustafsson (2020) further stated that even though several industries such as travel and tourism, MICE tourism, vehicle and electronics and other general services faced temporary or permanent bankruptcy, the internet-based companies such as online entertainment, online shopping, online education, food delivery and remote working were booming during the pandemic. This is mainly due to the cognitive reactions of the customers to Covid-19 such as the fear and threat of going outside and getting infected by the disease and the government rules and regulations such as lockdowns which forced them to shift towards online shopping (Kim et al., 2022).

Wellness Tourism in Post Covid-19

Moncloa (2021, cited in Nel-lo Andreu et al., 2021) stated that the new tourism trends have been risen around the world in post pandemic such as traveling to less crowded destinations, increasing demand for wellness tourism, innovating technologically developed tourism products for new generations, creating awareness regarding sustainability, and providing more attention to the environment and humanity. Although, the wellness tourism sector was rapidly improving within the international market before the pandemic, there was a temporary halt during the Covid-19 (Datta, 2022). On the other hand, it is expected to grow as a special niche market of the tourism industry which forced the countries to modify their strategies to create competitive advantage for wellness segment (Mandeep & Mohan, 2021). For instance, the Sri Lankan government along with the National Operation Center for Prevention of Covid-19 have presented that the Sri Lankan indigenous medicine and practices could be used to treat this disease as a curative method, prevention method or a post-treatment method (Ranasinghe et al., 2020).

Furthermore, many destinations tend to position themselves based on the natural and cultural elements of their wellness products and services such as Ayurveda medicine in India, spa retreats in Costa Rica, and hot springs in Vietnam etc. (Datta, 2022). In reality, the modern tourists are now interested in wellness tourism activities rather than other tourism segments since they are more concerned about their physical and mental health, seeking relaxation and rejuvenation from the stress caused by Covid-19, healing, recovering and long life (Dini & Pencarelli, 2022). In addition, among the elements of wellness tourism the major focus has been given to yoga and meditation followed by Ayurveda, religiousness, pilgrimage, contentment, privacy, indigenous medicine, spas, hot springs, faith healing and gastronomy (Dillette et al., 2021).

CONCLUSION

Social media is defined as "a group of internet-based applications that builds on the ideological and technological foundations of Web 2.0, and that allow the creation and exchange of user generated content" (Kaplan & Haenlein, 2010). In addition, Van Dijck (2013, cited in Zerman, 2022) defined social media as "culture of connectivity" which further interpreted as a multiway communication such as business to business, business to consumer, consumer to consumer and consumer to machines (Tuten, 2020). Therefore, it has been used in the business context for marketing purposes to create, communicate, and deliver online marketing offerings via social media platforms to build and maintain stakeholder relationships that enhance stakeholders' value by facilitating interaction, information sharing, offering personalized purchase recommendations, and word of mouth creation among stakeholders about existing and trending products and services (Yadav & Rahman, 2017). The most popular social media platforms are blogs, microblogs, social networks, media sharing domains, and review sites (Zerman, 2022).

The hospitality and tourism companies are extensively using social media platforms for their marketing purposes since it is a powerful marketing tool which provides an international reach for their organizations at a relatively low cost (Songur & Turktarhan, 2022). Facebook is the most used social media channel among the wellness tourism business where they have connected their official website and their mobile application to their Facebook page enabling integrated marketing (Lagrosen & Grundén, 2014). On the other hand, it provides unfiltered data from various travelers around the world which will benefit the potential travelers to get an idea about the tourism products and services before consuming since it is intangible and therefore cannot evaluate before actual consumption and require high involvement when purchasing since the buying process is not routine (Zerman, 2022). Moreover, it will facilitate the tourists to search, organize, and share their travel experiences as well (Leung et al., 2013).

Voigt et al, (2011, cited by Okumus & Linton-Kelly, 2022) defined wellness tourism as "the sum of all the relationships resulting from a journey by people whose motive, in whole or on part, is to maintain or promote their health and well-being, and who stay at least one night at a facility that is specifically designed to enable and enhance peoples' physical, psychological, spiritual and/or social well-being". Other than that, it contains several lifestyle dimensions such as health and body, mind and spirit, self-sufficiency, physical strength, esthetics, healthy nutrition, relaxation, meditation, mental activity, education, environmental awareness, and sensitivity to social relationships (Smith & Puczko, 2014). Therefore, Earth Changers (2021) has partnered with wellness spa and retreats in Costa Rica, Nicaragua, Indonesia, Galapagos Islands, Kenya, Croatia, Malawi, and Tanzania to explore their organic and local food, de-stress, relax and recharge themselves, explore the nature, improve fitness, and practice yoga.

This book chapter elaborated the role of social media towards ensuring good health and well-being of the tourists by promoting wellness tourism. The mission of this book chapter was to identify the ways of achieving sustainability in relation to the health and well-being of individuals through wellness tourism and to recognize the contribution of social media to promote wellness tourism. The first section of the book chapter presented a few definitions of social media to provide the reader an understanding of what is social media and the uses of social media in general. Next, it discussed how social media has been utilized in the tourism industry overall and in the wellness tourism sector with specific information. Finally, it covered how wellness tourism benefits tourists to ensure their good health and well-being which is one of the sustainable development goals introduced by United Nations.

REFERENCES

Agarwal, B., Kumar, A., & Arora, T. (2020). Impact of Social Media Advertising on Millennials Buying Behaviour. *International Journal of Intelligent Enterprise*, *1*(1), 1. doi:10.1504/IJIE.2020.110795

Ali, F., Terrah, A., Dogan, S., & Cobanoglu, C. (2022). Social media marketing activities: Studying social identification, trust, value and loyalty. In *Digital Marketing and Social Media Strategies for Tourism and Hospitality Organizations* (pp. 35–56). Goodfellow Publishers. https://ebookcentral.proquest.com/lib/sunderland/detail.action?docID=29182557

Anannukul, N., & Yoopetch, C. (2022). The determinants of intention to visit wellness tourism destination of young tourists. *Kasetsart Journal of Social Sciences*, *43*(2), 417–424. doi:10.34044/j.kjss.2022.43.2.20

Brown, G., Howat, G., & Voigt, C. (2011). *Wellness tourists: in search of transformation*. Emerald Insight. doi:10.1108/16605371111127206

Chu, S.-C. (2009). *Determinants of Consumer Engagement in Electronic Word-of-Mouth in Social Networking Sites*.

Datta, B. (2022). PREFERENCES AND CHANGING NEEDS OF WELLNESS TOURISTS: A STUDY FROM INDIAN PERSPECTIVE POST COVID-19. *Geo Journal of Tourism and Geosites*, *42*(2 supplement), 782–786. doi:10.30892/gtg.422spl18-889

Davis, F. D. (1989). Perceived Usefulness, Perceived Ease of Use, and User Acceptance of Information Technology. *IT Usefulness and Ease of Use*, 319–339.

Del Chiappa, G. (2011). *Trustworthiness of Travel 2.0 applications and their influence on tourist behaviour: an empirical investigation in Italy*. Information and Communication Technologies in Tourism.

Delone, W. H., & Mclean, E. R. (2003). The DeLone and McLean Model of Information Systems Success: A Ten-Year Update. *Information Systems Research. Journal of Management Information Systems*, *19*(4), 9–30. doi:10.1080/07421222.2003.11045748

Dillette, A. K., Douglas, A. C., & Andrzejewski, C. (2021). Dimensions of holistic wellness as a result of international wellness tourism experiences. *Current Issues in Tourism*, *24*(6), 794–810. doi:10.1080/13683500.2020.1746247

Dini, M., & Pencarelli, T. (2022). Wellness tourism and the components of its offer system: a holistic perspective. In Tourism Review, 77(2), 394–412. Emerald Group Holdings Ltd. doi:10.1108/TR-08-2020-0373

Donthu, N., & Gustafsson, A. (2020). Effects of COVID-19 on business and research. In *Journal of Business Research* (Vol. 117, pp. 284–289). Elsevier Inc. doi:10.1016/j.jbusres.2020.06.008

Dubbelink, S. I., Soria, C. H., & Constantinides, E. (2021). Social media marketing as a branding strategy in extraordinary times: Lessons from the covid-19 pandemic. In Sustainability (Switzerland), 13(18). MDPI. doi:10.3390u131810310

Global Wellness Institute. (2019). *Understanding Wellness: Opportunities and Impacts of the Wellness Economy for Regional Development*. Global Wellness Institute. https://globalwellnessinstitute.org/industry-research/understanding-wellness-opportunities-impact-wellness-economy-for-regional-development/

Global Wellness Institute. (2021). *The Global Wellness Economy: Looking Beyond COVID*. Global Wellness Institute. https://globalwellnessinstitute.org/press-room/statistics-and-facts/

Ho, C. I., & Lee, Y. L. (2007). The development of an e-travel service quality scale. *Tourism Management, 28*(6), 1434–1449. doi:10.1016/j.tourman.2006.12.002

Kaplan, A. M., & Haenlein, M. (2010). Users of the world, unite! The challenges and opportunities of Social Media. *Business Horizons, 53*(1), 59–68. doi:10.1016/j.bushor.2009.09.003

Kim, J., Yang, K., Min, J., & White, B. (2022). Hope, fear, and consumer behavioral change amid COVID-19: Application of protection motivation theory. *International Journal of Consumer Studies, 46*(2), 558–574. doi:10.1111/ijcs.12700 PMID:34220343

Lagrosen, S. O., & Grundén, K. (2014). Social media marketing in the wellness industry. *The TQM Journal, 26*(3), 253–260. doi:10.1108/TQM-12-2013-0129

Lane, M., & Coleman, P. (2012). Journal of Technology Research Technology ease of use. *Journal of Technology Research, 3*, 1–12.

Leung, D., Law, R., van Hoof, H., & Buhalis, D. (2013). Social Media in Tourism and Hospitality: A Literature Review. In Journal of Travel and Tourism Marketing, 30(1–2), 3–22. doi:10.1080/10548408.2013.750919

Mandeep, S. L., & Mohan, D. (2021). *HVS Monday Musings: Wellness Tourism will Flourish in the Post-COVID Era*. Hospitality Net. https://www.hospitalitynet.org/opinion/4102574.html

Necka, R., Cacioppo, E. A., & John, T. (2017). Article Loneliness and Social Internet Use: Pathways to Reconnection in a Digital World? *Perspectives on Psychological Science, 13*(1), 70–87. doi:10.1177/1745691617713052 PMID:28937910

Nel-lo Andreu, M. G., Font-Barnet, A., & Espasa Roca, M. (2021). Wellness tourism-new challenges and opportunities for tourism in Salou. *Sustainability (Basel), 13*(15), 8246. Advance online publication. doi:10.3390u13158246

Nunes, A. R., Lee, K., & O'riordan, T. (2016). The importance of an integrating framework for achieving the Sustainable Development Goals: The example of health and well-being. *BMJ Global Health, 1*(3), e000068. Advance online publication. doi:10.1136/bmjgh-2016-000068 PMID:28588955

OECD. (2006). Innovation and Growth in Tourism. In Innovation and Growth: Chasing a Moving Frontier. Organisation for Economic Cooperation and Development (OECD). doi:10.1787/9789264073975-10-en

Okumus, B., & Linton-Kelly, H. (2022). *Introduction to Wellness Management in Hospitality and Tourism*.

Ranasinghe, R., Damunupola, A., Wijesundara, W., & Karunarathne, C. (2020). *TOURISM AFTER CORONA: IMPACTS OF COVID 19 PANDEMIC AND WAY FORWARD FOR TOURISM, HOTEL AND MICE INDUSTRY IN SRI LANKA*. Research Gate. https://doi.org/ doi:10.13140/RG.2.2.27955.17442

Rauniar, R., Rawski, G., Yang, J., & Johnson, B. (2014). Technology acceptance model (TAM) and social media usage: An empirical study on Facebook. *Journal of Enterprise Information Management, 27*(1), 6–30. doi:10.1108/JEIM-04-2012-0011

Saravanakumar, M., & Suganthalakshmi, T. (2012). Social Media Marketing. *Life Science Journal, 9*(4), 1097–8135. http://www.lifesciencesite.comhttp://www.lifesciencesite.com.670

Shen, B., & Bissell, K. (2013). Social Media, Social Me: A Content Analysis of Beauty Companies' Use of Facebook in Marketing and Branding. *Journal of Promotion Management, 19*(5), 629–651. doi:10.1080/10496491.2013.829160

Smith, M., & Puczko, L. (2014). History of Health Tourism. In *Health, Tourism and Hospitality*. Routledge. https://books.google.co.uk/books?hl=en&lr=&id=p0bIAgAAQBAJ&oi=fnd&pg=PP1&dq=Health,+Tourism+and+Hospitality:+Spas,+Wellness+and+Medical+Travel&ots=1Kf6yfyQSa&sig=xUqjKWxF7Oubwap861XF_wYVkfo&redir_esc=y#v=onepage&q=Health%2C%20Tourism%20and%20Hospitality%3A%20Spas%2C%20Wellness%20and%20Medical%20Travel&f=false doi:10.4324/9780203083772

Songur, A. G., & Turktarhan, G. (2022). The role of social media marketing in the travel planning and decision-making processes of today's travelers. In *Digital Marketing and Social Media Strategies for Tourism and Hospitality Organizations*. Goodfellow Publishers. https://ebookcentral.proquest.com/lib/sunderland/detail.action?docID=29182557

Statista. (2022). *Social media platforms used by marketers*. Statista. https://www.statista.com/statistics/259379/social-media-platforms-used-by-marketers-worldwide/

Statista. (2023). *Number of worldwide social network users 2027*. Statista. https://www.statista.com/statistics/278414/number-of-worldwide-social-network-users/

Tuten, T. L. (2020). *Social media marketing* (4th ed.). Sage Publications.

United Nation. (2023). *Goal 3 | Department of Economic and Social Affairs*. UN. https://sdgs.un.org/goals/goal3

Wen, J., Kozak, M., Yang, S., & Liu, F. (2021). COVID-19: Potential effects on Chinese citizens' lifestyle and travel. *Tourism Review, 76*(1), 74–87. doi:10.1108/TR-03-2020-0110

Yadav, M., & Rahman, Z. (2017). Measuring consumer perception of social media marketing activities in e-commerce industry: Scale development & validation. *Telematics and Informatics, 34*(7), 1294–1307. doi:10.1016/j.tele.2017.06.001

Zerman, S. (2022). Definition and functionality of social media. In *Digital Marketing and Social Media Strategies for Tourism and Hospitality Organizations*. Goodfellow Publishers. https://ebookcentral.proquest.com/lib/sunderland/detail.action?docID=29182557

Chapter 15
Early Damage Direction in a Structural Health Monitoring Environment

N. Ambika
https://orcid.org/0000-0003-4452-5514
St. Francis College, India

ABSTRACT

Probabilistic FFS assessments are carried out by integrating damage detection data gathered from inspections and permanently installed monitoring systems. After a negative measurement, it determines the likelihood of a postulated severe defect being present. It is crucial to point out that this distribution of the size of a postulated fault differs from the distribution of the size of a defect. A negative measurement merely eliminates the possibility that defects of the specified size do not exist. As a result, rather than estimating the dimensions of a defect, the distribution gives an estimate of the possible sizes of defects in the component of interest. The work is suggested to make early detection and future prediction damages in the structures. The database considers the initial images of the structure. The present images are mapped to the initial images to estimate the damage that can be caused in the future. It increases the detection by 13.69%.

INTRODUCTION

Structural health monitoring (Balageas, Fritzen, & Güemes, 2010) is a strategy for identifying damage in aerospace, civil, and mechanical engineering infrastructure. Changes to these systems' material and geometric properties, boundary conditions, and connectivity harm the system's performance. The five closely related fields of SHM, condition monitoring, non-destructive evaluation, statistical process control, and damage prognosis are all involved in damage identification.

It monitors changes in the material and geometric features of engineering structures like bridges and buildings, and structural health monitoring (SHM) includes the observation and analysis of a system over time utilizing periodically sampled response measurements. It involves carrying out a plan for identifying

DOI: 10.4018/979-8-3693-2065-5.ch015

damage, damages connected to an adverse change in the material qualities, geometry, support conditions, or loading that affects the structure's performance or durability now or in the future.

Structural Health Monitoring (SHM) is a field of engineering that involves using various sensors and technologies to continuously or periodically assess the condition and performance of structures, such as buildings, bridges, dams, pipelines, and aircraft. The primary goal of SHM is to ensure safety, reliability, and longevity by detecting and assessing any damage, defects, or deterioration in real time or through regular inspections. Some crucial aspects of structural health monitoring:

1. **Sensors**: SHM relies on many sensors to collect data about a structure's behavior. These sensors include accelerometers, strain gauges, displacement sensors, temperature sensors, and more. They are strategically placed on or within the structure to capture relevant data.
2. **Data Collection**: Data collected from sensors are typically processed and analyzed in real-time or periodically. This data may include measurements of stress, strain, vibration, temperature, corrosion, and other relevant parameters.
3. **Data Analysis**: Advanced data analysis techniques, such as signal processing, machine learning, and statistical methods, are often used to interpret the data and identify anomalies or potential issues. This analysis helps in understanding the structural condition and predicting potential failures.
4. **Damage Detection**: SHM systems are designed to detect damage or anomalies in structures, including cracks, corrosion, fatigue, and other forms of deterioration. Early detection can prevent catastrophic failures and costly repairs.
5. **Performance Monitoring**: SHM can also assess the overall performance of a structure, including its response to external forces such as wind, earthquakes, and traffic loads. This information can help optimize maintenance and improve structural safety.
6. **Remote Monitoring**: Some SHM systems are equipped with remote monitoring capabilities, allowing engineers and maintenance personnel to access real-time data from anywhere, useful for large or remotely located structures.
7. **Predictive Maintenance**: By continuously monitoring a structure's health, SHM enables predictive maintenance strategies. The maintenance activities can be scheduled based on actual condition data rather than fixed schedules, reducing downtime and costs.
8. **Applications**: SHM is used in civil engineering, aerospace, automotive, energy, and other industries where the integrity of structures is critical. For example, it monitors the health of bridges, assesses the integrity of aircraft components, tracks the condition of offshore oil rigs, and more.
9. **Challenges**: Implementing effective SHM systems can be challenging due to issues such as sensor placement, data interpretation, and system integration. Additionally, ensuring the security of data collected from SHM systems is crucial.

Overall, structural health monitoring plays a vital role in improving the safety and longevity of infrastructure and industrial assets by enabling timely maintenance and reducing the risk of unexpected failures. Advances in sensor technology and data analytics continue to enhance the capabilities of SHM systems.

The SHM process (Ciang, Lee, & Bang, 2008) (Chang, Markmiller, Yang, & Kim, 2011) entails monitoring a system over time using dynamic response measurements, periodically sampled from various sensors, extracting damage-sensitive features from these measurements, and statistically analyzing these features to ascertain the current structural health. The outcome of this process provides long-term SHM with frequently updated information on the structure's capacity to carry out its intended function in light of the inevitable aging and degradation brought on by operational settings. After dramatic occurrences like earthquakes or blast loading, SHM is utilized for quick condition screening and seeks to deliver trustworthy information on structural integrity in close to real-time.

The installation of dense sensor (Nagaraj A., 2021) (Nagaraj A., 2022) arrays on civil infrastructure has been hampered by the restrictions on sensor measurement capabilities and difficulties in implementing sensor networks owing to the power and data connection requirements. As these restrictions have been removed, a large quantity of heterogeneous data is made available from many types of sensors. Large sensor datasets may make it difficult for standard SHM techniques, which rely on verified multi-physics models, to be successful in health monitoring.

Probabilistic FFS assessments (Hey Leung & Corcoran, 2022) are carried out by integrating damage detection data gathered from inspections and permanently installed monitoring systems. After a negative measurement, it determines the likelihood of a postulated severe defect being present. It is crucial to point out that this distribution of the size of a postulated fault differs from the distribution of the size of a defect. A negative measurement merely eliminates the possibility that defects of the specified size do not exist. As a result, rather than estimating the dimensions of a defect, the distribution gives an estimate of the possible sizes of defects in the component of interest. When the inspection or monitoring system's output, X, falls below a predetermined threshold value, determined by requirements regarding the likelihood of a false alarm, this results in a negative measurement.

The work is suggested to make early detection and future prediction damages in the structures. The database considers the initial images of the structure. The present images are mapped to the initial images to estimate the damages that can be caused in the future. It increases the detection by 13.69%.

BENEFITS OF FAULT DETECTION SYSTEM

- *Avoidance of premature breakdown –*

A wind turbine management paradigm (Kromanis & Arab) is supported by the suggested method. Like any structural system, a wind turbine shows reactions that change depending on the applied loads. The system's comprehensive structural reaction to all applied loads is monitored continuously. After a possible preliminary examination, the obtained measurements are sent to distant servers. The processes may be used to analyze these measurements. The goal is to create measurement interpretation techniques to aid in this phase of wind turbine management. So that engineers may plan and prioritize actions, results from measurement interpretation may be provided via appropriate interfaces.

- *Reduced maintenance cost –*

The creation of a vehicle health management system revolves around structural health monitoring (SHM). A built-in sensor network that can offer information about the structure's real-time situation and damage level makes up an SHM system. Data on structural status might be made available in real-time through a health management system. According to an examination of the data on the actual structural state, maintenance might be planned and carried out.

- *Supervision at remote sites and diagnosis*

SHM can retain the same degree of safety as manual inspection and have equivalent quality. It is necessary to remove internal surrounding facilities to provide inspectors access to the internal structures to do a manual reevaluation. This process takes person-hours for labor, and airlines lose revenue due to maintenance downtime. It might be considered a cost-benefit for the SHM-based examination.

- *Support for future development*

The compositions of composite materials were used to categorize the many types of composite constructions that were investigated. This knowledge contributes to a basic understanding of how damage in such structures might advance when these components age or fail.

Literature Survey

The following section talks about various contributions to similar domain.

Probabilistic FFS assessments (Hey Leung & Corcoran, 2022) are carried out by integrating damage detection data gathered from inspections and permanently installed monitoring systems. After a negative measurement, it determines the likelihood of a postulated severe defect being present. It is crucial to point out that this distribution of the size of a postulated fault differs from the distribution of the size of a defect. A negative measurement merely eliminates the possibility that defects of the specified size do not exist. As a result, rather than estimating the dimensions of a defect, the distribution gives an estimate of the possible sizes of defects in the component of interest. When the inspection or monitoring system's output, X, falls below a predetermined threshold value, determined by requirements regarding the likelihood of a false alarm, this results in a negative measurement.

This method (Bao, Tang, Li, & Zhang, 2019) mimics the biological eyesight and rational thought processes of humans. The time series signals are converted into picture vectors during the data visualization stage and then piecewise plotted as grayscale graphics. The second phase involves feeding a training dataset of randomly chosen and manually labeled picture vectors into a deep neural network (DNN), trained using the stacked autoencoder and greedy layer-wise training methods. Large volumes of unmanaged structural health monitoring data may be scanned for possible problems using trained deep neural networks. The suggested method's framework consists of two key components. Data visualization is the initial step in automatically identifying many abnormalities in SHM data. The neural network's input is the picture vector created by successively joining pixel columns. Training samples labeled with an index are chosen. The stacked autoencoder DNN, which is quick and efficient, is used. To illustrate the two-stage training process, a two-hidden-layer stacked autoencoder neural network is built. Pre-training phase is the initial step in building a two-hidden-layer stacked autoencoder neural network. The project takes into account a Chinese long-span cable-stayed bridge. The bridge has a 1088 m main span, two side spans (300 m long), and two towers 306 m high. The accelerometers on the deck and the towers employ 38 channels. It has 16 two-channel accelerometers on the deck and two three-channel accelerometers at the base of the towers. The acceleration data measured by the SHM system and the acceleration data anomalies are categorized into six patterns: missing, minor, outlier, square, trend, and drift. The fusion DNN architecture disseminates the labeled data anomaly patterns.

It is a brand-new approach (Tang, Chen, Bao, & Li, 2019) to detecting data anomalies that mimic human decision-making and perception using a convolutional neural network (CNN). The research divided the unprocessed time series data into segments and displayed the information in the time and frequency domains. The photos from each part are combined into a single dual-channel image and labeled with graphical features. A CNN was created and trained, and convolutional learning was used to learn the descriptions and visual representations of the anomalies' characteristics. It took the impacts of balanced and unbalanced training sets and training ratios.

The research (Gui, Pan, Lin, Li, & Yuan, 2017) introduces three support vector machines for damage identification that are based on optimization algorithms. The parameters for the Gaussian kernel function and the penalty parameters are optimized using various optimization techniques, such as grid search, partial swarm optimization, and genetic algorithms. Two categories of feature extraction techniques using time-series data are used. The 17 diverse situations from the literature were utilized as benchmark experimental data to validate the suggested data-driven methodologies. All three improved machine learning techniques outperformed traditional techniques w.r.t sensitivity, accuracy, and efficacy. Compared to other approaches, the SVM based on genetic algorithms provided a superior forecast. The study's has two distinct feature techniques also showed how picking the characteristics may increase sensitivity in spotting damage and gauging structural health.

The study (Johnson, Lam, Katafygiotis, & Beck, 2001) describes the initial stage of a benchmark structural health monitoring challenge run under the direction of the IASC-ASCE Structural Health Monitoring Task Group. It discusses to scale-model structure used in this benchmark challenge. Two analytical models are based on the structure. One is a 12DOF shear-building model, and the other is a 120DOF model. The types and numbers of sensors, the amount of sensor data, and information are presented together with the damage patterns that need to be recognized.

The skeleton (Zhang, Schulz, Naser, Ferguson, & Pai, 1999) is equipped with accelerometers or piezoceramic patches for sensing, and inertial actuators or piezoceramic actuators are employed to excite the framing. Broadband excitation is used by the sensor-actuator system to actively probe the structure. The historical data is recorded for transmittance functions between successive sensors from the sound structure. The structure's damage is then found, located, and evaluated using changes in the functions. It is possible to calculate transmittance functions using many sorts of measurable structural responses. Structural translations and curvatures are employed to look for deterioration. The best frequency range to detect damage is found experimentally after comparing the sensitivity of the two distinct approaches. In order to calculate the frequency at length piezoceramic sensor can measure the structural response, the wavelengths of the structural mode shapes are also computed.

The recommendation (Ying, et al., 2013) is the framework for detecting damage in a steel pipe works under various operating and environmental conditions. Ultrasonic wave-generating and -sensing piezoelectric wafers were used to equip the pipe. A mass scatterer grease-coupled to the pipe's surface physically imitated damage. Benign fluctuations included changing ambient temperature and interior air pressure over time. The scatterer was positioned at various points along the pipe on three distinct days over the course of the ultrasonic tests. Even if the wave patterns are complicated and challenging to read, it might be challenging to distinguish between changes brought on by the scatterer and changes brought on by benign fluctuations. 365 characteristics are taken from various signal-processing methods and applied to the observed data helped to characterise them. The best features for damage identification were then identified using automated feature selection techniques created utilising an adaptive boosting algorithm. Five machine learning classifiers were created using the chosen characteristics and are based on adaptive boosting and support vector machines. They had an average accuracy of 98.5-99.8% during random testing and an accuracy of 84.2-89% during systematic testing.

It is a decentralized, autonomous defect detection strategy for wireless SHM systems using embedded machine learning (Smarsly, Dragos, & Wiggenbrock, 2016). The reliability and accuracy of SHM systems may be jeopardized by sensor errors and miscalibrations. It improves the dependability and accuracy of SHM system outputs and the resilience of algorithms used for structural health monitoring. The integrity of the sensor data must be maintained. Based on correlations between the response data of several sensor nodes, or "analytical redundancy," the effective identification of sensor defects and miscalibrations is carried out using an integrated machine learning technique based on artificial neural networks. The design of a wireless SHM system includes wireless sensor nodes with integrated 3-axis accelerometers, a base station, and a host computer. The monitoring activities that the SHM system does. Sensor node samples acceleration response data during operation and a built-in Cooley-Tukey FFT algorithm performs a local transformation into the frequency domain. The basic eigenfrequency is chosen as the highest peak in the frequency spectrum by a peak detection algorithm. The modal amplitudes are shared across the sensor nodes. It uses the modal peak amplitudes of associated sensor nodes. The sensor node predicts the modal amplitude of its acceleration response data and determines the presence of sensor failures based on differences between the predicted and the actual modal peak amplitude. The results of the sensor nodes' fault detection process are sent to the host computer through the base station for archival and decision-making. The correlations between the modal peak amplitudes from various sensors serve as the foundation for the decentralized autonomous fault detection approach suggested in this paper. An embedded machine-learning technique with a supervised learning framework is shown to map these associations.

PREVIOUS WORK

The work is Probabilistic Fitness-for-Service (FFS) assessments (Hey Leung & Corcoran, 2022), which are used to evaluate the structural integrity and reliability of components and structures in various industries, such as oil and gas, aerospace, and civil engineering.

1. **Integration of Damage Detection Data**: Probabilistic FFS assessments involve the integration of data obtained from two sources: inspections and permanently installed monitoring systems. These sources provide information about the condition of a component or structure over time.
2. **Negative Measurement**: When a negative measurement occurs, it means that the data obtained from inspections or monitoring systems does not indicate the presence of a severe defect or damage above a certain threshold size.
3. **Distribution of Postulated Fault Size**: It's important to note that the distribution being discussed here relates to the size of a postulated fault, not the actual size of a defect. In other words, it provides an estimate of the possible sizes of defects that could be present in the component of interest.
4. **Elimination of Possibilities**: A negative measurement eliminates the possibility that defects of a specified size, exist within the component. It doesn't provide an estimate of the precise dimensions of a defect but narrows down the range of possible defect sizes.
5. **Threshold Value**: The decision to classify a measurement as negative is based on a predetermined threshold value. This threshold is determined by considering factors such as the likelihood of a false alarm, which means mistakenly identifying a defect when it doesn't exist.

Overall, Probabilistic FFS assessments help in making informed decisions about the structural integrity and safety of components and structures. By integrating inspection and monitoring data and considering the probability distribution of possible defect sizes, engineers can assess the risk associated with the continued operation of a component or structure. This approach is valuable in ensuring the safety and reliability of critical infrastructure and industrial assets.

PROPOSED WORK

Probabilistic FFS assessments (Hey Leung & Corcoran, 2022) are carried out by integrating damage detection data gathered from inspections and permanently installed monitoring systems. After a negative measurement, it determines the likelihood of a postulated severe defect being present. It is crucial to point out that this distribution of the size of a postulated fault differs from the distribution of the size of a defect. A negative measurement merely eliminates the possibility that defects of the specified size do not exist. As a result, rather than estimating the dimensions of a defect, the distribution gives an estimate of the possible sizes of defects in the component of interest. When the inspection or monitoring system's output, X, falls below a predetermined threshold value, determined by requirements regarding the likelihood of a false alarm, this results in a negative measurement.

The proposal deploys IoT devices (Ambika .. N., 2022) (Ambika N., 2022) which monitor the damage of the structures. The devices are programmed to measure initial water leakage in the building. The following images are exacted to measure the damages at an initial stage. The devices are equipped with initial constructed images. The images are captured by the devices and compared with the initial images. The images are fed into machine learning algorithm to measure the next stages of damage. This system helps to measure the damage at the early stage. Table 1. Provides the machine learning algorithm that aids in detecting early damages by measuring the decolouration of the structure. The future damages are predicted based on the number of damages at the collected stage. Figure 1. Portrays the pictures of images collected at various stages. Stage 1 image is collected after 15 years of construction. Stage 2 is collected after 19 years of construction. Stage 3 is collected after 25 years of construction. Figure 1 portrays the same. Table 1 represents the algorithm used to estimate early detection and future prediction of the damages.

It is an improved CNN-based method (Abdeljaber, et al., 2018) that, regardless of the size of the structure, only calls for two measurement sets. The generation of data for training the 1D CNN classifiers that this algorithm uses is the first phase of the suggested evaluation approach. When the structure is undamaged, the first set of necessary data is collected by measuring the vibration response with the n accelerometers. The information obtained from accelerometers are the entirely damaged and unharmed scenarios. The suggested CNN-based technique was tested using the acceleration data gathered under the benchmark problem's nine structural scenarios. The accelerations observed at all floors comprise the data into account in this investigation. Therefore, 12 accelerometers were considered to represent the entire number. Each case's acceleration measurements used a 200 Hz sampling rate. The vibration response was assessed for 120 seconds in Case 1, 300 seconds in Case 6, and 360 seconds in the other examples.

Figure 1. Water leakage

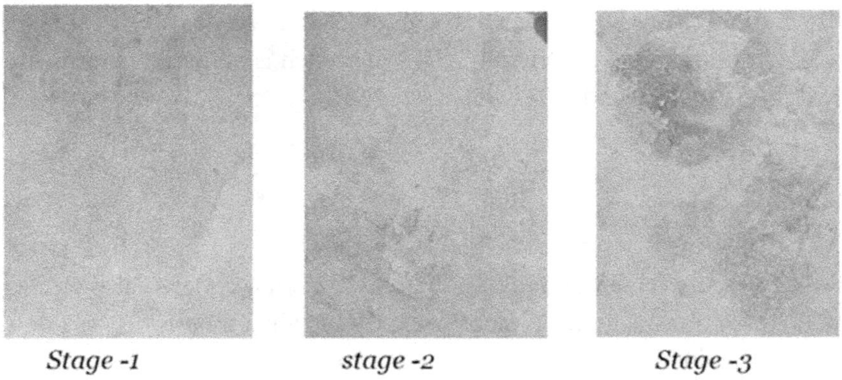

Table 1. Algorithm to estimate future damage and early detection of damages

Step 1: Maintain the database of the previous taken images Step 1: Insert the image Step 2: Estimate the texture in terms of pixels and resolution Step 3: Estimate the dimension of the damage Step 4: Estimate the decolouration Step 5: Compare the readings with the previous images stored in the database. Step 6: Increase the damage rate by 2 for every 5 years. Step 7: Estimate the future damage by analysing the time taken for the damage since the initial readings.

Simulation

The work is implemented using Python. JPEG files are used in the work. Table 2 contains the details of simulation. Table 2 portrays the same.

Table 2. Samples taken to evaluate the work

Parameters used	*Description*
Dimensions of the images	87kb to 203 kb
Width of the image	1200 pixel
Height of the image	1600 pixel
Resolution	96dpi
Bit depth	24
Previous image store	5 different images of a sample (initial readings)

Analysis of the Work

Probabilistic FFS assessments (Hey Leung & Corcoran, 2022) are carried out by integrating damage detection data gathered from inspections and permanently installed monitoring systems. After a negative measurement, it determines the likelihood of a postulated severe defect being present. It is crucial to point out that this distribution of the size of a postulated fault differs from the distribution of the size of a defect. A negative measurement merely eliminates the possibility that defects of the specified size do not exist. As a result, rather than estimating the dimensions of a defect, the distribution gives an estimate of the possible sizes of defects in the component of interest. When the inspection or monitoring system's output, X, falls below a predetermined threshold value, determined by requirements regarding the likelihood of a false alarm, this results in a negative measurement.

The work is suggested to make early detection and future prediction damages in the structures. The database considers the initial images of the structure. The present images are mapped to the initial images to estimate the damages that can be caused in the future.

Early Detection

The structures images are compared with the initial images to detect the discolouration of the building. It increases the detection by 13.69%. Figure 2 portrays the same. Figure 3 represents the future prediction.

Figure 2. Early detection of damages

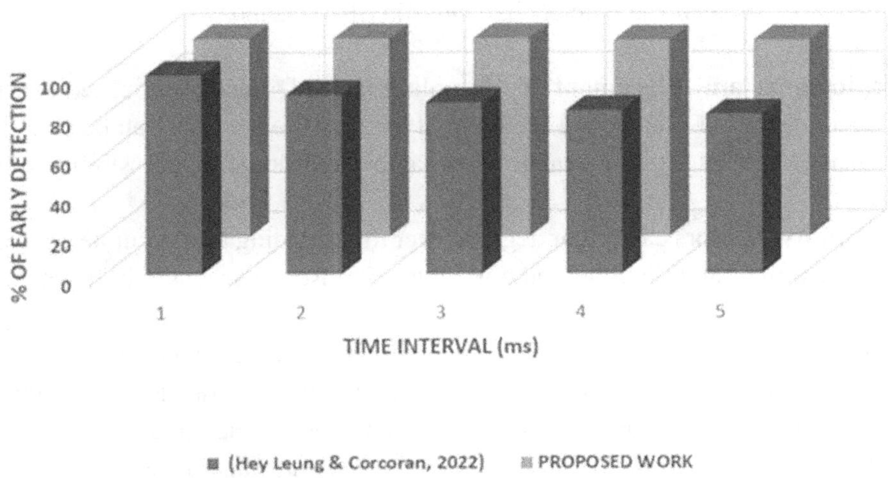

Figure 3. Future detection

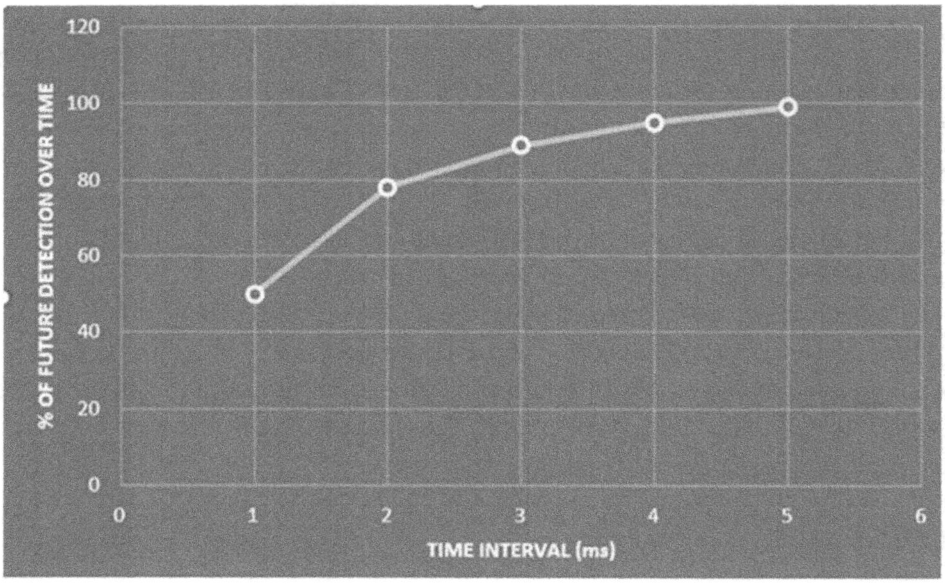

CHALLENGES

While Structural Health Monitoring (SHM) offers numerous benefits for infrastructure and asset management, it also faces several challenges that need to be addressed for its successful implementation and continued improvement. Some of the crucial challenges in SHM include:

1. **Sensor Deployment and Placement**: Proper placement of sensors on structures is critical to collecting accurate data. Determining the optimal locations for sensors can be complex and may require extensive knowledge of the structure's behavior. Additionally, accessibility to structure can be a challenge.
2. **Sensor Reliability**: Sensors can fail or degrade over time, leading to inaccurate data and potential false alarms. Ensuring the reliability and durability of sensors, especially in harsh environments, is a challenge.
3. **Data Interpretation**: Collecting vast amounts of data from sensors is one thing, but making sense of that data is another. Data interpretation requires advanced analytics and modeling techniques, and the complexity of some structures can make this process challenging.
4. **False Positives and Negatives**: SHM systems may generate false positives or false negatives (missing actual issues). Reducing these errors and improving the accuracy of damage detection algorithms is a significant challenge.
5. **Data Security**: The data collected by SHM systems can be sensitive, especially for critical infrastructure. Ensuring the security and privacy of this data is essential to protect against cyber threats and unauthorized access.

6. **Cost and Scalability**: Implementing SHM systems can be expensive, particularly for large or complex structures. Finding cost-effective solutions to be scaled to fit various applications is a challenge.
7. **Integration with Existing Structures**: Retrofitting existing structures with SHM systems can be challenging due to design constraints and the need to minimize disruption to ongoing operations.
8. **Power Supply**: Many sensors require power sources, such as batteries, which need periodic replacement or recharging. Finding sustainable and long-lasting power solutions, particularly for remote or hard-to-reach locations.
9. **Standardization**: Lack of standardized protocols and data formats in SHM can hinder interoperability between different systems and make it challenging to share data across organizations or regions.
10. **Environmental Factors**: Extreme weather conditions, vibrations, and other environmental factors can affect sensor performance and data accuracy, posing challenges for consistent monitoring.
11. **Regulatory and Ethical Issues**: Compliance with regulations and ethical considerations related to data collection and privacy can be complex, especially when SHM systems are deployed in public or shared spaces.
12. **Human Expertise**: Skilled personnel with expertise in SHM are required to design, implement, and maintain these systems. A shortage of qualified professionals can be a limiting factor.
13. **Long-Term Data Management**: Managing and archiving large volumes of historical data generated by SHM systems can be challenging. This data is valuable for trend analysis and long-term asset management.

Addressing these challenges in Structural Health Monitoring will require ongoing research, innovation, collaboration between experts in various fields, and the development of standardized practices and guidelines. As technology advances and the benefits of SHM become more evident, overcoming these challenges will be crucial for the continued growth and effectiveness of SHM systems.

FUTURE SCOPE

The future of Structural Health Monitoring (SHM) holds significant promise and is likely to see several developments and trends that will further enhance its capabilities and applications. Here are some potential directions for the future of SHM:

1. **Integration of IoT and Wireless Technologies**: SHM systems will increasingly incorporate Internet of Things (IoT) devices and wireless sensors, allowing for more extensive and cost-effective monitoring of structures. These sensors can provide real-time data, reducing the need for manual inspections and improving data accuracy.
2. **Advanced Sensor Technology**: Ongoing advancements in sensor technology, including miniaturization, improved sensitivity, and durability, will make it easier to deploy sensors in challenging environments and on a range of structures.
3. **Machine Learning and AI**: Machine learning and artificial intelligence (AI) will play a more significant role in SHM. These technologies can help in automated data analysis, anomaly detec-

tion, and predictive maintenance, making SHM systems more intelligent and capable of identifying subtle structural issues.

4. **Data Fusion and Multimodal Sensors**: Combining data from various sensors, including visual cameras, acoustic sensors, and environmental sensors, will provide a more comprehensive view of a structure's health. Data fusion techniques will enable more accurate and holistic assessments.
5. **Real-time Monitoring and Remote Control**: SHM systems will continue to move towards real-time monitoring and remote control capabilities, allowing engineers and maintenance teams to make immediate decisions and take preventive actions when needed.
6. **Wireless Power Transfer**: Developing wireless power transfer technologies can eliminate the need for batteries in remote sensors, reducing maintenance requirements and expanding the lifespan of SHM systems.
7. **Structural Health Monitoring for Smart Cities**: SHM will be integral to the development of smart cities, ensuring the safety and longevity of critical infrastructure such as bridges, roads, and buildings. SHM data optimize traffic flow, improve energy efficiency, and enhance urban planning.
8. **Energy Harvesting**: Integration of energy harvesting techniques, such as utilizing vibrations or environmental energy sources, can help power autonomous sensors, reducing the need for frequent battery replacements.
9. **Blockchain for Data Security**: As the amount of sensitive structural data collected increases, blockchain technology enhances the security and integrity of SHM data, preventing tampering or unauthorized access.
10. **Environmental Impact Assessment**: SHM systems will also focus on assessing the environmental impact of structures. It includes monitoring emissions, resource consumption, and the overall sustainability of infrastructure.
11. **Global Standardization**: As SHM technology matures, there may be efforts to standardize data formats, sensor deployment methods, and analysis techniques, making it easier for different systems to communicate and share data.
12. **Autonomous Drones and Robotics**: The use of autonomous drones and robotics equipped with sensors will become more common for inspecting and maintaining structures that are difficult to access or in hazardous locations.

Overall, the future of Structural Health Monitoring characterized by increased automation, enhanced data analytics, improved sensor technology, and broader applications across various industries. These developments will contribute to safer and more efficient infrastructure and asset management.

CONCLUSION

Civil infrastructure is managed and maintained using structural health monitoring (SHM). Although SHM systems have generated enormous volumes of data, further research is still required to monitor, mine, and use this data. In general, SHM data contains a variety of abnormalities that might impede structural analysis and assessment and are brought on by sensor errors or system blunders.

Probabilistic FFS assessments are carried out by integrating damage detection data gathered from inspections and permanently installed monitoring systems. After a negative measurement, it determines the likelihood of a postulated severe defect being present. It is crucial to point out that this distribution of the size of a postulated fault differs from the distribution of the size of a defect. A negative measurement merely eliminates the possibility that defects of the specified size do not exist. As a result, rather than estimating the dimensions of a defect, the distribution gives an estimate of the possible sizes of defects in the component of interest. When the inspection or monitoring system's output, X, falls below a predetermined threshold value, determined by requirements regarding the likelihood of a false alarm, this results in a negative measurement.

The work is suggested to make early detection and future prediction damages in the structures. The database considers the initial images of the structure. The present images are mapped to the initial images to estimate the damages that can be caused in the future. It increases the detection by 13.69%.

REFERENCES

Abdeljaber, O., Avci, O., Kiranyaz, M. S., Boashash, B., Sodano, H., & Inman, D. J. (2018). 1-D CNNs for structural damage detection: Verification on a structural health monitoring benchmark data. *Neurocomputing*, *275*, 1308–1317. doi:10.1016/j.neucom.2017.09.069

Ambika, N. (2022). An Augmented Edge Architecture for AI-IoT Services Deployment in the Modern Era. In *Handbook of Research on Technical, Privacy, and Security Challenges in a Modern World* (pp. 286–302). IGI Global.

Ambika, N. (2022). Enhancing Security in IoT Instruments Using Artificial Intelligence. In V. J.K., S. D., & G.-P. V. (eds), IoT and Cloud Computing for Societal Good (pp. 259-276). Cham: Springer. doi:10.1007/978-3-030-73885-3_16

Balageas, D., Fritzen, C. P., & Güemes, A. (2010). *Structural health monitoring* (Vol. 90). John Wiley & Sons.

Bao, Y., Tang, Z., Li, H., & Zhang, Y. (2019). Computer vision and deep learning–based data anomaly detection method for structural health monitoring. *Structural Health Monitoring*, *18*(2), 401–421. doi:10.1177/1475921718757405

Chang, F. K., Markmiller, J. F., Yang, J., & Kim, Y. (2011). Structural health monitoring. *System health management: with aerospace applications*, 419-428.

Ciang, C. C., Lee, J. R., & Bang, H. J. (2008). Structural health monitoring for a wind turbine system: A review of damage detection methods. *Measurement Science & Technology*, *19*(12), 122001. doi:10.1088/0957-0233/19/12/122001

Gui, G., Pan, H., Lin, Z., Li, Y., & Yuan, Z. (2017). Data-driven support vector machine with optimization techniques for structural health monitoring and damage detection. *KSCE Journal of Civil Engineering*, *21*(2), 523–534. doi:10.100712205-017-1518-5

Hey Leung, M. S., & Corcoran, J. (2022). A probabilistic method for structural integrity assurance based on damage detection structural health monitoring data. *Structural Health Monitoring*, *21*(4), 1608–1625. doi:10.1177/14759217211038881

Johnson, E. A., Lam, H. F., Katafygiotis, L. S., & Beck, J. L. (2001). A benchmark problem for structural health monitoring and damage detection. *Structural control for civil and infrastructure engineering*, 317-324.

Kromanis, R., & Arab, M. Z. (n.d.). *Structural health monitoring of wind turbines: Characterizing response using a regression-based approach.*

Nagaraj, A. (2021). *Introduction to Sensors in IoT and Cloud Computing Applications*. Bentham Science Publishers. doi:10.2174/97898114793591210101

Nagaraj, A. (2022). Adapting Blockchain for Energy Constrained IoT in Healthcare Environment. In K. Kaushik, S. Tayal, S. Dahiya, & A. O. Salau (Eds.), *Sustainable and Advanced Applications of Blockchain in Smart Computational Technologies* (p. 103). CRC press. doi:10.1201/9781003193425-7

Smarsly, K., Dragos, K., & Wiggenbrock, J. (2016). Machine learning techniques for structural health monitoring. *8th European workshop on structural health monitoring (EWSHM 2016)*, (pp. 5-8). Bilbao, Spain.

Tang, Z., Chen, Z., Bao, Y., & Li, H. (2019). Convolutional neural network-based data anomaly detection method using multiple information for structural health monitoring. *Structural Control and Health Monitoring*, *26*(1), e2296. doi:10.1002tc.2296

Ying, Y., Garrett, J. H. Jr, Oppenheim, I. J., Soibelman, L., Harley, J. B., Shi, J., & Jin, Y. (2013). Toward data-driven structural health monitoring: Application of machine learning and signal processing to damage detection. *Journal of Computing in Civil Engineering*, *27*(6), 667–680. doi:10.1061/(ASCE)CP.1943-5487.0000258

Zhang, H., Schulz, M. J., Naser, A., Ferguson, F., & Pai, P. F. (1999). Structural health monitoring using transmittance functions. *Mechanical Systems and Signal Processing*, *13*(5), 765–787. doi:10.1006/mssp.1999.1228

Chapter 16
Digital Health Revolution: Enhancing Well-Being Through Technology

Vipin Singh
https://orcid.org/0000-0001-5566-0151
Vellore Institute of Technology, India

Amrik Singh
https://orcid.org/0000-0003-3598-8787
Lovely Professional University, India

ABSTRACT

The rapid advancement of digital technologies has revolutionized various sectors, including healthcare, fostering novel approaches to promote health and well-being. This book chapter provides a comprehensive overview of the integration and application of digital technologies in health and well-being, exploring their transformative potential and the challenges they pose. These innovations have not only enhanced healthcare delivery but also empowered individuals to actively participate in managing their well-being. Mobile health apps, for instance, allow users to monitor their fitness levels, track nutrition, and manage stress, fostering a culture of self-care and health awareness. However, there are issues that need to be resolved among the advantages of digital technologies. The chapter clarifies the significance of data privacy and security in light of the massive sharing of private health information on digital platforms. To keep patients' trust and preserve their personal information,

DIGITAL HEALTH REVOLUTION: ENHANCING WELL-BEING THROUGH TECHNOLOGY

The integration of digital technologies in various sectors has catalyzed transformative changes, and healthcare is no exception. In recent years, the healthcare industry has witnessed a digital revolution that has reshaped the way health and well-being are managed and promoted (Lee& Lee 2021). This

DOI: 10.4018/979-8-3693-2065-5.ch016

chapter provides an in-depth exploration of the integration and application of digital technologies in the realm of health and well-being, highlighting their potential to revolutionize healthcare delivery, empower individuals, and foster a culture of self-care. While acknowledging the remarkable advantages these technologies offer, the chapter also delves into the importance of data privacy and security in the digital health landscape. The 21st century has ushered in an era of rapid technological advancement, impacting various sectors of society. Among the sectors profoundly transformed is healthcare, which has undergone a digital revolution that is reshaping how health and well-being are managed, monitored, and promoted. The integration of digital technologies has given rise to innovative approaches that empower individuals, enhance healthcare delivery, and foster a culture of self-care (Hird, Ghosh, & Kitano, 2016), In this chapter, we delve into the multifaceted landscape of the digital health revolution, exploring its transformative potential and the challenges it brings to light.

Empowering Individuals: Mobile Health Apps and Beyond: A hallmark of the digital health revolution is the proliferation of mobile health apps. These applications have transcended their role as mere tools, evolving into essential companions for health-conscious individuals. Fitness tracking apps allow users to monitor their physical activities, heart rates, and sleep patterns in real time. Nutrition tracking apps facilitate informed dietary choices, empowering users to make healthier food selections. This democratization of health data empowers individuals to take ownership of their well-being and instills a sense of agency in health management (Balapour et al. 2019).

Personalized Healthcare Insights: The Role of Data Analytics: Digital health technologies enable the collection and analysis of massive amounts of health-related data. Wearable devices, sensors, and EHRs generate a rich tapestry of information that, when harnessed by advanced analytics and artificial intelligence, produces personalized healthcare insights. These insights can range from early disease detection to predictive analytics, aiding both individuals and healthcare providers in making informed decisions about treatment and prevention strategies.

The digital health revolution is reshaping healthcare paradigms by placing individuals at the forefront of their well-being. Mobile health apps, personalized insights, and data-driven decision-making are the cornerstones of this revolution. However, it is imperative to strike a balance between technological innovation and the protection of individuals' privacy. By addressing challenges related to data security, the digital divide, and health literacy, we can forge a path toward a future where technology and well-being coexist harmoniously, enriching lives and improving health outcomes (Hassan et al. 2022).

Digital Technologies in Healthcare: A Transformative Shift

The advent of digital technologies has revolutionized healthcare in unprecedented ways. The convergence of mobile devices, wearable sensors, data analytics, and artificial intelligence has led to the development of innovative solutions that enhance health and well-being. These technologies enable seamless communication, real-time data monitoring, and personalized health insights. One of the most prominent outcomes of the digital health revolution is the proliferation of mobile health apps. These apps empower individuals to actively engage in managing their health and well-being. Fitness-tracking apps allow users to monitor their physical activity levels, heart rate, and sleep patterns while nutrition-tracking apps help individuals make informed dietary choices. The accessibility of these apps has transformed health monitoring into a daily habit, promoting a culture of proactive self-care (Boll et al.2021).

Digital technologies enable the collection and analysis of vast amounts of health data. Wearable devices and electronic health records provide a comprehensive view of an individual's health status. Advanced analytics and machine learning algorithms can process this data to generate personalized health recommendations and predictions. For instance, individuals with chronic conditions can receive timely alerts and guidance based on their health data, contributing to early intervention and improved health outcomes. In today's digital landscape, the convergence of technology and healthcare has ushered in a transformative era, where the amalgamation of digital technologies enables the collection, analysis, and strategic utilization of an extensive array of health-related data. This revolutionary shift has been made possible through wearable devices and electronic health records (EHRs), which collectively furnish an all-encompassing perspective on an individual's health status. Wearable devices, spanning from fitness trackers to smartwatches, serve as continuous monitors, meticulously capturing vital signs, physical activities, sleep patterns, and more. In parallel, electronic health records establish a digital repository housing an individual's medical history, diagnoses, treatment records, and test results, amalgamating these fragments into a holistic portrayal of the patient's healthcare journey (Hulsen, 2021).

However, the true potential of this amassed health data emerges when coupled with the prowess of advanced analytics and machine learning. These technologies possess the ability to sift through the voluminous data and unearth intricate patterns and insights. Employing intricate algorithms, machine learning systems decode correlations, identify trends, and even predict prospective health outcomes. This analytical finesse holds substantial implications, particularly for individuals grappling with chronic conditions.

The seamless synergy between wearable devices and EHRs weaves an intricate narrative of their daily life – blood sugar levels, dietary habits, physical exertion, and sleep quality. Enter advanced analytics, bolstered by the might of machine learning algorithms. These algorithms scrutinize the real-time data streams, enabling individuals to receive tailored, precise health recommendations calibrated to their distinct circumstances. In practice, this translates into timely alerts in response to fluctuations in blood sugar levels, prompting personalized suggestions for dietary adjustments or medication recalibrations. The net result is the empowerment of individuals to proactively engage in their health management (Hassan et al.2022).

Data Privacy and Security

As individuals share personal health information on digital platforms, data privacy and security become paramount. The massive collection of health data raises concerns about the unauthorized access and misuse of sensitive information. To build and maintain trust, healthcare providers and technology developers must implement robust data protection measures. Compliance with privacy laws and regulations is essential to ensure the safe handling of personal health data. In the rapidly evolving landscape of digital health, where personal health information is increasingly being shared on digital platforms, the significance of data privacy and security has reached paramount importance. The sheer magnitude of health data being collected raises legitimate concerns about the potential for unauthorized access and misuse of sensitive information. This issue goes beyond mere inconveniences; it delves into the core of individuals' privacy and personal integrity.

To navigate this intricate terrain, two critical players bear the mantle of responsibility: healthcare providers and technology developers. Both entities are entrusted with safeguarding the confidentiality of individuals' health data. Robust data protection measures emerge as the cornerstone of this endeavor.

From encryption protocols that shield data during transmission to stringent access controls that limit who can view sensitive information, the arsenal of protection mechanisms must be both advanced and comprehensive (Paul et al.,2023).

Integral to this quest for data security is a steadfast commitment to compliance with privacy laws and regulations. Adhering to established norms and regulations is not just a legal requirement, but a moral imperative. Regulations such as the Health Insurance Portability and Accountability Act (HIPAA) in the United States and the General Data Protection Regulation (GDPR) in the European Union provide a framework for protecting personal health data. Complying with these regulations not only ensures the safe handling of sensitive information but also nurtures a culture of trust between healthcare providers, technology developers, and individuals. Data privacy and security reverberate beyond mere technical aspects; it is a fundamental component of ethical healthcare practices. Individuals must be assured that their health information is handled with the utmost care and that their rights to privacy are respected in the digital realm. As health systems increasingly transition towards digitization, the commitment to robust data protection measures and unwavering adherence to privacy regulations will serve as the bedrock upon which the future of healthcare is built – a future that harmoniously balances technological advancements with the ethical duty to protect and honor individuals' personal health information (Awotunde et al.2021: Deshmukh & Croasdell. 2008)

Digital Divide and Accessibility

Despite the rapid proliferation of digital technologies, a digital divide still exists, preventing equal access to health-enhancing tools. Socioeconomic factors and limited digital literacy can hinder certain populations from benefiting fully from digital health solutions. Bridging this divide requires efforts to ensure accessibility, affordability, and education about digital health tools. In the era of rapid digital transformation, characterized by the pervasive integration of technology into various aspects of life, a sobering reality persists: the digital divide continues to cast its shadow, posing barriers to equitable access to health-enhancing tools. Despite the widespread proliferation of digital technologies, a significant portion of the population remains on the outskirts of this technological revolution. Socioeconomic factors and disparities in digital literacy play a pivotal role in shaping this divide, creating an imbalance in the distribution of benefits derived from digital health solutions (Pick, & Azari, 2008).

Socioeconomic factors, including income levels and access to resources, often determine an individual's ability to access and utilize digital health tools effectively. Affordability becomes a pivotal concern as some segments of society find themselves unable to acquire the necessary devices or afford the costs associated with digital health applications. Moreover, limited access to reliable internet connections in certain regions exacerbates the issue, further isolating marginalized communities from the potential benefits of these tools. The disparity in digital literacy compounds the problem. While digital natives adeptly navigate the intricacies of technology, others may struggle to engage with digital health platforms due to a lack of familiarity or understanding. This knowledge gap can hinder individuals from making the most of the health-enhancing opportunities that digital tools offer (Vicente & Lopez, 2010). .

Addressing the digital divide in the context of healthcare demands concerted efforts aimed at ensuring accessibility, affordability, and education. Initiatives that provide subsidized or free access to devices and applications can play a pivotal role in expanding digital health outreach to underserved communities. Equally important is investing in digital literacy programs that empower individuals with the skills needed to navigate digital platforms confidently.

In this pursuit of equitable digital health access, collaboration between governments, non-profit organizations, and technology developers becomes indispensable. It is a collective responsibility to bridge the gap and create an environment where all individuals, regardless of socioeconomic status or digital proficiency, can harness the benefits of digital health solutions. By laying the groundwork for equal access, society can unleash the potential of technology to uplift health outcomes for all, transcending the barriers that the digital divide presents (Fairlie, 2004).

Empowering Patients and Professionals

Digital health technologies empower patients to take an active role in their health management. Patients can access personalized health information, communicate with healthcare providers, and make informed decisions about their well-being. Moreover, healthcare professionals can leverage digital tools for accurate diagnosis, data-driven treatment plans, and remote patient monitoring, thereby enhancing patient outcomes. In the contemporary healthcare landscape, the convergence of digital health technologies with patient-centered care has birthed a transformational dynamic that empowers both patients and healthcare professionals. At the forefront of this shift lies the empowerment of patients, as digital health technologies bestow upon them an active role in their health management. This empowerment stems from the ability to access personalized health information at their fingertips, creating a bridge between medical insights and individual well-being. Patients are now equipped to engage directly with their health data, track their progress, and gain a holistic understanding of their health status (Calvillo, Roman & Roa, 2015).

Furthermore, the advent of digital health has redefined the patient-provider relationship by fostering seamless communication between individuals and healthcare professionals. This real-time interaction enables patients to consult their providers, seek clarifications, and gain valuable guidance remotely, transcending geographical constraints. Informed decision-making becomes a hallmark of this empowerment, as individuals armed with comprehensive information can actively participate in determining their treatment plans, choosing suitable interventions, and optimizing their overall well-being.

In parallel, healthcare professionals stand to reap substantial benefits from this paradigm shift. Digital tools facilitate precision and efficiency in diagnosis, enabling clinicians to access a comprehensive digital footprint of patients' health history. This holistic overview facilitates informed decision-making and reduces the likelihood of oversight or medical errors. Moreover, data-driven treatment plans guided by advanced analytics equip professionals with insights into the most effective interventions, thereby enhancing the quality of care provided. Beyond diagnosis and treatment, digital health technologies have revolutionized the concept of remote patient monitoring. Healthcare professionals can now monitor patients' health statuses in real-time, irrespective of their physical location. This empowerment not only enhances patient outcomes by enabling early detection and timely interventions but also fosters a sense of security and well-being among patients (Chang, 2020).

In essence, the marriage of digital health technologies with patient care has sculpted an ecosystem where patients are informed and proactive stakeholders in their health journeys, and healthcare professionals are empowered with tools that elevate the precision, quality, and accessibility of care. This symbiotic relationship underscores the potential of digital health to usher in a new era of patient-centered care, redefining the boundaries of healthcare interaction and engendering positive outcomes for both patients and professionals.

CONCLUSION: A PATIENT-CENTRIC DIGITAL HEALTH LANDSCAPE

The digital health revolution has ushered in a patient-centric paradigm, empowering individuals and reshaping healthcare delivery. Mobile health apps, personalized insights, and seamless data sharing are catalysts for proactive health management. However, it's imperative to maintain a balance between innovation and privacy. Ensuring data security, addressing the digital divide, and promoting digital health literacy are vital steps in harnessing the potential of digital technologies for holistic well-being.

As we navigate the intricacies of the digital health landscape, embracing these technologies while safeguarding individuals' privacy will pave the way for a future where technology and well-being coexist harmoniously. In the ever-evolving landscape of healthcare, the advent of the digital health revolution has inaugurated a transformative era characterized by patient-centricity. This paradigm shift has redefined the traditional healthcare model, placing individuals at the epicenter of their health management journey. Mobile health apps, personalized insights, and seamless data sharing have emerged as potent catalysts, fueling a proactive approach to health maintenance. The empowerment of individuals through accessible and intelligible health data engenders a sense of ownership, as they navigate their well-being armed with informed decisions and personalized guidance.

However, as we embrace the dynamic potential of digital health, a delicate equilibrium between innovation and privacy must be preserved. The paramount importance of data security becomes evident in an era marked by heightened data sharing. Similarly, the spectre of the digital divide reminds us of the ethical imperative to ensure that the benefits of digital health are universally accessible. This mandates concerted efforts to bridge disparities in access and knowledge, fostering inclusivity and equality in health empowerment.

As the threads of this digital tapestry are woven, the intertwining of technology and holistic well-being must be skilfully managed. The legacy of the digital health revolution lies not merely in its technical advancements, but in its seamless coexistence with the very essence of human health. The future we aspire to construct harmoniously intertwines technology and well-being, where digital tools enhance lives without compromising privacy, and individuals are equipped with the literacy to navigate the evolving landscape adeptly. With unwavering commitment to these principles, we forge a path toward a future where technology amplifies wellness, and a patient-centric ethos becomes the cornerstone of healthcare delivery.

REFERENCES

Awotunde, J. B., Jimoh, R. G., Folorunso, S. O., Adeniyi, E. A., Abiodun, K. M., & Banjo, O. O. (2021). Privacy and security concerns in IoT-based healthcare systems. In *The Fusion of Internet of Things, Artificial Intelligence, and Cloud Computing in Health Care* (pp. 105–134). Springer International Publishing. doi:10.1007/978-3-030-75220-0_6

Balapour, A., Reychav, I., Sabherwal, R., & Azuri, J. (2019). Mobile technology identity and self-efficacy: Implications for the adoption of clinically supported mobile health apps. *International Journal of Information Management*, *49*, 58–68. doi:10.1016/j.ijinfomgt.2019.03.005

Boll, S., Meyer, J., & O'Connor, N. E. (2018). Health media: From multimedia signals to personal health insights. *IEEE MultiMedia*, *25*(1), 51–60. doi:10.1109/MMUL.2018.011921235

Calvillo, J., Roman, I., & Roa, L. M. (2015). How technology is empowering patients? A literature review. *Health Expectations*, *18*(5), 643–652. doi:10.1111/hex.12089 PMID:23711169

Chang, A. C. (2020). *Intelligence-based medicine: artificial intelligence and human cognition in clinical medicine and healthcare*. Academic Press.

Deshmukh, P., & Croasdell, D. (2008). HIPAA: Privacy and security in health care networks. In Information Security and Ethics: Concepts, Methodologies, Tools, and Applications (pp. 2770-2781). IGI Global.

Fairlie, R. W. (2004). Race and the digital divide. *Contributions to Economic Analysis & Policy*, *3*(1), 1–38. doi:10.2202/1538-0645.1263

Hassan, M., Awan, F. M., Naz, A., deAndrés-Galiana, E. J., Alvarez, O., Cernea, A., & Kloczkowski, A. (2022). Innovations in genomics and big data analytics for personalized medicine and health care: A review. *International Journal of Molecular Sciences*, *23*(9), 4645. doi:10.3390/ijms23094645 PMID:35563034

Hird, N., Ghosh, S., & Kitano, H. (2016). Digital health revolution: Perfect storm or perfect opportunity for pharmaceutical R&D? *Drug Discovery Today*, *21*(6), 900–911. doi:10.1016/j.drudis.2016.01.010 PMID:26821131

Hulsen, T. (2021). Challenges and solutions for big data in personalized healthcare. In Big Data in Psychiatry# x0026; Neurology (pp. 69-94). Academic Press. doi:10.1016/B978-0-12-822884-5.00016-7

Johnson, K. B., Wei, W. Q., Weeraratne, D., Frisse, M. E., Misulis, K., Rhee, K., & Snowdon, J. L. (2021). Precision medicine, AI, and the future of personalized health care. *Clinical and Translational Science*, *14*(1), 86–93. doi:10.1111/cts.12884 PMID:32961010

Lee, S. M., & Lee, D. (2021). Opportunities and challenges for contactless healthcare services in the post-COVID-19 Era. *Technological Forecasting and Social Change*, *167*, 120712. doi:10.1016/j.techfore.2021.120712 PMID:33654330

Paul, M., Maglaras, L., Ferrag, M. A., & AlMomani, I. (2023). *Digitization of healthcare sector: A study on privacy and security concerns*. ICT Express.

Pick, J. B., & Azari, R. (2008). Global digital divide: Influence of socioeconomic, governmental, and accessibility factors on information technology. *Information Technology for Development*, *14*(2), 91–115. doi:10.1002/itdj.20095

Vicente, M. R., & López, A. J. (2010). A multidimensional analysis of the disability digital divide: Some evidence for Internet use. *The Information Society*, *26*(1), 48–64. doi:10.1080/01615440903423245

Compilation of References

(Social Sustainability | UN Global Compact) https://www.sustain.ucla.edu/wp-content/uploads/UCLA-Sustainability-Charter.pdf

Abbou, T. (2022). The Pilgrimage to the Grand Magal in Ṭūbā, Senegal. International Journal of Religious Tourism and Pilgrimage, 10(4).

Abdeljaber, O., Avci, O., Kiranyaz, M. S., Boashash, B., Sodano, H., & Inman, D. J. (2018). 1-D CNNs for structural damage detection: Verification on a structural health monitoring benchmark data. *Neurocomputing*, *275*, 1308–1317. doi:10.1016/j.neucom.2017.09.069

Adekunle, P. A., Omoba, R. O., & Tella, A. (2007). Attitudes of librarians in selected Nigerian universities toward the use of ICT. *Library Philosophy and Practice*, *9*(2), 1–8.

Agarwal, B., Kumar, A., & Arora, T. (2020). Impact of Social Media Advertising on Millennials Buying Behaviour. *International Journal of Intelligent Enterprise*, *1*(1), 1. doi:10.1504/IJIE.2020.110795

Aguolu, C. C., & Aguolu, L. E. (2007). *A force in library development in Nigeria*. World Libraries. https://worldlibraries.dom.edu/index.php/worldlib/article/view/199/154

Ahmed, N. (2013). Sustainable Tourism Development in Uttarakhand Region of India. *International Journal of Management and Social Sciences Research, 2*(4).

Ajzen, I. (1991). The theory of planned behavior. *Organizational Behavior and Human Decision Processes*, *50*(2), 179–211. doi:10.1016/0749-5978(91)90020-T

Alazaizeh, M. M., Jamaliah, M. M., Mgonja, J. T., & Ababneh, A. (2019). Tour guide performance and sustainable visitor behavior at cultural heritage sites. *Journal of Sustainable Tourism*, *27*(11), 1708–1724. doi:10.1080/09669582.2019.1658766

Alghazi, S. S., Wong, S. Y., Kamsin, A., Yadegaridehkordi, E., & Shuib, L. (2020). Towards sustainable mobile learning: A brief review of the factors influencing acceptance of the use of mobile phones as learning tools. *Sustainability (Basel)*, *12*(24), 10527. doi:10.3390u122410527

Ali, F., Terrah, A., Dogan, S., & Cobanoglu, C. (2022). Social media marketing activities: Studying social identification, trust, value and loyalty. In *Digital Marketing and Social Media Strategies for Tourism and Hospitality Organizations* (pp. 35–56). Goodfellow Publishers. https://ebookcentral.proquest.com/lib/sunderland/detail.action?docID=29182557

Ali, H., & Jabeen, A. (2015). Effects of Education on Economic Growth: Evidence from Pakistan. American Journal of Economics. *Financial Management*, *1*(6), 579–585.

Alla, L., Bentalha, B., & Bouhtati, N. (2022). Assessing Supply Chain Performance in the Covid 19 Context: A Prospective Model. In *2022 14th International Colloquium of Logistics and Supply Chain Management (LOGISTIQUA)* (pp. 1-6). IEEE.

Almaiah, M. A., Ayouni, S., Hajjej, F., Lutfi, A., Almomani, O., & Awad, A. B. (2022). Smart mobile learning success model for higher educational institutions in the context of the COVID-19 pandemic. *Electronics (Basel), 11*(8), 1278. doi:10.3390/electronics11081278

ALmasoodi, M. F., & Rahman, S. (2023). International Tourists' Satisfaction with Tour Guide's Service Quality at Babylon Archaeological Site. *International Journal of Sustainable Development and Planning, 18*(1), 17–28. doi:10.18280/ijsdp.180102

Altinay, M., & Hussain, K. (2005). Sustainable tourism development: A case study of North Cyprus. *International Journal of Contemporary Hospitality Management, 17*(3), 272–280. doi:10.1108/09596110510591963

Alvarez Alday, M., & Fernández-Villaran, A. (2012). Economic Impact of Leisure in the 21st Century. *Arbor, 188*(754), 351–363. doi:10.3989/arbor.2012.754n2008

Ambika, N. (2022). Enhancing Security in IoT Instruments Using Artificial Intelligence. In V. J.K., S. D., & G.-P. V. (eds), IoT and Cloud Computing for Societal Good (pp. 259-276). Cham: Springer. doi:10.1007/978-3-030-73885-3_16

Ambika, N. (2022). An Augmented Edge Architecture for AI-IoT Services Deployment in the Modern Era. In *Handbook of Research on Technical, Privacy, and Security Challenges in a Modern World* (pp. 286–302). IGI Global.

Anannukul, N., & Yoopetch, C. (2022). The determinants of intention to visit wellness tourism destination of young tourists. *Kasetsart Journal of Social Sciences, 43*(2), 417–424. doi:10.34044/j.kjss.2022.43.2.20

Anser, M. K., Yousaf, Z., Usman, M., & Yousaf, S. (2020). Towards Strategic Business Performance of the Hospitality Sector: Nexus of ICT, E- Marketing and Organisational Readiness. *Sustainability (Basel), 12*(4), 1346. doi:10.3390u12041346

Anup, K. C., & Fernandez, M. (2022). Tourism and Himalayan Indigenous Communities. *Tourism and Development in the Himalaya*, 149–169. https://doi.org/ doi:10.4324/9781003030126-12/TOURISM-HIMALAYAN-INDIGENOUS-COMMUNITIES-ANUP-MARIELA-FERNANDEZ

Apaolaza, V., Hartmann, P., D'Souza, C., & López, C. M. (2018). Eat organic – Feel good? The relationship between organic food consumption, health concern and subjective wellbeing. *Food Quality and Preference, 63*, 51–62. doi:10.1016/j.foodqual.2017.07.011

Ap, J., & Wong, K. K. F. (2001). Case study on tour guiding: Professionalism, issues and problems. *Tourism Management, 22*(5), 551–563. doi:10.1016/S0261-5177(01)00013-9

Aref, F., & Gill, S. S. (2009). Rural tourism development through rural cooperatives. *Nature and Science, 7*(10), 68–73.

Ares, G., de Saldamando, L., Giménez, A., Claret, A., Cunha, L. M., Guerrero, L., de Moura, A. P., Oliveira, D. C. R., Symoneaux, R., & Deliza, R. (2015). Consumers' associations with wellbeing in a food-related context: A cross-cultural study. *Food Quality and Preference, 40*(PB), 304–315. doi:10.1016/j.foodqual.2014.06.001

Ares, G., De Saldamando, L., Giménez, A., & Deliza, R. (2014). Food and wellbeing. Towards a consumer-based approach. *Appetite, 74*, 61–69. doi:10.1016/j.appet.2013.11.017 PMID:24295927

Arica, R. (n.d.). *A Review of Barriers of Tour Operators Sustainable Tourism Activities*. Academia. https://www.academia.edu/31115290/A_Review_of_Barriers_of_Tour_Operators_Sustainable_Tourism_Activities

Arida, N. S. N. S., & Sunarta, N. (2017). *Pariwisata berkelanjutan.* Pariwisata Berkelanjutan.

Ataei, P., Gholamrezai, S., Movahedi, R., & Aliabadi, V. (2021). An analysis of farmers' intention to use green pesticides: The application of the extended theory of planned behavior and health belief model. *Journal of Rural Studies*, *81*, 374–384. doi:10.1016/j.jrurstud.2020.11.003

Ates, H. (2019). Elementary school teachers' behavioral intentions for healthy nutrition: Extending theory of planned behavior. *Health Education*, *119*(2), 133–149. doi:10.1108/HE-11-2018-0056

Awan, K. A., Din, I. U., Almogren, A., & Rodrigues, J. J. (2022). AutoTrust: A privacy-enhanced trust-based intrusion detection approach for internet of smart things. *Future Generation Computer Systems*, *137*, 288–301. doi:10.1016/j.future.2022.07.026

Awotunde, J. B., Jimoh, R. G., Folorunso, S. O., Adeniyi, E. A., Abiodun, K. M., & Banjo, O. O. (2021). Privacy and security concerns in IoT-based healthcare systems. In *The Fusion of Internet of Things, Artificial Intelligence, and Cloud Computing in Health Care* (pp. 105–134). Springer International Publishing. doi:10.1007/978-3-030-75220-0_6

Ayazlar, G. & Ayazlar, R. (2015). *Rural Tourism: A Conceptual Approach*. Research Gate.

Baddeley, J., & Font, X. (2011). Barriers to tour operator sustainable supply chain management. *Tourism Recreation Research*, *36*(3), 4. doi:10.1080/02508281.2011.11081667

Baguio, J. B. (2019). Outcomes-based education: Teachers' attitude and implementation. *University of Bohol Multidisciplinary Research Journal*, *7*(1), 110–127. doi:10.15631/ubmrj.v7i1.113

Bairwa, M. K. (2021). Festivals for Sustainable Tourism Development: A case study of Marwar Region of Rajasthan. In *Local Food and Community Empowerment through Tourism* (*Vol. 1*, pp. 82–96). Eureka Publication. https://www.researchgate.net/publication/354061838_Festivals_for_Sustainable_Tourism_Development_A_case_study_of_Marwar_Region_of_Rajasthan

Bakaloudi, D. R., Jeyakumar, D. T., Jayawardena, R., & Chourdakis, M. (2021). The impact of COVID-19 lockdown on snacking habits, fast-food and alcohol consumption: A systematic review of the evidence. *Clinical Nutrition (Edinburgh, Lothian)*. doi:10.1016/j.clnu.2021.04.020 PMID:34049747

Bakare, O. D. (2023). Emerging Technologies as a Panacea for Sustainable Provision of Library Services in Nigeria. In *Global Perspectives on Sustainable Library Practices* (pp. 1–21). IGI Global.

Bakare, O. D., & Ademakinwa, M. A. (2021). The Impact of COVID-19 on Mentorship of Graduate Students in Nigerian Universities. *Journal of the Nigerian Pastoral Counselling Association*, *1*(1), 15–19.

Bakare, O., & Okuonghae, N. (2022). Information Managers as Change Agents in Achieving Sustainable Development in the 21st Century. *Journal of Environmental Science and Economics*, *1*(2), 58–66. doi:10.56556/jescae.v1i2.97

Balageas, D., Fritzen, C. P., & Güemes, A. (2010). *Structural health monitoring* (Vol. 90). John Wiley & Sons.

Balapour, A., Reychav, I., Sabherwal, R., & Azuri, J. (2019). Mobile technology identity and self-efficacy: Implications for the adoption of clinically supported mobile health apps. *International Journal of Information Management*, *49*, 58–68. doi:10.1016/j.ijinfomgt.2019.03.005

Balle, M. (2022). The Social and Organisational Life of a Nocturnalilgr image in Mallorca From Palma to Lluc. *International Journal of Religious Tourism and Pilgrimage, 10*(4).

Baloglu, S., & Mangaloglu, M. (2001). Tourism destination images of Turkey, Egypt, Greece, and Italy as perceived by US-based tour operators and travel agents. *Tourism Management*, *22*(1), 1–9. doi:10.1016/S0261-5177(00)00030-3

Bansal, S. P., Gautam, P. K., & Kulshreestha, S. (n.d.). *THE DEVELOPMENT TEAM Principal Investigator Co-Principal Investigator Paper Coordinator Content Reviewer.*

Bao, Y., Tang, Z., Li, H., & Zhang, Y. (2019). Computer vision and deep learning–based data anomaly detection method for structural health monitoring. *Structural Health Monitoring, 18*(2), 401–421. doi:10.1177/1475921718757405

Baralla, G., Ibba, S., Marchesi, M., Tonelli, R., & Missineo, S. (2018) A blockchain based system to ensure transparency and reliability in food supply chain. In: *European conference on parallel processing.* Springer, Cham, pp 379–391

Barrett, E. M., Foster, S. I., & Beck, E. J. (2020). Whole grain and high-fibre grain foods: How do knowledge, perceptions and attitudes affect food choice? *Appetite, 149*, 104630. doi:10.1016/j.appet.2020.104630 PMID:32057840

Barua, B., &Urme, U. N. (2023). Assessing the online teaching readiness of faculty member. *Journal of Research in Innovative Teaching & Learning.*

Bauske, D. (n.d.). *B., von Münchhausen, M., Plitharas, A., Tsoukalas, K., Bauer, U., Köberich, T., WWF Deutschland, & WWF Deutschland.* Stoppt die Plastikflut Wirksame Maßnahmen zur Vermeidung von Einwegplastik und Verpackung im Hotel.

Beedie, P. (2011). Mountain guiding and adventure tourism: reflections on the choreography of the experience. L*eisure Studies, 22*(2), 147–167. doi:10.1080/026143603200068991

Ben-Eli, M. (2015). *Sustainability: The Five Core Principles–A New Framework.* Buckminster Fuller Institute. http://bfi-internal. org/sustainability/principles.

Bentalha, B. (2023). Motivating Factors for Hotel Employees: A Fuzzy Logic Approach. In Strategic Human Resource Management in the Hospitality Industry: A Digitalized Economic Paradigm (pp. 159-178). IGI Global. doi:10.4018/978-1-6684-7494-5.ch008

Bentalha, B., Hmioui, A., & Alla, L. (2023). Green Transportation Balanced Scorecard: A VIKOR Fuzzy Method for Evaluating Green Logistics Initiatives. In *International Conference on Digital Technologies and Applications* (pp. 916-925). Cham: Springer Nature Switzerland. 10.1007/978-3-031-29857-8_91

Bentalha, B. (2022). Green Transportation Balanced Scorecard Model: A Fuzzy-Delphi Approach During COVID-19. In *Computational Intelligence Techniques for Green Smart Cities* (pp. 107–127). Springer. doi:10.1007/978-3-030-96429-0_5

Bentalha, B. (2022). Smart Technologies for a Sustainable Service Supply Chain: A Prospective Perspective. *Journal of Environmental Issues and Climate Change, 1*(1), 77–89. doi:10.59110/jeicc.v1i1.81

Bentalha, B., Hmioui, A., & Alla, L. (2019). The digitalization of the supply chain management of service companies: a prospective approach. In *Proceedings of the 4th International Conference on Smart City Applications* (pp. 1-8). ACM. 10.1145/3368756.3369005

Bentalha, B., Hmioui, A., & Alla, L. (2020). Digital service supply chain management: current realities and prospective visions. In *The Proceedings of the Third International Conference on Smart City Applications* (pp. 808-822). Springer, Cham. 10.1007/978-3-030-37629-1_58

Bentalha, B., Hmioui, A., & Alla, L. (2021). The global performance of a service supply chain: a simulation-optimization under arena. In *The Proceedings of the Third International Conference on Smart City Applications* (pp. 489-502). Springer, Cham. 10.1007/978-3-030-66840-2_37

Bergada, À. (1997). Stradin: A strategic dynamic and interactive decision-making process. *Group Decision and Negotiation, 6*(1), 61–75. doi:10.1023/A:1008688508836

Bergadaà, M. (1999). Strategic Decisions and Implementation: PRODIN™, a Prospective Dialectic Interpersonal Method. *Journal of Business Research*, *45*(2), 211–220. doi:10.1016/S0148-2963(97)00225-7

Bhalla, P., Coghlan, A., & Recreation, P. B.-T. (2016). Homestays' contribution to community-based ecotourism in the Himalayan region of India. *Taylor & Francis, 41*(2), 213–228. doi:10.1080/02508281.2016.1178474

Binita, C. (2020). Homestay as a reliable promotional tool for Cultural Tourism and Security in Indian context. *IJSSTH, 21*(5). https://dialnet.unirioja.es/servlet/articulo?codigo=7962192

Boakye Agyeman, Y., Boaa Antwi-Bosiako, N., Box, P. O., & Wong, J. (2022). Visitor perceptions of the roles of tour guides in Kakum National Park in Ghana. *Cogent Social Sciences*, *8*(1), 2052403. doi:10.1080/23311886.2022.2052403

Bochkovskaya, A. V, & Bochkovskaya, A. (2022). Emotions at the Border : Verbal Aspects of the Attari-Wagah Patriotic Pilgrimage. *International Journal of Religious Tourism and Pilgrimage, 10*(4).

Bollen, K. (1987). Total, direct, and indirect effects in structural equation models. In C. Clogg (Ed.), *Sociological methodology* (pp. 37–69). American Sociological Association. doi:10.2307/271028

Boll, S., Meyer, J., & O'Connor, N. E. (2018). Health media: From multimedia signals to personal health insights. *IEEE MultiMedia*, *25*(1), 51–60. doi:10.1109/MMUL.2018.011921235

Bolton, A. D., Goosen, L., & Kritzinger, E. (2023). Embracing Business Sustainability Through Innovation and Productivity in the Automotive Sector: Creativity, Collaboration, and Generating Savings. In P. Tyagi, V. Nadda, V. Bharti, & E. Kemer (Eds.), Embracing Business Sustainability Through Innovation and Creativity in the Service Sector (pp. 184-204). IGI Global. doi:10.4018/978-1-6684-6732-9.ch012

Bompard, E., Estebsari, A., Mazza, A., Pons, E., & Solida, L. (2023). Innovative Higher Education Approaches for Power System Courses. *Education Sciences*, *13*(1), 92. doi:10.3390/educsci13010092

Bond, M. (2021). Schools and emergency remote education during the COVID-19 pandemic: A living rapid systematic review. *Asian Journal of Distance Education*, *15*(2), 191–247.

Boobalan, K., & Nawaz, N., M, H. R., & Gajenderan, V. (. (2021). Influence of Altruistic Motives on Organic Food Purchase: Theory of Planned Behavior. *Sustainability*, *13*. doi:10.3390u13116023

Borsoto, et al. (2014). Status of implementation and usefulness of outcomes-based education in the engineering department of an Asian university. *International Journal of Multidisciplinary Academic Research,* 14-25

Botha, R. J. (2002). Outcomes-based education and educational reform in South Africa. *International Journal of Leadership in Education*, *5*(4), 361–371. doi:10.1080/13603120110118831

Bramwell, B., & Lane, B. (2012). Towards Innovation in Sustainable Tourism Research? *Journal of Sustainable Tourism*, *20*(1), 1–7. doi:10.1080/09669582.2011.641559

Bravo, R., Martinez, E., & Pina, J. M. (2019). Effects of service experience on customer responses to a hotel chain. *International Journal of Contemporary Hospitality Management*, *31*(1), 389–405. doi:10.1108/IJCHM-09-2017-0569

Brown, G., Howat, G., & Voigt, C. (2011). *Wellness tourists: in search of transformation*. Emerald Insight. doi:10.1108/16605371111127206

Brown, R. L. (1997). Assessing specific mediational effects in complex theoretical models. *Structural Equation Modeling*, *4*(2), 142–156. doi:10.1080/10705519709540067

Bryon, J. (2012). Tour Guides as Storytellers – From Selling to Sharing. *Scandinavian Journal of Hospitality and Tourism, 12*(1), 27–43. doi:10.1080/15022250.2012.656922

Buckley, R. (2012). Sustainable tourism: Research and reality. *Annals of Tourism Research, 39*(2), 528–546. doi:10.1016/j.annals.2012.02.003

Budeanu, A. (2005). Impacts and responsibilities for sustainable tourism: A tour operator's perspective. *Journal of Cleaner Production, 13*(2), 89–97. https://www.academia.edu/8505736/Impacts_and_responsibilities_for_sustainable_tourism_a_tour_operators_perspective. doi:10.1016/j.jclepro.2003.12.024 PMID:32288344

Buhalis, D., & Laws, D. (2001). Tourism distribution channels: Practices, issues and transformations. London: Continuum International Publishing Group.

Buhalis, D., & Amaranggana, A. (2013). *Smart tourism destinations. Information and Communication Technologies in Tourism 2014*. Springer International Publishing.

Butler, R. W. (1999). Sustainable Tourism: A State-of-the-Art Review. *Tourism Geographies, 1*(1), 7–25. doi:10.1080/14616689908721291

Byrd, E. T. (2007). Stakeholders in Sustainable Tourism Development and Their Roles: Applying Stakeholder Theory to Sustainable Tourism Development. *Tourism Review, 62*(2), 6–13. doi:10.1108/16605370780000309

Byrd, E. T., Bosley, H. E., & Dronberger, M. G. (2009). Comparisons of Stakeholder Perceptions of Tourism Impacts in Rural Eastern North Carolina. *Tourism Management, 30*(5), 693–703. doi:10.1016/j.tourman.2008.10.021

Calvillo, J., Roman, I., & Roa, L. M. (2015). How technology is empowering patients? A literature review. *Health Expectations, 18*(5), 643–652. doi:10.1111/hex.12089 PMID:23711169

Camilleri, M. A., & Camilleri, A. C. (2022). The acceptance of learning management systems and video conferencing technologies: Lessons learned from COVID-19. *Technology. Knowledge and Learning, 27*(4), 1311–1333. doi:10.100710758-021-09561-y

Casado, S. G., Manuel, Á. F. G., Fernández, I. A., & Palomo, D. R. (2019). Competitive Intelligence and Sustainable Competitive Advantage in the Hotel Industry [March.]. *Sustainability, MDPI, Open Access Journal, 11*(6), 1–12.

Castillo, R. (2014). A paradigm shift to outcomes-based higher education: Policies, principles and preparations. [R]. *International Journal of Sciences, Basic and Applied Research*, 174–186.

Cattell, R. B. (1966). The scree test for the number of factors. *Multivariate Behavioral Research, 1*(2), 245–276. doi:10.120715327906mbr0102_10 PMID:26828106

Chakraborty, B. (2019). Homestay And Women Empowerment: A Case Study Of Women Managed Tourism Product In Kasar Devi, Uttarakhand, India. *Tourism International Scientific Conference Vrnjačka Banja - TISC, 4*(1), 202–216. https://www.tisc.rs/proceedings/index.php/hitmc/article/view/252

Chakraborty, B. (2019). *Homestay and women empowerment: A case study of women managed tourism product in Kasar Devi*. Uttarakhand.

Champion, V. L., & Skinner, C. S. (2008). The health belief model. *Health Behavior and Health Education: Theory, Research, and Practice, 4*, 45–65.

Chang, F. K., Markmiller, J. F., Yang, J., & Kim, Y. (2011). Structural health monitoring. *System health management: with aerospace applications*, 419-428.

Chang, A. C. (2020). *Intelligence-based medicine: artificial intelligence and human cognition in clinical medicine and healthcare*. Academic Press.

Chang, H. P., Ma, C. C., & Chen, H. S. (2020). The impacts of young consumers' health values on functional beverages purchase intentions. *International Journal of Environmental Research and Public Health, 17*(10), 3479. doi:10.3390/ijerph17103479 PMID:32429409

Chauhan, H. & Jain, V. (2022). *Destination branding as new tool for economic development: a qualitative approach with reference to JaunsarBawar Region, Uttarakhand.* Taylor & Francis. doi:10.1080/24721735.2022.2115331

Chen, D. (2009). *Innovation of Tourism Supply Chain Management. 2009 International Conference on Management of e-Commerce and e-Government*, Nanchang. 10.1109/ICMeCG.2009.79

Chen, J., Guan, J., Xu, J., & Clergeau, C. (2018). Constructing the Green Supply Chain for Rural Tourism, in China: Perspective of Front–Back Stage Decoupling. *Sustainability (Basel), 10*(11), 4276–4293. doi:10.3390u10114276

Cheung, M. W. (2007). Comparison of approaches to constructing confidence intervals for mediating effects using structural equation models. *Structural Equation Modeling, 14*(2), 227–246. doi:10.1080/10705510709336745

Chithradevi, S. N., & Nadda, V. (2022). Impact of Mobile Technology to Enhance the Customer Service Experience in SME Hotels. In *Disruptive Innovation and Emerging Technologies for Business Excellence in the Service Sector* (pp. 1–22). IGI Global. doi:10.4018/978-1-7998-9194-9.ch001

Choi, H.-S. C., & Sirakaya, E. (2005). Measuring residents. attitude toward sustainable tourism: Development of sustainable tourism attitude scale. *Journal of Travel Research, 43*(4), 380–394. doi:10.1177/0047287505274651

Christie, M. F., & Mason, P. A. (2010). Transformative Tour Guiding: Training Tour Guides to be Critically. *Journal of Ecotourism, 2*(1), 1–16. Https://Doi.Org/10.1080/14724040308668130. doi:10.1080/14724040308668130

Chu, S.-C. (2009). *Determinants of Consumer Engagement in Electronic Word-of-Mouth in Social Networking Sites.*

Chu, S. (2010). *Applying outcomes-based teaching and learning framework in the BSc Information Management Program in the Faculty of Education. Centre for information Technology in Education.* The University of Hong Kong.

Ciang, C. C., Lee, J. R., & Bang, H. J. (2008). Structural health monitoring for a wind turbine system: A review of damage detection methods. *Measurement Science & Technology, 19*(12), 122001. doi:10.1088/0957-0233/19/12/122001

Ciolac, R., Adamov, T., Iancu, T., Popescu, G., Lile, R., Rujescu, C., & Marin, D. (2019). Agritourism - A Sustainable Development Factor for Improving the "Health" of Rural Settlements. Case Study Apuseni Mountains Area. *Sustainability (Basel), 11*(5), 1467–1490. doi:10.3390u11051467

Clarkson, M. B. E. (1995). A Stakeholder Framework for Analyzing and Evaluating Corporate Social Performance. *Academy of Management Review, 20*(1), 92–117. doi:10.2307/258888

Clemente-Suárez, V. J., Beltrán-Velasco, A. I., Ramos-Campo, D. J., Mielgo-Ayuso, J., Nikolaidis, P. A., Belando, N., & Tornero-Aguilera, J. F. (2022). Physical activity and COVID-19. The basis for an efficient intervention in times of COVID-19 pandemic. *Physiology & Behavior, 244*, 113667. doi:10.1016/j.physbeh.2021.113667 PMID:34861297

Cohen, E. (1985). The tourist guide: The origins, structure and dynamics of a role. *Annals of Tourism Research, 12*(1), 5–29. doi:10.1016/0160-7383(85)90037-4

Cohen, J., Cohen, P., West, S. G., & Aiken, L. S. (1983). *Applied regression/correlation analysis for the behavioral sciences*. Routledge.

Crawford, J., & Cifuentes-Faura, J. (2022). Sustainability in higher education during the COVID-19 pandemic: A systematic review. *Sustainability (Basel), 14*(3), 1879. doi:10.3390u14031879

Creswell, J. W. (2009). Qualitative procedures. In *Research Design: Qualitative, Quantitative and Mixed-Methods Approaches* (pp. 173–202). Sage Publications.

Creswell, J. W., & Poth, C. N. (2016). *Qualitative inquiry and research design: Choosing among five approaches*. Sage publications.

Cronbach, L. J. (1951). Coefficient alpha and the internal structure of tests. *Psychometrika*, *16*(3), 297–334. doi:10.1007/BF02310555

Currie, R. R., Seaton, S., & Wesley, F. (2009). Determining Stakeholders for Feasibility Analysis. *Annals of Tourism Research*, *36*(1), 41–63. doi:10.1016/j.annals.2008.10.002

Daneva, A., & Nadda, V. (2023). Community Development Through Ecotourism: A Stakeholder Analysis of Botevgrad, Bulgaria. In Inclusive Community Development Through Tourism and Hospitality Practices (pp. 20-48). IGI Global.

Daniel, J., &Ndumbaro, F. (2022). An assessment of human resource capabilities in supporting digital records preservation: a case of RAMD and RITA, Tanzania. *Records Management Journal*.

Datta, B. (2022). PREFERENCES AND CHANGING NEEDS OF WELLNESS TOURISTS: A STUDY FROM INDIAN PERSPECTIVE POST COVID-19. *Geo Journal of Tourism and Geosites*, *42*(2 supplement), 782–786. doi:10.30892/gtg.422spl18-889

Davis, F. D. (1989). Perceived Usefulness, Perceived Ease of Use, and User Acceptance of Information Technology. *IT Usefulness and Ease of Use*, 319–339.

Daymon, C., & Holloway, I. (2010). *Qualitative research methods in public relations and marketing communications*. Routledge. doi:10.4324/9780203846544

De Jong, J. P., & Den Hartog, D. N. (2010). Measuring innovative work behaviour. *Creativity and Innovation Management*, *19*(1), 23–36. doi:10.1111/j.1467-8691.2010.00547.x

Deacon, B., Laufer, M., & Schäfer, L. O. (2023). Infusing educational technologies in the heart of the university—A systematic literature review from an organisational perspective. *British Journal of Educational Technology*, *54*(2), 441–466. doi:10.1111/bjet.13277

Del Chiappa, G. (2011). *Trustworthiness of Travel 2.0 applications and their influence on tourist behaviour: an empirical investigation in Italy*. Information and Communication Technologies in Tourism.

Delone, W. H., & Mclean, E. R. (2003). The DeLone and McLean Model of Information Systems Success: A Ten-Year Update. *Information Systems Research. Journal of Management Information Systems*, *19*(4), 9–30. doi:10.1080/07421222.2003.11045748

Dempsey, N., Bramley, G., Power, S., & Brown, C. (2009). The social dimension of sustainable development: Defining urban social sustainability. *Sustainable Development (Bradford)*, *19*(5), 289–300. doi:10.1002d.417

Deshmukh, P., & Croasdell, D. (2008). HIPAA: Privacy and security in health care networks. In Information Security and Ethics: Concepts, Methodologies, Tools, and Applications (pp. 2770-2781). IGI Global.

Dey, B., Mathew, J., & Chee-Hua, C. (2020). Influence of destination attractiveness factors and travel motivations on rural homestay choice: The moderating role of need for uniqueness. *International Journal of Culture, Tourism and Hospitality Research*, *14*(4), 639–666. doi:10.1108/IJCTHR-08-2019-0138

Dillette, A. K., Douglas, A. C., & Andrzejewski, C. (2021). Dimensions of holistic wellness as a result of international wellness tourism experiences. *Current Issues in Tourism*, *24*(6), 794–810. doi:10.1080/13683500.2020.1746247

Dimitrov, D. M. (2014). *Statistical methods for validation of assessment scale data in counseling and related fields.* John Wiley & Sons.

Dini, M., & Pencarelli, T. (2022). Wellness tourism and the components of its offer system: a holistic perspective. In Tourism Review, 77(2), 394–412. Emerald Group Holdings Ltd. doi:10.1108/TR-08-2020-0373

Dogru, T., Mody, M., & Leonardi, C. (2018). *Blockchain technology & its implications for the hospitality industry.* Boston University.

Doll, W. J., & Xia, W. (1997). Confirmatory factor analysis of the end-user computing satisfaction instrument: A replication. [JOEUC]. *Journal of Organizational and End User Computing*, *9*(2), 24–31. doi:10.4018/joeuc.1997040103

Donthu, N., & Gustafsson, A. (2020). Effects of COVID-19 on business and research. In *Journal of Business Research* (Vol. 117, pp. 284–289). Elsevier Inc. doi:10.1016/j.jbusres.2020.06.008

DroliM.OstiL. (2013). Developing health tourism in healthier rural areas: the role of matrix-resources. doi:10.13140/2.1.4023.9685

Dubbelink, S. I., Soria, C. H., & Constantinides, E. (2021). Social media marketing as a branding strategy in extraordinary times: Lessons from the covid-19 pandemic. In Sustainability (Switzerland), 13(18). MDPI. doi:10.3390u131810310

Dubey, R., Gunasekaran, A., Papadopoulos, T., Childe, S. J., Shibin, K. T., & Wamba, S. F. (2016). Sustainable supply chain management: Framework and further research directions. *Journal of Cleaner Production.*

Ebrahimi, M. & Eizad, E. (2018). *Effects of rural tourism: A case study of Iran.* Isfahan University of Technology.

Eccles, R. G., & Serafeim, G. (2013). A tale of two stories: Sustainability and the quarterly earnings call. *The Bank of America Journal of Applied Corporate Finance*, *25*(3), 8–19. doi:10.1111/jacf.12023

Ecotourism policy and planning. (2003). *Ecotourism Policy and Planning.* Ecotourism policy and Planning. doi:10.1079/9780851996097.0000

Eizenberg, E., & Jabareen, Z. (2017). Social sustainability: A new conceptual framework. *Sustainability (Basel)*, *9*(1), 68–82. doi:10.3390u9010068

Ezema, I., Izobo-Martins, O., & Owoseni, A. (2020). Promoting ICT and Digital Education in Public Schools in Lagos, Nigeria Using Affordable Clean Energy Solutions. *13th annual International Conference of Education, Research and Innovation (ICERI) Proceedings* (pp. 9585-9590). International Academy of Technology, Education and Development (IATED). https://library.iated.org/view/EZEMA2020PRO

Ezeuduji, I. O. (2015). Strategic event-based rural tourism development for sub-Saharan Africa. *Current Issues in Tourism*, *18*(3), 212–228. doi:10.1080/13683500.2013.787049

Fairlie, R. W. (2004). Race and the digital divide. *Contributions to Economic Analysis & Policy*, *3*(1), 1–38. doi:10.2202/1538-0645.1263

Ferdig, R. E., Kosko, K. W., & Gandolfi, E. (2022). Using the COVID-19 pandemic to create a vision for XR-based teacher education field experiences. *Journal of Technology and Teacher Education*, *30*(2), 239–252.

Feroz, H. M. B., Zulfiqar, S., Noor, S., & Huo, C. (2022). Examining multiple engagements and their impact on students' knowledge acquisition: The moderating role of information overload. *Journal of Applied Research in Higher Education*, *14*(1), 366–393. doi:10.1108/JARHE-11-2020-0422

Field, A. (2009). *Discovering Statistics Using SPSS (Introducing Statistical Methods).* Sage Publications Ltd.

Font, X., Tapper, R., Schwartz, K., & Kornilaki, M. (2008). Sustainable supply chain management in tourism. *Business Strategy and the Environment, 17*(4), 260–271. doi:10.1002/bse.527

Forgas, J. P., Baumeister, R. F., & Tice, D. M. (2009). The psychology of self-regulation: An introductory review. In J. P. Forgas, R. F. Baumeister, & D. M. Tice (Eds.), *Psychology of Self-Regulation: Cognitive, Affective and Motivational Processes* (pp. 1–20). Psychology Press.

Forrester, J. (1958). Industrial Dynamics A Major Breakthrough for Decision Makers. *Harvard Business Review, 36*, 37–66.

Freeman, R. E. (1984). *Strategic Management: A Stakeholder Approach*. Pitman.

Frischmann, P. (2011). *Konza Technology City: Where Africa's silicon savannah begins.* Do It In Kenya. www.doitinkenya.co.ke/pdf/Konza%20Summary%20Document.pdf

Gain, V. (2023). Informality as a resource: A systems-theoretical take on the open method of coordination in education. *European Educational Research Journal*, 14749041231168952. doi:10.1177/14749041231168952

George, T. (2022). *Semi-Structured Interview.* Scribbr. https://www.scribbr.com/methodology/semi-structured-interview/

Ghobakhloo, M., Fathi, M., Iranmanesh, M., Maroufkhani, P., & Morales, M. E. (2021). Industry 4.0 ten years on: A bibliometric and systematic review of concepts, sustainability value drivers, and success determinants. *Journal of Cleaner Production, 302*, 127052. doi:10.1016/j.jclepro.2021.127052

Ghobrini, R. E. A., Benzert, F. Z., & Balas, M. (2022). Educationalizinginstagram for virtual instruction in COVID-19: A pragmatic framework. [IJWLTT]. *International Journal of Web-Based Learning and Teaching Technologies, 17*(6), 1–16. doi:10.4018/IJWLTT.287621

Ghosh, P. (2021). Model Village Development in Indian Himalayan Region: An Overview of Initiatives and Activities. *International Journal of Social Sciences Citation*, 315–328. doi:10.46852/2249-6637.04.2021.4

Giancaspro, M. (2017). Is a 'smart contract' really a smart idea? Insights from a legal perspective. *Computer Law & Security Report, S026736491730167X*(6), 825–835. https://www.sciencedirect.com/science/article/pii/. doi:10.1016/j.clsr.2017.05.007

Gibsen, B. (2013). *Definitive Guide to Integrated Supply Chain Management*. Pearson.

Giessen-Hood, C. (1999). *Teacher'sattitudes towards the implementation of outcomes based education (OBE) in South Africa* [Doctoral dissertation University of the Witwatersrand].

Global Wellness Institute. (2019). *Understanding Wellness: Opportunities and Impacts of the Wellness Economy for Regional Development.* Global Wellness Institute. https://globalwellnessinstitute.org/industry-research/understanding-wellness-opportunities-impact-wellness-economy-for-regional-development/

Global Wellness Institute. (2021). *The Global Wellness Economy: Looking Beyond COVID.* Global Wellness Institute. https://globalwellnessinstitute.org/press-room/statistics-and-facts/

Goodyear, V. A., & Armour, K. M. (2021). Young People's health-related learning through social media: What do teachers need to know? *Teaching and Teacher Education, 102*, 103340. doi:10.1016/j.tate.2021.103340 PMID:34083866

Goosen, L. (2015a). Educational Technologies for an ICT4D MOOC in the 21st Century. In D. Nwaozuzu, & S. Mnisi (Ed.), *Proceedings of the South Africa International Conference on Educational Technologies* (pp. 37-48). Pretoria: African Academic Research Forum.

Goosen, L. (2015b). Educational Technologies for Growing Innovative e-Schools in the 21st Century: A Community Engagement Project. In D. Nwaozuzu, & S. Mnisi (Ed.), *Proceedings of the South Africa International Conference on Educational Technologies* (pp. 49-61). Pretoria: African Academic Research Forum.

Goosen, L. (2016, February 18). *"We don't need no education"? Yes, they DO want e-learning in Basic and Higher Education!* UIR. https://uir.unisa.ac.za/handle/10500/20999

Goosen, L., & Mukasa-Lwanga, T. (2017). Educational Technologies in Distance Education: Beyond the Horizon with Qualitative Perspectives. In U. I. Ogbonnaya, & S. Simelane-Mnisi (Ed.), *Proceedings of the South Africa International Conference on Educational Technologies* (pp. 41 - 54). Pretoria: African Academic Research Forum.

Goosen, L., & Ngugi, J. K. (2018). Rethinking Teaching and Learning in the 21st Century: Course Design Characteristics towards Innovative Behaviour. In M. M. Dichaba, & M. A. Sotayo (Ed.), *Proceedings of the South Africa International Conference on Education* (pp. 376 - 394). Pretoria: African Academic Research Forum.

Goosen, L., & Ngugi, J. K. (2019b). Towards Innovative Behaviour For Technology Students. In J. Kriek, A. Ferreira, K. Padayachee, S. Van Putten, D. Mogashana, W. Raucher, & M. Speight Vaughn (Ed.), *Proceedings of the 10th Institute of Science and Technology Education (ISTE) International Conference on Mathematics, Science and Technology Education* (pp. 333 - 342). Mopani Camp, Kruger National Park: UNISA. https://uir.unisa.ac.za/handle/10500/26055

Goosen, L. (2008). A Brief History of Choosing First Programming Languages. In J. Impagliazzo (Ed.), *History of Computing and Education 3* (Vol. 269, pp. 167–170). Springer. doi:10.1007/978-0-387-09657-5_11

Goosen, L. (2018). Students' Access to an ICT4D MOOC. In S. Kabanda, H. Suleman, & S. Jamieson (Ed.), *Proceedings of the 47th Annual Conference of the Southern African Computer Lectures' Association (SACLA 2018)* (pp. 183-201). Cape Town: University of Cape Town.

Goosen, L. (2019a). Research on Technology-Supported Teaching and Learning for Autism. In L. Makewa, B. Ngussa, & J. Kuboja (Eds.), *Technology-Supported Teaching and Research Methods for Educators* (pp. 88–110). IGI Global., doi:10.4018/978-1-5225-5915-3.ch005

Goosen, L. (2019b). Technology-Supported Teaching and Research Methods for Educators: Case Study of a Massive Open Online Course. In L. Makewa, B. Ngussa, & J. Kuboja (Eds.), *Technology-Supported Teaching and Research Methods for Educators* (pp. 128–148). IGI Global., doi:10.4018/978-1-5225-5915-3.ch007

Goosen, L., Mentz, E., & Nieuwoudt, H. (2007). Choosing the "Best" Programming Language?! In E. Cohen (Ed.), *Proceedings of the 2007 Computer Science and IT Education Conference* (pp. 269-282). Santa Rosa: Informing Science Press.

Goosen, L., & Ngugi, J. K. (2019a). Innovation for Computing Students Matter, of Course! In B. L. Tait & J. H. Kroeze (Eds.), *Proceedings of 48th Annual Conference of the Southern African Computer Lecturers' Association (SACLA 2019)* (pp. 19–36). University of South Africa. http://osprey.unisa.ac.za/sacla2019/SACLA2019%20Proceedings.pdf#page=31

Gössling, S., Hall, C. M., & Scott, D. (2015). *Tourism and Water*. Academia. https://www.academia.edu/9394033/Tourism_and_Water

Gretzel, U., Sigala, M., Xiang, Z., & Koo, C. (2015a). Smart tourism: Foundations and developments. *Electronic Markets, 25*(3), 179–188. doi:10.100712525-015-0196-8

Gretzel, U., Werthner, H., Koo, C., & Lamsfus, C. (2015b). Conceptual foundations for understanding smart tourism ecosystems. *Computers in Human Behavior, 50*, 558–563. doi:10.1016/j.chb.2015.03.043

Gui, G., Pan, H., Lin, Z., Li, Y., & Yuan, Z. (2017). Data-driven support vector machine with optimization techniques for structural health monitoring and damage detection. *KSCE Journal of Civil Engineering*, *21*(2), 523–534. doi:10.100712205-017-1518-5

Güler, M., Bütüner, S. Ö., Danişman, Ş., & Gürsoy, K. (2022). A meta-analysis of the impact of mobile learning on mathematics achievement. *Education and Information Technologies*, *27*(2), 1–21. doi:10.100710639-021-10640-x

Gursoy, D., & Chi, C. G. (2021). Celebrating 30 years of excellence amid the COVID-19 pandemic — An update on the effects of COVID-19 pandemic and COVID-19 vaccines on hospitality industry: Overview of the current situation and a research agenda. *Journal of Hospitality Marketing & Management*, *30*(3), 277–281. doi:10.1080/19368623.2021.1902052

Gurung, R. K. (2016). *Marketing Religious Tourism Destination, Case study: The Birthplace of Gautama Buddha, Lumbini, Nepal*. Research Gate.

Güzel, Ö. (n.d.). *Sustainable Tourism and The Roles of Tour Guides in Destinations: A Qualitative Case Study in Turkey*. Academia. https://www.academia.edu/44606413/Sustainable_Tourism_and_The_Roles_of_Tour_Guides_in_Destinations_A_Qualitative_Case_Study_in_Turkey

Hackman, J. R., & Oldham, G. R. (1980). *Work redesign*. Addison-Wesley.

Hagger, M. S., Wood, C., Stiff, C., & Chatzisarantis, N. L. (2009). The strength model of self-regulation failure and health-related behaviour. *Health Psychology Review*, *3*(2), 208–238. doi:10.1080/17437190903414387

Haidabrus, B. (2022). Information technology and management in higher education and science. *Futurity Education*, *2*(4), 26–35.

Hair, J. F., Anderson, R. E., Babin, B. J., & Black, W. C. (2010). *Multivariate data analysis: A global perspective* (Vol. 7). Pearson.

Hall, C. M. (2013). *Green growth and tourism for a sustainable future: "We just need to put the right policies in place", or, the lunatics have taken over the asylum*. Presented at International Critical Tourism Studies, Canterbury, NZ. http://canterbury-nz.academia.edu/CMichaelHall

Haller, S. F., & Haller, S. (2022). A Changed Understanding of Miracles in Religious Tourism A Changed Understanding of Miracles in Religious Tourism. *International Journal of Religious Tourism and Pilgrimage, 10*(4).

Hall, M. C., Sharples, L., Mitchell, R., Macionis, N., & Cambourne, B. (2003). *Food Tourism around the World*. Development, Management and Markets, Elsevier Butterworth-Heinemann.

Harden, R. M. (2002). Developments in outcome-based education. *Medical Teacher*, *24*(2), 117–120. doi:10.1080/01421590220120669 PMID:12098427

Hassan, M., Awan, F. M., Naz, A., deAndrés-Galiana, E. J., Alvarez, O., Cernea, A., & Kloczkowski, A. (2022). Innovations in genomics and big data analytics for personalized medicine and health care: A review. *International Journal of Molecular Sciences*, *23*(9), 4645. doi:10.3390/ijms23094645 PMID:35563034

Hassan, T., Carvache-Franco, M., Carvache-Franco, W., & Carvache-Franco, O. (2022). Segmentation of Religious Tourism by Motivations: A Study of the Pilgrimage to the City of Mecca. *Sustainability (Basel)*, *14*(13), 1–19. doi:10.3390u14137861

Hawkins, D., & Cunningham, J. (1996). It Is 'Never-Never Land' When Interest Groups Prevail: Disney's America Project, Prince William County, Virginia, USA. In L. Harrison & W. Husbands (Eds.), *Practicing Responsible Tourism: International Case Studies in Tourism Planning, Policy and Development* (pp. 350–365). John Wiley.

Heckmann, P., Shorten, D., & Engel, H. (2003). *Supply Chain Management at 21*. Chief Logistics Officer.

Heck, R. H., & Wolcott, L. P. (1997). Beginning teachers: A statewide study of factors explaining successful completion of the probationary period. *Educational Policy, 11*(1), 111–133. doi:10.1177/0895904897011001005

Herrera, F. & Blanco, C. (2012). Gastronomy's importance in the development of tourism destinations in the world. *Ref. Revista: Global Report on Food Tourism.* [UNWTO]. *World Tourism Organization.*

Herro, D., Kiger, D., & Owens, C. (2013). Mobile technology: Case-based suggestions for classroom integration and teacher educators. *Journal of Digital Learning in Teacher Education, 30*(1), 30–40. doi:10.1080/21532974.2013.10784723

Hey Leung, M. S., & Corcoran, J. (2022). A probabilistic method for structural integrity assurance based on damage detection structural health monitoring data. *Structural Health Monitoring, 21*(4), 1608–1625. doi:10.1177/14759217211038881

Hird, N., Ghosh, S., & Kitano, H. (2016). Digital health revolution: Perfect storm or perfect opportunity for pharmaceutical R&D? *Drug Discovery Today, 21*(6), 900–911. doi:10.1016/j.drudis.2016.01.010 PMID:26821131

Hmioui, A., Bentalha, B., & Alla, L. (2020). Service supply chain: A prospective analysis of sustainable management for global performance. In *2020 IEEE 13th International Colloquium of Logistics and Supply Chain Management (LOGISTIQUA)* (pp. 1-7). IEEE. 10.1109/LOGISTIQUA49782.2020.9353940

Hmioui, A., Alla, L., & Bentalha, B. (2017). *Pilotage de la touristicité territoriale au Maroc Proposition d'un indice de touriscticité pour la destination Fès. ntrepreneuriat, Innovation, Gouvernance et Développement territorial.* Faculté Polydisciplinaire de TAZA.

Hmioui, A., & Bentalha, B. (2020). Service Supply Chain Management et performance commerciale: Esquisse d'une synthèse théorique. *Alternatives Managériales Economiques*, 2(2), 1–21.

Hmioui, A., & Bentalha, B. (2021). Service supply chain management: A literature review. *International Journal of Logistics Systems and Management, 40*(3), 332–353. doi:10.1504/IJLSM.2021.120253

Ho, C. I., & Lee, Y. L. (2007). The development of an e-travel service quality scale. *Tourism Management, 28*(6), 1434–1449. doi:10.1016/j.tourman.2006.12.002

Hochbaum, G., Rosenstock, I., & Kegels, S. (1952). Health belief model. United States Public Health Service, 1.

Hoffman, R. R., Mueller, S. T., Klein, G., & Litman, J. (2023). Measures for explainable AI: Explanation goodness, user satisfaction, mental models, curiosity, trust, and human-AI performance. *Frontiers of Computer Science, 5*, 1096257. doi:10.3389/fcomp.2023.1096257

Horwath, C. C., Hagmann, D., & Hartmann, C. (2020). The Power of Food: Self-control moderates the association of hedonic hunger with overeating, snacking frequency and palatable food intake. *Eating Behaviors, 38*, 101393. doi:10.1016/j.eatbeh.2020.101393 PMID:32497904

Howley, D. (2022). Experiences of teaching and learning in K-12 physical education during COVID-19: An international comparative case study. *Physical Education and Sport Pedagogy, 27*(6), 608–625. doi:10.1080/17408989.2021.1922658

Huang, A., & George, Q. (2003). Huang, Jason S. K. LAU, K. L. Mak (2003), The impacts of sharing production information on supply chain dynamics: A review of the literature. *International Journal of Production Research, 41*(7), 1483–1517. doi:10.1080/0020754031000069625

Huang, X., Dai, S., & Xu, H. (2020). Predicting tourists' health risk preventative behaviour and travelling satisfaction in Tibet: Combining the theory of planned behaviour and health belief model. *Tourism Management Perspectives, 33*, 100589. doi:10.1016/j.tmp.2019.100589

Hulsen, T. (2021). Challenges and solutions for big data in personalized healthcare. In Big Data in Psychiatry# x0026; Neurology (pp. 69-94). Academic Press. doi:10.1016/B978-0-12-822884-5.00016-7

Hunter, C. (1997). Sustainable Tourism as an Adaptive Paradigm. *Annals of Tourism Research*, *24*(4), 850–867. doi:10.1016/S0160-7383(97)00036-4

Hunter, C. J. (1995). On the need to re-conceptualise sustainable tourism development. [Google Scholar] [CrossRef]. *Journal of Sustainable Tourism*, *3*(3), 155–165. doi:10.1080/09669589509510720

Hunter, W. C., Chung, N., Gretzel, U., & Koo, C. (2015). Constructivist research in smart tourism. *Asia Pacific Journal of Information Systems*, *25*(1), 105–120. doi:10.14329/apjis.2015.25.1.105

IBEF. (2022). *Uttarakhand State Report.* Delhi: India Brand Equity Foundation (IBEF). https://www.ibef.org/states/uttarakhand

Igbinovia, M. O., & Osuchukwu, N. P. (2018). Predictors of knowledge sharing behaviour on Sustainable Development Goals among library personnel in Nigeria. *IFLA Journal*, *44*(2), 119–131. doi:10.1177/0340035218763445

Iliev, D. (2020, December). The evolution of religious tourism: Concept, segmentation and development of new identities. *Journal of Hospitality and Tourism Management*, *45*, 131–140. doi:10.1016/j.jhtm.2020.07.012

Imran, M. M., & Ngyuen, N. (2018). A Community Response to Tourism, Focusing on the Home-stay Program in K Village in Nainital. *Journal of Urban and Rgional Studies on Contemporary India*, *4*(2), 55–62. https://home.hiroshima-u.ac.jp/hindas/index.html

Imran, S., Alam, K., & Beaumont, N. (2014). Environmental Orientations and Environmental Behaviour: Perceptions of Protected Area Tourism Stakeholders. *Tourism Management*, *40*, 290–299. doi:10.1016/j.tourman.2013.07.003

Intojunyomg, S., Kaewkitipong, L., & Ractham, P. (2016). *Thailand's tourism industry: Demystifying the supply chain.* SMU. https://cmp.smu.edu.sg/amb/article. [Accessed 01 February 2023].

Irenoa, K. O., Emilian, B., & Eru, J. (2019). Funding Academic Libraries in Nigeria for Effective Services: Alternatives to Resource Development and Library Management. *Communicate: Journal of Library and Information Science*, *21*(1), 104–111.

Ivona, A., Claval, P., Pagnini, P. & Scaini, M. (2006). *Farm tourism and rural development. a successful combination? a local experience.* OpenStarTs.

Jamal, T., & Stronza, A. (2009). Collaboration Theory and Tourism Practice in Protected Areas: Stakeholders, Structuring and Sustainability. *Journal of Sustainable Tourism*, *17*(2), 169–189. doi:10.1080/09669580802495741

Jasim, M. M. (2021). Universities to adopt outcome-based education system. *The Business Standard.* https://www.tbsnews.net/bangladesh/education/universities-adopt-outcome-based-education-system-215209

Jastrow, F., Greve, S., Thumel, M., Diekhoff, H., & Süßenbach, J. (2022). Digital technology in physical education: A systematic review of research from 2009 to 2020. *German Journal of Exercise and Sport Research*, *52*(4), 504–528. doi:10.100712662-022-00848-5

Jayara, J. (2017). *Home-Stay Tourism in Uttarakhand: Opportunities and Challenges.* Researchgate.Net. https://www.researchgate.net/profile/Jaswant-Jayara/publication/354143118_Home_Stay_Tourism_In_Uttarakhand-_Opportunities_Challenges/links/61272bd72b40ec7d8bc4677c/Home-Stay-Tourism-In-Uttarakhand-Opportunities-Challenges.pdf

Jayara, J. (2018). *Home-Stay Tourism in Uttarakhand: Opportunities and Challenges*. Researchgate.Net. https://www.researchgate.net/profile/Jaswant-Jayara/publication/354143118_Home_Stay_Tourism_In_Uttarakhand-_Opportunities_Challenges/links/61272bd72b40ec7d8bc4677c/Home-Stay-Tourism-In-Uttarakhand-Opportunities-Challenges.pdf

Ji, G., & Guo, B. (2009). *Study on the performance evaluation of sustainable tourism supply chain based on balanced scorecard*. 2009 6th International Conference on Service Systems and Service Management, Xiamen.

John F. Kenedy Quotes . (2023). Goodreads. https://www.goodreads.com/quotes/48906-if-this-nation-is-to-be-wise-as-well-as

Johnson, E. A., Lam, H. F., Katafygiotis, L. S., & Beck, J. L. (2001). A benchmark problem for structural health monitoring and damage detection. *Structural control for civil and infrastructure engineering*, 317-324.

Johnson, K. B., Wei, W. Q., Weeraratne, D., Frisse, M. E., Misulis, K., Rhee, K., & Snowdon, J. L. (2021). Precision medicine, AI, and the future of personalized health care. *Clinical and Translational Science*, *14*(1), 86–93. doi:10.1111/cts.12884 PMID:32961010

Jones, S. (2005). Community-Based Ecotourism the Significance of Social Capital. *Annals of Tourism Research*, *32*(2), 303–324. doi:10.1016/j.annals.2004.06.007

Jung, S. E., Shin, Y. H., & Dougherty, R. (2020). A Multi Theory–Based Investigation of College Students' Underlying Beliefs About Local Food Consumption. *Journal of Nutrition Education and Behavior*, *52*(10), 907–917. doi:10.1016/j.jneb.2020.07.002 PMID:32859527

Kakabadse, N. K., Kakabadse, A., & Kouzmin, A. (2002). Ethical considerations in management research: A truth seekers guide. *International Journal of Value-Based Management*, *15*(2), 105–138. doi:10.1023/A:1015246111906

Kala, D. (2018). Barriers to local community participation in tourism development: Evidence from mountainous state Uttarakhand, India. *Hrcak.Srce.Hr*, *66*(3). https://hrcak.srce.hr/clanak/303072

Kapil, S., & Planning, B. V. T. (n.d.). *Territorial Planning Models in Homestays: An Indian Context*. IGI Global. https://www.igi-global.com/chapter/territorial-planning-models-in-homestays/317827

Kaplan, A. M., & Haenlein, M. (2010). Users of the world, unite! The challenges and opportunities of Social Media. *Business Horizons*, *53*(1), 59–68. doi:10.1016/j.bushor.2009.09.003

Kapoor, S. (2016) Rural Tourism In India: Relevance, Prospects And Promotional Strategies. *International Journal of Tourism and Travel*, *9*(1, 2).

Kaukal, M., Werthner, H., & Hoepken, W. (2000). An approach to enable interoperability in electronic tourism markets. ECIS 2000 Proceedings. ACM.

Kavaratzis, M. (2012). From "necessary evil" to necessity: Stakeholders' involvement in place branding. *Journal of Place Management and Development*, *5*(1), 7–19. doi:10.1108/17538331211209013

Kavaratzis, M., & Hatch, M. J. (2013). The dynamics of place brands: An identity-based approach to place branding theory. *Marketing Theory*, *13*(1), 69–86. doi:10.1177/1470593112467268

Kember, D., & Leung, D. (2005). The Influence of the Teaching and Learning Environment on the Development of Generic Capabilities Needed for a Knowledge-Based Society. *Learning Environments Research*, *8*(3), 245–266. doi:10.100710984-005-1566-5

Kemer, E., & Tyagi, P. K. (2023). Application of Artificial Intelligence and Robotics in Tourism and Hospitality Marketing. In *Embracing Business Sustainability Through Innovation and Creativity in the Service Sector* (pp. 125–140). IGI Global. doi:10.4018/978-1-6684-6732-9.ch008

Khan, A., Bibi, S., Ardito, L., Lyu, J., Hayat, H., & Arif, A. M. (2020). Revisiting the Dynamics of Tourism, Economic Growth, and Environmental Pollutants in the Emerging Economies—Sustainable Tourism Policy Implications. *Sustainability (Basel)*, *12*(6), 2533. doi:10.3390u12062533

Khan, S. A., & Parveen, A. (2020). Professional competencies for librarians working in special libraries: The case of Pakistan. *The Electronic Library*, *38*(5/6), 1135–1148. doi:10.1108/EL-02-2020-0030

Kim, J., Yang, K., Min, J., & White, B. (2022). Hope, fear, and consumer behavioral change amid COVID-19: Application of protection motivation theory. *International Journal of Consumer Studies*, *46*(2), 558–574. doi:10.1111/ijcs.12700 PMID:34220343

Kiss, A. (2004). Is community-based ecotourism a good use of biodiversity conservation funds? *Trends in Ecology & Evolution*, *19*(5), 232–237. doi:10.1016/j.tree.2004.03.010 PMID:16701261

Km, D. M., & Munro, D. (2022). A Semi-autoethnographical Account of the Order of Malta ' s Annual Pilgrimage to Lourdes. *International Journal of Religious Tourism and Pilgrimage, 10*(4).

Kokkoris, M. D., & Stavrova, O. (2021). Meaning of food and consumer eating behaviors. *Food Quality and Preference*, *94*, 104343. doi:10.1016/j.foodqual.2021.104343

Kone, M. L., & Samayamanthula, D. R. (2021). Significance of conventional Indian foods acting as immune boosters to overcome COVID-19. *Environmental Resilience and Transformation in Times of COVID-19, 385*. doi:10.1016/B978-0-323-85512-9.00034-6

Korstanje, M. E. (2012). The Darker Side of Travel: The Theory and Practice of Dark Tourism. *International Journal of Contemporary Hospitality Management*, *24*(1), 160–162. doi:10.1108/09596111211197854

Ko, T. G. (2005). Development of a Tourism Sustainability Assessment Procedure: A Conceptual Approach. *Tourism Management*, *26*(3), 431–445. doi:10.1016/j.tourman.2003.12.003

Krepps, K. (2018). *An Appalachia Abroad: Connecting to International Mountain Cultures in India's Uttarakhand.* MDS. https://mds.marshall.edu/asa_conference/2018/accepted_proposals/145/

Krippendorff, K. (2018). *Content analysis: An introduction to its methodology*. Sage publications.

Kromanis, R., & Arab, M. Z. (n.d.). *Structural health monitoring of wind turbines: Characterizing response using a regression-based approach.*

Kuhn, L. (2007). Sustainable tourism as emergent discourse. *World Futures*, *63*(3–4), 286–297. doi:10.1080/02604020601174950

Kumar, S. (2019). *Kedarnath temple in Rainy season.* OpenVerse. https://openverse.org/image/78936110-af1e-4549-9a39-98c690268c5c?q=kedarnath%20temple.

Kumar, S., Rana, G., & Mairaj, H. (2017). *Status and Scenario of Tourism Industry in India-A Case Study of Uttarakhand.* Academia. https://www.academia.edu/download/52174384/STATUS_AND_SCENARIO_OF_TOURISM_INDUSTRY_IN_INDIA_-_A_CASE_STUDY_OF_UTTARAKHAND.pdf

Kusa, R. (2009). *Analiza łańcucha dostaw produktu turystycznego, w: Konkurencja i kooperacja w strategiach zarządzania organizacjami, red.* Jana Pyki, Towarzystwo Naukowe Organizacji i Kierownictwa. Oddział w Katowicach.

Kwaah, C. Y., Adu-Yeboah, C., Amuah, E., Essilfie, G., & Somuah, B. A. (2022). Exploring preservice teachers' digital skills, stress, and coping strategies during online lessons amid covid-19 pandemic in Ghana. *Cogent Education*, *9*(1), 2107292. doi:10.1080/2331186X.2022.2107292

Lagrosen, S. O., & Grundén, K. (2014). Social media marketing in the wellness industry. *The TQM Journal*, *26*(3), 253–260. doi:10.1108/TQM-12-2013-0129

Lambert, D. M., Stock, J. R., & Ellram, L. M. (1998). *Fundamentals of Logistics Management*. Irwin/McGraw-Hill.

Lane, M., & Coleman, P. (2012). Journal of Technology Research Technology ease of use. *Journal of Technology Research*, *3*, 1–12.

Laririt, M. R. I. (2011) *Sustainable tourism for biodiversity conservation - case study: El Nido Resorts, Palawan, Philippines*. Ten Knots Group. https://environment.elnidoresorts.com/2012/01/05/ sustainable-tourism-for-biodiversity-conservation/

Lasi, H., Fettke, P., Kemper, H. G., Feld, T., & Hoffmann, M. (2014). Industry 4.0. *Business & Information Systems Engineering*, *6*(4), 239–242. doi:10.100712599-014-0334-4

Lateef Ahmad, M. (2014). An Economic Evaluation of Indian Tourism Industry. *International Journal of Scientific and Research Publications, 4*(12).

Lebedev, O. T., Mokeeva, T. V., & Rodionov, D. G. (2018) Matrix Structures of Science and Technology Innovations Development and Implementation Trajectory. In *Proc. of the 31st Int. Business Information Management Association Conf.* IOP Science.

Lee, H., Woo, D., & Yu, S. (2022). Virtual reality metaverse system supplementing remote education methods: Based on aircraft maintenance simulation. *Applied Sciences (Basel, Switzerland)*, *12*(5), 2667. doi:10.3390/app12052667

Lee, J., Kao, H. A., & Yang, S. (2014). Service innovation and smart analytics for industry 4.0 and big data environment. *Procedia CIRP*, *16*, 3–8. doi:10.1016/j.procir.2014.02.001

Lee, S. M., & Lee, D. (2021). Opportunities and challenges for contactless healthcare services in the post-COVID-19 Era. *Technological Forecasting and Social Change*, *167*, 120712. doi:10.1016/j.techfore.2021.120712 PMID:33654330

Le, H. T. C. H., Dang, T. N., Ware, R., Phung, D., Thai, P. K., Sly, P. D., & Le An, P. (2021). Using the health beliefs model to explore children's attitudes and beliefs on air pollution. *Public Health*, *196*, 4–9. doi:10.1016/j.puhe.2021.04.026 PMID:34126559

Leung, D., Law, R., van Hoof, H., & Buhalis, D. (2013). Social Media in Tourism and Hospitality: A Literature Review. In Journal of Travel and Tourism Marketing, 30(1–2), 3–22. doi:10.1080/10548408.2013.750919

Li, J., Lee, T. J., Chen, N., & Park, K. S. (2022). Pro-environmental behaviour of the residents in sensitive tourism destinations. *Sage, 29*(2), 291–308. doi:10.1177/13567667221101406

Library inspired my love for education, says LG Chairman (2009, August 13). Vanguard. https://www.vanguardngr.com/2009/08/library-inspired-my-love-for-education-says-lg-chairman/

Lim, H. R., & An, S. (2021). Intention to purchase wellbeing food among Korean consumers: An application of the Theory of Planned Behavior. *Food Quality and Preference*, *88*, 104101. doi:10.1016/j.foodqual.2020.104101 PMID:33071469

Limongelli, C., Marani, A., Sciarrone, F., & Temperini, M. (2022). Measuring the similarity of concept maps according to pedagogical criteria. *IEEE Access : Practical Innovations, Open Solutions*, *10*, 27655–27669. doi:10.1109/ACCESS.2022.3156662

Line, N. D., & Wang, Y. (2017). A multi-stakeholder market oriented approach to destination marketing. J. Destin. [CrossRef]. *Mark. Manag.*, *6*, 84–93.

Ling, R. (2015). A review of Tourism Supply Chain based on the Perspective of sustainable development. *J Econ Sustain Develop*, *6*, 128–13.

Lin, T.-C. (2004). The role of higher education in economic development: An empirical study of Taiwan case. *Journal of Asian Economics*, *15*(2), 355–371. doi:10.1016/j.asieco.2004.02.006

Lizarraga, M., Villanueva, O. A., & Baquedano, M. (2011). Self-regulation of learning supported by web 2.0 tools: An example of raising competence on creativity and innovation. In G. Dettori & D. Persico (Eds.), *Fostering self-regulated learning through ICT* (pp. 295–314). Information Science Reference. doi:10.4018/978-1-61692-901-5.ch018

Lu, J., & Nepal, S. K. (2009). Sustainable Tourism Research: An Analysis of Papers Published in the Journal of Sustainable Tourism. *Journal of Sustainable Tourism*, *17*(1), 5–16. doi:10.1080/09669580802582480

Lu, J., Schmidt, M., Lee, M., & Huang, R. (2022). Usability research in educational technology: A state-of-the-art systematic review. *Educational Technology Research and Development*, *70*(6), 1951–1992. doi:10.100711423-022-10152-6

Lund, B. D., Omame, I., Tijani, S., & Agbaji, D. (2020). Perceptions toward artificial intelligence among academic library employees and alignment with the diffusion of innovations' adopter categories. *College & Research Libraries*, *81*(5), 865. doi:10.5860/crl.81.5.865

Lynch, P. A. (1999). Host attitudes towards guests in the homestay sector. *Tourism and Hospitality Research*, *1*(2), 119–144. doi:10.1177/146735849900100203

Macek, I. C. (2012). *Homestays as livelihood strategies in rural economies: The case of Johar Valley, Uttarakhand, India*. Proquest. https://search.proquest.com/openview/60d93a96583095eaa262583a4ab60097/1?pq-origsite=gscholar&cbl=18750

Maheshwari, A. (2020). Attitude and Perception of the Local Community Towards Community based Tourism Development in Har Ki Dun Valley Uttarakhand. *EM International*, *27*(1), 2021–2115. http://www.envirobiotechjournals.com/EEC/v27i121/EEC-16.pdf

Mandeep, S. L., & Mohan, D. (2021). *HVS Monday Musings: Wellness Tourism will Flourish in the Post-COVID Era*. Hospitality Net. https://www.hospitalitynet.org/opinion/4102574.html

Martha, H. (1999). *Ecotourism and sustainable development: Who owns paradise?* Washington, D.C.: Trove.

Mate, M. J. (2022). *Improving the Teaching Staff Capacity to Integrate EdTech in the Teaching and Learning Processes at Eduardo Mondlane University* [Master's thesis, Faculty of Humanities].

McDermott, M. S., Oliver, M., Simnadis, T., Beck, E. J., Coltman, T., Iverson, D., Caputi, P., & Sharma, R. (2015). The Theory of Planned Behaviour and dietary patterns: A systematic review and meta-analysis. *Preventive Medicine*, *81*, 150–156. doi:10.1016/j.ypmed.2015.08.020 PMID:26348455

McGrath, G. (2007). *Towards developing tour guides as interpreters of cultural heritage: The case of Cusco*. Quality Assurance and Certification in Ecotourism., doi:10.1079/9781845932374.0364

Mcintosh, I. S., & Mcintosh, I. S. (2022). Working Paper Part 1 : The Very First Pilgrimage - An Inspired Trajectory Out of Africa Working Paper Part 1. *International Journal of Religious Tourism and Pilgrimage*, *10*(4).

Mehdi, S. A. (2018), Sustainable Supply Chain Management in Pithoragarh: Prospects of Rural Tourism. *The IUP Journal of Supply Chain Management*. https://ssrn.com/abstract=3191710

Menon, D. (2022). Uses and gratifications of educational apps: A study during COVID-19 pandemic. *Computers and Education Open*, *3*, 100076. doi:10.1016/j.caeo.2022.100076

Michaels, S. (2022). *Eligibility, Preparation and Administration of the PASA (Pennsylvania Alternate System of Assessment): Special Education Teacher Perceptions of the Alternate Assessment*. Immaculata University.

Midraj, S. (2018). Outcome-Based Education (OBE). The TESOL Encyclopedia of English Language Teaching, 1-7.

Mikayilov, J. I., Mukhtarov, S., Mammadov, J., & Azizov, M. (2019). Re-evaluating the environmental impacts of tourism: Does EKC exist? *Environmental Science and Pollution Research International*, *26*(19), 19389–19402. doi:10.100711356-019-05269-w PMID:31073834

Ming-Chou, L., & Ming-Hsiao, C. (2012). Investigating learner affective performance in web-based learning by using entrepreneurship as a metaphor. *Journal of Educational Technology & Society*, *15*(3), 202–213.

Misra, L. (2012). *Role of Homestay in the Promotion of Rural Tourism in India*.

Mohayidin, M. G., Suandi, T., Mustapha, G., Konting, M., Kamaruddin, N., Man, N. A., Adam, A., & Abdullah, S. N. (2008). Implementation of Outcome-Based Education in Universiti Putra Malaysia: A Focus on Students' Learning Outcomes. *International Education Studies*, *1*(4), 147–160. doi:10.5539/ies.v1n4p147

Molefe, P., Tauoatsoala, P., Sifolo, P., Pfarelo, S., Unathi, M., & Henama, U. (2018). The effects of tourism supply chain management practices on tourism operations in Pretoria, South Africa. *African Journal of Hospitality, Tourism and Leisure*, 7.

Moniz Vieira, R. (2022). *The tourism and lifestyle mobilities of the Madeiran community in the Channel Island of Jersey*. [PhD thesis, Edinburgh Napier University..

Moropa, R. (2010). Academic libraries in transition: Some leadership issues–a viewpoint. *Library Management*, *31*(6), 381–390. doi:10.1108/01435121011066144

MoT. (2022). INDIA TOURISM STATISTICS. Delhi: Market Research Division, Ministry of Tourism, Government of India. https://tourism.gov.in/sites/default/files/2023-01/India%20Tourism%20Statistics%20English%202022%20%28Revise%29.pdf

Murphy, P. E. (1983). Perceptions and Attitudes of Decisionmaking Groups in Tourism Centers. *Journal of Travel Research*, *21*(3), 8–12. doi:10.1177/004728758302100302

Nadda, V. (2022a). Employability Skills Development in Hospitality. In Employability and Skills Development in the Sports, Events, and Hospitality Industry (pp. 25-46). IGI Global. doi:10.4018/978-1-7998-7781-3.ch002

Nadda, V. (2022b). Problem-Based Learning (PBL) and Employability Skills Development in the Hospitality Sector. In Employability and Skills Development in the Sports, Events, and Hospitality Industry (pp. 139-151). IGI Global.

Nadda, V. (2023). The Role of Information and Communication Technology (ICT) in Global Higher Education Institutions (HEIs). In Knowledge Management and Research Innovation in Global Higher Education Institutions (pp. 61-74). IGI Global.

Nadda, V., & Pospíšilová, M. (2023). Airbnb in the Local Neighbourhood: Innovaiton vs. Disruption. In Embracing Business Sustainability Through Innovation and Creativity in the Service Sector (pp. 249-252). IGI Global.

Nadda, V., Arnott, I., Sealy, W., & Delaney, E. (Eds.). (2022). *Employability and Skills Development in the Sports, Events, and Hospitality Industry*. IGI Global. https://www.igi-global.com/gateway/book/265889 doi:10.4018/978-1-7998-7781-3

Nadda, V., Gonzo, F., Batta, R., & Sharma, A. (Eds.). (2023). *Inclusive community development through tourism and hospitality practices.* IGI Global. https://www.igi-global.com/book/inclusive-community-development-through-tourism/304337 doi:10.4018/978-1-6684-6796-1

Nagaraj, A. (2021). *Introduction to Sensors in IoT and Cloud Computing Applications.* Bentham Science Publishers. doi:10.2174/97898114793591210101

Nagaraj, A. (2022). Adapting Blockchain for Energy Constrained IoT in Healthcare Environment. In K. Kaushik, S. Tayal, S. Dahiya, & A. O. Salau (Eds.), *Sustainable and Advanced Applications of Blockchain in Smart Computational Technologies* (p. 103). CRC press. doi:10.1201/9781003193425-7

Nagaraju, L. G., & Chandrashekara, B. (2014). Rural Tourism and Rural Development in India. [IJIMS]. *International Journal of Interdisciplinary and Multidisciplinary Studies, 1*(6), 42–48.

Nair, V., Munikrishnan, U. T., Rajaratnam, S. D., & King, N. (2015). Redefining rural tourism in Malaysia: A conceptual perspective. *Asia Pacific Journal of Tourism Research, 23*(3), 314–337. doi:10.1080/10941665.2014.889026

Najafqolinejad, A., & Hassanzadeh, M. (2016). National libraries and regional cooperations: A framework for ECO national libraries. *The Electronic Library, 34*(2), 196–212. doi:10.1108/EL-07-2014-0118

Nakamoto, S. (2008). *Bitcoin: a peer-to-peer electronic cash system.* Bitcoin.org. https:// bitcoin.org/bitcoin.pdf

Nakhoul, S. (2019). Banks are promoting digital solutions to cut costs. *Business News.* http://www.businessnews.com.lb/cms/Story/StoryDetails/7149

Nam, K., Dutt, C. S., Chathoth, P., & Khan, M. S. (2019). Blockchain technology for smart city and smart tourism: Latest trends and challenges. *Asia Pacific Journal of Tourism Research, 60,* 1–15.

Narayanan, A., Bonneau, J., Felten, E., Miller, A., & Goldfeder, S. (2016). *Bitcoin and cryptocurrency technologies: a comprehensive introduction.* Princeton University Press.

Nathaniel, S. P., & Adedoyin, F. F. (2020). Tourism development, natural resource abundance, and environmental sustainability: Another look at the ten most visited destinations. *Journal of Public Affairs,* 25–53.

National tourism policy. (2002) Tourism.gov. https://tourism.gov.in/sites/default/files/2019-11/National_tourism_Policy_2002.pdf

Nazar, R., Chaudhry, I. S., Ali, S., & Faheem, M. (2018). Role Of Quality Education For Sustainable Development Goals (SDGS). PEOPLE. *The International Journal of Social Sciences (Islamabad), 4*(2), 486–501. doi:10.20319/pijss.2018.42.486501

Necka, R., Cacioppo, E. A., & John, T. (2017). Article Loneliness and Social Internet Use: Pathways to Reconnection in a Digital World? *Perspectives on Psychological Science, 13*(1), 70–87. doi:10.1177/1745691617713052 PMID:28937910

Negi, J. M. (1990). *Tourism development and nature conservation.* Metropolitan Publishers.

Negruşa, A. L., Toader, V., Sofică, A., Tutunea, M. F., & Rus, R. V. (2015). Exploring gamification techniques and applications for sustainable tourism. *Sustainability (Basel), 7*(8), 11160–11189. doi:10.3390u70811160

Nel-lo Andreu, M. G., Font-Barnet, A., & Espasa Roca, M. (2021). Wellness tourism-new challenges and opportunities for tourism in Salou. *Sustainability (Basel), 13*(15), 8246. Advance online publication. doi:10.3390u13158246

Nelson, F. (2007). *Emergent or illusory? Community wildlife management in Tanzania.* Russell Press.

Neuman, L. W. (2006). *Social research methods: Qualitative and quantitative Approaches* (6th ed.). Pearson Education Inc.

Ngugi, J. K., & Goosen, L. (2021c). Computer Science and Information Technology Students' Self-regulated Learning and Knowledge Sharing Behavior as Drivers of Individual Innovative Behavior. (R. Silhavy, Ed.) Lecture Notes in Networks and Systems, 230, 593-608. doi:10.1007/978-3-030-77442-4_50

Ngugi, J. K., & Goosen, L. (2022). Digitalization and Drivers of Innovative Behavior for a Smart Economy in the Post-COVID-19 Era: Technology Student Course Design Characteristics. In L. Reis, L. Carvalho, C. Silveira, & D. Brasil (Eds.), Digitalization as a Driver for Smart Economy in the Post-COVID-19 Era (pp. 176-197)). IGI Global. doi:10.4018/978-1-7998-9227-4.ch010

Ngugi, J., & Goosen, L. (2017). The Effects of Course Design Characteristics, Self-Regulated Learning and Knowledge Sharing in Facilitating the Development of Innovative Behaviour among Technology Students at Universities. *Proceedings of the Institute of Science and Technology Education (ISTE) Conference on Mathematics, Science and Technology Education* (pp. 80-86). Mopani Camp, Kruger National Park: UNISA Press.

Ngugi, J., & Goosen, L. (2019, October 25). Towards Smart Innovation for Information Systems and Technology Students: Modelling Motivation, Metacognition and Affective Aspects of Learning. (Á. Rocha, & M. Serrhini, Eds.) Smart Innovation, Systems and Technologies, 111, 90-99. doi:10.1007/978-3-030-03577-8_11

Ngugi, J. K., & Goosen, L. (2021a). Knowledge Sharing Mediating Information Technology Student Innovation. In M. Khosrow-Pour (Ed.), *Handbook of Research on Modern Educational Technologies, Applications, and Management* (Vol. II, pp. 645–663). IGI Global. doi:10.4018/978-1-7998-3476-2.ch040

Ngugi, J. K., & Goosen, L. (2021b). Innovation, Entrepreneurship, and Sustainability for ICT Students Towards the Post-COVID-19 Era. In L. C. Carvalho, L. Reis, & C. Silveira (Eds.), *Handbook of Research on Entrepreneurship, Innovation, Sustainability, and ICTs in the Post-COVID-19 Era* (pp. 110–131). IGI Global. doi:10.4018/978-1-7998-6776-0.ch006

Ngugi, J., & Goosen, L. (2018). Modelling Course-Design Characteristics, Self-Regulated Learning and the Mediating Effect of Knowledge-Sharing Behavior as Drivers of Individual Innovative Behavior. *Eurasia Journal of Mathematics, Science and Technology Education*, *14*(8). doi:10.29333/ejmste/92087

Niedlich, S., Kallfaß, A., Pohle, S., & Bormann, I. (2021). A comprehensive view of trust in education: Conclusions from a systematic literature review. *Review of Education*, *9*(1), 124–158. doi:10.1002/rev3.3239

Nulty, P. M. (2004). *Keynote Presentation: Establishing the Principles for Sustainable Rural Tourism, Rural Tourism in Europe: Experiences, Development, and Perspectives*. WTO.

Nunes, A. R., Lee, K., & O'riordan, T. (2016). The importance of an integrating framework for achieving the Sustainable Development Goals: The example of health and well-being. *BMJ Global Health*, *1*(3), e000068. Advance online publication. doi:10.1136/bmjgh-2016-000068 PMID:28588955

Nyaupane, G. P., & Poudel, S. (2011). Linkages among Biodiversity, Livelihood, and Tourism. *Annals of Tourism Research*, *38*(4), 1344–1366. doi:10.1016/j.annals.2011.03.006

OECD. (2006). Innovation and Growth in Tourism. In Innovation and Growth: Chasing a Moving Frontier. Organisation for Economic Cooperation and Development (OECD). doi:10.1787/9789264073975-10-en

Okumus, B., & Linton-Kelly, H. (2022). *Introduction to Wellness Management in Hospitality and Tourism*.

Önder, E., & Kabadayi, N. (2015). Supplier Selection in Hospitality Industry Using ANP. *International Journal of Academic Research in Business & Social Sciences*, *5*(1). Advance online publication. doi:10.6007/IJARBSS/v5-i1/1417

Otsonu, A. S., Asom, F., Zuwaira, A., & Olije, O. A. (2016). Challenges and strategies to enhance staff development for effective library services in special libraries in Benue State, Nigeria. *International Journal of Education, Learning and Development*, *4*(4), 12–20.

Ozdamli, F., & Karagozlu, D. (2022). Online Education During the Pandemic: A Systematic Literature Review. *International Journal of Emerging Technologies in Learning*, *17*(16), 167–193. doi:10.3991/ijet.v17i16.32287

Ozdemir, A. I., Ar, I. M., & Erol, I. (2019). Assessment of blockchain applications in travel and tourism industry. *Quality & Quantity*, *54*, 1–15.

OzturkI. (2008). The role of education in economic development: a theoretical perspective. *SSRN*. doi:10.2139/ssrn.1137541

Pacific Policy Research Center. (2010). *21st Century Skills for Students and Teachers. Honolulu: Kamehameha Schools, Research & Evaluation Division.* Resource Center. http://resourcecentre.foodrisc.org/surveys_32.html

Page, S. J. (2014). *Tourism management: Managing for change.* Routledge. doi:10.4324/9781315768267

Page, S. J., & Connell, J. (2014). *Tourism: A Modern Synthesis* (4th ed.). Thomson Learning.

Pakhomova, T., Hryhorieva, V., Omelchenko, A., Kalenyk, M., & Semak, L. (2023). The formation of digital competence by means of information and communication technologies among students of higher education. *RevistaEduweb*, *17*(2), 78–88.

Pal, A. (n.d.). Potential and Planning for Ecotourism Development in Dehradun District (Uttarakhand). *Essence-Journal.* https://essence-journal.com/wp-content/uploads/Archives/Volume_VII/Issue_1/Potential-and-Planning-for-Ecotourism-Development-in-Dehradun-District-Uttarakhand.pdf

Pankaj. (2016). Rural Tourism a Solution for Ghost Villages of Uttarakhand. *International Journal of New Technology and Research, 2*(6).

Pan, S. Y., Gao, M., Kim, H., Shah, K. J., Pei, S. L., & Chiang, P. C. (2018). Advances and challenges in sustainable tourism toward a green economy. *The Science of the Total Environment*, *635*, 452–469. doi:10.1016/j.scitotenv.2018.04.134 PMID:29677671

Panyik, E., Costa, C., & Rátz, T. (2011). Panyik. E., Costa, c., and Rátz, T, (2011). Implementing integrated rural tourism: An event-based approach. *Tourism Management*, *32*(6), 1352–1363. doi:10.1016/j.tourman.2011.01.009

Patel, P. H., Angrish, A. K., & Nadda, V. (2023). A Cross-Sector Comparison of Industry 5.0: Digital Technologies in Supply Chain Management of FMCG and the Automotive Sector. In *Opportunities and Challenges of Business 5.0 in Emerging Markets* (pp. 99–123). IGI Global. doi:10.4018/978-1-6684-6403-8.ch006

Paul, M., Maglaras, L., Ferrag, M. A., & AlMomani, I. (2023). *Digitization of healthcare sector: A study on privacy and security concerns.* ICT Express.

Payal, M. (2021). *Overview of tourist behavior with respect to environmental sustainability of tourism in the context of a developing economy-a case study of Mussoorie, India.* Researchgate.Net. https://www.researchgate.net/profile/Ashish-Jangid/publication/356378409_Overview_of_Tourist_Behavior_with_Respect_to_Environmental_Sustainability_of_Tourism_in_the_Context_of_a_Developing_Economy_A_Case_Study_of_Mussoorie_India/links/61976b0061f0987720b297fe/Overview-of-Tourist-Behavior-with-Respect-to-Environmental-Sustainability-of-Tourism-in-the-Context-of-a-Developing-Economy-A-Case-Study-of-Mussoorie-India.pdf

Pearcy, H. D., Gorodina, D., & Lester, J. (2011). *Using the Resource-Based View to Explore the Jamaican Health Tourism Sector as a Service: A Preliminary Examination.* 2011 Las Vegas International Academic Conference Conference Proceedings. Caesars Palace, Las Vegas.

Peceny, U. S., Urbančič, J., Mokorel, S., Kuralt, V., & Ilijaš, T. (2019). Tourism 4.0: Challenges in Marketing a Paradigm Shift. In Consumer Behavior and Marketing. IntechOpen.

Pechlaner, H., & Fischer, E. (2006). Alpine Wellness: A Resource-based View. *Tourism Recreation Research, 31*(1), 67–77. doi:10.1080/02508281.2006.11081248

Pick, J. B., & Azari, R. (2008). Global digital divide: Influence of socioeconomic, governmental, and accessibility factors on information technology. *Information Technology for Development*, *14*(2), 91–115. doi:10.1002/itdj.20095

Point 1. website: https://travel.economictimes.indiatimes.com/news/research-and-statistics/figures/indian-hospitality-sector-witnessed-90-yoy-revpar-growth-in-q3-2022-jll/95375678

Polese, M., & Stren, R. (2000). *The Social Sustainability of Cities: Diversity and the Management of Change*. University of Toronto Press. doi:10.3138/9781442682399

Pomering, A., Noble, G., & Lester, W.J. (2011). Conceptualising a contemporary marketing mix for sustainable tourism. *J Sustain Tour 19*(8), 953–969. https://doi.org/. 584625 doi:10.1080/09669582.2011

Porter, M. E., & Heppelmann, J. E. (2014). How smart, connected products are transforming competition. *Harvard Business Review*, *92*(11), 64–88.

Portnov-Neeman, Y., & Barak, M. (2013). Exploring Students' Perceptions about Learning in School: An Activity Theory Based Study. *Journal of Education and Learning*, *2*(3), 9–25. doi:10.5539/jel.v2n3p9

Prajapati, V., Dhodi, R., & Journal, R. D.-I. (2018). *Women Empowerment Through Participation In Homestay In Sari Village Of Uttarakhand*. Researchgate.Net. https://www.researchgate.net/profile/Vijay-Prajapati-18/publication/363703460_Women_empowerment_through_participation_in_homestay_in_sari_village_of_Uttarakhand/links/632b0a98071ea12e364e9502/Women-empowerment-through-participation-in-homestay-in-sari-village-of-Uttarakhand.pdf

Pregowska, A., Masztalerz, K., Garlińska, M., & Osial, M. (2021). A worldwide journey through distance education—From the post office to virtual, augmented and mixed realities, and education during the COVID-19 pandemic. *Education Sciences*, *11*(3), 118. doi:10.3390/educsci11030118

Preuss, L. (2005). Rhetoric and reality of corporate greening: A view from the supply chain management function. *Business Strategy and the Environment*, *14*(2), 123–139. doi:10.1002/bse.435

Progano, R. N., & Progano, R. N. (2022). Roles of Religious Guides in Tourism : A Qualitative Study from Japan Roles of Religious Guides in Tourism. *International Journal of Religious Tourism and Pilgrimage, 10*(4).

Pu, P., Cheng, L., Samarathunga, W. H. M. S., & Wall, G. (2023). Tour guides' sustainable tourism practices in host-guest interactions: When Tibet meets the west. *Tourism Review*, *78*(3), 808–833. doi:10.1108/TR-04-2022-0182

Purvis, B., Mao, Y., & Robinson, D. (2019). Three pillars of sustainability: In search of conceptual origins. *Sustainability Science*, *14*(3), 681–695. doi:10.100711625-018-0627-5

Qiao, X., Ji, L., Jin, Y., Si, H., Bian, Y., Wang, W., & Wang, C. (2021). Development and validation of an instrument to measure beliefs in physical activity among (pre)frail older adults: An integration of the Health Belief Model and the Theory of Planned Behavior. *Patient Education and Counseling*, *104*(10), 2544–2551. doi:10.1016/j.pec.2021.03.009 PMID:33722429

Quinn, E. M., & Quinn, E. M. (2022). Making History Visible : Ireland ' s National Famine Way Told Through Models and Interactive Digital Narratives Making History Visible. *International Journal of Religious Tourism and Pilgrimage, 10*(4).

Quote Park. (1996, December 23). *Carl Sagan Quotes*. Quote Park. https://quotepark.com/quotes/687730-carl-sagan-books-permit-us-to-voyage-through-time-to-tap-the/

Radha, R., Mahalakshmi, K., Kumar, V. S., &Saravanakumar, A. R. (2020). E-Learning during lockdown of Covid-19 pandemic: A global perspective. *International journal of control and automation, 13*(4), 1088-1099.

Radhika, V. (2020). RURAL TOURISM – Features, Components and Key drivers for its Growth. *IJCRT, 8*(10).

Rahman, F., & Amir, P. (2019). Trends in Reading Literary Fiction in Print and Cyber Media by Undergraduate Students of Hasanuddin University. *International Journal of Education and Practice, 7*(2), 66–77. doi:10.18488/journal.61.2019.72.66.77

Rahman, M. S. (2013). Relationship among GDP, per capita GDP, literacy rate and unemployment rate. *British Journal of Arts and Social Sciences, 14*(2), 169–177.

Raman, V., & Hellerstein, J. M. (2000). *An interactive framework for data cleaning*. Digital Assets. https://digitalassets.lib.berkeley.edu/techreports/ucb/text/CSD-00-1110.pdf

Ramirez, C., & Rangel, J. (2018). Sustainable Tourism:The New Engine for the Economic Development of the 21st Century in APEC. *International Journal of Sustainable Economies Management, 7*(4), 29–36. doi:10.4018/IJSEM.2018100103

Ranasinghe, R., Damunupola, A., Wijesundara, W., & Karunarathne, C. (2020). *TOURISM AFTER CORONA: IMPACTS OF COVID 19 PANDEMIC AND WAY FORWARD FOR TOURISM, HOTEL AND MICE INDUSTRY IN SRI LANKA*. Research Gate. https://doi.org/ doi:10.13140/RG.2.2.27955.17442

Rao, N. J. (2020). Outcome-based education: An outline. *Higher Education for the Future, 7*(1), 5–21. doi:10.1177/2347631119886418

Rao, P., & Holt, D. (2005). Do green supply chains lead to competitiveness and economic performance. *International Journal of Operations & Production Management, 25*(9), 898–916. doi:10.1108/01443570510613956

Rauniar, R., Rawski, G., Yang, J., & Johnson, B. (2014). Technology acceptance model (TAM) and social media usage: An empirical study on Facebook. *Journal of Enterprise Information Management, 27*(1), 6–30. doi:10.1108/JEIM-04-2012-0011

Ray, N. & Das, D. (2020). *Relationship among Influencing Factors of Tourism Infrastructure: An Empirical Assessment at Kamarpukur, India*. IGI Global. . doi:10.4018/978-1-7998-2469-5.ch039

Reichel, A., Lowengart, O., & Milman, A. (2000). Rural tourism in Israel: Service quality and orientation. *Tourism Management, 21*(5), 451–459. doi:10.1016/S0261-5177(99)00099-0

Republic of Kenya. (2007a). *Kenya Vision 2030: A globally competitive and prosperous Kenya*. Government Printer.

Republic of Kenya. (2007b). Sector Plan for Science [Nairobi: Government Printer.]. *Technology and Innovation*.

Republic of Kenya. (2012). *Universities Act. Kenya Gazette Supplement No. 192 (Acts No. 42)*. Nairobi: Government Printer.

Richards, G. (n.d.). *Cultural tourism : global and local perspectives*. Routledge. https://www.routledge.com/Cultural-Tourism-Global-and-Local-Perspectives/Richards/p/book/9780789031174

Robertson, V. J. (2021). *UNESCO Statement for the World Summit on Ecotourism*. UNESCO. http://www.unep.fr/shared/publications/cdrom/WEBx0139xPA/statmnts/pdfs/rouneef

Robinson, M., & Picard, D. (2011). Tourism, Culture and Sustainable Development. *Sustainable Development, 54*(1&2), 97.

Roblek, V., Drpić, D., Meško, M., & Milojica, V. (2021). Evolution of Sustainable Tourism Concepts. *Sustainability (Basel), 13*(22), 12829. doi:10.3390u132212829

Rodrigue, J. (2020). *The Geography of Transport Systems*. Routledge.

Rowley, T. J. (1997). Moving Beyond Dyadic Ties: A Network Theory of Stakeholder Influences. *Academy of Management Review, 22*(4), 887–910. doi:10.2307/259248

Roxas, F. M. Y., Rivera, J. P. R., & Gutierrez, E. L. M. (2020). Framework for creating sustainable tourism using systems thinking. *Current Issues in Tourism, 23*(3), 280–296. doi:10.1080/13683500.2018.1534805

Samoggia, A., & Riedel, B. (2020). Assessment of nutrition-focused mobile apps' influence on consumers' healthy food behaviour and nutrition knowledge. *Food Research International, 128*, 108766. doi:10.1016/j.foodres.2019.108766 PMID:31955740

Sanfiel-Fumero, A., Armas-Cruz, Y., & González-Morales, O. (2017). Sustainability of the tourist supply chain and governance in an insular biosphere reserve destination: The perspective of tourist accommodation. *European Planning Studies, 25*(7), 1256–1274. doi:10.1080/09654313.2017.1319466

Saravanakumar, M., & Suganthalakshmi, T. (2012). Social Media Marketing. *Life Science Journal, 9*(4), 1097–8135. http://www.lifesciencesite.comhttp://www.lifesciencesite.com.670

Sati, V. P. (2020). A Sustainable Homestay Tourism and Its Prospects. In *Sustainable Tourism Development in the Himalaya: Constraints and Prospects*. Springer. https://link.springer.com/chapter/10.1007/978-3-030-58854-0_9

Sautter, E. T., & Leisen, B. (1999). Managing Stakeholders a Tourism Planning Model. *Annals of Tourism Research, 26*(2), 312–328. doi:10.1016/S0160-7383(98)00097-8

Saville, P., & MacIver, R. (2017). A very good question. *Psychometric Testing: Critical Perspectives*, 29–42.

Schizas, N., Karras, A., Karras, C., & Sioutas, S. (2022). TinyML for Ultra-Low Power AI and Large Scale IoT Deployments: A Systematic Review. *Future Internet, 14*(12), 363. doi:10.3390/fi14120363

Schwab, K. (2016) *The Fourth Industrial Revolution: what it means, how to respond.* World Economic Forum. https://www.weforum.org/agenda/2 016/01/the-fourth-industrial revolution- what it- means-and-how to- respond/

Secundo, G., Gioconda, M. E. L. E., Del Vecchio, P., Gianluca, E. L. I. A., Margherita, A., & Valentina, N. D. O. U. (2021). Threat or opportunity? A case study of digital-enabled redesign of entrepreneurship education in the COVID-19 emergency. *Technological Forecasting and Social Change, 166*, 120565. doi:10.1016/j.techfore.2020.120565 PMID:33518821

Seffinga, J., Lyons, L., & Bachman, A. (2017). *The blockchain (r)evolution - the Swiss perspective*. Deloitte.

Semwal, R. (2022). Preserving and Marketing Rural Cultural Heritage through Homestays of Uttarakhand State. In *Recent Trends in Tourism and Hospitality* (1st ed., Vol. 1, pp. 85–97). Eureka Publications., https://www.researchgate.net/publication/365635848_Preserving_and_Marketing_Rural_Cultural_Heritage_through_Homestays_of_Uttarakhand_State

Sen, A. (2013). *A survey of sustainable development: social and economic dimensions* (Vol. 6). Island Press.

Seyedabolghasemi, M. A., Kilic, H., Avci, T., Eluwole, K. K., & Lasisi, T. T. (2022). Residents' perceptions of sustainable tourism destination recovery: The case of Northern Cyprus. [CrossRef]. *Land (Basel), 11*(1), 94. doi:10.3390/land11010094

Shamim, S., Cang, S., Yu, H., & Li, Y. (2016). Management approaches for Industry 4.0: A human resource management perspective. In *2016 IEEE Congress on Evolutionary Computation (CEC)* (pp. 5309-5316). IEEE. 10.1109/CEC.2016.7748365

Shen, B., & Bissell, K. (2013). Social Media, Social Me: A Content Analysis of Beauty Companies' Use of Facebook in Marketing and Branding. *Journal of Promotion Management, 19*(5), 629–651. doi:10.1080/10496491.2013.829160

Shultz, J., & Shultz, J. A. (2022). The Epic Pilgrimage : The Way of the Ascetics of El Capitan. *International Journal of Religious Tourism and Pilgrimage, 10*(4).

Siakalli, M., Mousoulidou, M., Christodoulou, A., Savvidou, A., & Kouppa, K. (2022). Secondary Education and COVID-19. *Encyclopedia, 2*(1), 409–427. doi:10.3390/encyclopedia2010025

Sidola, A., Kumar, P., & Kumar, D. (2012). System dynamics investigation of information technology in small and medium enterprise supply chain. *Journal of Advances in Management Research, 9*(2), 199–207. doi:10.1108/09727981211271940

Silva, A. S., Nascimento, L. P., Ribeiro, J. R., & Belderrain, M. C. N. (2009). ANP and ratings model applied to supplier selection problem. *Proceedings of the International Symposium on the Analytic Hierarchy Process.* Semantic Scholar.

Singh, A. (2022). Conceptual framework on Smart Learning Environment for the present and new century-An Indian perspective. *Revista de educación y derecho= Education and law review*, (25), 2.

Singh, A., & Bathla, G. (2023). Fostering Creativity and Innovation: Tourism and Hospitality Perspective. In Embracing Business Sustainability Through Innovation and Creativity in the Service Sector (pp. 70-83). IGI Global.

Singh, A. K., Tyagi, P. K., Irshad, A., Singh, A. K., Tyagi, P., & Benedict, B. (2023b, March). Use of Internet of Things in the Tourism and Hospitality Realm: A Descriptive Bibliometric Study using Bibliometrix R-Tool. *Second International Conference on Electronics and Renewable Systems (ICEARS)* (pp. 619-626). IEEE. 10.1109/ICEARS56392.2023.10085341

Singh, A. K., Tyagi, P., Tyagi, P. K., Chanchal, H. K., Singh, A. K., & Arora, B. (2023a, January). Green Technology and Sustainability: A Review and Future Research Agenda. *5th International Conference on Smart Systems and Inventive Technology (ICSSIT)* (pp. 239-246). IEEE. 10.1109/ICSSIT55814.2023.10061015

Smarsly, K., Dragos, K., & Wiggenbrock, J. (2016). Machine learning techniques for structural health monitoring. *8th European workshop on structural health monitoring (EWSHM 2016)*, (pp. 5-8). Bilbao, Spain.

Smith, M., & Puczko, L. (2014). History of Health Tourism. In *Health, Tourism and Hospitality*. Routledge. https://books.google.co.uk/books?hl=en&lr=&id=p0bIAgAAQBAJ&oi=fnd&pg=PP1&dq=Health,+Tourism+and+Hospitality:+Spas,+Wellness+and+Medical+Travel&ots=1Kf6yfyQSa&sig=xUqjKWxF7Oubwap861XF_wYVkfo&redir_esc=y#v=onepage&q=Health%2C%20Tourism%20and%20Hospitality%3A%20Spas%2C%20Wellness%20and%20Medical%20Travel&f=false doi:10.4324/9780203083772

Sofaer, S. (1999). Qualitative methods: What are they and why use them? *Health Services Research, 34*(5 Pt 2), 1101–1118. http://www.ncbi.nlm.nih.gov/pubmed/10591275%0Ahttp://www.pubmedcentral.nih.gov/articlerender.fcgi?artid=PMC1089055 PMID:10591275

Song, D., & Xu, Y. (2011). Integrated Design of Service Supply Chain in the Perspective of Producer Service Outsourcing. *International Conference on Management and Service Science (MASS),* IEEE, pp. 1-4. 10.1109/ICMSS.2011.5998333

Song, H., Li, G., Witt, S. F., & Athanasopoulos, G. (2011). Forecasting tourist arrivals using time-varying parameter structural time series models. *International Journal of Forecasting, 27*(3), 855–869. doi:10.1016/j.ijforecast.2010.06.001

Song, H., Liu, J., & Chen, G. (2012). Tourism Value Chain Governance. *Review and Prospects Journal of Travel Research, 2012*, 96–107.

Songur, A. G., & Turktarhan, G. (2022). The role of social media marketing in the travel planning and decision-making processes of today's travelers. In *Digital Marketing and Social Media Strategies for Tourism and Hospitality Organizations*. Goodfellow Publishers. https://ebookcentral.proquest.com/lib/sunderland/detail.action?docID=29182557

Sorokina, A. (2016).. . *Typology of Gastronomy Tourists and Tourism.*, (January), 99.

Spady, W. (2020). *Outcome-Based Education's Empowering Essence*. Mason Works Press. https://williamspady.com/index.php/products/

Spady, W. G. (1994). *Outcome-based education: Critical issues and answers*. American Association of School Administrators.

Spasic, V. (2012). Integrating sustainable tourism in tour operators' supply chain. *Singidunum Journal of Applied Sciences.*, *9*(1), 60–66. doi:10.5937jas1201060S

Statista. (2022). *Social media platforms used by marketers*. Statista. https://www.statista.com/statistics/259379/social-media-platforms-used-by-marketers-worldwide/

Statista. (2023). *Number of worldwide social network users 2027*. Statista. https://www.statista.com/statistics/278414/number-of-worldwide-social-network-users/

Stoddard, J. E., Pollard, C. E., & Evans, M. R. (2012). The Triple Bottom Line: A Framework for Sustainable Tourism Development. *International Journal of Hospitality & Tourism Administration*, *13*(3), 233–258. doi:10.1080/15256480.2012.698173

Streiner, D. L., Norman, G. R., & Cairney, J. (2015). *Health measurement scales: a practical guide to their development and use*. Oxford University Press. doi:10.1093/med/9780199685219.001.0001

Syakier, W. A., & Hanafiah, M. H. (2021). Tour Guide Performances, Tourist Satisfaction And Behavioural Intentions: A Study On Tours In Kuala Lumpur City Centre. *Journal of Quality Assurance in Hospitality and Tourism, 23*(3), 597–614. doi:10.1080/1528008X.2021.1891599

Szpilko, D. (2017), Tourism Supply Chain–Overview of Selected Literature. *Procedia Engineering, 182*.

Szpilko, D. (2017). Tourism Supply Chain–overview of selected literature. *Procedia Engineering*, *182*, 687–693. doi:10.1016/j.proeng.2017.03.180

Tadić, S., & Veljović, M. (2020). LOGISTICS OF RURAL TOURISM. *International Journal for Traffic and Transport Engineering*, *10*(3), 323–350. doi:10.7708/ijtte.2020.10(3).06

Tadić, S., Zečević, S., & Krstić, M. (2012). Logistics and Supply Chain Management in tourism: Present state and limitations. *Tehnika*, *67*(6), 1018–1025.

Tam, M. (2014). Outcomes-based approach to quality assessment and curriculum improvement in higher education. *Quality Assurance in Education*, *22*(2), 158–168. doi:10.1108/QAE-09-2011-0059

Tanguay, G. A., Rajaonson, J., & Therrien, M. C. (2013). Sustainable tourism indicators: Selection criteria for policy implementation and scientific recognition. *Journal of Sustainable Tourism*, *21*(6), 862–879. doi:10.1080/09669582.2012.742531

Tang, Z., Chen, Z., Bao, Y., & Li, H. (2019). Convolutional neural network-based data anomaly detection method using multiple information for structural health monitoring. *Structural Control and Health Monitoring*, *26*(1), e2296. doi:10.1002tc.2296

Tapper, R., & Font, X. (2004). *Tourism supply chains: Report of a desk research project for the travel foundation*. Leeds Metropolitan University, Environment Business & Development Group. http://www.lmu.ac.uk/lsif/the/Tourism-Supply-Chains.pdf

Tasya, D. H. (2023). The Role Of Technology In English Curriculum Design. *PUSTAKA: Jurnal Bahasa danPendidikan, 3*(4), 42-57.

Tigu, G., & Calareţu, B. (2013). Supply Chain Management Performance in Tourism. Continental Hotels Chain Case. *Amfiteatru Economic, 15*, 103–115.

Treiblmaier, H. (2019) Toward more rigorous blockchain research: recommendations for writing blockchain case studies. *Front Blockchain, 2*(3), 1–15. https://doi.org/. 2019.00003 doi:10.3389/fbloc

Triši'c, I., Šteti'c, S., Privitera, D., Petrovi'c, M. D., Maksin, M., Vujovi'c, S., Jovanovi'c, Z., & Kalini'c, M. Perspectives on sustainable tourism development in the hotel industry—A case study from Southern Europe. Sustainability, 13, 5563.

Troshina, E. P., Dobrova, V. V., & Kozyreva, M. P. (2022). Digital educational platforms: Advantages and disadvantages. In *Digital Technologies in the New Socio-Economic Reality* (pp. 183–188). Springer International Publishing. doi:10.1007/978-3-030-83175-2_25

Tsironis, C. N. (2022). Pilgrimage and Religious Tourism in Society, in the Wake of the COVID-19 Pandemic: A Paradigmatic Focus on 'St. Paul's Route' in the Central Macedonia Region, Greece. *Religions, 13*(10), 887. doi:10.3390/rel13100887

Tuten, T. L. (2020). *Social media marketing* (4th ed.). Sage Publications.

Tyagi, P. K., Nadda, V., Bharti, V., & Kemer, E. (Eds.). (2023). *Embracing Business Sustainability Through Innovation and Creativity in the Service Sector*. IGI Global. https://www.igi-global.com/book/embracing-business-sustainability-through-innovation/303947 doi:10.4018/978-1-6684-6732-9

Tyagi, P. K., Tyagi, P., Pandey, U., Upadhyay, R., Sharma, D., & Arora, B. (2023, March). Evaluation of the Value of the Employee Tourist Interaction using Big Data Analytics. *10th International Conference on Computing for Sustainable Global Development (INDIACom)* (pp. 1289-1294). IEEE.

Udegbe, S. (2017). E: impact of blockchain technology in enhancing customer loyalty programs in airline business. *Int J Innov Res Adv Stud, 4*(6), 257–263.

UKEssays. (2018). *Supply Chain Management in Tourism*. UKEssays. https://www.ukessays.com/essays/business/supply-chain-in-tourism-services.php?vref=1

UKGov. (2022). *Economic Survey 2021-22 (Vol-1)*. Dehradun: DIRECTORATE OF ECONOMICS & STATISTICS. https://des.uk.gov.in/pages/display/177-economic-survey-2021-22

UNEP & UNWTO. (2005). *Making Tourism More Sustainable: A Guide for Policy Makers*. UNEP and UNWTO.

UNEP and UNWTO. (2005). *Making tourism more sustainable - a guide for policy makers*. UN.http://www.unep.fr/shared/publications/pdf/DTIx0592xPA-TourismPolicyEN.pdf

United Nation. (2023). *Goal 3 | Department of Economic and Social Affairs*. UN. https://sdgs.un.org/goals/goal3

United Nations. (2021). *Rio+20. Report on the UN Conference on Sustainable Development*. UN. https://www.uncsd2012.org/content/documents/814UNCSD%20REPORT%20final%20revs.pdf

UNWTO—United Nations World Tourism Organisation. (2021). *The Guidebook "Sustainable Tourismfor Development" Brussels*. UNWTO. http://icr.unwto.org/content/guidebook-sustainable-tourism-development

Vega-Muñoz, A., Estrada-Muñoz, C., Andreucci-Annunziata, P., Contreras-Barraza, N., & Bilbao-Cotal, H. (2022). Validation of a measurement scale on technostress for university students in Chile. *International Journal of Environmental Research and Public Health, 19*(21), 14493. doi:10.3390/ijerph192114493 PMID:36361366

Verevka, T. (2018). Key performance indicators of high-tech enterprises. *The Convergence of Digital and Physical Worlds: Technological, Economic, and Social Challenges (CC-TESC2018).* EDP Sciences.

Vicente, M. R., & López, A. J. (2010). A multidimensional analysis of the disability digital divide: Some evidence for Internet use. *The Information Society*, *26*(1), 48–64. doi:10.1080/01615440903423245

Vikuk, A. L. (2021). *Handbook of Sustainable Development andLeisur e Services.* Springer Science and Business Media LLC. doi:10.1007/978-3-030-59820-4

Villalón-Fonseca, R., Mora-Castro, A., Bartels-González, R., Carballo-Chavarría, M., & Marín-Raventós, G. (2016). Promoting quality e-government solutions by applying a comprehensive information assurance model: Use cases for digital signature. *ICT for Promoting Human Development and Protecting the Environment: 6th IFIP World Information Technology Forum (WITFOR)* (pp. 223-234). San José, Costa Rica: Springer International Publishing.

Vongsaroj, R. (2013). *Sustainable Tourism Supply Chain Management Of Tour Operator And Its Deteminants: A Case of Thailand.* Semantic Scholar.

Voon, J. P., Sing Ngui, K., & Agrawal, A. (2011). Determinants of Willingness to Purchase Organic Food: An Exploratory Study Using Structural Equation Modeling. *Agribusiness Management Review, 14*(2).

Vorster, J., & Goosen, L. (2017). A Framework for University Partnerships Promoting Continued Support of e-Schools. In J. Liebenberg (Ed.), *Proceedings of the 46th Annual Conference of the Southern African Computer Lecturers' Association (SACLA)* (pp. 118 - 126). Magaliesburg: North-West University.

Waligo, V. M., Clarke, J., & Hawkins, R. (2013). Implementing sustainable tourism: A multi-stakeholder involvement management framework. *Tourism Management*, *36*, 342–353. doi:10.1016/j.tourman.2012.10.008

Wang, H. Y. (2012). Value as a medical tourism driver. *Managing Service Quality*, *22*(5), 465–491. doi:10.1108/09604521211281387

Wang, M., Huang, L., Pan, C., & Bai, L. (2021). Adopt proper food-handling intention: An application of the health belief model. *Food Control*, *127*, 108169. doi:10.1016/j.foodcont.2021.108169

Wassler, P., Wang, L., & Hung, K. (2019). Identity and destination branding among residents: How does brand self-congruity influence brand attitude and ambassadorial behavior? [CrossRef]. *International Journal of Tourism Research*, *21*(4), 437–446. doi:10.1002/jtr.2271

Watty, K., McKay, J., & Ngo, L. (2016). Innovators or inhibitors? Accounting faculty resistance to new educational technologies in higher education. *Journal of Accounting Education*, *36*, 1–15. doi:10.1016/j.jaccedu.2016.03.003

WCED. (1987). *Our Common Future*. WCED.

Weiler, B., & Kim, A. K. (2011). Tour guides as agents of sustainability: Rhetoric, reality and implications for research. *Tourism Recreation Research*, *36*(2), 113–125. doi:10.1080/02508281.2011.11081313

Wen, J., Kozak, M., Yang, S., & Liu, F. (2021). COVID-19: Potential effects on Chinese citizens' lifestyle and travel. *Tourism Review*, *76*(1), 74–87. doi:10.1108/TR-03-2020-0110

West, M. A., & Farr, J. L. (1990). Innovation at work. In M. A. West & J. L. Farr (Eds.), *Innovation and creativity at work: Psychological and organizational strategies* (pp. 3–13). Wiley.

Widari, D. A. D. S. (2020). Kebijakan Pengembangan Pariwisata Berkelanjutan: Kajian Teoretis dan Empiris. *Jurnal Kajian Dan Terapan Pariwisata*, *1*(1), 1–11. doi:10.53356/diparojs.v1i1.12

Williams, M. (2008). *Components of self-regulated learning in high school students with learning disabilities* [Unpublished Doctoral Thesis, USA: Indiana University of Pennsylvania].

Wolverton, A. (2018). Promoting Exercise and Activity in Children: Challenges and Solutions to Today's Digital Society. *Journal of Pediatric Surgical Nursing*, *7*(1), 4–5. doi:10.1097/JPS.0000000000000160

Woo, Y., Kim, E., & Lim, J. (2017). The impact of education and R&D investment on regional economic growth. *Sustainability (Basel)*, *9*(5), 676. doi:10.3390u9050676

World Summit on Sustainable Development. (2002). *Tourism and the Earth Summit, World Summit on Sustainable Development.* Tourism Concern UK. www.tourismconcern.org.uk

WTO. (2001). Sustainable Development of Tourism. A Compilation of Good Practices. WTO.

Xu, M., David, J. M., & Kim, S. H. (2018). The fourth industrial revolution: Opportunities and challenges. *International journal of financial research*, *9*(2), 90-95.

Yadav, M., & Rahman, Z. (2017). Measuring consumer perception of social media marketing activities in e-commerce industry: Scale development & validation. *Telematics and Informatics*, *34*(7), 1294–1307. doi:10.1016/j.tele.2017.06.001

Yadav, R., & Pathak, G. S. (2016). Intention to purchase organic food among young consumers: Evidences from a developing nation. *Appetite*, *96*, 122–128. doi:10.1016/j.appet.2015.09.017 PMID:26386300

Ying, Y., Garrett, J. H. Jr, Oppenheim, I. J., Soibelman, L., Harley, J. B., Shi, J., & Jin, Y. (2013). Toward data-driven structural health monitoring: Application of machine learning and signal processing to damage detection. *Journal of Computing in Civil Engineering*, *27*(6), 667–680. doi:10.1061/(ASCE)CP.1943-5487.0000258

Yu, Z. (2022). A meta-analysis and bibliographic review of the effect of nine factors on online learning outcomes across the world. *Education and Information Technologies*, *27*(2), 2457–2482. doi:10.100710639-021-10720-y PMID:34456608

Zago, R., Block, T., Dessein, J., & Brunori, G. (2014). Participatory democracy in integrated rural development: the case of LEADER programme: towards Europe 2020 and community-led local development. In *ILVP Winter school 'Place base approaches in regional development'. Proceedings.* Universiteit Gent. https://biblio.ugent.be/publication/6845538

Zakaria, S., & Yusoff, W. W. (2010). Outcome-based education in a private HIL: Perceptions of students. *Advances in Management*, *3*, 31.

Zerman, S. (2022). Definition and functionality of social media. In *Digital Marketing and Social Media Strategies for Tourism and Hospitality Organizations*. Goodfellow Publishers. https://ebookcentral.proquest.com/lib/sunderland/detail.action?docID=29182557

Zhang, H., Schulz, M. J., Naser, A., Ferguson, F., & Pai, P. F. (1999). Structural health monitoring using transmittance functions. *Mechanical Systems and Signal Processing*, *13*(5), 765–787. doi:10.1006/mssp.1999.1228

Zhang, X., Song, H., & Huang, G. Q. (2009, June). Tourism Supply Chain Management: A New Research Agenda. *Tourism Management*, *30*(3), 345–358. doi:10.1016/j.tourman.2008.12.010 PMID:32287729

Zheng, L., Long, M., Zhong, L., & Gyasi, J. F. (2022). The effectiveness of technology-facilitated personalized learning on learning achievements and learning perceptions: A meta-analysis. *Education and Information Technologies*, *27*(8), 11807–11830. doi:10.100710639-022-11092-7

Zhu, D., & Xu, H. (2021). Guides' handling of multiple roles in interactions with tourists: The prism of impression management. *Tourism Management*, *85*, 104306. doi:10.1016/j.tourman.2021.104306

Zurick, D. N. (1992). Adventure travel and sustainable tourism in the peripheral economy of Nepal. *Annals of the Association of American Geographers*, *82*(4), 606–628. doi:10.1111/j.1467-8306.1992.tb01720.x

Zviagintsev, R., Kersha, Y., Bysik, N., & Kosaretsky, S. (2023). Response to COVID-19 in Remote Russian Schools: Readiness to Online Education and Coping Strategies. In Global Perspectives on Education Research, (pp. 34-65). Routledge.

Żywiołek, J., & Schiavone, F. (2021, September). Perception of the quality of smart city solutions as a sense of residents' safety. *Energies*, *14*(17), 5511. doi:10.3390/en14175511

Related References

To continue our tradition of advancing academic research, we have compiled a list of recommended IGI Global readings. These references will provide additional information and guidance to further enrich your knowledge and assist you with your own research and future publications.

Ababio, G. K. (2018). Nutraceuticals: The Dose Makes the Difference – It's All in the Dose. In A. Verma, K. Srivastava, S. Singh, & H. Singh (Eds.), *Nutraceuticals and Innovative Food Products for Healthy Living and Preventive Care* (pp. 24–47). Hershey, PA: IGI Global. doi:10.4018/978-1-5225-2970-5.ch002

Adams, M. G. (2018). Systematically Investigating Instructor Impact on Student Satisfaction in Graduate Programs. In D. Polly, M. Putman, T. Petty, & A. Good (Eds.), *Innovative Practices in Teacher Preparation and Graduate-Level Teacher Education Programs* (pp. 200–214). Hershey, PA: IGI Global. doi:10.4018/978-1-5225-3068-8.ch012

Akgül, Y., & Tunca, M. Z. (2018). Proliferating View of Knowledge Management and Balanced Scorecard Outcome Linkage. In N. Baporikar (Ed.), *Global Practices in Knowledge Management for Societal and Organizational Development* (pp. 168–193). Hershey, PA: IGI Global. doi:10.4018/978-1-5225-3009-1.ch008

Alcaraz-Valencia, P. A., Gaytán-Lugo, L. S., & Gallardo, S. C. (2018). An Exploratory Study on the Interaction Beyond Virtual Environments to Improve Listening Ability When Learning English as a Second Language. In F. Cipolla-Ficarra (Ed.), *Optimizing Human-Computer Interaction With Emerging Technologies* (pp. 306–331). Hershey, PA: IGI Global. doi:10.4018/978-1-5225-2616-2.ch013

Altıntaş, F. Ç., & Kavurmacı, C. (2018). Value Statements in Web Pages of Turkish State Universities: A Basic Classification. In U. Thomas (Ed.), *Advocacy in Academia and the Role of Teacher Preparation Programs* (pp. 302–316). Hershey, PA: IGI Global. doi:10.4018/978-1-5225-2906-4.ch017

Amoroso, D. L. (2018). The Importance of Advocacy on Reputation and Loyalty: Comparison of Japanese, Chinese, and the Filipino Consumers. In P. Ordóñez de Pablos (Ed.), *Management Strategies and Technology Fluidity in the Asian Business Sector* (pp. 114–125). Hershey, PA: IGI Global. doi:10.4018/978-1-5225-4056-4.ch007

Atiku, S. O., & Fields, Z. (2018). Organisational Learning Dimensions and Talent Retention Strategies for the Service Industries. In N. Baporikar (Ed.), *Global Practices in Knowledge Management for Societal and Organizational Development* (pp. 358–381). Hershey, PA: IGI Global. doi:10.4018/978-1-5225-3009-1.ch017

Ayoola-Amale, A. (2018). Women in Leadership: Why We Need More Women Leaders. In B. Cook (Ed.), *Handbook of Research on Examining Global Peacemaking in the Digital Age* (pp. 211–222). Hershey, PA: IGI Global. doi:10.4018/978-1-5225-3032-9.ch015

Baran, A. G. (2018). Through the Syrians Refuge in Turkey Towards the Creation of the War Migration Theory. In Ş. Erçetin (Ed.), *Social Considerations of Migration Movements and Immigration Policies* (pp. 178–196). Hershey, PA: IGI Global. doi:10.4018/978-1-5225-3322-1.ch011

Beckett-Camarata, J. (2018). Public Choice and Financing Local Government Fiscal Reform in Albania. In H. Levine & K. Moreno (Eds.), *Positioning Markets and Governments in Public Management* (pp. 197–208). Hershey, PA: IGI Global. doi:10.4018/978-1-5225-4177-6.ch015

Bedford, D. A. (2018). Sustainable Knowledge Management Strategies: Aligning Business Capabilities and Knowledge Management Goals. In N. Baporikar (Ed.), *Global Practices in Knowledge Management for Societal and Organizational Development* (pp. 46–73). Hershey, PA: IGI Global. doi:10.4018/978-1-5225-3009-1.ch003

Benaouda, A., & García-Peñalvo, F. J. (2018). Towards an Intelligent System for the Territorial Planning: Agricultural Case. In F. García-Peñalvo (Ed.), *Global Implications of Emerging Technology Trends* (pp. 158–178). Hershey, PA: IGI Global. doi:10.4018/978-1-5225-4944-4.ch010

Beneventi, P. (2018). When Technology Becomes Popular: A Multimedia, Shared Production for the Information Age. In *Technology and the New Generation of Active Citizens: Emerging Research and Opportunities* (pp. 23–44). Hershey, PA: IGI Global. doi:10.4018/978-1-5225-3770-0.ch002

Bernal, L. D., & Cusi, M. L. (2018). Corporate Entrepreneurship in Colombia: Contrast Cases of Two Colombian Manufacturing SMEs. In R. Perez-Uribe, C. Salcedo-Perez, & D. Ocampo-Guzman (Eds.), *Handbook of Research on Intrapreneurship and Organizational Sustainability in SMEs* (pp. 368–390). Hershey, PA: IGI Global. doi:10.4018/978-1-5225-3543-0.ch017

Berning, S. C., & Ambrosius, J. (2018). How the Human Resource Practices of Chinese MNEs in Africa Create Economic Growth and Livelihood Options. In S. Hipsher (Ed.), *Examining the Private Sector's Role in Wealth Creation and Poverty Reduction* (pp. 85–109). Hershey, PA: IGI Global. doi:10.4018/978-1-5225-3117-3.ch005

Bharti, A., & Mittal, A. (2018). Perishable Goods Supply Cold Chain Management in India. In A. Kumar & S. Saurav (Eds.), *Supply Chain Management Strategies and Risk Assessment in Retail Environments* (pp. 232–246). Hershey, PA: IGI Global. doi:10.4018/978-1-5225-3056-5.ch013

Bhattacharya, S., Kumar, R. V., & Dutta, A. (2018). Exploring Kapferer's Brand Identity Prism Applicability in Indian Political Marketing Aspect With Special Focus to Youth Voters. In Rajagopal, & R. Behl (Eds.), Start-Up Enterprises and Contemporary Innovation Strategies in the Global Marketplace (pp. 136-152). Hershey, PA: IGI Global. doi:10.4018/978-1-5225-4831-7.ch010

Bhattarai, R. K. (2018). Enterprise Immune System. In *Enterprise Resiliency in the Continuum of Change: Emerging Research and Opportunities* (pp. 88–111). Hershey, PA: IGI Global. doi:10.4018/978-1-5225-2627-8.ch003

Bhattarai, R. K. (2018). Enterprise Philosophy. In *Enterprise Resiliency in the Continuum of Change: Emerging Research and Opportunities* (pp. 1–43). Hershey, PA: IGI Global. doi:10.4018/978-1-5225-2627-8.ch001

Bhattarai, R. K. (2018). Enterprise Resiliency. In *Enterprise Resiliency in the Continuum of Change: Emerging Research and Opportunities* (pp. 112–137). Hershey, PA: IGI Global. doi:10.4018/978-1-5225-2627-8.ch004

Bisen, S. S., & Deshpande, Y. (2018). The Impact of the Internet in Twenty-First Century Addictions: An Overview. In B. Bozoglan (Ed.), *Psychological, Social, and Cultural Aspects of Internet Addiction* (pp. 1–19). Hershey, PA: IGI Global. doi:10.4018/978-1-5225-3477-8.ch001

Biswal, S. K. (2018). Branding Culture: A Study of Telugu Film Industry. In S. Dasgupta, S. Biswal, & M. Ramesh (Eds.), *Holistic Approaches to Brand Culture and Communication Across Industries* (pp. 1–23). Hershey, PA: IGI Global. doi:10.4018/978-1-5225-3150-0.ch001

Blake, S., & Burkett, C. M. (2018). Individual Creativity: Predictors and Characteristics. In *Creativity in Workforce Development and Innovation: Emerging Research and Opportunities* (pp. 88–104). Hershey, PA: IGI Global. doi:10.4018/978-1-5225-4952-9.ch005

Blomeley, S., & Hamilton, A. H. (2018). Writing Partners: Bridging the Personal and Social in the Service-Learning Classroom. In O. Delano-Oriaran, M. Penick-Parks, & S. Fondrie (Eds.), *Culturally Engaging Service-Learning With Diverse Communities* (pp. 202–222). Hershey, PA: IGI Global. doi:10.4018/978-1-5225-2900-2.ch012

Bohra, M., & Visen, A. (2018). Nutraceutical Properties in Flowers. In A. Verma, K. Srivastava, S. Singh, & H. Singh (Eds.), *Nutraceuticals and Innovative Food Products for Healthy Living and Preventive Care* (pp. 217–235). Hershey, PA: IGI Global. doi:10.4018/978-1-5225-2970-5.ch010

Boyd, L. N. (2018). Fortifying Parent Partnerships Through the Black Church Space. In K. Norris & S. Collier (Eds.), *Social Justice and Parent Partnerships in Multicultural Education Contexts* (pp. 118–137). Hershey, PA: IGI Global. doi:10.4018/978-1-5225-3943-8.ch007

Bozoglan, B. (2018). The Role of Family Factors in Internet Addiction Among Children and Adolescents: An Overview. In B. Bozoglan (Ed.), *Psychological, Social, and Cultural Aspects of Internet Addiction* (pp. 146–168). Hershey, PA: IGI Global. doi:10.4018/978-1-5225-3477-8.ch008

Briz-Ponce, L., Juanes-Méndez, J. A., & García-Peñalvo, F. J. (2018). Current Situation and Appraisal Tendencies of M-Learning. In F. García-Peñalvo (Ed.), *Global Implications of Emerging Technology Trends* (pp. 115–129). Hershey, PA: IGI Global. doi:10.4018/978-1-5225-4944-4.ch007

Brkljačić, T., Majetić, F., & Wertag, A. (2018). I'm Always Online: Well-Being and Main Sources of Life Dis/Satisfaction of Heavy Internet Users. In B. Bozoglan (Ed.), *Psychological, Social, and Cultural Aspects of Internet Addiction* (pp. 72–89). Hershey, PA: IGI Global. doi:10.4018/978-1-5225-3477-8.ch004

Brown, M. A. Sr. (2018). Defining Your Team. In *Motivationally Intelligent Leadership: Emerging Research and Opportunities* (pp. 1–22). Hershey, PA: IGI Global. doi:10.4018/978-1-5225-3746-5.ch001

Brown, M. A. Sr. (2018). Empowering Leaders With Tools. In *Motivationally Intelligent Leadership: Emerging Research and Opportunities* (pp. 72–96). Hershey, PA: IGI Global. doi:10.4018/978-1-5225-3746-5.ch006

Brown, M. A. Sr. (2018). Sensemaking Theory. In *Motivationally Intelligent Leadership: Emerging Research and Opportunities* (pp. 46–55). Hershey, PA: IGI Global. doi:10.4018/978-1-5225-3746-5.ch004

Brown, S., & Bousalis, R. (2018). Best Practices in K-12 Arts Integration: Curricular Connections. In *Curriculum Integration in Contemporary Teaching Practice: Emerging Research and Opportunities* (pp. 95–124). Hershey, PA: IGI Global. doi:10.4018/978-1-5225-4065-6.ch004

Brown, S., & Bousalis, R. (2018). Interdisciplinary Curriculum in K-12 Schools: Current Practices in the Field. In *Curriculum Integration in Contemporary Teaching Practice: Emerging Research and Opportunities* (pp. 125–143). Hershey, PA: IGI Global. doi:10.4018/978-1-5225-4065-6.ch005

Bullock, C. A. (2018). Collaboration: Academes, Government, and Community to Drive Economic Uplift and Empowerment. In S. Burton (Ed.), *Engaged Scholarship and Civic Responsibility in Higher Education* (pp. 1–24). Hershey, PA: IGI Global. doi:10.4018/978-1-5225-3649-9.ch001

Burdenko, E. V., & Mudrova, S. V. (2018). Indicators System as a Measure of Development Level of Knowledge Economy: Application of World Bank Methodology. In N. Baporikar (Ed.), *Global Practices in Knowledge Management for Societal and Organizational Development* (pp. 74–105). Hershey, PA: IGI Global. doi:10.4018/978-1-5225-3009-1.ch004

Burston, B., & Collier-Stewart, S. (2018). STEM for All: The Importance of Parent/School/Community Partnerships Across the K-12 Pipeline and Beyond. In K. Norris & S. Collier (Eds.), *Social Justice and Parent Partnerships in Multicultural Education Contexts* (pp. 274–288). Hershey, PA: IGI Global. doi:10.4018/978-1-5225-3943-8.ch015

Carboni, M., & Perelli, C. (2018). "Beyond" Religious Tourism: The Case of Fez. In H. El-Gohary, D. Edwards, & R. Eid (Eds.), *Global Perspectives on Religious Tourism and Pilgrimage* (pp. 71–83). Hershey, PA: IGI Global. doi:10.4018/978-1-5225-2796-1.ch005

Cascella, M., Muzio, M. R., Bimonte, S., & Cuomo, A. (2018). Nutraceuticals for Prevention of Chemotherapy-Induced Peripheral Neuropathy. In A. Verma, K. Srivastava, S. Singh, & H. Singh (Eds.), *Nutraceuticals and Innovative Food Products for Healthy Living and Preventive Care* (pp. 236–259). Hershey, PA: IGI Global. doi:10.4018/978-1-5225-2970-5.ch011

Cena, F., Rapp, A., Likavec, S., & Marcengo, A. (2018). Envisioning the Future of Personalization Through Personal Informatics: A User Study. *International Journal of Mobile Human Computer Interaction, 10*(1), 52–66. doi:10.4018/IJMHCI.2018010104

Chandiramani, J., & Airy, A. (2018). Urbanization and Socio-Economic Growth in South Asia Region. In U. Benna & I. Benna (Eds.), *Urbanization and Its Impact on Socio-Economic Growth in Developing Regions* (pp. 130–154). Hershey, PA: IGI Global. doi:10.4018/978-1-5225-2659-9.ch007

Chang, Y., Choi, S. B., Lee, J., & Jin, W. C. (2018). Population Size vs. Number of Crimes: Is the Relationship Superlinear? *International Journal of Information Systems and Social Change*, *9*(1), 26–39. doi:10.4018/IJISSC.2018010102

Chaudhary, N. S., & Yadav, R. (2018). Cross-Cultural Conflicts: Concept, Causes, and Elucidations. In N. Sharma, V. Singh, & S. Pathak (Eds.), *Management Techniques for a Diverse and Cross-Cultural Workforce* (pp. 79–96). Hershey, PA: IGI Global. doi:10.4018/978-1-5225-4933-8.ch005

Chirisa, I., Mukarwi, L., & Matamanda, A. R. (2018). Social Costs and Benefits of the Transformation of the Traditional Families in an African Urban Society. In U. Benna & I. Benna (Eds.), *Urbanization and Its Impact on Socio-Economic Growth in Developing Regions* (pp. 179–197). Hershey, PA: IGI Global. doi:10.4018/978-1-5225-2659-9.ch009

Chitima, S. S., & Ndlovu, I. (2018). Incorporating Indigenous Knowledge in the Preservation of Collections at the Batonga Community Museum in Zimbabwe. In P. Ngulube (Ed.), *Handbook of Research on Heritage Management and Preservation* (pp. 396–407). Hershey, PA: IGI Global. doi:10.4018/978-1-5225-3137-1.ch019

Choudhury, D. K., & Rao, P. (2018). Determinants of FDI Inflows in Developing Countries: A Dynamic Panel Approach. In V. Malepati & C. Gowri (Eds.), *Foreign Direct Investments (FDIs) and Opportunities for Developing Economies in the World Market* (pp. 25–45). Hershey, PA: IGI Global. doi:10.4018/978-1-5225-3026-8.ch002

Cipolla-Ficarra, F. V., Carré, J., Quiroga, A., & Ficarra, V. M. (2018). Anti-Models for Architectural Graphic Expression and UX Education. In F. Cipolla-Ficarra, M. Ficarra, M. Cipolla-Ficarra, A. Quiroga, J. Alma, & J. Carré (Eds.), *Technology-Enhanced Human Interaction in Modern Society* (pp. 218–233). Hershey, PA: IGI Global. doi:10.4018/978-1-5225-3437-2.ch011

Cipolla-Ficarra, F. V., Ficarra, V. M., & Cipolla-Ficarra, M. (2018). Inverted Semanteme Into Financial Information Online. In F. Cipolla-Ficarra, M. Ficarra, M. Cipolla-Ficarra, A. Quiroga, J. Alma, & J. Carré (Eds.), *Technology-Enhanced Human Interaction in Modern Society* (pp. 263–283). Hershey, PA: IGI Global. doi:10.4018/978-1-5225-3437-2.ch013

Cipolla-Ficarra, F. V., Quiroga, A., & Ficarra, V. M. (2018). Kernel of the Labyrinths Hypertextuals. In F. Cipolla-Ficarra, M. Ficarra, M. Cipolla-Ficarra, A. Quiroga, J. Alma, & J. Carré (Eds.), *Technology-Enhanced Human Interaction in Modern Society* (pp. 122–142). Hershey, PA: IGI Global. doi:10.4018/978-1-5225-3437-2.ch006

Coffey, S. M. (2018). Unveilings Through Transformative Pedagogy: Striving for Realization of Du Bois' Educational Paradigm. In U. Thomas (Ed.), *Advocacy in Academia and the Role of Teacher Preparation Programs* (pp. 206–224). Hershey, PA: IGI Global. doi:10.4018/978-1-5225-2906-4.ch012

da Rocha, J. P. (2018). Process Outcomes. In *Political Mediation in Modern Conflict Resolution: Emerging Research and Opportunities* (pp. 155–164). Hershey, PA: IGI Global. doi:10.4018/978-1-5225-5118-8.ch004

Dahiya, K., & Dhankhar, R. (2018). Role of Nutraceuticals in Cancer. In A. Verma, K. Srivastava, S. Singh, & H. Singh (Eds.), *Nutraceuticals and Innovative Food Products for Healthy Living and Preventive Care* (pp. 176–194). Hershey, PA: IGI Global. doi:10.4018/978-1-5225-2970-5.ch008

Dasgupta, S., & Kothari, R. (2018). The Impact of Digital Word-of-Mouth Communication on Consumer Decision-Making Processes: With Special Reference to Fashion Apparel Industry. In S. Dasgupta, S. Biswal, & M. Ramesh (Eds.), *Holistic Approaches to Brand Culture and Communication Across Industries* (pp. 176–198). Hershey, PA: IGI Global. doi:10.4018/978-1-5225-3150-0.ch010

Dávila, F. A. (2018). Relationship Lending and Entrepreneurial Behavior: A Game-Theoretic-Based Modeling. In Rajagopal, & R. Behl (Eds.), Start-Up Enterprises and Contemporary Innovation Strategies in the Global Marketplace (pp. 65-86). Hershey, PA: IGI Global. doi:10.4018/978-1-5225-4831-7.ch006

de Sousa, J. C. (2018). Memory. In *Neuromarketing and Big Data Analytics for Strategic Consumer Engagement: Emerging Research and Opportunities* (pp. 92–100). Hershey, PA: IGI Global. doi:10.4018/978-1-5225-4834-8.ch006

de Sousa, J. C. (2018). Sensory and Motor System. In *Neuromarketing and Big Data Analytics for Strategic Consumer Engagement: Emerging Research and Opportunities* (pp. 68–91). Hershey, PA: IGI Global. doi:10.4018/978-1-5225-4834-8.ch005

Deka, D. B., & Jadeja, M. (2018). Childhood Sexual Abuse: Prevention and Intervention. In R. Gopalan (Ed.), *Social, Psychological, and Forensic Perspectives on Sexual Abuse* (pp. 127–146). Hershey, PA: IGI Global. doi:10.4018/978-1-5225-3958-2.ch010

Dobell, E., Herold, S., & Buckley, J. (2018). Spreadsheet Error Types and Their Prevalence in a Healthcare Context. *Journal of Organizational and End User Computing*, *30*(2), 20–42. doi:10.4018/JOEUC.2018040102

Donert, K., & Papoutsis, P. (2018). School on the Cloud: Connecting Education to the Cloud for Digital Citizenship. In K. Koutsopoulos, K. Doukas, & Y. Kotsanis (Eds.), *Handbook of Research on Educational Design and Cloud Computing in Modern Classroom Settings* (pp. 157–182). Hershey, PA: IGI Global. doi:10.4018/978-1-5225-3053-4.ch008

Downton, M. P. (2018). Preparation for Future Teaching: Authentic Activities in a Teacher Education Classroom. In D. Polly, M. Putman, T. Petty, & A. Good (Eds.), *Innovative Practices in Teacher Preparation and Graduate-Level Teacher Education Programs* (pp. 293–305). Hershey, PA: IGI Global. doi:10.4018/978-1-5225-3068-8.ch016

Drivas, G., Sotiriou, C., Bonanou, H., Saliari, S., Balafouti, M., & Tsevi, H. (2018). The Sky Is the Limit! In K. Koutsopoulos, K. Doukas, & Y. Kotsanis (Eds.), *Handbook of Research on Educational Design and Cloud Computing in Modern Classroom Settings* (pp. 101–121). Hershey, PA: IGI Global. doi:10.4018/978-1-5225-3053-4.ch006

Erçetin, Ş. Ş., & Bisaso, S. M. (2018). Migration and Refugee Crisis: Structural and Managerial Implications for Education. In Ş. Erçetin (Ed.), *Educational Development and Infrastructure for Immigrants and Refugees* (pp. 47–71). Hershey, PA: IGI Global. doi:10.4018/978-1-5225-3325-2.ch003

Erçetin, Ş. Ş., & Kubilay, S. (2018). Educational Expectations of Refugee Mothers for Their Children. In Ş. Erçetin (Ed.), *Educational Development and Infrastructure for Immigrants and Refugees* (pp. 171–195). Hershey, PA: IGI Global. doi:10.4018/978-1-5225-3325-2.ch009

Erçetin, Ş. Ş., Potas, N., Açıkalın, Ş. N., Özdemir, N., & Doğan, A. M. (2018). Municipalities and Refugee Crisis: Ansar Policies and Numbers. In Ş. Erçetin (Ed.), *Social Considerations of Migration Movements and Immigration Policies* (pp. 46–57). Hershey, PA: IGI Global. doi:10.4018/978-1-5225-3322-1.ch003

Erkekoğlu, L. C., & Madi, İ. (2018). The Hashemite Kingdom of Jordan. In S. Ozdemir, S. Erdogan, & A. Gedikli (Eds.), *Handbook of Research on Sociopolitical Factors Impacting Economic Growth in Islamic Nations* (pp. 95–121). Hershey, PA: IGI Global. doi:10.4018/978-1-5225-2939-2.ch006

Essien, E. D. (2018). Strengthening Performance of Civil Society Through Dialogue and Critical Thinking in Nigeria: Its Ethical Implications. In S. Chhabra (Ed.), *Handbook of Research on Civic Engagement and Social Change in Contemporary Society* (pp. 82–102). Hershey, PA: IGI Global. doi:10.4018/978-1-5225-4197-4.ch005

Feza, N. N. (2018). The Socioeconomic Status Label Associated With Mathematics. In I. Tshabangu (Ed.), *Global Ideologies Surrounding Children's Rights and Social Justice* (pp. 186–203). Hershey, PA: IGI Global. doi:10.4018/978-1-5225-2578-3.ch012

Fleener, J., Lu, L., Dun, J., & Mingquan, Y. (2018). Sustaining a Teacher Professional Learning Community in China Through Technology. In H. Spires (Ed.), *Digital Transformation and Innovation in Chinese Education* (pp. 80–99). Hershey, PA: IGI Global. doi:10.4018/978-1-5225-2924-8.ch005

Forge, J. (2018). Defence. In *The Morality of Weapons Design and Development: Emerging Research and Opportunities* (pp. 52–77). Hershey, PA: IGI Global. doi:10.4018/978-1-5225-3984-1.ch004

Forge, J. (2018). Justification. In *The Morality of Weapons Design and Development: Emerging Research and Opportunities* (pp. 78–93). Hershey, PA: IGI Global. doi:10.4018/978-1-5225-3984-1.ch005

Forge, J. (2018). Projectile Weapons. In *The Morality of Weapons Design and Development: Emerging Research and Opportunities* (pp. 94–117). Hershey, PA: IGI Global. doi:10.4018/978-1-5225-3984-1.ch006

Forge, J. (2018). Proportionality, Just War Theory, and Weapons Design. In *The Morality of Weapons Design and Development: Emerging Research and Opportunities* (pp. 139–154). Hershey, PA: IGI Global. doi:10.4018/978-1-5225-3984-1.ch008

Forge, J. (2018). Purposes and Means. In *The Morality of Weapons Design and Development: Emerging Research and Opportunities* (pp. 34–51). Hershey, PA: IGI Global. doi:10.4018/978-1-5225-3984-1.ch003

Fudge, M. (2018). The Inequity of User Fees and the Overreliance by Communities to Generate Revenue. In H. Levine & K. Moreno (Eds.), *Positioning Markets and Governments in Public Management* (pp. 147–158). Hershey, PA: IGI Global. doi:10.4018/978-1-5225-4177-6.ch011

Furumoto, R. R. (2018). Mexican-American Parents Using Critical Literacy to Address Climate Change. In K. Norris & S. Collier (Eds.), *Social Justice and Parent Partnerships in Multicultural Education Contexts* (pp. 187–208). Hershey, PA: IGI Global. doi:10.4018/978-1-5225-3943-8.ch010

Gabay, D. (2018). Who's Represented in Canadian Teaching and Learning Centres? In B. Blummer, J. Kenton, & M. Wiatrowski (Eds.), *Promoting Ethnic Diversity and Multiculturalism in Higher Education* (pp. 172–198). Hershey, PA: IGI Global. doi:10.4018/978-1-5225-4097-7.ch010

Garner, G. (2018). Foundations for Yoga Practice in Rehabilitation. In S. Telles & N. Singh (Eds.), *Research-Based Perspectives on the Psychophysiology of Yoga* (pp. 263–307). Hershey, PA: IGI Global. doi:10.4018/978-1-5225-2788-6.ch015

Geethanjali, P. (2018). Bio-Inspired Techniques in Human-Computer Interface for Control of Assistive Devices: Bio-Inspired Techniques in Assistive Devices. In D. Lopez & M. Durai (Eds.), *HCI Challenges and Privacy Preservation in Big Data Security* (pp. 23–46). Hershey, PA: IGI Global. doi:10.4018/978-1-5225-2863-0.ch002

Gharote, M. (2018). Common Features Between Findings in Traditional Texts and Contemporary Science: Yoga Texts and Contemporary Science. In S. Telles & N. Singh (Eds.), *Research-Based Perspectives on the Psychophysiology of Yoga* (pp. 309–315). Hershey, PA: IGI Global. doi:10.4018/978-1-5225-2788-6.ch016

Giosi, A., Zaccaro, E., & Testarmata, S. (2018). Social Responsibility, Shared Value, and Business Modelling: An Integrated Approach. In M. Risso & S. Testarmata (Eds.), *Value Sharing for Sustainable and Inclusive Development* (pp. 100–121). Hershey, PA: IGI Global. doi:10.4018/978-1-5225-3147-0.ch005

Grădinaru, C., Toma, S. I., & Marinescu, P. I. (2018). Entrepreneurial Thinking in the Educational System. In M. Risso & S. Testarmata (Eds.), *Value Sharing for Sustainable and Inclusive Development* (pp. 29–48). Hershey, PA: IGI Global. doi:10.4018/978-1-5225-3147-0.ch002

Güler, A. (2018). PKK-Related Asylum Applications from Turkey: Counter-Terrorism Measures vs. Refugee Status. In Ş. Erçetin (Ed.), *Social Considerations of Migration Movements and Immigration Policies* (pp. 117–142). Hershey, PA: IGI Global. doi:10.4018/978-1-5225-3322-1.ch008

Gupta, S. K. (2018). Sexual Abuse of Children and Adults With Intellectual Disabilities: Preventive, Supportive, and Intervention Strategies for Clinical Practice. In R. Gopalan (Ed.), *Social, Psychological, and Forensic Perspectives on Sexual Abuse* (pp. 197–206). Hershey, PA: IGI Global. doi:10.4018/978-1-5225-3958-2.ch014

Gürcan, Ö. F., & Gümüşsoy, Ç. A. (2018). Factors Influencing Effective Knowledge Transfer in Organizations. In N. Baporikar (Ed.), *Global Practices in Knowledge Management for Societal and Organizational Development* (pp. 271–292). Hershey, PA: IGI Global. doi:10.4018/978-1-5225-3009-1.ch013

Hagen, I., Kofoed, S., & Nayar, U. (2018). Yoga for Psychological Wellbeing in Modern Life and Contexts. In S. Telles & N. Singh (Eds.), *Research-Based Perspectives on the Psychophysiology of Yoga* (pp. 316–334). Hershey, PA: IGI Global. doi:10.4018/978-1-5225-2788-6.ch017

Handayani, B. (2018). The Paradox of Authenticity and Its Implications for Contemporary and "Bizarre" Tourism Campaigns. In S. Sarma (Ed.), *Global Observations of the Influence of Culture on Consumer Buying Behavior* (pp. 48–65). Hershey, PA: IGI Global. doi:10.4018/978-1-5225-2727-5.ch003

Huamaní, G. A., Fernández-López, S., Gómez, I. N., Rey-Ares, L., Rodríguez-Gulías, M. J., & Rodeiro-Pazos, D. (2018). The Role Models as Determinants of New Technology-Based Firms: An Exploratory Study. In A. Carrizo Moreira, J. Guilherme Leitão Dantas, & F. Manuel Valente (Eds.), *Nascent Entrepreneurship and Successful New Venture Creation* (pp. 272–288). Hershey, PA: IGI Global. doi:10.4018/978-1-5225-2936-1.ch013

Hucks, D., Sturtz, T., & Tirabassi, K. (2018). Building, Shaping, and Modeling Tools for Literacy Development and Civic Engagement. In *Fostering Positive Civic Engagement Among Millennials: Emerging Research and Opportunities* (pp. 22–35). Hershey, PA: IGI Global. doi:10.4018/978-1-5225-2452-6.ch002

Hucks, D., Sturtz, T., & Tirabassi, K. (2018). Insights, Next Steps, and Future Research. In *Fostering Positive Civic Engagement Among Millennials: Emerging Research and Opportunities* (pp. 65–72). Hershey, PA: IGI Global. doi:10.4018/978-1-5225-2452-6.ch005

Iguisi, O. V. (2018). Comparative Analysis of Hofstede's Culture Dimensions for West African Regions (WAF) and Nigeria. In S. Sarma (Ed.), *Global Observations of the Influence of Culture on Consumer Buying Behavior* (pp. 190–205). Hershey, PA: IGI Global. doi:10.4018/978-1-5225-2727-5.ch012

Islam, M. R. (2018). Abuse Among Child Domestic Workers in Bangladesh. In I. Tshabangu (Ed.), *Global Ideologies Surrounding Children's Rights and Social Justice* (pp. 1–21). Hershey, PA: IGI Global. doi:10.4018/978-1-5225-2578-3.ch001

Ito, K., & Hilliker, S. M. (2018). Supporting University International Students Through Supportive ESL Instruction and Corrective Feedback. In B. Blummer, J. Kenton, & M. Wiatrowski (Eds.), *Promoting Ethnic Diversity and Multiculturalism in Higher Education* (pp. 40–58). Hershey, PA: IGI Global. doi:10.4018/978-1-5225-4097-7.ch003

Iurato, G. (2018). A Brief Account of Ignacio Matte Blanco Theory and Other Related Psychoanalytic Themes. In *Computational Psychoanalysis and Formal Bi-Logic Frameworks* (pp. 114–135). Hershey, PA: IGI Global. doi:10.4018/978-1-5225-4128-8.ch003

Iurato, G. (2018). First Attempts to Formalize Some Main Aspects of Psychoanalysis: Towards a Computational Psychoanalysis. In *Computational Psychoanalysis and Formal Bi-Logic Frameworks* (pp. 136–205). Hershey, PA: IGI Global. doi:10.4018/978-1-5225-4128-8.ch004

Jacobsen, M., Friesen, S., & Brown, B. (2018). Teachers' Professional Learning Focused on Designs for Early Learners and Technology. In D. Polly, M. Putman, T. Petty, & A. Good (Eds.), *Innovative Practices in Teacher Preparation and Graduate-Level Teacher Education Programs* (pp. 417–438). Hershey, PA: IGI Global. doi:10.4018/978-1-5225-3068-8.ch022

Jensen, A. A., & Thomassen, A. O. (2018). Teachers' Reflective Practice in Lifelong Learning Programs. In Z. Djoub (Ed.), *Fostering Reflective Teaching Practice in Pre-Service Education* (pp. 25–45). Hershey, PA: IGI Global. doi:10.4018/978-1-5225-2963-7.ch002

Jiang, K., Barnett, G. A., Taylor, L. D., & Feng, B. (2018). Dynamic Co-Evolutions of Peace Frames in the United States, Mainland China, and Hong Kong: A Semantic Network Analysis. In B. Cook (Ed.), *Handbook of Research on Examining Global Peacemaking in the Digital Age* (pp. 145–168). Hershey, PA: IGI Global. doi:10.4018/978-1-5225-3032-9.ch010

Jiménez-González, S. G., Mendoza-González, R., & Luna-García, H. (2018). Guidelines Based on Need-Findings Study and Communication Types to Design Interactions for MOOCs. In F. Cipolla-Ficarra (Ed.), *Optimizing Human-Computer Interaction With Emerging Technologies* (pp. 210–231). Hershey, PA: IGI Global. doi:10.4018/978-1-5225-2616-2.ch008

Johnson, N. N. (2018). Effectively Managing Bias in Teacher Preparation. In U. Thomas (Ed.), *Advocacy in Academia and the Role of Teacher Preparation Programs* (pp. 146–160). Hershey, PA: IGI Global. doi:10.4018/978-1-5225-2906-4.ch008

Joseph, C. (2018). The Role of Government in a Liberal Market Economy: A Double-Edge Sword. In H. Levine & K. Moreno (Eds.), *Positioning Markets and Governments in Public Management* (pp. 53–61). Hershey, PA: IGI Global. doi:10.4018/978-1-5225-4177-6.ch005

Kade, D., Lindell, R., Ürey, H., & Özcan, O. (2018). Supporting Motion Capture Acting Through a Mixed Reality Application. In F. Cipolla-Ficarra (Ed.), *Optimizing Human-Computer Interaction With Emerging Technologies* (pp. 248–273). Hershey, PA: IGI Global. doi:10.4018/978-1-5225-2616-2.ch010

Karataş, S., Kukul, V., & Özcan, S. (2018). How Powerful Is Digital Storytelling for Teaching?: Perspective of Pre-Service Teachers. In D. Polly, M. Putman, T. Petty, & A. Good (Eds.), *Innovative Practices in Teacher Preparation and Graduate-Level Teacher Education Programs* (pp. 511–529). Hershey, PA: IGI Global. doi:10.4018/978-1-5225-3068-8.ch027

Kavaklı, N. (2018). Hate Speech Towards Syrian Refugees in Turkish Online Reader Comments. In C. Akrivopoulou (Ed.), *Global Perspectives on Human Migration, Asylum, and Security* (pp. 127–142). Hershey, PA: IGI Global. doi:10.4018/978-1-5225-2817-3.ch007

Kaynak, S. (2018). Pakistan. In S. Ozdemir, S. Erdogan, & A. Gedikli (Eds.), *Handbook of Research on Sociopolitical Factors Impacting Economic Growth in Islamic Nations* (pp. 293–313). Hershey, PA: IGI Global. doi:10.4018/978-1-5225-2939-2.ch015

Korstanje, M. E. (2018). Thana-Capitalism and the Sense of Reality: Lessons Unlearned. In C. Akrivopoulou (Ed.), *Global Perspectives on Human Migration, Asylum, and Security* (pp. 1–20). Hershey, PA: IGI Global. doi:10.4018/978-1-5225-2817-3.ch001

Korstanje, M. E. (2018). The Lost Paradise: The Religious Nature of Tourism. In H. El-Gohary, D. Edwards, & R. Eid (Eds.), *Global Perspectives on Religious Tourism and Pilgrimage* (pp. 129–141). Hershey, PA: IGI Global. doi:10.4018/978-1-5225-2796-1.ch008

Korstanje, M. E., & George, B. P. (2018). Emotionality, Reason, and Dark Tourism: Discussions Around the Sense of Death. In M. Korstanje & B. George (Eds.), *Virtual Traumascapes and Exploring the Roots of Dark Tourism* (pp. 1–25). Hershey, PA: IGI Global. doi:10.4018/978-1-5225-2750-3.ch001

Kougioumtzis, G. A., & Louka, D. (2018). Advocacy and Teacher Mentoring. In U. Thomas (Ed.), *Advocacy in Academia and the Role of Teacher Preparation Programs* (pp. 65–87). Hershey, PA: IGI Global. doi:10.4018/978-1-5225-2906-4.ch004

Kousar, H. (2018). Gender Violence in Academia. In N. Mahtab, T. Haque, I. Khan, M. Islam, & I. Wahid (Eds.), *Handbook of Research on Women's Issues and Rights in the Developing World* (pp. 144–155). Hershey, PA: IGI Global. doi:10.4018/978-1-5225-3018-3.ch009

Koutsafti, M., & Politi, N. (2018). Career Counseling: The "Model of Personal Career Management". In K. Koutsopoulos, K. Doukas, & Y. Kotsanis (Eds.), *Handbook of Research on Educational Design and Cloud Computing in Modern Classroom Settings* (pp. 410–429). Hershey, PA: IGI Global. doi:10.4018/978-1-5225-3053-4.ch020

Koutsopoulos, K. (2018). From Ground to Cloud: The School on the Cloud. In K. Koutsopoulos, K. Doukas, & Y. Kotsanis (Eds.), *Handbook of Research on Educational Design and Cloud Computing in Modern Classroom Settings* (pp. 1–21). Hershey, PA: IGI Global. doi:10.4018/978-1-5225-3053-4.ch001

Kovacevic, Z., Klimek, B., & Drower, I. S. (2018). Refugee Children and Parental Involvement in School Education: A Field Model. In K. Norris & S. Collier (Eds.), *Social Justice and Parent Partnerships in Multicultural Education Contexts* (pp. 139–161). Hershey, PA: IGI Global. doi:10.4018/978-1-5225-3943-8.ch008

Kratky, A. (2018). Personal Touch: A Viewing-Angle-Compensated Multi-Layer Touch Display. In F. Cipolla-Ficarra (Ed.), *Optimizing Human-Computer Interaction With Emerging Technologies* (pp. 232–247). Hershey, PA: IGI Global. doi:10.4018/978-1-5225-2616-2.ch009

Kuang, Y. (2018). Application of the "Teaching Innovation Practice Platform" in English Reading Instruction: A Case Study of a Public Middle School in Shanghai. In H. Spires (Ed.), *Digital Transformation and Innovation in Chinese Education* (pp. 249–271). Hershey, PA: IGI Global. doi:10.4018/978-1-5225-2924-8.ch014

Kubilay, S., & Yardibi, N. (2018). Refugee Parents' Preferential Values in Education. In Ş. Erçetin (Ed.), *Educational Development and Infrastructure for Immigrants and Refugees* (pp. 72–84). Hershey, PA: IGI Global. doi:10.4018/978-1-5225-3325-2.ch004

Kumar, T. P. (2018). Impact of Corporate Social Responsibility on Service Performance in Mediating Effect of Brand Equity With Reference To Banks in India. In Rajagopal, & R. Behl (Eds.), Start-Up Enterprises and Contemporary Innovation Strategies in the Global Marketplace (pp. 88-99). Hershey, PA: IGI Global. doi:10.4018/978-1-5225-4831-7.ch007

LaPlante, J. M. (2018). Unequal Opportunities and Inequitable Outcomes: Rethinking Education Finance Policy Design for a Global Society. In H. Levine & K. Moreno (Eds.), *Positioning Markets and Governments in Public Management* (pp. 209–239). Hershey, PA: IGI Global. doi:10.4018/978-1-5225-4177-6.ch016

Lau, B. T., & Win, K. M. (2018). Differentiated Animated Social Stories to Enhance Social Skills Acquisition of Children With Autism Spectrum Disorder. In V. Bryan, A. Musgrove, & J. Powers (Eds.), *Handbook of Research on Human Development in the Digital Age* (pp. 300–329). Hershey, PA: IGI Global. doi:10.4018/978-1-5225-2838-8.ch014

Lee, J. K., & Chirino-Klevans, I. (2018). Cosmopolitanism in a World of Teachers: American Student Teachers in a Chinese School. In H. Spires (Ed.), *Digital Transformation and Innovation in Chinese Education* (pp. 232–248). Hershey, PA: IGI Global. doi:10.4018/978-1-5225-2924-8.ch013

Lee, S. (2018). Expatriate Cantonese Learners in Hong Kong: Adult L2 Learning, Identity Negotiation, and Social Pressure. In D. Velliaris (Ed.), *Study Abroad Contexts for Enhanced Foreign Language Learning* (pp. 151–168). Hershey, PA: IGI Global. doi:10.4018/978-1-5225-3814-1.ch007

Lee, S. C. (2018). Mother America: Cold War Maternalism and the Origins of Korean Adoption. In F. Topor (Ed.), *Ethical Standards and Practice in International Relations* (pp. 157–186). Hershey, PA: IGI Global. doi:10.4018/978-1-5225-2650-6.ch007

Li, Y., & Wang, X. (2018). Seeking Health Information on Social Media: A Perspective of Trust, Self-Determination, and Social Support. *Journal of Organizational and End User Computing*, *30*(1), 1–22. doi:10.4018/JOEUC.2018010101

Livers, S. D., & Lin, L. (2018). Elementary Teacher Candidates' Perspectives on the Teaching and Learning of English Learners. In U. Thomas (Ed.), *Advocacy in Academia and the Role of Teacher Preparation Programs* (pp. 23–41). Hershey, PA: IGI Global. doi:10.4018/978-1-5225-2906-4.ch002

López-Cózar-Navarro, C., & Priede-Bergamini, T. (2018). Nascent Social Entrepreneurship: Economic, Legal, and Financial Framework. In A. Carrizo Moreira, J. Guilherme Leitão Dantas, & F. Manuel Valente (Eds.), *Nascent Entrepreneurship and Successful New Venture Creation* (pp. 132–152). Hershey, PA: IGI Global. doi:10.4018/978-1-5225-2936-1.ch006

Lu, S. (2018). Financial Literacy Education Program Post Financial Housing Crisis: Community Based Financial Literacy Education Program. In S. Burton (Ed.), *Engaged Scholarship and Civic Responsibility in Higher Education* (pp. 49–66). Hershey, PA: IGI Global. doi:10.4018/978-1-5225-3649-9.ch003

Luyombya, D. (2018). Management of Records and Archives in Uganda's Public Sector. In P. Ngulube (Ed.), *Handbook of Research on Heritage Management and Preservation* (pp. 275–297). Hershey, PA: IGI Global. doi:10.4018/978-1-5225-3137-1.ch014

Luyombya, D., Kiyingi, G. W., & Naluwooza, M. (2018). The Nature and Utilisation of Archival Records Deposited in Makerere University Library, Uganda. In P. Ngulube (Ed.), *Handbook of Research on Heritage Management and Preservation* (pp. 96–113). Hershey, PA: IGI Global. doi:10.4018/978-1-5225-3137-1.ch005

Lytras, M. D., Papadopoulou, P., Marouli, C., & Misseyanni, A. (2018). Higher Education Out-of-the-Box: Technology-Driven Learning Innovation in Higher Education. In S. Burton (Ed.), *Engaged Scholarship and Civic Responsibility in Higher Education* (pp. 67–100). Hershey, PA: IGI Global. doi:10.4018/978-1-5225-3649-9.ch004

Mafumbate, R. (2018). Child Resilience, Survival, and Development: Voices of Orphans in Zimbabwe. In I. Tshabangu (Ed.), *Global Ideologies Surrounding Children's Rights and Social Justice* (pp. 239–252). Hershey, PA: IGI Global. doi:10.4018/978-1-5225-2578-3.ch015

Malmierca, M. J. (2018). Cloud Computing for Rural and Isolated Schools. In K. Koutsopoulos, K. Doukas, & Y. Kotsanis (Eds.), *Handbook of Research on Educational Design and Cloud Computing in Modern Classroom Settings* (pp. 376–394). Hershey, PA: IGI Global. doi:10.4018/978-1-5225-3053-4.ch018

Maroofi, F. (2018). Knowledge Management and Organizational Performance in Service Industry: Transformational Leadership Versus Transactional Leadership. In N. Baporikar (Ed.), *Global Practices in Knowledge Management for Societal and Organizational Development* (pp. 194–212). Hershey, PA: IGI Global. doi:10.4018/978-1-5225-3009-1.ch009

Mattson, T., & Aurigemma, S. (2018). Running with the Pack: The Impact of Middle-Status Conformity on the Post-Adoption Organizational Use of Twitter. *Journal of Organizational and End User Computing*, *30*(1), 23–43. doi:10.4018/JOEUC.2018010102

Medhekar, A., & Haq, F. (2018). Urbanization and New Jobs Creation in Healthcare Services in India: Challenges and Opportunities. In U. Benna & I. Benna (Eds.), *Urbanization and Its Impact on Socio-Economic Growth in Developing Regions* (pp. 198–218). Hershey, PA: IGI Global. doi:10.4018/978-1-5225-2659-9.ch010

Meletiou-Mavrotheris, M., & Koutsopoulos, K. (2018). Projecting the Future of Cloud Computing in Education: A Foresight Study Using the Delphi Method. In K. Koutsopoulos, K. Doukas, & Y. Kotsanis (Eds.), *Handbook of Research on Educational Design and Cloud Computing in Modern Classroom Settings* (pp. 262–290). Hershey, PA: IGI Global. doi:10.4018/978-1-5225-3053-4.ch012

Miller, J. (2018). Causes and Ramifications of Public Pension Fund Underfunding: A Case Study of the New Jersey Pension Funds. In H. Levine & K. Moreno (Eds.), *Positioning Markets and Governments in Public Management* (pp. 114–146). Hershey, PA: IGI Global. doi:10.4018/978-1-5225-4177-6.ch010

Milović, B. (2018). Developing Marketing Strategy on Social Networks. In S. Sarma (Ed.), *Global Observations of the Influence of Culture on Consumer Buying Behavior* (pp. 66–82). Hershey, PA: IGI Global. doi:10.4018/978-1-5225-2727-5.ch004

Mosweu, O., & Kenosi, L. S. (2018). Theories of Appraisal in Archives: From Hillary Jenkinson to Terry Cook's Times. In P. Ngulube (Ed.), *Handbook of Research on Heritage Management and Preservation* (pp. 24–46). Hershey, PA: IGI Global. doi:10.4018/978-1-5225-3137-1.ch002

Mukherjee, S., & Pradeep, K. (2018). Does Internationalization of Business-Group-Affiliated Firms Depend on Their Performance? In Rajagopal, & R. Behl (Eds.), Start-Up Enterprises and Contemporary Innovation Strategies in the Global Marketplace (pp. 153-165). Hershey, PA: IGI Global. https://doi.org/doi:10.4018/978-1-5225-4831-7.ch011

Mutisya, P. M., & Conway, C. S. (2018). Quality Mentoring: A Prerequisite for Faculty at HBCUs. In C. Conway (Ed.), *Faculty Mentorship at Historically Black Colleges and Universities* (pp. 15–34). Hershey, PA: IGI Global. doi:10.4018/978-1-5225-4071-7.ch002

Nagabhushan, P. (2018). Mean Level Changes in College Students' Academic Motivation and Engagement. In *Engaging Adolescent Students in Contemporary Classrooms: Emerging Research and Opportunities* (pp. 142–174). Hershey, PA: IGI Global. doi:10.4018/978-1-5225-5155-3.ch006

Naranjo, J. (2018). Meeting the Need for Inclusive Educators Online: Teacher Education in Inclusive Special Education and Dual-Certification. In D. Polly, M. Putman, T. Petty, & A. Good (Eds.), *Innovative Practices in Teacher Preparation and Graduate-Level Teacher Education Programs* (pp. 106–122). Hershey, PA: IGI Global. doi:10.4018/978-1-5225-3068-8.ch007

Nirmala, T., & Aram, I. A. (2018). Newspaper Framing of Climate Change and Sustainability Issues in India. *International Journal of E-Politics*, *9*(1), 15–28. doi:10.4018/IJEP.2018010102

Novak, J. I., & Loy, J. (2018). Digital Technologies and 4D Customized Design: Challenging Conventions With Responsive Design. In V. Bryan, A. Musgrove, & J. Powers (Eds.), *Handbook of Research on Human Development in the Digital Age* (pp. 403–426). Hershey, PA: IGI Global. doi:10.4018/978-1-5225-2838-8.ch018

Ögeyik, M. C. (2018). Measuring Phonological and Orthographic Similarity: The Case of Loanwords in Turkish and English. In D. Buğa & M. Coşgun Ögeyik (Eds.), *Psycholinguistics and Cognition in Language Processing* (pp. 49–67). Hershey, PA: IGI Global. doi:10.4018/978-1-5225-4009-0.ch003

Oling-Sisay, M. (2018). Don't Touch My Hair: Culturally Responsive Engagement in Service-Learning. In O. Delano-Oriaran, M. Penick-Parks, & S. Fondrie (Eds.), *Culturally Engaging Service-Learning With Diverse Communities* (pp. 43–55). Hershey, PA: IGI Global. doi:10.4018/978-1-5225-2900-2.ch003

Ololube, N. P., Ingiabuna, E. T., & Dudafa, U. J. (2018). Effective Decision Making for Knowledge Development in Higher Education: A Case Study of Nigeria. In N. Baporikar (Ed.), *Global Practices in Knowledge Management for Societal and Organizational Development* (pp. 382–399). Hershey, PA: IGI Global. doi:10.4018/978-1-5225-3009-1.ch018

Oritsejafor, E. O. (2018). Enhancing Competitiveness of Public Utilities in Nigeria: The Case of the Power Holding Company of Nigeria (PHCN). In H. Levine & K. Moreno (Eds.), *Positioning Markets and Governments in Public Management* (pp. 240–252). Hershey, PA: IGI Global. doi:10.4018/978-1-5225-4177-6.ch017

Otunla, A. O., & Olatunji, O. T. (2018). Clients' Perception, Extent of Adoption, and Level of Satisfaction With Multi-Platform Advertising Media Strategies (MuPAMS): Among Business Organisations in Ibadan, South-Western Nigeria. In K. Yang (Ed.), *Multi-Platform Advertising Strategies in the Global Marketplace* (pp. 54–80). Hershey, PA: IGI Global. doi:10.4018/978-1-5225-3114-2.ch003

Owuor, N. A. (2018). Oil and Gas Discoveries in Kenya: Important Global Exploration and Production Value Chain Lessons for the Society. In M. Risso & S. Testarmata (Eds.), *Value Sharing for Sustainable and Inclusive Development* (pp. 322–337). Hershey, PA: IGI Global. doi:10.4018/978-1-5225-3147-0.ch015

Özdemir, E., & Yılmaz, M. (2018). Omni-Channel Retailing: The Risks, Challenges, and Opportunities. In A. Kumar & S. Saurav (Eds.), *Supply Chain Management Strategies and Risk Assessment in Retail Environments* (pp. 97–118). Hershey, PA: IGI Global. doi:10.4018/978-1-5225-3056-5.ch006

Panko, T. R., & George, B. P. (2018). Animal Sexual Abuse and the Darkness of Touristic Immorality. In M. Korstanje & B. George (Eds.), *Virtual Traumascapes and Exploring the Roots of Dark Tourism* (pp. 175–189). Hershey, PA: IGI Global. doi:10.4018/978-1-5225-2750-3.ch009

Paraschiv, M. M. (2018). Elif Shafak's Works: A Means of Preventing Honor Based Violence. In M. Badea & M. Suditu (Eds.), *Violence Prevention and Safety Promotion in Higher Education Settings* (pp. 36–49). Hershey, PA: IGI Global. doi:10.4018/978-1-5225-2960-6.ch003

Paravastu, N., Simmers, C. A., & Anandarajan, M. (2018). Non-Compliant Mobile Device Usage and Information Systems Security: A Bystander Theory Perspective. *International Journal of Information Systems and Social Change, 9*(1), 1–25. doi:10.4018/IJISSC.2018010101

Pathak, B. (2018). Process Documentation of Interfaith Peacebuilding Cycle: A Case Study From Nepal. In B. Cook (Ed.), *Handbook of Research on Examining Global Peacemaking in the Digital Age* (pp. 70–93). Hershey, PA: IGI Global. doi:10.4018/978-1-5225-3032-9.ch006

Pathak, S. J. (2018). Women Painters of Mithila: A Quest for Identity. In N. Mahtab, T. Haque, I. Khan, M. Islam, & I. Wahid (Eds.), *Handbook of Research on Women's Issues and Rights in the Developing World* (pp. 370–381). Hershey, PA: IGI Global. doi:10.4018/978-1-5225-3018-3.ch023

Patro, C. S., & Raghunath, K. M. (2018). Corporate Social Responsibility: A Conscientious Take. In M. Risso & S. Testarmata (Eds.), *Value Sharing for Sustainable and Inclusive Development* (pp. 75–99). Hershey, PA: IGI Global. doi:10.4018/978-1-5225-3147-0.ch004

Pérez-Uribe, R. I., Torres, D. A., Jurado, S. P., & Prada, D. M. (2018). Cloud Tools for the Development of Project Management in SMEs. In R. Perez-Uribe, C. Salcedo-Perez, & D. Ocampo-Guzman (Eds.), *Handbook of Research on Intrapreneurship and Organizational Sustainability in SMEs* (pp. 95–120). Hershey, PA: IGI Global. doi:10.4018/978-1-5225-3543-0.ch005

Perrotta, K. A., & Mattson, M. F. (2018). Using Counterstories and Reflective Writing Assignments to Promote Critical Race Consciousness in an Undergraduate Teacher Preparation Course. In U. Thomas (Ed.), *Advocacy in Academia and the Role of Teacher Preparation Programs* (pp. 42–64). Hershey, PA: IGI Global. doi:10.4018/978-1-5225-2906-4.ch003

Poli, A., Gambini, A., Pezzotti, A., Broglia, A., Mazzola, A., Muschiato, S., ... Costa, F. (2018). Digital Diorama: An Interactive Multimedia Resource for Learning the Life Sciences. In F. Cipolla-Ficarra (Ed.), *Optimizing Human-Computer Interaction With Emerging Technologies* (pp. 52–82). Hershey, PA: IGI Global. doi:10.4018/978-1-5225-2616-2.ch003

Presadă, D. (2018). Literature and Aesthetic Reading as Means of Promoting Nonviolence. In M. Badea & M. Suditu (Eds.), *Violence Prevention and Safety Promotion in Higher Education Settings* (pp. 94–109). Hershey, PA: IGI Global. doi:10.4018/978-1-5225-2960-6.ch006

Punetha, H., Kumar, S., Mudila, H., & Prakash, O. (2018). Brassica Meal as Source of Health Protecting Neuraceutical and Its Antioxidative Properties. In A. Verma, K. Srivastava, S. Singh, & H. Singh (Eds.), *Nutraceuticals and Innovative Food Products for Healthy Living and Preventive Care* (pp. 108–131). Hershey, PA: IGI Global. doi:10.4018/978-1-5225-2970-5.ch005

Puri, R., & Sengupta, P. (2018). Application of Statistics in Human Resource Management. In D. Bhattacharyya (Ed.), *Statistical Tools and Analysis in Human Resources Management* (pp. 15–37). Hershey, PA: IGI Global. doi:10.4018/978-1-5225-4947-5.ch002

Putnik, N., & Milošević, M. (2018). Trends in Peace Research: Can Cyber Détente Lead to Lasting Peace? In B. Cook (Ed.), *Handbook of Research on Examining Global Peacemaking in the Digital Age* (pp. 1–18). Hershey, PA: IGI Global. doi:10.4018/978-1-5225-3032-9.ch001

Rana, S., & Sharma, R. (2018). An Overview of Employer Branding With Special Reference to Indian Organizations. In N. Sharma, V. Singh, & S. Pathak (Eds.), *Management Techniques for a Diverse and Cross-Cultural Workforce* (pp. 116–131). Hershey, PA: IGI Global. doi:10.4018/978-1-5225-4933-8.ch007

Randa, I. O. (2018). Leveraging Knowledge Management for Value Creation in Service-Oriented Organisations of Namibia. In N. Baporikar (Ed.), *Global Practices in Knowledge Management for Societal and Organizational Development* (pp. 145–167). Hershey, PA: IGI Global. doi:10.4018/978-1-5225-3009-1.ch007

Rekun, M. S. (2018). A Swift Kick: Russian Diplomatic Practice in Bulgaria, 1879-1883. In F. Topor (Ed.), *Ethical Standards and Practice in International Relations* (pp. 49–72). Hershey, PA: IGI Global. doi:10.4018/978-1-5225-2650-6.ch003

Rodil, K., Nielsen, E. B., & Nielsen, J. B. (2018). Sharing Memories: Co-Designing Assistive Technology with Aphasic Adults and Support Staff. *International Journal of Sociotechnology and Knowledge Development, 10*(1), 21–36. doi:10.4018/IJSKD.2018010102

Samli, R. (2018). A Review of Internet Addiction on the Basis of Different Countries (2007–2017). In B. Bozoglan (Ed.), *Psychological, Social, and Cultural Aspects of Internet Addiction* (pp. 200–220). Hershey, PA: IGI Global. doi:10.4018/978-1-5225-3477-8.ch011

Sánchez-García, J. C., & Hernández-Sánchez, B. R. (2018). Nascent Entrepreneurs, Psychological Characteristics, and Sociocultural Background: Psycho-Sociocultural Background of Nascent Entrepreneurs. In A. Carrizo Moreira, J. Guilherme Leitão Dantas, & F. Manuel Valente (Eds.), *Nascent Entrepreneurship and Successful New Venture Creation* (pp. 111–131). Hershey, PA: IGI Global. doi:10.4018/978-1-5225-2936-1.ch005

Santana-Mansilla, P., Costaguta, R., & Schiaffino, S. (2018). A Multi-Agent Model for Personalizing Learning Material for Collaborative Groups. In F. Cipolla-Ficarra (Ed.), *Optimizing Human-Computer Interaction With Emerging Technologies* (pp. 343–375). Hershey, PA: IGI Global. doi:10.4018/978-1-5225-2616-2.ch015

Santos, C. E., Lima de Oliveira, D., & Freitas, M. D. (2018). The Role of Pibid in Graduation Courses: Discussing Teachers' Education. In Z. Djoub (Ed.), *Fostering Reflective Teaching Practice in Pre-Service Education* (pp. 218–234). Hershey, PA: IGI Global. doi:10.4018/978-1-5225-2963-7.ch012

Sarkar, J. (2018). Methodological Considerations for Research in Compensation Management. In D. Bhattacharyya (Ed.), *Statistical Tools and Analysis in Human Resources Management* (pp. 142–168). Hershey, PA: IGI Global. doi:10.4018/978-1-5225-4947-5.ch007

Sarofim, S., & Tolba, A. (2018). When Age, Religion, and Culture Matter: The Impact of Aging, Religiosity, and Cultural Differences on Consumers' Emotions and Behavior. In S. Sarma (Ed.), *Global Observations of the Influence of Culture on Consumer Buying Behavior* (pp. 261–278). Hershey, PA: IGI Global. doi:10.4018/978-1-5225-2727-5.ch015

Schroth, S. T., & Helfer, J. A. (2018). Differentiated Fieldwork and Practicum Experiences: Matching Teacher Candidate Assignments to Their Skills and Needs. In D. Polly, M. Putman, T. Petty, & A. Good (Eds.), *Innovative Practices in Teacher Preparation and Graduate-Level Teacher Education Programs* (pp. 306–326). Hershey, PA: IGI Global. doi:10.4018/978-1-5225-3068-8.ch017

Schwartz, H. M. (2018). States via Markets and Markets via States: Symbiosis and Change, Not Conflict. In H. Levine & K. Moreno (Eds.), *Positioning Markets and Governments in Public Management* (pp. 1–10). Hershey, PA: IGI Global. doi:10.4018/978-1-5225-4177-6.ch001

Semali, L. M. (2018). Indigenous Knowledge as Resource to Sustain Self-Employment in Rural Development. In S. Chhabra (Ed.), *Handbook of Research on Civic Engagement and Social Change in Contemporary Society* (pp. 142–158). Hershey, PA: IGI Global. doi:10.4018/978-1-5225-4197-4.ch008

Seraphin, H., & Gowreesunkar, V. (2018). On the Use of Qualitative Comparative Analysis to Identify the Bright Spots in Dark Tourism. In M. Korstanje & B. George (Eds.), *Virtual Traumascapes and Exploring the Roots of Dark Tourism* (pp. 67–83). Hershey, PA: IGI Global. doi:10.4018/978-1-5225-2750-3.ch004

Shahidi, N., Tossan, V., & Cacho-Elizondo, S. (2018). Assessment of A Mobile Educational Coaching App: Exploring Adoption Patterns and Barriers in France. *International Journal of Technology and Human Interaction, 14*(1), 22–43. doi:10.4018/IJTHI.2018010102

Sikira, A. N., Matekere, T., & Urassa, J. K. (2018). Engaging Men in Women's Economic Empowerment in Butiama District, Mara Region, Tanzania. In N. Mahtab, T. Haque, I. Khan, M. Islam, & I. Wahid (Eds.), *Handbook of Research on Women's Issues and Rights in the Developing World* (pp. 252–268). Hershey, PA: IGI Global. doi:10.4018/978-1-5225-3018-3.ch015

Silveira, D. G. (2018). Diffusion of Innovation and Role of Opinion Leaders. In S. Sarma (Ed.), *Global Observations of the Influence of Culture on Consumer Buying Behavior* (pp. 83–93). Hershey, PA: IGI Global. doi:10.4018/978-1-5225-2727-5.ch005

Simard, D. A., Martin, M., Mockry, J., Puliatte, A., & Squires, M. E. (2018). Introduction: Mental Health and Well-Being of College Students. In M. Martin, J. Mockry, A. Puliatte, D. Simard, & M. Squires (Eds.), *Raising Mental Health Awareness in Higher Education: Emerging Research and Opportunities* (pp. 1–20). Hershey, PA: IGI Global. doi:10.4018/978-1-5225-3793-9.ch001

Sosnin, P. (2018). Experimental Actions With Conceptual Objects. In *Experience-Based Human-Computer Interactions: Emerging Research and Opportunities* (pp. 47–97). Hershey, PA: IGI Global. doi:10.4018/978-1-5225-2987-3.ch003

Sosnin, P. (2018). Lack of Naturalness in Human-Computer Interactions. In *Experience-Based Human-Computer Interactions: Emerging Research and Opportunities* (pp. 9–46). Hershey, PA: IGI Global. doi:10.4018/978-1-5225-2987-3.ch002

Spaseski, N. (2018). Fractal and Wavelet Market Analysis in Pattern Recognition. In *Alternative Decision-Making Models for Financial Portfolio Management: Emerging Research and Opportunities* (pp. 254–309). Hershey, PA: IGI Global. doi:10.4018/978-1-5225-3259-0.ch007

Spaseski, N. (2018). Theory and Modelling. In *Alternative Decision-Making Models for Financial Portfolio Management: Emerging Research and Opportunities* (pp. 1–19). Hershey, PA: IGI Global. doi:10.4018/978-1-5225-3259-0.ch001

Spires, H. A., Green, K. E., & Liang, P. (2018). Chinese Parents' Perspectives on International Higher Education and Innovation. In H. Spires (Ed.), *Digital Transformation and Innovation in Chinese Education* (pp. 272–287). Hershey, PA: IGI Global. doi:10.4018/978-1-5225-2924-8.ch015

Spires, H. A., Himes, M., & Wang, L. (2018). Designing a State-of-the-Art High School in Suzhou, China: Connecting to the Future. In H. Spires (Ed.), *Digital Transformation and Innovation in Chinese Education* (pp. 191–210). Hershey, PA: IGI Global. doi:10.4018/978-1-5225-2924-8.ch011

Squires, M. E., Martin, M., Mockry, J., Puliatte, A., & Simard, D. A. (2018). Campus-Wide Initiatives. In M. Martin, J. Mockry, A. Puliatte, D. Simard, & M. Squires (Eds.), *Raising Mental Health Awareness in Higher Education: Emerging Research and Opportunities* (pp. 77–104). Hershey, PA: IGI Global. doi:10.4018/978-1-5225-3793-9.ch005

Standing, K., & Parker, S. L. (2018). Girls' and Women's Rights to Menstrual Health in Nepal. In N. Mahtab, T. Haque, I. Khan, M. Islam, & I. Wahid (Eds.), *Handbook of Research on Women's Issues and Rights in the Developing World* (pp. 156–168). Hershey, PA: IGI Global. doi:10.4018/978-1-5225-3018-3.ch010

Stępień, B., & Hinner, M. (2018). From Love to Rebuff: How Culture Shapes the Perception of Luxury Goods Among Consumers. In S. Sarma (Ed.), *Global Observations of the Influence of Culture on Consumer Buying Behavior* (pp. 24–47). Hershey, PA: IGI Global. doi:10.4018/978-1-5225-2727-5.ch002

Tantau, A. D., & Frăţilă, L. C. (2018). Trends and Conclusions for Business Development in the Renewable Energy Industry. In *Entrepreneurship and Business Development in the Renewable Energy Sector* (pp. 351–376). Hershey, PA: IGI Global. doi:10.4018/978-1-5225-3625-3.ch010

Terry, D. L., & Amudalat, E. A. (2018). Data Documentation and Informed Consent in Research. In C. Sibinga (Ed.), *Ensuring Research Integrity and the Ethical Management of Data* (pp. 127–154). Hershey, PA: IGI Global. doi:10.4018/978-1-5225-2730-5.ch008

Toma, S. I., Marinescu, P., & Grădinaru, C. (2018). Creating Shared Value in the 21st Century: The Case of Toyota Motor Company. In M. Risso & S. Testarmata (Eds.), *Value Sharing for Sustainable and Inclusive Development* (pp. 155–184). Hershey, PA: IGI Global. doi:10.4018/978-1-5225-3147-0.ch007

Travis, F. T. (2018). Long-Term Changes in Experienced Yoga Practitioners: Growth of Higher States of Consciousness. In S. Telles & N. Singh (Eds.), *Research-Based Perspectives on the Psychophysiology of Yoga* (pp. 35–51). Hershey, PA: IGI Global. doi:10.4018/978-1-5225-2788-6.ch003

Tripp, L. O., Love, A., Thomas, C. M., & Russell, J. (2018). Teacher Education Advocacy for Multiple Perspectives and Culturally Sensitive Teaching. In U. Thomas (Ed.), *Advocacy in Academia and the Role of Teacher Preparation Programs* (pp. 161–181). Hershey, PA: IGI Global. doi:10.4018/978-1-5225-2906-4.ch009

Tshabangu, I. (2018). Child Poverty and Social Inequalities in Africa: A Social Justice Perspective. In I. Tshabangu (Ed.), *Global Ideologies Surrounding Children's Rights and Social Justice* (pp. 74–87). Hershey, PA: IGI Global. doi:10.4018/978-1-5225-2578-3.ch005

Tugjamba, N., Yembuu, B., Gantumur, A., & Gezel, U. (2018). Research Study on Climate Change Education for Sustainable Development in Mongolia. In P. Ordóñez de Pablos (Ed.), *Management Strategies and Technology Fluidity in the Asian Business Sector* (pp. 192–214). Hershey, PA: IGI Global. doi:10.4018/978-1-5225-4056-4.ch012

Upadhye, B. D., & Bandopadhyay, N. (2018). The Taxonomy of Methodological Approaches in Marketing Research: Retrospect and Prospect. In Rajagopal, & R. Behl (Eds.), Start-Up Enterprises and Contemporary Innovation Strategies in the Global Marketplace (pp. 276-293). Hershey, PA: IGI Global. https://doi.org/ doi:10.4018/978-1-5225-4831-7.ch021

Uvanesh, K., Nayak, S. K., Sagiri, S. S., Banerjee, I., Ray, S. S., & Pal, K. (2018). Effect of Non-Ionic Hydrophilic and Hydrophobic Surfactants on the Properties on the Stearate Oleogels: A Comparative Study. In A. Verma, K. Srivastava, S. Singh, & H. Singh (Eds.), *Nutraceuticals and Innovative Food Products for Healthy Living and Preventive Care* (pp. 260–279). Hershey, PA: IGI Global. doi:10.4018/978-1-5225-2970-5.ch012

Vallverdú, J., Nishida, T., Ohmoto, Y., Moran, S., & Lázare, S. (2018). Fake Empathy and Human-Robot Interaction (HRI): A Preliminary Study. *International Journal of Technology and Human Interaction, 14*(1), 44–59. doi:10.4018/IJTHI.2018010103

Van Deur, P. (2018). Assessing Self-Directed Learning at School Level. In *Managing Self-Directed Learning in Primary School Education: Emerging Research and Opportunities* (pp. 61–77). Hershey, PA: IGI Global. doi:10.4018/978-1-5225-2613-1.ch003

Van Deur, P. (2018). Case Study: The Relationship Between Curriculum Focus on Inquiry and Self-Directed Learning. In *Managing Self-Directed Learning in Primary School Education: Emerging Research and Opportunities* (pp. 95–111). Hershey, PA: IGI Global. doi:10.4018/978-1-5225-2613-1.ch005

Van Deur, P. (2018). Describing Self-Directed Learning in Primary Students. In *Managing Self-Directed Learning in Primary School Education: Emerging Research and Opportunities* (pp. 33–59). Hershey, PA: IGI Global. doi:10.4018/978-1-5225-2613-1.ch002

Vargas-Hernández, J. G., Almanza-Jiménez, R., Calderón, P. C., & Casas-Cardenaz, R. (2018). Organizational Learning and Performance Under the Approach of Organizational Theories. In N. Baporikar (Ed.), *Global Practices in Knowledge Management for Societal and Organizational Development* (pp. 106–125). Hershey, PA: IGI Global. doi:10.4018/978-1-5225-3009-1.ch005

Vega, J. A., Arquette, C. M., Lee, H., Crowe, H. A., Hunzicker, J. L., & Cushing, J. (2018). Ensuring Social Justice for English Language Learners: An Innovative English as a Second Language (ESL) Endorsement Program. In D. Polly, M. Putman, T. Petty, & A. Good (Eds.), *Innovative Practices in Teacher Preparation and Graduate-Level Teacher Education Programs* (pp. 48–66). Hershey, PA: IGI Global. doi:10.4018/978-1-5225-3068-8.ch004

Verma, A. K., Singh, A., & Negi, M. S. (2018). Nutriproteomics: An Advance Methodology of Nutrichemical Analysis. In A. Verma, K. Srivastava, S. Singh, & H. Singh (Eds.), *Nutraceuticals and Innovative Food Products for Healthy Living and Preventive Care* (pp. 1–23). Hershey, PA: IGI Global. doi:10.4018/978-1-5225-2970-5.ch001

Verma, J., & Verma, R. (2018). Innovation in the Provision of Medical Services in India. In Rajagopal, & R. Behl (Eds.), Start-Up Enterprises and Contemporary Innovation Strategies in the Global Marketplace (pp. 16-27). Hershey, PA: IGI Global. doi:10.4018/978-1-5225-4831-7.ch002

Verrini, A. (2018). Strategists From the Past, as Encrypted Cognitive Maps, Whose Access Code Is the Will of Learning Solutions. In L. dall'Acqua, & D. Lukose (Eds.), Improving Business Performance Through Effective Managerial Training Initiatives (pp. 196-209). Hershey, PA: IGI Global. https://doi.org/ doi:10.4018/978-1-5225-3906-3.ch009

Veselinova, E., & Samonikov, M. G. (2018). Driving Brand Equity With Radical Transparency. In *Building Brand Equity and Consumer Trust Through Radical Transparency Practices* (pp. 18–62). Hershey, PA: IGI Global. doi:10.4018/978-1-5225-2417-5.ch002

Veselinova, E., & Samonikov, M. G. (2018). Henkel: Radical Transparency and Sustainability. In *Building Brand Equity and Consumer Trust Through Radical Transparency Practices* (pp. 337–389). Hershey, PA: IGI Global. doi:10.4018/978-1-5225-2417-5.ch009

Veselinova, E., & Samonikov, M. G. (2018). The 3M Company: How to Use Radical Transparency to Generate Value for the Company. In *Building Brand Equity and Consumer Trust Through Radical Transparency Practices* (pp. 185–318). Hershey, PA: IGI Global. doi:10.4018/978-1-5225-2417-5.ch007

Vila, A. R. (2018). Latin American and Caribbean Literature Transposed Into Digital: Corpus, Ecosystem, Canon, and Cartonera Publishing. In F. García-Peñalvo (Ed.), *Global Implications of Emerging Technology Trends* (pp. 34–58). Hershey, PA: IGI Global. doi:10.4018/978-1-5225-4944-4.ch003

Vorkapic, C. F. (2018). Yoga for Children. In S. Telles & N. Singh (Eds.), *Research-Based Perspectives on the Psychophysiology of Yoga* (pp. 104–120). Hershey, PA: IGI Global. doi:10.4018/978-1-5225-2788-6.ch007

Vu, N. T. (2018). Pros and Cons of Integrating Non-Financial Services in Microfinance. In S. Hipsher (Ed.), *Examining the Private Sector's Role in Wealth Creation and Poverty Reduction* (pp. 171–199). Hershey, PA: IGI Global. doi:10.4018/978-1-5225-3117-3.ch008

Wani, K. A., Manzoor, J., Anjum, J., Bashir, M., & Mamta. (2018). Pesticides in Vegetables: Their Impact on Nutritional Quality and Human Health. In A. Verma, K. Srivastava, S. Singh, & H. Singh (Eds.), *Nutraceuticals and Innovative Food Products for Healthy Living and Preventive Care* (pp. 132-157). Hershey, PA: IGI Global. https://doi.org/ doi:10.4018/978-1-5225-2970-5.ch006

Weiss-Randall, D. (2018). DOI Theoretical Framework: Adopting Innovative Technologies. In *Utilizing Innovative Technologies to Address the Public Health Impact of Climate Change: Emerging Research and Opportunities* (pp. 144–166). Hershey, PA: IGI Global. doi:10.4018/978-1-5225-3414-3.ch005

Weiss-Randall, D. (2018). Sustainable Development. In *Utilizing Innovative Technologies to Address the Public Health Impact of Climate Change: Emerging Research and Opportunities* (pp. 167–203). Hershey, PA: IGI Global. doi:10.4018/978-1-5225-3414-3.ch006

Whitelaw, L., & Taddei, L. M. (2018). Using Reflection to Explore Cultural Responsiveness of Preservice Teachers. In Z. Djoub (Ed.), *Fostering Reflective Teaching Practice in Pre-Service Education* (pp. 166–188). Hershey, PA: IGI Global. doi:10.4018/978-1-5225-2963-7.ch009

Wongsurawat, W., & Shrestha, V. (2018). Information Technology, Globalization, and Local Conditions: Implications for Entrepreneurs in Southeast Asia. In P. Ordóñez de Pablos (Ed.), *Management Strategies and Technology Fluidity in the Asian Business Sector* (pp. 163–176). Hershey, PA: IGI Global. doi:10.4018/978-1-5225-4056-4.ch010

Woodman, K., & Kourtis-Kazoullis, V. (2018). Facebook, Tele-Collaboration, and International Access to Technology in the Classroom. In F. Cipolla-Ficarra (Ed.), *Optimizing Human-Computer Interaction With Emerging Technologies* (pp. 274–286). Hershey, PA: IGI Global. doi:10.4018/978-1-5225-2616-2.ch011

Woods, R. J., Johnson, S., & Pope, M. L. (2018). Teaching in an Anti-Deficit Pedagogical Mindset. In U. Thomas (Ed.), *Advocacy in Academia and the Role of Teacher Preparation Programs* (pp. 190–205). Hershey, PA: IGI Global. doi:10.4018/978-1-5225-2906-4.ch011

Wright, M. (2018). Cyberbullying: Description, Definition, Characteristics, and Outcomes. In F. Cipolla-Ficarra (Ed.), *Optimizing Human-Computer Interaction With Emerging Technologies* (pp. 161–182). Hershey, PA: IGI Global. doi:10.4018/978-1-5225-2616-2.ch006

Xu, D. (2018). Multimodal Semiotics in China. In H. Spires (Ed.), *Digital Transformation and Innovation in Chinese Education* (pp. 60–79). Hershey, PA: IGI Global. doi:10.4018/978-1-5225-2924-8.ch004

Yaokumah, W., & Kumah, P. (2018). Exploring the Impact of Security Policy on Compliance. In F. García-Peñalvo (Ed.), *Global Implications of Emerging Technology Trends* (pp. 256–274). Hershey, PA: IGI Global. doi:10.4018/978-1-5225-4944-4.ch014

Yaokumah, W., & Okai, E. S. (2018). Inter-Organizational Study of Access Control Security Measures. *International Journal of Technology and Human Interaction, 14*(1), 60–79. doi:10.4018/IJTHI.2018010104

Zheng, X., Liu, H., Lin, D., & Li, J. (2018). Achieving Rural Teachers' Development Through a WeChat Professional Learning Community: Two Cases From Guangdong Province. In H. Spires (Ed.), *Digital Transformation and Innovation in Chinese Education* (pp. 307–318). Hershey, PA: IGI Global. doi:10.4018/978-1-5225-2924-8.ch017

About the Contributors

Vipin Nadda is working as Lecturer and Programme Manager (Postgraduate-Tourism & Hospitality) with University of Sunderland in London. Some of his previous responsibilities involved Lecturer for tourism and hospitality management at Oxford House College, London and Kurukshetra University in India. He also freelance as 'consultant' for University of East London, Confederation of tourism and Hospitality, Anglia Ruskin University, BPP University and Cardiff Metropolitan University. He has more than twenty years of experience in education, Industry and research and besides PhD in tourism, also written book Chapters, published two books and attended and presented papers in various international conferences/ seminars. As an experienced academician, he has been Lecturing/teaching a variety of subjects ranging from, Strategic tourism development, Destination branding, global tourism, sustainable tourism development, hospitality management studies, Tourism Marketing and International Hospitality Marketing, Marketing strategy, International business environment, Applied Research Methods, supervising MBA, MSc, and PhD Dissertation projects in UK as well as overseas. Dr. Nadda has been also actively involved in development of Programme at different awarding bodies. He has been working with confederation of tourism and hospitality awarding body based at London as an exam board member, external examiner and assessor for last seven years and has helped to develop level-5/6 qualifications for them which are Ofqual recognised and delivered globally. Also, developed level-5/6 qualifications for global examination board, University of East London and assessment for undergraduate and postgraduate tourism and hospitality qualifications for University of Sunderland. He has international exposure having taught students from various nationalities which evidences his adaptability, diversity and multi-levelled skills.

Pankaj Tyagi is an accomplished academician, researcher, and consultant. He is presently working as Professor at Chandigarh University, Mohali, India. Dr. Tyagi is an alumnus of Hemwati Nandan Bahuguna Garhwal University (Central University), India and Kurukshetra University, India. He has more than 20 years of experience in the industry, teaching, training, consultancy, and expertise in destination management, travel process and disruptive technologies. He has published over 30 research papers in international journals indexed in the quality database and authored/edited 6 books. He is a reviewer for many international journals in tourism, management, and technology.

Rubina Moniz Vieira is a Lecturer of Business and Tourism Management at St. Mary's University and has been lecturing at independent colleges and universities for several years. She has a degree in International Relations from Universidade de Lisboa and a PG Diploma in Written Journalism. Prior to starting a career as a lecturer, Rubina worked as journalist and has written numerous articles about the Tourism and Hospitality industry before completing an MA in Tourism Management at the University of

Westminster. She has worked as an associate lecturer for the University of Sunderland and Anglia Ruskin University and completed a PhD on 'Tourism, Diaspora and Mobilities' at Edinburgh Napier University.

Priyanka Tyagi is a Tourism & Hospitality Skill Council (India) Certified Master Trainer & Assessor. She is also associated as Lead Assessor and Trainer with Management & Entrepreneurship and Professional Skill Council (India). She has earned Master of Tourism Administration degree from Hemwati Nandan Bahuguna Garhwal Central University, India, Master of Business Administration Degree from Maharishi Dayanand University, India and M.Phil from Madurai Kamaraj University, India. She has 14 years of experience in the industry, academics & skill-based vocational training. Ms Priyanka has published many research papers in international peer-reviewed journals and edited 4 books. She has expertise in product development, resources management, human resources practice and cultural tourism.

***

Oluwabunmi Bakare-Fatungase is an Information Professional/Researcher in the Department of Information Management, Faculty of Communication & Information Sciences, Lead City University. Her research interest covers emerging technologies, digital & virtual libraries, information use and user communities, bullying and mobile bullying, etc. She is passionate about emphasizing the significant roles of Librarians in solving different societal issues with the arsenal of information at their disposal. She is a fellow of the Council for the Development of Social Science Research in Africa and a Queen Elizabeth Scholar in the Advanced Scholars West Africa (QES-AS-WA) program, Carleton University, Canada.

Badr Bentalha received his PhD in Service Logistics and performance at Sidi Mohammed Ben Abdellah University, Fez, Morocco. He is a Professor in Economics and Management. He has written several articles and participated in various international conferences. He is a member of numerous scientific committees of international journals and conferences. Since 2009, Mr. Bentalha has helped sundry companies implement an audit system, resolve issues and improve performance. Disciplines Managerial Economics Business Administration Supply chain management Qualitative Social Research Skills and expertise Management Marketing Management Management studies AuditSupply Chain Supply Chain Management Green Supply Chain Account Management Operations Research Organization and Administration Service Service Operations Management Service Supply Chain Languages English French

Shivam Bhartiya is an Assistant Professor, Commerce & Management, Centre for Distance and Online Education, Jain University.

Devendra Krishana Bhatt is a seasoned professional with 14 years' experience in Sales, business building & client development for top travel multinationals. Expertise in Business Development, Corporate connect, Team Management, Possess Adroit communication, Interpersonal and people management skills. Currently working as Vice-president in Nesta group of companies, also undertaking his Ph.D in Tourism from Department of Tourism, Kumaun University Nainital.

Vaibhav Bhatt is an Assistant Professor Department of Tourism and Hospitality Management Central University of Tamil Nadu.

Leila Goosen is a full professor in the Department of Science and Technology Education of the University of South Africa. Prof. Goosen was an Associate Professor in the School of Computing, and the module leader and head designer of the fully online signature module for the College for Science, Engineering and Technology, rolled out to over 92,000 registered students since the first semester of 2013. She also supervises ten Masters and Doctoral students, and has successfully completed supervision of 43 students at postgraduate level. Previously, she was a Deputy Director at the South African national Department of Education. In this capacity, she was required to develop ICT strategies for implementation. She also promoted, coordinated, managed, monitored and evaluated ICT policies and strategies, and drove the research agenda in this area. Before that, she had been a lecturer of Information Technology (IT) in the Department for Science, Mathematics and Technology Education in the Faculty of Education of the University of Pretoria. Her research interests have included cooperative work in IT, effective teaching and learning of programming and teacher professional development.

Rupali Gupta is presently working as Assistant Professor at School of Business, Dr. Vishwanath Karad MIT World Peace University, Pune (Only Private University in India with 1st rank in Maharashtra, 26th Rank in India and 426 Rank in world, Under UI Green Metric World in 2021). She has 5 years of teaching experience. Her areas of interest for research are Corporate Finance, Financial Statement Analysis and Accounting. She has completed her PhD from Banaras Hindu University, NET-JRF. She has done her Masters in Financial Management (MFM), and B.Com (Hons.) from BHU and completed M.Com from IGNOU. Dr. Rupali has more than 8 research papers to her acclaim published in national and international journals. She is also a proud Gold-medalist in Masters in Financial Management from Banaras Hindu University in the year 2012.

Sunita Jatav is presently working as Assistant Professor with School of Management (PG) MIT WPU, Pune. She has a flair for Research and has contributed and presented Research Papers in various National / International Conferences and Journals. Her areas of interest include International Business, Service Marketing and Research Methodology.

Rashmi Jha is a UGC-JRF qualified Research Scholar at the Department of History of Art, Banaras Hindu University. She previously worked as a Research Assistant in an IoE Incentive Grant, B.H.U. (MoE, Govt. of India) sponsored project, "Developing a Digital Archive of the Art Heritage of Varanasi (Newly Discovered Group of Ancient Temples and Musical Traditions of Varanasi)". Her research interests are Indian vernacular (religious and non-religious) architecture, and ancient and contemporary craft traditions of Varanasi

Tasleem Khanam is an Assistant Professor, Dept. of Economics, GD Goenka University

Aman Kumar did his graduation in Tourism Studies and post graduation in Tourism Management from IGNOU, Delhi, and MScHMCTT-LE from IKGPTU, Jalandhar, UGC-NET Qualified, and Ph.D. In Tourism Management from Lovely Professional University (LPU) Phagwara, Jalandhar (Punjab). He is working in the field of Airlines and Airport Management, Research in tourism, culture tourism, hospitality management, Tourism education and adventure tourism. He is guiding four Ph. D research scholars. At present He is working as an Associate Professor of Airlines and Airport Management of UITHM at Chandigarh University –Gharuan. He has published 20 Research Papers, Publishing edited book, Patents and attended more than 7 conferences. His work has been recognized internationally and nationally at various journals, conferences and seminars. He has also organized the international conference at CT University in 2022. Before joining Chandigarh University, he has worked in wide spectrum of reputed institutes viz. Chandigarh College of Hospitality Landran, CT University Ludhiana as Associate Prof. in Tourism Management. He is a passionate researcher and delivered Expert lectures on Tourism and Hospitality Research at different Institutions. His love for Tourism education and research is evident from his research papers, book chapters and conferences.

Ashok Kumar is Associate Professor and is heading Department of Tourism and Hospitality, Kumaun University Nainital. He has worked with various research project, guided a number of Ph.D scholars and have good number of published paper under his name.

Ambika N. is a MCA, MPhil, Ph.D. in computer science. She completed her Ph.D. from Bharathiar university in the year 2015. She has 16 years of teaching experience and presently working for St.Francis College, Bangalore. She has guided BCA, MCA and M.Tech students in their projects. Her expertise includes wireless sensor network, Internet of things, cybersecurity. She gives guest lectures in her expertise. She is a reviewer of books, conferences (national/international), encyclopaedia and journals. She is advisory committee member of some conferences. She has many publications in National & international conferences, international books, national and international journals and encyclopaedias. She has some patent publications (National) in computer science division.

James Ngugi is at Kenyatta University Commission for University Education, Kenya.

Sandeep Paatlan: Nurturing Academia and Fostering Research in Tourism Management Sandeep Paatlan, an accomplished academic and dedicated researcher, has made an indelible mark on the field of Tourism & Hospitality. His passion for education, coupled with an unyielding commitment to research and development, has propelled him on a trajectory of excellence, inspiring students and professionals alike. Early Years and Academic Pursuits: Born on December 6th, 1987, Sandeep Paatlan began his academic journey with a thirst for knowledge that would shape his future. Graduating with distinction in B.Sc. Tourism from ITFT-Chandigarh, affiliated with Panjab Technical University, India, in 2008, Sandeep showcased an early aptitude for academic excellence. This initial success laid the foundation for his subsequent achievements. A Career in Academia: Sandeep's journey into academia began when he assumed the role of an Assistant Professor in the Department of Tourism Management at Maharaja Agrasen University, Baddi, H.P., in September 2013. His dedication to nurturing young minds and fostering their growth earned him recognition and admiration. During his tenure, Sandeep contributed significantly to the department's growth and development. In November 2017, Sandeep's trajectory took him to Chandigarh University, where he assumed the dual role of Training and Placement Incharge along with Assistant Professor in the Department of Tourism & Hospitality.

Sachin Pandey is a graduate and postgraduate in History of Art from Banaras Hindu University, Varanasi. Presently, he is working as a Project Fellow under the affiliation of Department of Archaeology and Museums, Government of Gujarat, with the supervision of Prof. Atul Tripathi.

Ashish Raina is working as Dean in the School of Hotel management, Airlines and Tourism, CT University and a chef by profession with specializations in Indian, Italian, and French cuisines.

Jayati Ranga currently working with Amity University, Mohali. She is a dedicated professional with a passion for business education and learning. Her career objective is to contribute to the advancement of business education and be part of a dynamic team that thrives on challenges and nurtures creativity. With a remarkable 9-year career in teaching business-related courses at both the professional graduate and post-graduate levels, Jayati has honed her skills as an educator. Her expertise extends to training senior executives from various sectors. She excels in contemporary teaching pedagogy and boasts a diverse teaching portfolio. Her areas of interest include Business English, Organizational Behavior, Human Resources Management, Import and Export Documentation, Labor Welfare and Industrial Hygiene, Training and Development, Supply Chain Management, Contemporary Issues in Tourism, Tourism Products of India, Customer Service in the Tourism Industry, Project Management, and Retail Management. Jayati's educational journey is characterized by excellence. She is currently pursuing her Ph.D. in Management from Banasthali Vidyapith, Rajasthan. Her academic qualifications include an MBA in Human Resource Management from Sikkim Manipal University, a PGDM in Port Development and Management from the Institute of Rail Transport, and a PGDM in International Business/Tourism from the Indian Institute of Tourism and Travel Management (Government of India), Gwalior.

Rajeev Ranjan is an Assistant Professor, currently working with the Mangalayatan University Aligarh(Uttar Pradesh). He has six years of working experience in industry and academics. He has published several research papers in National and International Journals. He is UGC- JRF & SRF in Tourism Administration & Management, pursued his undergraduate from Jamia Millia Islamia (New Delhi) and Post graduate and Doctorate from Banaras Hindu University. He has keen interest in Heritage Management, Cultural Management, Destination Management as well as Policy and Planning of Indian Tourism & Hospitality.

Swati Shah is a Ph.D in Tourism with specialization in the area of customer satisfaction, employee satisfaction in the service Industry. She holds experience of approximately 10 years in academics. In her academic career, she has worked with reputed institutions like Amity University, Noida, Kalindi College Delhi University, CVS Delhi University and Kumaun University Nainital. She has been actively involved with students from teaching, training, placements and designing of the course curriculum. In her academic career she has also participated in research workshops, seminar and conferences. Some of her research work is published in journals of international repute.

Ridhima Sharma, Assistant Professor, Vivekananda Institute of Professional Studies is an avid reader and believer of hard work. She earned MPhil(Economics) from Thapar University & did her doctorate from Banasthali Vidyapith. She has contributed several articles to the journals of national & international repute and have presented papers in national and international conferences apart from authoring one book. She has a rich eight years of teaching experience. And also holds a rich corporate work experience working at managerial positions with AXIS Bank, HOC Enterprises & Focus Corporate Alliance for 3 years.

Ajit Kumar Singh is an accomplished academician and researcher. He is currently working as an Associate Professor in Chandigarh University, India. He earned his PhD in Management from Magadh University, Bodhgaya, India. With a distinguished career spanning over 14 years in teaching and training within the tourism and hospitality industry, Dr. Singh has made significant contributions to the field. He has authored over 30 research papers, which have been recognized and indexed in reputable databases. Moreover, his expertise is sought after, and he actively serves as a reviewer for numerous IEEE conferences, contributing to the evaluation and selection of high-quality research.

Amrik Singh is working as Professor in the School of Hotel Management and Tourism at Lovely Professional University, Punjab, India. He obtained his Ph.D. degree in Hotel Management from Kurukshetra University, Kurukshetra. He started his academic career at Lovely Professional University, Punjab, India in the year 2007. He has published more than 30 research papers in UGC and peer-reviewed journals and 10 publications (Scopus/Web of Science). He has published 12 patents and 01 patent has been granted in the inter-disciplinary domain. Dr. Amrik Singh participated and acted as a resource person in various national and international conferences, seminars, research workshops, and industry talks. His area of research interest is accommodation management, ergonomics, green practices, human resource management in hospitality, waste management, AR VR in hospitality, etc. He is currently guiding 8Ph.D. scholars and 2 Ph.D. scholars have been awarded Ph.D.

Sujay Vikram Singh is a Senior Research Fellow currently pursuing a doctorate from Banaras Hindu University. Graduated and post-graduated from IHM Lucknow. His research interest includes Hospitality, CRM, Service Marketing, Service Quality, and Systematic Literature reviews. Published papers in various handbooks and journals. His Recent journal publications include International Journal of Market Research (Sage publishing), ABDC-A,Scopus Journal of Global information management (IGI Publishing) Scopus, ABDC-A .Presented papers at various conferences,seminars. Achieved best papers in various conferences.At present working on projects for Shri Kashi Vishwanath corridor and monograph on the heritage relevance of karkotaka vapi

Vijeta Singh is a research-driven faculty with broader experience in research areas of energy and finance area. She completed her PhD from IIT Bombay in 2018 in the area of microfinance. She has published in ABDC and Scopus-indexed journals and her research interests broadly lie in topics like renewable energy, sustainable development goals (SDGs), green growth, hydrogen economy, green finance, and clean fuels.Relevant skills and expertise include working on statistics and econometric modelling over various ranges of micro and macroeconomic issues. She has experience in heading/co-heading of funded projects and organizing of research workshops. Apart from that she has been actively collaborating with international academicians in the area of her research interest and has published papers in reputed publications.

Vipin Singh is a distinguished expert in the field of Tourism and Hospitality Management, known for his in-depth knowledge and extensive experience.r. With over a decade of diversified experience, Dr. Vipin Singh has made significant contributions both in the hotel industry and academia. His expertise spans a wide range of areas, making him a valuable asset in the field. In his illustrious career, Dr. Vipin Singh has had the privilege of working with renowned establishments like Taj Hotel and Domino's Pizza. During his time in the hotel industry, he has successfully managed operations, ensuring the seamless functioning of the establishments under his care. His hands-on approach and leadership skills have proven instrumental in enhancing efficiency and guest satisfaction.

Index

I

K

L

M

N

O

P

R

S

T

U

W

www.ingramcontent.com/pod-product-compliance
Lightning Source LLC
LaVergne TN
LVHW062154300926
849161LV00010B/2661
* 9 7 9 8 3 6 9 3 2 0 6 5 5 *